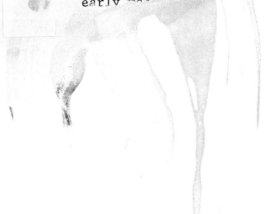

THE PRISON EXPERIENCE

A VOLUME IN THE
CRIME, LAW, and DEVIANCE
SERIES

Pieter Spierenburg

THE**PRISON**
EXPERIENCE

Disciplinary Institutions and Their
Inmates in Early Modern Europe

RUTGERS UNIVERSITY PRESS   **RUTGERS**   NEW BRUNSWICK AND LONDON

Library of Congress Cataloging-in-Publication Data

Spierenburg, Petrus Cornelis.
    The prison experience: disciplinary institutions and their
  inmates in early modern Europe / Pieter Spierenburg.
    p.   cm.—(Crime, law, and deviance series)
    Includes bibliographical references and index.
    ISBN 0-8315-1639-0
    1. Prisons—Europe—History—17th century. 2. Prisons—Europe—His-
  tory—18th century. I. Title. II. Series.
  HV9637.S65 1991
  365′.94—dc20   90-42138
                                                                      CIP

British Cataloging-in-Publication information available.

CONTENTS

PART ONE: THE ORIGINS

PART TWO: PRISONERS AND FORCED LABOR

PART THREE: PRISONS AND FAMILY DISCIPLINE

PART FOUR: THE EARLY MODERN LEGACY

Illustrations appear between pages **170** and **171**.

LIST OF FIGURES AND TABLES

PREFACE

This book has been in the making for quite some time. My interest in the history of imprisonment dates back to the beginning of 1975, when I had just embarked upon the research for what was to become a thesis on executions. Perusing the literature on punishment and discipline in early modern Europe, I encountered a number of references to, though few extensive discussions of, the emergence and spread of various types of carceral institutions. This phenomenon fascinated me because of its implications for the study of such subjects as deviance, the family, madness, and state formation processes. At that time only one example of the 'social control' historiography of prisons, Rothman's *The Discovery of the Asylum*, had been published, so I basically had to develop my own ideas on the subject. Using empirical evidence from Amsterdam court records, I included a chapter on imprisonment in my 1978 dissertation.

When I became a member of the Department of the History of Society at Erasmus University, I chose this subject for a major project. Following an extensive reading of the literature and preliminary investigation in Dutch archives, I prepared a paper that was presented at the First International Conference on the History of Crime and Criminal Justice held at the University of Maryland in 1980. This paper was published by my department (Spierenburg 1984b). The first analysis of the data was presented in that publication. Part of the analysis, with corrected data, is included in several chapters of the present book. During the 1980s the project was continued at a slower pace, because I was also pursuing other interests. With regard to imprisonment, I concentrated on the theme of confinement at the request of relatives and its implications for family discipline. This resulted, among other publications, in an article in *Social Science History* (Spierenburg 1986). Some of the evidence presented there is included in chapters 9 and 10. The bulk of the research for this book, however, was performed during the period 1986–1989, and the data are analyzed here for the first time.

For assistance received in the course of so many years, I owe numerous debts of gratitude. The first is to my department, for providing working facilities and for financing several research trips to Bremen, Hamburg, and Lübeck. Also, a number of students provided assistance in gathering and processing data. For this book, the contributions of Mila Davids and Jan Bruggeman were important. In archives I visited, my queries always received a sympathetic reply, and for this a few persons should be mentioned in particular. Florence Koorn came up with valuable sources from

Haarlem archives still in the process of being inventoried, while Rob Huy-brecht offered similar help at the Algemeen Rijksarchief at The Hague. Originally a stranger to German record offices, I was grateful for guidance by Frau Breitenfeldt and Dr. Lührs in Bremen and Dr. Eckard in Hamburg. In Lübeck, Frau dr. Grassmann took the trouble to search for me in a pile of recently recovered archive boxes that had not yet been catalogued due to the fact that a city proud of its historical past was reluctant to pay for its conservation.

Scholarly suggestions and criticism were freely given from various sides. Rudolf Dekker and I have exchanged references for years, and the present book is one of the products that has profited from this exchange. Sjoerd Faber provided me with quantitative data that he had not included in his own book. Valuable help also came from Bengt Ankarloo, Lee Beier, Johannes Feest, Mary Elizabeth Perry, Lotte van de Pol, Herbert Reinke, and Jan Sundin. Peter Burke and Joanna Innes commented on an early draft of the manuscript, while Peter Klein did the same for chapter 6. David Greenberg and James Murray, who read the manuscript for Rutgers University Press, made helpful comments. The book's preliminary version was discussed during a session at my home one September night. Present were two of the persons already mentioned—Dekker and Faber—and Herman Diederiks, Floor Egmond, Herman Franke, and Jean Jüngen. We reflected on the subject informally but seriously over a glass of good wine and some French cheese, proving that scholarship can also be fun.

A NOTE ON SPELLING

The early modern period lacked a standard spelling of words; notably, names were spelled differently by the same person at various times. I have chosen, therefore, to adhere to the following principles: Dutch names are always written in modern fashion, while German ones are rendered the way they appear in the majority of instances in the records. Although it is the rule in modern German to capitalize every noun, in my sources this was never done consistently. This provides legitimation for keeping German nouns in lower case, which allows easier reading. Geographic names have not been anglicized, save for a few very familiar ones.

THE PRISON EXPERIENCE

PART ONE:

THE ORIGINS

1

INTRODUCTION
A Process Approach to Prison History

The prison experience profoundly influenced the lives of ordinary inmates, but it also affected guards, managers, and policymakers. In a second sense, the concept refers to the experience of every group in society with a new punitive institution. Most European nations became accustomed to it in the course of the seventeenth and eighteenth centuries. The overall impact of imprisonment in early modern Europe is the subject of this book. Such a wide perspective makes it imperative to begin with a statement that certain themes will not be dealt with. The purpose of this chapter is threefold: 1) to locate the present study in the historiography of carceral institutions; 2) to introduce the empirical evidence and discuss its limitations; and 3) to define a few key concepts and explain my point of departure.

Processes versus Modernization   It is customary to state that a major reorientation in the historiography of prisons and incarceration took place in the 1970s. With a few exceptions, works published before that date are branded as 'narratives of reform.'[1] This is not entirely justified. As I will explain in the next chapter, some valuable work on prisons had been done by legal historians, but their contributions were restricted in size. Indeed, most of the older work can be described as a historiography by relative outsiders to this profession: amateur historians; students of local institutions; lawyers or criminologists with an interest in the past. They presented a factual story, often naïvely, with an emphasis on the benevolent motives of the actors involved. The implicit, heavily value-laden conceptual framework can easily be deduced from their writings: since prisons appeared on the scene as an alternative to corporal and capital punishments, they were wonderful institutions that deserved to be applauded by everyone.[2]

Major studies published from about 1970 on adopted a more detached historical approach. They took account of the social context of changes in punishment and discipline, and traced the interrelated history of prisons and other carceral institutions. This revisionist literature often stressed the repressive functions of penitentiaries and asylums and the desire for control on the part of penal reformers. As I have argued elsewhere, such an approach, although valid up to a point, tends to create a mirror image of the one the authors are reacting to.[3] The revisionist historians were biased in two respects. First, they took their predecessors too seriously, so that the latter negatively determined the direction of their inquiries. Second, they overemphasized the motives of the champions of imprisonment. Important as these motives are, the question is why prisons became accepted in a particular society at a particular time. That question refers to a wider context of historical processes, which may be relatively independent of the motives of the prison founders. The 'mentalities' approach adopted here is also a method of exploring this wider context.

Another criterion to subdivide historical studies of imprisonment is more relevant to my discussion. To explain it, I have to begin with the trivial subject of chronology. Most recent work on prisons deals with the nineteenth century and especially its first half. The initial book in this category is by David Rothman (1971). He shows that the beginnings of imprisonment in America in the 1820s were accompanied by the spread of related institutions such as poorhouses and insane asylums. Rothman explains the rise of this network with reference to Jacksonian democracy. Foucault (1975) devotes the first part of his book to the spectacle of capital executions and discusses imprisonment as an entirely new mode of repression to replace capital punishment. He strongly suggests that there was a neat transition from one penal system to the other around 1800, although he pays ample attention to control techniques developed earlier in schools and the army. French historians who are critical of Foucault's method do not question his basic chronology. Michelle Perrot calls the period 1815 to 1848 "the age of the triumphant prison," and a collection of essays edited by her focuses on the first part of the nineteenth century.[4] In England, Michael Ignatieff studied the model penitentiaries established in that period and situated them in a sociopolitical context. Although he briefly refers to the houses of correction which preceded them, he tends to underplay their significance. Like Foucault, Ignatieff depicts a penal system quickly shifting from a reliance on public executions to a confidence in imprisonment.[5] DeLacy (1986), investigating Lancashire developments, also focuses on the years 1800–1850 and refers to the preceding century as "the period of the old jail." Bender (1987) argues that from about 1720 onward English novelists shaped the attitudes that led to the creation of penitentiaries toward 1800. He, too, sees these prisons as lacking precursors. In the case of Geneva, Roth (1981) has a similar chronological emphasis.[6]

The desire to link the development of prisons and related institutions is certainly justified. Consequently, the study of madness should be reviewed, too. Standard histories of psychiatry consider the first half of the nineteenth century a crucial period of change, when 'moral treatment' was initiated and physicians increased their hold over asylums. Social histories of madness likewise tend to focus on the nineteenth century. Dörner (1969) considers the period 1650–1800 merely an age of transition and relates every important change to the rise of the bourgeoisie. Scull (1979) deals with Victorian England and argues that urbanization and industrialization caused an increased demand for committals as many families were no longer able to take care of insane members. Binneveld (1985) argues that developments in the Netherlands deviated from those in the surrounding countries in certain respects, notably with regard to the role of religious organizations. But he, too, identifies the nineteenth century as the classic age of confinement of the insane.

Chronology is not important for its own sake, since any period can be legitimately investigated by historians. My criticism aims at the suggestion that something entirely new was created from about 1800 on. Notably the authors who see imprisonment quickly succeeding a penal system based on public executions and physical punishments construct such a view. Their approach may be called 'modernization-oriented.' The concept of modernization is usually defined, if at all, very loosely. But scholars employing the concept usually stress a continuity in traditional society followed by a rapid transition to modern society. The transition is considered to have occurred in Western Europe and North America around 1800. The view that one penal system very quickly replaced another in the early nineteenth century fits into the modernization theory. However, the modernization theory is in itself inadequate, and consequently not useful as a guide to the history of punishment and discipline. This argument is subject to two restrictions. First, a relatively condensed transition did take place in America, due to the particular circumstances of its development.[7] Second, in Europe the period 1770–1870 was indeed one of crucial transformation, but it implied an acceleration of processes which had been initiated centuries earlier. It is the supposed continuity of traditional society with which I am taking issue. The evidence against such continuity is found in penal practices at both ends of the spectrum: the spectacle of the scaffold underwent several crucial changes since the early seventeenth century, and confinement played an important role in the penal system and among methods of repression and discipline generally since the late sixteenth century.

Another group of historians has shown an awareness of these early modern developments. This group includes the authors of descriptive studies of prisons, usually local prisons, from which part of my information is derived. I will briefly review a few books and articles of a somewhat general and theoretical perspective by these historians. Georg Rusche (1933) was the first to present a sociohistorical theory of changes in punishment.[8] He pays ample attention to the early modern period, focusing on galley servitude and forced labor in prisons. In his view, these penalties were connected with the beginnings of commercial capitalism and the prevalence of mercantilist policies. Melossi and Pavarini (1981) basically restate Rusche's thesis without adding much to it. Lis and Soly also interpret the rise of the use of confinement from an economic viewpoint, placing it in the context of contemporary attitudes toward poverty.[9] To some extent, Foucault (1960) adopts a similar approach. In that early work his perspective is quite different from what it was to become later. In a chapter called "The Great Confinement," Foucault discusses early modern carceral institutions. He emphasizes that these were primarily meant for the confinement of beggars and vagrants, and relates this policy to the economic circumstances of the period.[10] Tanghe (1986) follows Foucault in an attempt to integrate the history of human rights and of attitudes toward poverty. Langbein (1977), on the other hand, views confinement primarily as a penal option and explains its spread with reference to changes in legal theory. The efforts of Marzahn (1984) are directed at integrating the economic view of prison workhouses with a sociological approach. Herman Diederiks (1981) attempts to reconcile the first and second group of historians by arguing that there have been two prison movements: one in the seventeenth century, connected with commercial capitalism; the other in the nineteenth, connected with industrialization. Stekl (1978), is the only author who bridges the gap between both periods. His study of Austrian prisons extends from 1670 to 1920. He sees them as oscillating between charitable and punitive functions.[11]

The writings of the second group can be called 'process-oriented.' Their approach implies that changes in punishment, repression, and discipline constitute a series; they are phases in a long-term development. The evidence collected so far demonstrates that this approach is more congruent with historical reality than the modernization theory. My study, then, will be process-oriented. It is intended to confront a major shortcoming of the works just reviewed in providing an archival data base. The second group definitely lags behind the first with respect to its base of archival research. Stekl is the only member of the group who did a thorough investigation in the archives, but most of his evidence is on the nineteenth century. The others dealt with imprisonment in the context of a wider problem. Lacking research data of their own, they relied on published literature. Consequently, the institutional framework of prison history returns time and again, whereas little is known of what actually happened in the prisons. In this book I intend to remedy that state of affairs.

My study, to repeat, applies the process-oriented approach to the history of penal systems. Such an effort, of course, requires that the other side of the coin, the evolution of physical punishment, be considered, too. But in this work I restrict myself to confinement, because I have amply discussed the other side elsewhere.[12] This book has three main purposes:

1. To show that imprisonment was definitely a feature of European societies in the early modern period. I do not claim that in the seventeenth century the prison played a role in the penal system equal to the one it came to play in the nineteenth. That would be nonsense. I am postulating a relatively long period of coexistence of the scaffold and imprisonment as the most conspicuous elements in the system of repression. This was an intermediate phase, when publicity about and reliance on physical punishment were still dominant but not unchallenged. During this period imprisonment was also used for semipenal or nonpenal purposes, such as keeping vagrants off the streets and disciplining persons who behaved immorally.

2. But I am not content with presenting the bare framework which demonstrates the reality of this long period of coexistence. I also want to give it body by filling out the details. My selection of details will be guided by the modern perspective of a history of mentalities. What really went on in carceral institutions? Who was subjected to imprisonment, and why? How were prisons viewed by contemporaries, and what was the experience of the inmates? Up to now such questions have hardly been answered at all. The novelty of the enterprise makes it imperative to write the book from a full European perspective, but the emphasis will be on the Dutch Republic and the German Empire.

3. Finally, the book attempts to situate the evolution of imprisonment in a social context. It discusses the interdependence of penal developments and other social processes, such as state formation, urbanization, and commercialization. The ultimate aim is to contribute to our understanding of the development of European societies generally.

It should be emphasized that a process-orientation does not necessarily mean that subsequent chapters always deal with change and change alone. During the intermediate phase, some elements, such as the paternalistic conception of prisons, continued. A few crucial changes, on the other hand, may be anticipated in this period: prisons were gradually transformed from multipurpose institutions to purely judicial ones; in connection with this, their role in the penal system increased and they gained ascendancy over alternative forms of bondage; an inmate subculture came into being, based on the cumulative experiences of generations of prisoners; families increasingly made use of confinement on request, a practice which later declined under the influence of new ideas about personal liberty and the rise of a medical view of insanity.

Sources and Limitations   Certain practical objections imposed limits to the project of putting the process-oriented approach to the history of confinement on a firmer empirical base. Not every archive in Europe could be visited. Moreover, it would have been too big an undertaking to deal with the entire development of carceral institutions from the sixteenth century into the twentieth. Thus, I have restricted my research to the period before 1800, or for the Netherlands 1811, when the judicial Ancien Régime ended. There are three reasons for this chronological restriction. First, we are already reasonably well-informed about the period after 1800 through the social histories referred to above. Second, in order to illustrate the long-term process, it is necessary to show that the notion of traditional continuity is wrong. The third reason is more trivial: I happen to be a historian of preindustrial societies. Within the period studied there are differences of emphasis. I have tried to achieve what might be termed an economy of research. In archives where the material was too abundant to be dealt with completely, I concentrated on the early years. The reason for this choice was that it was important to gather data on the beginnings of a long-term development. The archives also yielded different kinds of information, but taken together, they covered most areas.

The selection of archives implied a geographical restriction as well. The primary decision was to investigate records in Continental Europe rather than in England, which had its own peculiar development. A few recent publications provide information with regard to British imprisonment.[13] On the Continent the natural choice for study was the oldest institutions in the Dutch and German territories. Especially the Dutch prisons were regarded as models all over Europe. This research was supplemented by a preliminary investigation in the archive of Antwerp, which had the first 'Catholic' prison. Within the Republic, I focused on the province of Holland. Amsterdam should have received special attention, but, unfortunately, the entire archive of its rasphouse, the first Continental prison, has been lost save for a few documents. The city's judicial records, which have been studied by myself and other historians, offer a partial compensation.[14] Within the Empire, I concentrated my archival research on the Hanseatic towns that pioneered in imprisonment, notably Bremen and Hamburg.[15] The picture of the German development was informed additionally by a number of local historical studies. The resulting geographical orientation can be justified on thematic grounds, too. It was especially in the Dutch and German territories where the 'classical' model of the workhouse with forced labor, the precursor of modern prisons, was elaborated. Forms of penal bondage other than imprisonment were prevalent in countries such as France and Spain.

The presentation of the data reflects the book's geographical orientation. The next chapter discusses the origins of imprisonment and deals with Europe as a whole. It is largely based on secondary literature. The two succeeding parts, devoted, respectively, to judicial imprisonment at hard labor and imprisonment as a form of family discipline, are based on my newly gathered empirical evidence. These sections present data on the Republic and the Empire and, when it seems appropriate, put them in a comparative context. The final part focuses again on Europe as a whole. It traces the overall development of imprisonment and other forms of bondage from the seventeenth century to the nineteenth and discusses the historical significance of this development.

The archival documents studied are varied in nature, but two types were especially important. The administrators of some prisons kept a record of their meetings and discussions.[16] These protocols inform us about important events, in the view of the administrators, in or around the institution from year to year and sometimes from day to day. I call this type of record a logbook. The other type of important archival document I call an entry book. It records data on individual prisoners from the date of entry until the date of exit, regardless of which court sentenced them to their prison term. While logbooks usually yield qualitative evidence, entry books permit a quantitative analysis of the prison population.

The novelty of the study of early modern imprisonment obliges me to specify to what extent the history is now documented and what remains to be done in this respect. The early evolution of prison workhouses in Continental Europe until about 1650 is relatively well-documented, although new evidence may still be gathered from the archives at Utrecht, Leeuwarden, and Lübeck.[17] For the period 1650–1800, the situation is as follows: the extant sources on the Amsterdam rasphouse have been dealt with, although further study of the city's court records may disclose new details. Concerning the Amsterdam spinhouse and workhouse, only the most important documents have been considered. The prison records of other major cities in Holland have been studied intensively; only a few small towns were left out. Several archives outside Holland still offer possibilities for research that may lead to a modification of some of my conclusions. Hallema's investigations of Dutch prisons are highly unreliable and historians should disregard them.[18] Bremen's prison archive has been consulted exhaustively up to about the middle of the eighteenth century; material on a proposed institutional reform in the 1780s and 1790s was not dealt with. The Hamburg records are more numerous, which obliged me to concentrate on the crucial, formative years. I consulted the logbook of the *zuchthaus* up to 1650 and the logbook and the entry books of the spinhouse up to 1709. Streng (1890) studied the logbooks of both houses, especially for the period I did not deal with. The Habsburg lands are covered by Stekl's exhaustive investigation. For the rest of the Empire there are local studies, but they generally fail to provide information on interesting subjects such as internal life in prisons. With regard to imprisonment outside the Republic and the Empire, no more than a bare framework is known. An exception has to be made for confinement at the request of relatives, on which a number of French studies have been published.

Words and Meanings   An international perspective makes correct understanding of terminology all the more imperative. A most important terminological distinction partly depends on chronology. It may be objected that my starting point comes too late, because imprisonment far antedates the early modern period. If we consider imprisonment the mere act of locking someone up in an enclosed space, there is no argument about this. But imprisonment in the sense we are intending involves more systematic practices. Buildings specifically designed for carceral purposes certainly existed before the sixteenth century. In medieval Europe kings, dukes, counts, bishops, and urban magistrates had their places of detention. The crucial difference between the Middle Ages and later periods is that in the medieval period these places were not primarily meant for punishment, though offenders might sometimes be imprisoned there. The punishment function became prevalent for the first time in the institutions established from the late sixteenth century onward called *bridewells* or *houses of correction* in England and *tuchthuizen* in the Netherlands. These new names testify that their new function was recognized. Contemporaries continued to differentiate between the new institutions and the old-type places of detention. In England the latter were denoted as *gaols*. German lawyers continued to employ the Latin term *carcer* to refer to strongholds not meant for punishment. The old Dutch and German words *gevangenis* and *gefängnis* continued to have such a meaning, too.[19]

This chronological sequence justifies distinguishing two Weberian ideal types: jail and prison.[20] A jail mainly holds debtors and persons under provisional detention; some inmates may have been incarcerated for penal purposes. Although a few inmates are detained for lengthy periods, the building is not expressly equipped for long-term stays. There are no arrangements for keeping inmates busy. A prison, on the other hand, primarily keeps delinquents or noncriminal offenders who have been sent there to serve a term for purposes of chastisement or correction. The inmates are subjected to a specific regime, often involving forced labor. The institution is equipped to occupy its inmates, although difficulties with this may arise in practice. This distinction of the two types of carceral institutions is an analytical one, because local terminology does not necessarily conform to it. In early modern France, for example, *la prison* usually denoted a jail. In the nineteenth century a *maison de correction* was a juvenile prison, while its English equivalent had for long been a synonym of bridewell.[21] Jails, too, might have a variety of specific, local names. Amsterdamers spoke of *de boeien;* Hamburg had its *Roggenkiste.*[22] Despite these differences in contemporary terminology, the places of detention had a similar character everywhere.

The remarkable continuity in the functions of jails, from the Middle Ages until the nineteenth century, underlines the distinction introduced here. Jails basically served for provisional detention, of various types of people including debtors. The latter were involved in civil cases; they were confined not to be punished but to be forced to satisfy their creditors. During their detention they were supposed to arrange to pay them back.

In English jails debtors were often granted a system of self-government.[23] In the Netherlands, jailed debtors were appropriately called *gijzelaars* (hostages), and it was considered exceptional when the distinction between jail and prison got blurred. In Haarlem in 1734, when the *schout*, the public prosecutor, had postponed his demand in a criminal case because the suspect was pregnant, he submitted an official request that she might be confined in prison for the duration. In 1754 a woman who was in debt but was also suspected of fraud was first detained in the 'hostage room' and then taken to prison for six weeks.[24] Debtors attempting to break out of Amsterdam's jail could be punished with a bread and water diet, but occasionally the sanction was a temporary transfer to the rasphouse.[25] The exceptional nature of these cases makes it clear that the jail-prison distinction was normally observed.

A regime was an essential component of life in prisons. As a rule, two regimes were possible. One consisted of separation from the outside world. Enforcement of this regime was recorded from the start in Amsterdam and Hamburg, where it was imposed upon a minority of inmates. These were usually persons from a well-to-do environment who had been admitted at the request of their families. In the eighteenth-century Netherlands this regime was also enforced in separate institutions, called *beterhuizen* or 'prisons for improvement.' Inmates had to serve a term to 'get better,' usually understood in a moral sense.

The most common regime, however, was of forced labor. The work program, the introduction of which was the rationale behind the establishment of prisons in the first place, was intended to discipline and punish the inmates. The obligation to work differentiated the institutions in question from hospitals, almshouses, and asylums, as well as from voluntary workhouses, where employment was not meant for punishment.[26] Beggars, vagrants, delinquents, and persons confined by less well-to-do families were all subjected to the regime of forced labor. Whenever I emphasize this aspect, I will use the term *prison workhouse,* rather than *house of correction.* It has become customary to use house of correction in English to refer to Continental prison workhouses, and I followed this practice in earlier publications. But I have come to realize that this is misleading. First, the term may give the impression that we are not dealing with places of confinement. To emphasize the contrary, I am designating the institutions I studied for what they were: prisons. Second, it is of doubtful validity to consider English houses of correction of the seventeenth and eighteenth centuries as counterparts of Dutch or German prisons. The most conspicuous difference is that in England a work program was often lacking. A literal translation of house of correction into Dutch would be *beterhuis.* The generic term for a carceral institution with forced labor, therefore, should be prison workhouse. When specifically referring to an individual institution, or just for stylistic variation, I will use local terms.

Present-day Dutch as well as German know the word *vrijheidsstraffen,* meaning punishments severely limiting the condemned's freedom of action and movement. The English language has no equivalent term. It is a useful term because it refers to a more general class of penal sanctions than imprisonment alone. The concept includes such penalties as transportation and the galleys that were widely used in the early modern period. The problem may be circumvented if we refer to the situation of being subjected to one of those penalties as 'bondage.'[27] A concept to be discarded, finally, is *the great confinement,* introduced by Foucault and adopted by subsequent authors.[28] It might convey the impression that a considerable share of the deviant or even the entire population was imprisoned in the seventeenth and eighteenth centuries. In fact, in most present-day societies a far higher percentage of the population is confined, in prisons, concentration camps, or psychiatric institutions. For the early modern period, we are not dealing with a quantitatively significant phenomenon. What is more important is the image of prisons in people's minds and their symbolic meaning in a society, matters that are relatively independent of numbers.

A History of Mentalities   This is my final confession. I am studying imprisonment in particular and punishment and discipline in general from the perspective of a history of mentalities. This is not because I am convinced that only the cultural aspects count, or that prisons should be studied primarily from that angle. It is the other way around. I happen to be interested in changes in experience, emotions, and world views, and my subject offers a possibility to investigate them. The following chapters present an integral story from the mentalities perspective. The word itself, I think, needs no special explanation. It is simply a sensitizing concept, differentiating my field of inquiry from the more traditional history of ideas. Neither does the use of the word mentalities imply that I am in complete agreement with the French school which first employed the concept.

My emphasis can also be justified using a theoretical argument. Revisionist historians regard prisons and related institutions primarily as tools of social control. From a short-term perspective, they are justified, but from a longer-term perspective, the social control motive is insufficient to explain change. Repression always implies attempts to control the population. The modes of repression, however, have changed considerably over time. These transformations, whatever else they meant, also reflected changes in mentalities. They had to do with notions about the appropriate treatment of offenders and the nature and purpose of punitive sanctions. Moreover, in preindustrial Europe the symbolic meaning of authorities' initiatives and directives was often found to be more important than actual enforcement or control. The paradox is that, although power differences between rulers and ruled were greater in the early modern period than they are today, the decisions of twentieth-century governments penetrate deeper into citizens' lives. Early modern rulers just attempted to keep things going, relying heavily on display. It is more useful, therefore, to study imprisonment and the evolution of repression as expressions of the cultural climate of a society than to assess the exact contribution of prisons to the enforcement of social norms.

2

IDLENESS AND LABOR
The Emergence of Prisons in
Early Modern Europe

The earliest prisons were established in the second half of the sixteenth century and the beginning of the seventeenth century in England, the Netherlands, and a handful of North German and Baltic towns. Simultaneously, other forms of bondage gained a foothold in Southern Europe. The purpose of this chapter is to explain these developments. To do so, we have to go back in time and take account of a broader context. Our first inquiry will be into the precursors of imprisonment; the second into the mental climate in which prisons were founded and the society.

The key word is idleness. The desire to adopt a more active policy toward people who failed to perform their daily tasks along expected lines was a major motivation behind the establishment of carceral institutions. Idleness might manifest itself in various ways, but two forms appear prominently in the historical record. The first was the idleness of specific groups, roaming around jobless and surviving by begging and possibly stealing. A second form of idleness consisted of living a life of pleasure or disobedience to authority, and thus neglecting one's proper tasks and duties. This form was not confined to a specific social group; it could manifest itself in individuals from all classes, rich or poor. The notion that idleness should be combated by forced labor lay behind the emergence of imprisonment and other forms of bondage. The following section of this chapter presents a factual account of the roots of imprisonment and the mental background to the rise of the prison workhouse. The next section inquires into the social context of these matters and attempts to explain them.

The Roots of Imprisonment

To begin with, we must look at imprisonment before establishment of the prison as an institution. Every starting point is relative, so analysis of in-

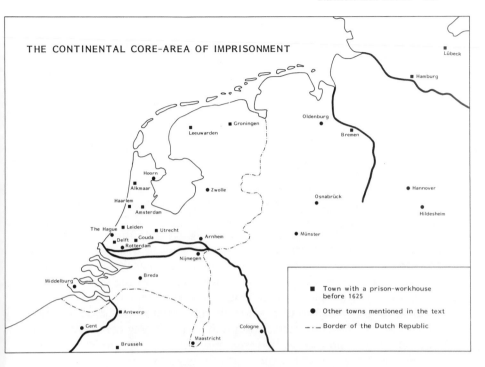

THE CONTINENTAL CORE-AREA OF IMPRISONMENT

■ Town with a prison-workhouse before 1625

● Other towns mentioned in the text

—.— Border of the Dutch Republic

stitutions should be preceded by a discussion of their precursors. Before the sixteenth century certain offenders were condemned to be locked up in jails. Simultaneously, other institutions served as prisons of a kind, at least for certain inmates.

Monasteries and Asylums   To the extent that persons living outside a regular household are best advised not to leave their place of residence, every institutional home resembles a prison. The earliest institutional homes in preindustrial Europe were monasteries and convents. They were also among the first communities observing a scheme of activities methodically spread over the day. Treiber and Steinert consider monastic discipline as the prototype of later forms of discipline, such as those imposed on factory workers or prisoners.[1] In theory, monks and nuns entered their holy places of residence voluntarily as a result of a vocational experience or because of godly inspiration. They were free to leave, although breaking their vow constituted a grave sin. In practice, however, free will could be restricted by convenience. During the early Middle Ages, for example, many boys and girls entered the religious community as *oblati* or *oblatae*. They were 'offered' by their parents when they were still very young. Brought up within the sacred walls, most of these monks must have been quite unfit for a life outside among peasants and knights. Moreover, there is evidence to suggest that, if they left the monastery, their abbots would track them down and return them to it.[2] The system of oblation declined from the twelfth century onward, but the idea that inhabitants of monasteries were not supposed to leave persisted. In an exemplary story written around 1230 about a young nun in a Frisian convent, it was said that she "constantly thought about flight."[3] Finally, seizing the opportunity, she ran away during the night. The equation of leaving the convent with escape is suggestive enough. It is impossible to tell how many monks and nuns perceived their home as a prison or how many were actually held forcibly.

At least a few were. What should an abbot do with a returned fugitive? Incarceration in a special cell was an obvious solution. Such cells, some of them quite unpleasant, had been in use in monasteries from an early date. They also were used as places of punishment for those who broke the rules within the institution, since the abbot, as father and lord, had a right of punishment over his dependents. It is understandable that religious establishments pioneered the use of imprisonment as a penalty. Because their leaders wished to retain those who entered their institutions, it seemed reasonable to physically restrain them. For a long time, this attitude was diametrically opposed to that of wordly rulers. For them, banishment of offenders was often the preferred option. A commonly observed rule in the case of runaway monks, however, was that they ought to be banished from monastic life only after they left for the third time.

Occasionally, secular authorities also imposed monastic imprisonment. As early as 751, Pepin the Short locked up the last Merovingian king in a monastery. Subsequently, he and his successors removed a number of political opponents in this way.[4] A Roman Council in 826, attempting to regulate the practice of oblation, stated that every entry into a monastery ought to be voluntary, except when it constituted punishment for a crime.[5] Throughout the Middle Ages ecclesiastical and secular judges imposed monastic imprisonment, but it is unknown how frequently.[6] Thus, religious establishments were the first places where penal imprisonment as a result of a judgment in a trial occurred. The confinement of offending monks and nuns continued in Catholic countries into the eighteenth century. Mabillon's famous *Réflexions sur les prisons des ordres religieux,* written around 1700 and first published in 1724, presents an historical overview and a criticism of the practice in his own time. Its influence on secular imprisonment had to wait until the nineteenth century, when the essay was referred to in the discussion of atonement and solitary confinement.[7]

The second form of imprisonment before the institution of the prison involves medieval hospitals. They were neither carceral institutions nor just homes for the sick, as are modern hospitals. Their existence has been recorded from the tenth century onward, but the principal foundation period was in the twelfth century and was connected with urbanization. In practically every medieval town, one or more hospitals were established, either by religious groups or lay people. Leprosaria and pesthouses should be mentioned in this context, too. Foucault (1960) considered the treatment of lepers as a blueprint for early modern imprisonment, but there are important differences. For one thing, we should not overestimate the isolation of leprosaria. They were often situated near main thorough-fares or places of pilgrimage, so that the inmates could go out and beg for their living.[8] The noncarceral character of hospitals within the city is also evident. They were charitable institutions that functioned as asylums for the aged, refuges for the homeless, inns sheltering pilgrims and other poor travellers, and secure places for the sick, the infirm, or women in labor. In some towns a distinction was made between hospitals for residents and for travellers, but both groups of hospital users were seen as proper objects of charity.[9]

Still, a few people may have been forbidden to leave the hospital.[10] An Amsterdam city ordinance of 30 December 1480 orders all *gasthuisboeven* (hospital rogues) and other able-bodied and unemployed people to leave the town forever. A year later some of them were found in the city and were banished again on penalty of losing both eyes.[11] In the second half of the eighteenth century, the historian Wagenaar, referring to these pas-sages, thought that the term 'hospital rogues' was used in the same sense in which he would use *rasphuisboeven* (prison rogues).[12] But the term might also refer to people who had earlier sought and maybe found a shelter in the hospital, but who were now denied it because they were considered criminals.

If medieval hospitals included sequestered areas, the inmates in which were not permitted to leave, then these inmates must primarily have been the insane. Which leads us to the third precursor of prisons. References to mad people who were committed to hospitals in various European coun-tries date back to the twelfth century. Those considered dangerous were probably kept in rooms with secure locks. The insane were the first type of deviants for whom separate institutions were built, probably from the fifteenth century onward. Charters of madhouses founded in the Dutch cities of Den Bosch and Utrecht in the middle of the fifteenth century refer to persons who are furious and out of their senses and cannot be restrained except in chains. Such institutions were the first places where a particular group of people were kept in custody for a relatively long period because of their behavior.[13] We might consider them as the first prisons. On the other hand, the fact that the insane were not usually held respon-sible for their deeds and the charitable character of these institutions make them rather different from the prison workhouses that emerged a century later.

Jails, of course, had never been viewed as charitable institutions. To the contrary, it was a traditional Christian duty to try to alleviate the sufferings of the unlucky ones detained there. Some of them were condemned offenders. Imprisonment had been practiced occasionally as an informal punishment by the ancient Romans, although the practice was not considered entirely legal.[14] Offenders who refused to pay a fine became debtors of a sort and their detention in jail may have been viewed as a penal measure.[15] Most of our information on medieval incarceration comes from England and Italy. In England penal imprisonment is said to have been a particularly ancient practice and already very common in the later Middle Ages.[16] Among the Italian cities, Venice made extensive use of penal imprisonment by the middle of the fourteenth century.[17] In England as well as Venice, prison terms were usually short. For Italy as a whole, until the sixteenth century, there is additional evidence from legal texts. Imprisonment was mentioned as a possible penalty in the statutes of thirty-seven out of eighty-one towns. Places of detention were usually called *carceri*.[18]

Little is known about life in medieval jails, though a few stereotypes exist. It is unlikely that all prisoners were chained to the wall or totally deprived of light. It is true, though, that contemporaries often regarded incarceration as a form of physical punishment. The most common aggravation of the penalty, no doubt, was the subjection to a diet of bread and water (or beer). This diet continued to be associated with jails. In early modern Netherlands it remained on the repertoire of penal sanctions, although it was imposed in a minority of cases. A bread and water sentence was never executed in a prison.

The fifth and last type of imprisonment before prisons consisted of prefigurations of what would be instituted later. Attempts to punish the two categories of idle persons were recorded from the end of the fifteenth century. The places where they were confined still resembled old-style jails. Two were established in Amsterdam in the 1490s.[19] In 1496 the court there imposed a fine that was characterized as a contribution to the financing of a *gayoel* for the confinement of "children or adolescents of evil conduct."[20] A charter of 1507 authorized Rotterdam to establish a house for the chastisement of undisciplined youths. Drinking and playing dice were explicitly mentioned as offenses. The building had already been constructed at the initiative of several families of citizens and residents.[21] A similar house, meant for "disobedient and evil-minded children and other persons," was planned in Gouda in 1530.[22] These projects were undertaken to provide for persons of immoral conduct. Comparable plans in other European countries were for beggars. Sometimes they were incarcerated in jail-like establishments before the foundation of prison workhouses. Such instances are discussed below.

Morals and the People   Terms such as disobedience, evil conduct, or disreputable behavior were to occur frequently in statements accompanying the foundation of prison workhouses. Their all-inclusiveness is remarkable. There was little differentiation, around 1600, between the categories of crime, sin, and immorality, between breaking laws made by mortals and breaking God's laws.[23] Another characteristic of these notions is their vagueness—they simply indicated a bad life-style. This is significant. A major attraction of confinement as a penalty lay in the fact that its execution was not restricted to one particular moment. It involved a long-term effort to change the behavior of offenders. Thus, the persons for whom prisons were originally established were considered appropriate candidates for this form of punishment because of their way of life. Bad habits, rather than concrete acts such as burglaries or a homicide, were penalized. Moral campaigns or 'civilization offensives' were an important background to the emergence of prison workhouses.

Organized efforts by clergymen as well as laymen to improve the morals of the population recurred throughout the early modern period. A number of authors refer to these movements. Elias shows that the sixteenth century witnessed a new impetus toward the refinement of manners. Erasmus's book on etiquette and the socialization of youths offered precepts for those confronted with problems of educating and teaching obedience to children.[24] Burke speaks of "the triumph of Lent," which began in the middle of the sixteenth century and included increased efforts by Protestant and Catholic moralists to reform the manners of the popular classes. The reformers pushed an ethic of decency, orderliness, and sobriety, in contrast to a more spontaneous way of life in which energy and money seemed to be more expendible.[25] Flandrin pays attention in particular to the effort to regulate sexual behavior during the early modern period. In his view, religious moralists were the main actors in this effort. They focused on such practices as concubinage and premarital intercourse.[26] Muchembled speaks of "the criminalization of the moral sphere" in the sixteenth and seventeenth centuries. He sees an intensification of the policing of people's behavior by judicial and administrative agencies.[27] These are only a few of the authors who might be mentioned. Historians generally agree that the early modern period was one of increasing moral entrepreneurship aimed at 'civilizing' people's behavior.[28] These regulation of morals movements continued after prisons had been established. In England, for example, moral concern received a new impetus with the societies for the reformation of manners that were in existence since the 1690s. They encouraged the imprisonment of drunks, gamblers, and similar offenders.[29]

Thus, early modern civilization offensives concerned the spheres of morality, handling financial resources, sexuality, and education. Persons who violated norms in those spheres were among the earliest to be singled out for imprisonment. These malefactors had something else in common: they opposed the ideal of the family. It is no coincidence that they were usually confined upon a request by one or more relatives. The nuclear family, benevolent but also authoritarian, was promoted as a pillar of good government from the sixteenth century onward. Secular and ecclesiastical authorities viewed it as a micromodel of the larger social hierarchy. The custom of confinement on request, wherein the authorities acted in concordance with private persons who wished to punish troublesome relatives, sprang from this worldview. The offenders were children who refused to stay at home, adulterous women, or drunken husbands. Imprisonment at the request of families was to become particularly popular in the eighteenth century. This is consistent with the observation that the civilization offensives reached a climax in that period.

Holy and Unholy Poverty   For the second of our target groups, the cultural background to the rise of imprisonment implied a greater change. This involved not merely an intensification of moral concern but a fundamental transformation of attitudes; an appreciation of the behavior of a whole social group, rather than of isolated individuals. The group consisted of beggars and vagabonds. In French it is customary to refer to them together as *les marginaux,* because they were eking out an existence on the margins of settled society. I will adopt this term and call them 'marginals' to avoid having to use the two words. Attitudes toward marginals changed fundamentally during a period from the end of the fifteenth century to the beginning of the seventeenth. Apart form marginals, the settled poor, too, were involved in this change to a certain extent. The transformation did not bring about an entirely new mentality. A cluster of attitudes that had previously remained submerged gradually surfaced, gained respectability, and became the majority view. Various authors deal with this change and it will suffice to summarize their findings.[30]

The older mentality was a deeply Christian one in which poverty was viewed as a kind of sacred state. Men and women without property were considered to be following in the footsteps of Christ; they were 'the poor of Jesus.' Consequently, their presence was not a source of anxiety. The poor provided the rich with an opportunity to give alms and so earn heaven. Whether they appeared as beggars, vagrants, or needy persons in one's parish, as poor lay persons or as members of mendicant religious orders, they all were considered to deserve charity. The popularity of pilgrimages and the frequent practice of begging one's way to the sanctuary contributed to a positive view of the itinerant poor. This attitude toward poor people must have led to a willingness to give alms to all kinds of persons in need. Although few would have argued that everyone was always deserving of alms, in practice the question of whether an individual beggar deserved alms was hardly ever posed. In principle, the scholastic doctrine on alms focused on the almsgiver. The receiver was just the occasion for an act that was pleasing to God, and it was found awkward to inquire into the causes of a beggar's misery.

In the newer cluster of attitudes the receiver of alms was at the center.

Some poor people, it was argued, were to be blamed for their condition. Increasingly, a distinction was made between the deserving and the undeserving poor, between able-bodied and disabled beggars. No longer did everyone automatically see the image of Christ in the poor. The state of poverty became a curse and the poor were considered a threat to the stability of society. Thus, they had to be strictly supervised, and beggars and vagabonds were liable to suspicion. With a few exceptions, idleness was only tolerated from the sick, the disabled, or the aged. It began to be considered inappropriate to give alms to beggars who could work instead. Charity was henceforth to be channeled into institutions that would distribute it to the deserving but not the undeserving poor.

To say that Western Europe moved from the first to the second mentality during the period of transition implies an analytical reconstruction. The two clusters of attitudes represent ideal types. In reality, individual views included a combination of both clusters. To complicate matters further, a third attitude, that poverty was a source of shame, coexisted with the other two. In that case we are not primarily concerned with general attitudes, but with a person's view of his poverty. Someone who had enjoyed a certain status but had moved down the social ladder because of sudden misfortune or for other factors he perceived to be beyond his control might still be ashamed of his new condition. He belonged to the *poveri vergognosi*, as they were called in Italy. Their poverty was relative; it consisted of an inability to live according to their former means. This notion is distinct from the new mentality just described; it could be quite compatible with the old. St. Francis, we are told, gave away his clothes to a knight who was poorly dressed. This was an act of double charity. It provided the knight with the means to hide his shame and it alleviated his misery.[31] In its passages associating poverty and shame, the *Roman de la Rose* primarily referred to *povertà vergognosa*. It was only from the late fifteenth century onward that the image of *poveri vergognosi* was gradually merged with that of the undeserving poor.[32]

Nor was the new mentality absent in medieval society. It can be traced back to the thirteenth century, at least, but it remained a minority view well into the fifteenth century.[33] Administrative measures introduced the change to the new mentality. The Black Death is often credited with causing a shift in official policies toward vagrants. In reality, the first to be chased away were the victims themselves. It was only later that urban authorities ordered the expulsion of beggars at the beginning of a plague epidemic. Biraben found the earliest reference to this policy in Bourg-en-Bresse in 1472.[34] Periods of economic crisis also caused temporary changes of attitudes. Although private individuals were usually compassionate toward unemployed people who roamed into the cities from the countryside, urban officials feared these multitudes. References to such fears are found in sources around 1400. Mollat concludes that in the fifteenth century resident beggars were still tolerated, while vagabonds had become objects of hate.[35]

The definitive ascendancy of the new mentality came around 1500. It was announced by clerics as well as laymen. Spokespersons for both groups were active in Strassburg in the 1490s. The popular preacher Johann Geiler von Kaysersberg was renowned for his sermons against unworthy beggars. Sebastian Brant, the city's syndic, in his *Ship of Fools,* used the metaphor of folly to denounce the vanities of this world, most of which he connected with idleness.[36] Other works criticizing the life-style of marginals appeared at about the same time. The most influential was the *Liber Vagatorum,* which also originated from the upper Rhineland. This anonymous work attempted to categorize numerous types of fraudulent beggars and vagrants, and illustrated the categories with supposedly authentic case histories. This work was translated into various languages and went through numerous editions in the course of the sixteenth century. Scherpner identified thirty-two editions before 1530. Both Martin Luther and the Franciscan Thomas Murner produced an edition with commentary.[37] The stereotypical descriptions in the *Liber Vagatorum* are perfect illustrations of the new mentality.

> About the *loseneeren:*
> Those are beggars saying that they have been imprisoned for vi or vii years. And they carry chains with them by which they were tied in Turkey, or by the pagans, or in Barbary in the Sunny Wood, all for the sake of faith in Christ. Item, that they were heavily chained at sea in a galley or in another big ship, as they say. But they are lying, because many of them never saw the sea.
> About the *clinckeneeren:*
> Those are beggars sitting in front of the churches when there is a mass or consecration with awfully broken limbs. One of them has no foot, the other has no shank and the third has no hand or arms. . . . And it is all a lie what they cry out, because one had his shank or foot infected or rotten away while in jail for some misdeed. Item, the other had his hand cut off in war, or in a brothel or tavern because of women. Item, many dress their shank or arm with bandages and bloodstained cloths and they walk on crutches, although they are not disabled.
> About the *dutsbetteren* or *dutsbetterinnen:*
> Those are beggars lying down in front of the churches in every country and they cover themselves with a linen cloth and they put wax and eggs before them, as if they were women who had just been lying-in. And they say that they have been delivered from a dead child xiiii days ago, but often they have not borne a child in x or xx years.[38]

Such stereotyping was no novelty around 1500. Comparable categories of false beggars had already been referred to in Augsburg ordinances of

1342–1343, but they had not been systematically enumerated in a literary work.[39] The *Liber Vagatorum* and the *Ship of Fools* were great successes in Continental Europe. Similar suspicious attitudes and moral criticisms of marginality were found in England, too. Edmund Dudley, writing in 1509, called idleness the mother of all vice. A rogue literature denouncing beggars and vagrants flourished from the 1530s.[40]

The rise of the new mentality was accompanied by institutional changes in charity and poor relief, including restrictions on begging and increased secular control of charity. By the later Middle Ages laymen—citizens as well as magistrates—had acquired greater influence over the management of charitable institutions. The Amsterdam magistrates, for example, appointed their first supervisors of the poor at the beginning of the fifteenth century, while a little later laymen founded hospitals.[41] In the neighboring towns of Strassburg, Freiburg, and Basel a number of charitable institutions were founded by private citizens, most of them town councilors, in the course of the fifteen century. The new institutions were put under the council's supervision. Shortly after 1500 special courts to judge resident beggars and recipients of relief were established. A few decades later a more extensive program leading to urban control over charity was implemented.[42] Such a program was not peculiar to the region in question; it belonged to a reform movement that swept over many parts of Europe. Between 1520 and 1550 a number of European towns reorganized the administration of charity, and the measures taken were similar everywhere. Begging was prohibited or restricted to special groups or certain situations. Relief was only available to residents, so the nonresident poor and vagrants had to leave the city. Control of the system by ecclesiastical authorities decreased in favor of control by secular magistrates. Thus, the shift away from a deeply Christian view of poverty and marginality was accompanied by laicization at the institutional level. In all, some sixty towns in Germany, the Netherlands, France, Switzerland, and Northern Italy instituted reforms.[43] Humanists such as Erasmus, Juan Luis Vives, and Thomas More supported the reforms. Passages in Erasmus's *Colloquia,* published 1522–1524, are a warning to marginals of coming events. In one of the colloquies an alchemist says to a beggar "Citizens are already muttering that beggars shouldn't be allowed to roam at will, but that each city should support its own beggars and all the able-bodied ones forced to work." When his mate says that this will happen "*ad calendas Graecas,*" the alchemist replies: "Sooner than you'd like, perhaps."[44]

The degree of lay control over charity should not be overemphasized. Ecclesiastical bodies continued to exert an influence and there was considerable regional variation. In France charity remained primarily a church affair throughout the years of the Ancien Régime. In the Dutch Republic a dual system of relief developed, with municipalities and the churches each having their own organizations. The institutional structure, however, is less important here than the accompanying mentality. Ecclesiastical relief in the early modern period was also based on restrictive policies and conditioned assistance. To be eligible for it, the poor had to exhibit a morally irreproachable conduct. This was in line with secular policies. In France ecclesiastical and worldly authorities were in league, although the intensity with which one or the other pursued their respective policies varied according to time and place.

The Pursuit of Marginals   The movement to reform charity led to experiments in several countries with the confinement of beggars. A well-documented case is that of the Aumône Générale of Lyon. It is one of the earliest of such experiments and it testifies to the link between the reform of poor relief in the first half of the sixteenth century and the rise of prison workhouses at the end of that century and the first decades of the next. The Aumône was founded in 1531 and became a permanent organization in 1534. It had a majority of laymen and coordinated the administration of the hospitals. It also ordered alien poor to leave town, and appointed special officials to catch beggars. Those arrested were put to forced labor, usually at the ramparts. In the 1550s the Aumône started to imprison beggars in several towers which had previously been in use as jails. Although terms were short and many escaped, this policy prefigured later developments.[45]

Elsewhere in France similar projects were recorded. Paris experimented with new ways of dealing with marginals from an early date. In 1545 the Trinity hospital for poor children was established. The inmates were barred from contact with the world outside, but spent the day in prayers, instruction, and labor.[46] The first systematic roundup of marginals took place between 1611 and 1617. Twenty *sergens* had the task of chasing after vagrants and other idle people. If they had been born outside Paris or its surrounding districts, they were put in jail and tried. Native Parisians were taken to 'hospitals of the confined poor,' where they were obliged to work about twelve hours a day. When the project was apparently discontinued in 1617, the bishop of Paris was requested to start it anew. The anonymous author of this request drew inspiration from policies in Amsterdam. His only criticism of that town concerned the nonobservance of the Catholic religion in its prison.[47] Plans for a program comparable to the one instituted in Paris were made in Rouen in the 1610s, but they were not put into practice. Lyon continued its program, however. The Aumône had always wanted a more suitable place than the old towers to lock up beggars, and found one in 1622. From then on confinement of marginals was institutionalized at Lyon.[48]

Related developments were recorded in Italy. In the second half of the sixteenth century a number of towns opened special beggars' hospitals, the character of which must have been halfway between traditional asylums and prisons. Rome's was established in 1587. Carlo Borromeo, cardinal-archbishop of Milan, championed these institutions. At least one case involved real imprisonment. Some 850 beggars were locked up first in a former Dominican monastery and later in another building in Rome from early 1581 until 1583, when Borromeo intervened on their behalf. Apparently he thought this treatment went too far.[49] This case confirms that similar underlying attitudes could lead to different practical solutions. In contrast to Northern Europe, Italy did not adopt the workhouse model at this time.

These episodes represent imprisonment before the institution of the prison, which occurred outside Italy and France, too. The Spanish Benedictine monk Juan de Medina, for example, advocated restricting begging and confining the poor in 1545. In Spain, however, at that time opposition to such plans was still strong.[50] In 1622 a prison for women where they were obliged to work was established at Madrid.[51] In the 1570s about a hundred marginals were locked up in Copenhagen's castle and put to forced labor. Some were sent to the galleys.[52] The Nürnberg magistrates promulgated an ordinance against begging in 1588. The ordinance threatened adult beggars with confinement in the *bettelstock*, while children were to be taken to a hospital. From then on beggars were confined in various places until the town opened a prison workhouse in 1670.[53]

The First Prisons   While these unfinished projects and early experiments were concentrated in the Latin countries, in the North a more permanent movement was initiated. Its beginnings in England were contemporaneous with the episodes in Lyon and Rome. National plans in England for the forcible employment of vagrants date back to the 1530s.[54] Urban authorities acted first to establish prison workhouses. In London the project followed directly on the reorganization of institutional charity. Four hospitals were established, so that in theory all the deserving poor were cared for. The fifth, the ancient palace of Bridewell, just outside the city walls, was destined for the undeserving poor. Able-bodied idlers, beggars, vagabonds, and prostitutes were to be confined there. The institution was unequivocally intended to be punitive, and the inmates were to be made to support themselves through compulsory labor. A strict disciplinary and work regime was instituted, with physical penalties supplementing regular discipline. Bridewell was chartered in 1553 and handed over to the city in February 1555. An ordinance of 1557 further regulated the hospital system. It designated beggars as the principal inmates-to-be of Bridewell and compared them to thieves. Just as in the Parisian project of 1611, however, the London prison received only natives and residents. Nonresident vagrants were taken to Bridewell, too, but they were whipped upon arrival and immediately sent back to their place of origin.[55]

Bridewells—the name was used generically—or houses of correction, as they came to be called, were soon established in other English towns. Norwich, the country's second largest city at the time, opened one in 1565. The Norwich bridewell is among the best-documented. Its punitive character is attested by an ordinance of 1571 referring to the inmates as "presonars."[56] Like their London model, the institutions in the other towns featured forced labor, discipline, and a strict daily routine.[57] For at least two decades the prison movement remained exclusively urban, but a statute of 1576 ordered the establishment of institutions in the provinces. Consequently, a number of county bridewells were opened, championed by the justices of the peace, who had the authority to confine offenders in them. Not every county bridewell had a work program. The inmate population resembled that in the towns; it included vagabonds who had been arrested elsewhere and sent back to their native area.[58]

On the Continent the movement also began as an urban one. The first prison on the Continent was opened at Amsterdam in 1596, following a decision of the city council in 1589. The institution had been promoted especially by the liberal faction within the city's patriciate. A number of towns in the Republic soon followed Amsterdam's example, as did Antwerp shortly after the truce between the Dutch and the Spanish. The Hanseatic towns of Bremen, Hamburg, Lübeck, and a little further away, Danzig, also were inspired by the institution of the Amsterdam prison. The movement even reached the Danish and Swedish capitals. With a few exceptions, the urban elite constituted the driving force behind the movement. As in England, the institutions in question had a punitive character, and they relied even more heavily than in England on a regime of compulsory labor. Marginals, persons failing to live up to moral standards, and a few petty thieves were their first inmates.

Imprisonment was not the only penalty and not even the oldest penalty that deprived delinquents or other offenders of their freedom or subjected them to forced labor. Early modern Europe witnessed three other forms of forced labor bondage: the galleys, public works, and transportation. The first is the most important for this discussion, because it preceded imprisonment and developed in close relationship with the repression of marginality. Its principal limitation was that women could not be subjected to it. Already in the fifteenth century French vagabonds served as oarsmen in the country's galleys for punishment or as a result of impressment. Originally, however, marginals and delinquents were a small minority among the oarsmen. The galley fleets employed by most Mediterranean states were manned by 'volunteers' and slaves. The latter were either Muslims captured at sea or persons bought at the slave markets of the Middle East. In France, Spain, and most Italian states, after about 1500, galley sentences became common.[59] On Italian galleys, for example, by the middle of the sixteenth century the condemned became the majority versus volunteers. In Venice a fairly ample supply of volunteer oarsmen from among lower-class natives and men from the Dalmatian and Greek coasts delayed this process a little. By the end of the century involuntary rowers dominated on the Venetian fleet, too.[60] Marginals constituted a substantial number of those receiving galley sentences. In France, Spain, and some Italian states, vagrants were occasionally rounded up to serve in the fleet. When Venice's hospitals became too crowded in the 1540s, a number of unlicensed beggars were condemned to the galleys.[61] This punishment, then, functioned as the Southern European equivalent to the workhouse of the North. That imprisonment and galley servitude were seen as akin can be deduced from the popular name of the prison for women opened at Madrid in 1622. Contemporaries referred to it as *la galera,* because it was supposed to be as frightening as the prospect of a term in the fleet for males.

In a broad sense, public works could include many forms of compulsory labor, even labor in prisons. Usually, though, it referred to forced employment building fortifications, in mines, on construction projects, or at such unpleasant jobs as collecting feces. Europeans probably adopted this form of punishment in imitation of the ancient Romans. Imperial laws distinguished between *metallum,* a life sentence to hard labor in the mines, and *opus publicum,* which involved lighter forms of servitude. Both were listed as official penalties since the time of Tiberius, but they were only imposed on low social status offenders.[62] In preindustrial Europe the Spanish monarchy was the first to employ delinquents at public works.[63] During the seventeenth century a number of German towns and territories followed. Transportation of convicts to colonies or other far-away places was practiced especially in England, and had its heyday still later. The evolution of these forms of bondage until about 1800 is dealt with in Chapter Eleven.

The Social Origins of the Prison Workhouse

Historical explanation means linking different phenomena. The previous section began this process by presenting the cultural background of the emergence of imprisonment and other forms of bondage. The purpose of this section is to inquire into the relationships of both phenomena with large-scale developments in European society. Two things must be explained and differentiated: the social context of the general transformation of mentalities; and the direct causes of the ultimate result of this transformation in Northern Europe, the institution of prison workhouses. Let us begin with the prison workhouses. The following is a complete list of prisons founded up to 1625:[64]

1555	London
1562	Oxford
1565–c. 1600	Other English towns
1596	Amsterdam

1598	Leiden, Leeuwarden
1604–c. 1620	Other towns in the Dutch Republic
1605	Copenhagen
1608	Bremen
1613	Lübeck, Antwerp
1618	Hamburg
1622	Lyon, Madrid
1624	Stockholm
1625	Brussels

The early prisons were concentrated in Europe's northern parts. The exceptions were Lyon and Madrid, and Madrid was untypical because its prison was for women only. Italy followed a different pattern than the northern European countries, establishing semivoluntary hospitals for marginals in the second half of the sixteenth century. The Latin countries relied on galley servitude for a penalty. Thus, the workhouse model mainly belonged to the North. However, the emergence of prisons was an international phenomenon that cannot be explained with reference to one country alone. The oldest theory linked it to Protestantism.

The Reformation   Since the turn of the century a school of German legal historians, headed by Robert von Hippel, has occupied itself with the origins of prison workhouses from an international perspective. They considered resocialization as the essence of modern imprisonment. Its purpose was to make prisoners 'better,' that is, to educate them in a moral and practical sense. This educational purpose was deduced from the prescription of religious exercises in prison ordinances and from a supposed implied switch away from a retributive idea of punishment. Forced labor was viewed as a contribution to practical education.[65] Since the earliest institutions were established in Protestant countries and religious instruction was so central to the resocialization argument, it was a natural step to the idea that Protestantism was somehow responsible for the emergence of imprisonment. This argument was introduced by Wilhelm Traphagen, who concluded that the educational purpose of the prisons had not come about as a result of changes in legal thinking but that it was part of a more general "protestant-humanistic reform movement."[66]

The humanistic component is removed by Hellmuth von Weber and Gustav Radbruch. They posit an intimate connection between Protestantism and the rise of prison workhouses. According to Von Weber, a number of Calvinist legal theorists wished to base criminal law upon Mosaic precepts. For most offenses this meant advocating more severe penalties, but in case of theft it led to a rejection of capital punishment and the recommendation to put delinquents to work. Calvinism, Von Weber concludes, led to a broad reform in criminal law, with the Amsterdam rasphouse, which was supposedly inaugurated by Calvinists, as its landmark.[67] Radbruch argues in a similar vein. According to him, the early prisons in England, the Netherlands, and Northern Germany had their roots in the Protestant ethic. More specifically, the London bridewell and the Amsterdam rasphouse were the spiritual children of groups of radical Protestants. In Amsterdam these are the Calvinists again, who are assumed to have been the ruling elite. In London Radbruch sees a faction favoring a radical Protestant theology responsible for the institutional reform of which Bridewell formed a part. Some of the members of this faction, he says, were burned at the stake during Queen Mary's reign. To Radbruch these events are a confirmation of Max Weber's theory. The Protestant ethic gave rise to institutions through which people were made accustomed to constant methodical labor. Radbruch goes so far as to call rasping wood an example of innerworldly asceticism.[68]

Such theories involve another, implicit idea, that the Reformation greatly reinforced the new mentality with regard to marginals and the poor. The connections seem easy to establish. Luther's doctrine of justification by faith alone lessened the need to do good works and give alms. Attacks on the mendicant orders could have reinforced the idea that all beggars were hypocrites. Condemnation of the cult of saints prevented vagabonds from posing as pilgrims. Finally, Calvinists saw poverty as a sign of not belonging to the elect. However, we should not overemphasize these associations. Although Protestant theology denied any beneficial effect for the almsgiver in the hereafter, Protestants still considered charity to be pleasing to God. Criticism of the mendicant orders as well as suspicion of pilgrims predated the Reformation. The Counter-Reformation led to a purification of the cult of saints and Catholic ritual generally of what had come to be recognized as abuses. At the same time, Catholics laid a greater emphasis upon disciplining the popular classes, which related to the second main purpose of prisons. Prostitution, which had been regulated but not criminalized during the later Middle Ages, came under heavy attack from Protestants, but Catholics soon adopted a more repressive attitude toward it, too. To conclude, it is fair to say that the Reformation accelerated the processes discussed here, but it did not produce them, and the Counter-Reformation soon caught up with the Reformation regarding the matters at issue.

The supposed link between radical Protestant factions and the emergence of prison workhouses fades upon inspection of the evidence from individual institutions.[69] There was no such link in London. The inauguration of Bridewell and the institutional reorganization of which it formed part had been advocated by churchmen like Nicholas Ridley as well as secular authorities such as Richard Dobbs and George Barnes, the lord mayors of 1551–1552. Barnes endorsed a petition from the citizens of London to the king to hand over his ancient palace. Only Ridley ended at the stake. He had been in the Tower for a year and a half when Bridewell was opened in 1555. The continuation of the project under Queen Mary proves that it was not considered especially Protestant at the time.[70] The continuation was owing to the interest in the project of London's ruling groups, whose interests were relatively independent of the politico-religious pendulum swings at the national level. There is even less evidence for an influential role of radical Protestant factions in the Hanseatic towns. These towns were ruled by patrician elites who were generally distrustful of religious radicalism. Although Bremen was officially Calvinist and Hamburg Lutheran, in both cities the anti-Catholic fervor and the impetus toward purity of faith came mainly from the lower-middle classes.

For Amsterdam and other Dutch towns the story is similar. It would be wrong to consider the Republic's political elite as Calvinists, at least in the early years. At the beginning the Reformed church included only a small minority of the population. Moreover, within this church a liberal and an orthodox current of thought held each other in balance until the Synod of Dordt. Most importantly, there existed a liberal ideological current within and outside the church. Its representatives included followers of other Protestant denominations and even Catholics. They cherished a policy of religious toleration and advocated the independence of the secular authorities from the prescriptions of the ministers. As the following chapter will demonstrate, the founding fathers of Amsterdam's prison were all associated with the liberal current.[71] This current almost always prevailed in Amsterdam. The only notable period of exception was during the 1610s, when the rasphouse had been in existence for some twenty years.

The final argument against the Reformation thesis is implied by the early prison foundations in a few Catholic towns. The first was the Antwerp *dwinghuis,* in 1613. An advice of June 1609 had recommended provisions to combat beggary and vagrancy, which were said to be on the increase due to the disbanding of troops.[72] Not only did the truce contribute to the problem, it facilitated the solution. The Antwerp founding fathers must have oriented themselves on this matter in Protestant Holland, since they collected copies of ordinances from the *tuchthuis* at Gouda. This proves that they considered the issue of the repression of marginality without regard to religion. In fact, the person who drew up the ordinance to create the *dwinghuis* closely followed the Gouda text, leaving a blank when he came to the passage listing the prayers to be recited by the prisoners. Another hand inserted: Pater Noster, Ave Maria, and the articles of faith. The Antwerp prison was to have a continuous existence throughout the early modern period.[73]

Events in Lyon have been discussed already. Although this town was exposed to Huguenot influences in the sixteenth century, Catholics participated in the reformed poor relief system, and the opening of a prison occurred during the heyday of the Counter-Reformation. Events elsewhere in France, although they occurred later, were significant, too. The Counter-Reformation was the prime mover behind the development of confinement in France before the monarchy took up the issue. Remember that the champions of the Paris experiment of 1611–1617 advocated a Catholic Amsterdam system. From the middle of the seventeenth century so-called *hôpitaux généraux,* housing the needy as well as offenders, were established in France. This system implied an adaptation of the old model of the hospital to the new one of the prison workhouse.[74] The inauguration of these *hôpitaux* had been championed by the Company of the Holy Sacrament, an association of fervent Catholics. It was dominated by nobles and magistrates of the *robe,* but religious people such as Vincent de Paul, Louise de Marillac, and Bossuet played important roles in the Company, too. Although Vincent placed the greatest emphasis on the asylum function and advocated voluntary entry, others had a more punitive institution in mind. The Company was bent on a campaign against popular license, which, in its view, consisted of blasphemy, nonattendance at Mass, prostitution, begging, and vagrancy. Mendicant Huguenots were mentioned among the categories to be imprisoned in the *hôpital* established under the aegis of the Company at Toulouse in 1647.[75]

The refutation of the Reformation thesis leads to a conclusion as to immediate causes of the rise of the prison workhouse. Protestantism may still be given partial credit. France developed the counter-model of the *hôpital* because its religious elite partially clung to traditional notions of charity. Next to the punishment of malefactors, they emphasized the provision of asylum for the needy. The institutions in Northern Europe had a more straightforward penal character. Although some of them were associated with voluntary workhouses, they all placed a strong emphasis on the value of hard labor. This element in the transformation of attitudes was first elaborated under the influence of the Reformation. It is one thing to downgrade the poor and view beggars with suspicion; it is another to believe that anyone who does not work should be forced to do so, rather than simply neglected or chased away. Although marginals had been subjected to galley servitude in the Mediterranean, the prison workhouses of the North inaugurated a more methodical use of forced labor for beggars and vagabonds. This reorientation may have come about more quickly under the influence of Protestant thinking.

Once the idea of the prison workhouse had been conceived, its implementation was independent of struggles between religious factions. Patricians agreed on policies to pursue. The second and more important explanation for the rise of prison workhouses is that it was a response by urban elites to problems they felt to be acute in the late sixteenth and early seventeenth centuries. Most of the early prisons were urban institutions. The bridewell movement in England began in the towns, only extending into the countryside after some decades. During the early years the houses at London and Norwich dominated the scene. The central government later added an impetus of its own. In Continental Europe the elites involved were usually autonomous or semiautonomous patriciates. They took pride in their relatively independent position and cherished their own institutions. The majority of Dutch prisons were inaugurated in the highly urbanized province of Holland. The rest of the first-wave foundations were also situated in maritime regions. More to the North, there were a few exceptions to this pattern. Copenhagen's *tugthus* of 1605 was founded by Christian IV and was intended as a central prison institution for the Danish-Norwegian monarchy.[76] In Stockholm the king and his advisors were involved, in the decision to establish a prison, along with the capital's magistrates.[77] However, the example of the North Sea and Baltic ports of Bremen, Hamburg, Lübeck, and Danzig (1629–1630) clearly predominated in this region. They were city-states which could completely determine their own policies in such respects.

To conclude, the inauguration of prison workhouses received a major impetus from relatively independent commercial and entrepreneurial elites. On a European scale, the beginnings of the movement were urban. In turn, this factor helped determine the form of bondage. The urban elites of the North did not own galley fleets. These ships mainly plied the Mediterranean, where the Valois/Bourbon and Habsburg monarchs contested with each other. French and Spanish judges, whether in the towns or in the countryside, had the option of pronouncing galley sentences. In Italy a process of rearistocratization took place, so that ruling groups around 1600 were territorial rather than urban elite. The geographic and urban-commercial factors were obviously connected. The first wave of prison foundations came out of the sea. It swept over commercial and industrial towns in Northern Europe at precisely the same time as the center of gravity in international trade definitely shifted from the South to the North. The Italian cities might have pioneered in imprisonment in the second half of the sixteenth century, but they chose to establish more strictly regulated hospitals instead. By the time prison workhouses became a familiar feature of Northern Europe, commercial activities and urban life had declined in Italy. In the end, however, imprisonment spread to Southern Europe, too. France, which introduced it during the time it was using galley servitude and then used the two forms of bondage contemporaneously, was the first country to imitate the pioneers. Eventually, imprisonment was felt to be superior. Sending morals offenders to the galleys was considered too severe a punishment, especially if they were punished at the behest of their families. Imprisonment, moreover, could also be imposed on women.

Finally, the geographical location of prison workhouses was not solely dependent on commercial considerations. The third factor among immediate causes for the rise of prison workhouses was regional cultural affinity.

Within a region, ruling groups were quick to imitate each other. This can explain why a town such as Stockholm, situated in a supposedly backward area, had a prison earlier than Paris or Rome. The first line of influence was probably from London or Norwich to Amsterdam. Numerous contacts existed between England and the Netherlands, though an exchange of ideas on imprisonment has not been demonstrated so far.[78] Such an exchange has been demonstrated in the case of Amsterdam and the Hanseatic towns. Interaction between the Dutch Republic and Northern Germany was not restricted to the economic sphere. They were adjacent cultural areas with numerous common characteristics at this time. Their cultural affinity was indicated most conspicuously by their common language.[79] The earliest documents relating to imprisonment in Bremen and Hamburg were written in local speech. It was only toward the middle of the seventeenth century that High German became the official language. The Amsterdam magistrates could have had no difficulty understanding the letter they received from their Bremen colleagues in 1604, stating that the latter were planning to establish a prison, following the Amsterdam example.[80] Thus cultural affinity was especially strong between Holland and the Hanseatic towns, and the latter in their turn influenced Scandinavia. Commercial and religious contacts did, of course, contribute to the cultural ties.

Secularization   With the question of the immediate causes for the emergence of the prison workhouse answered, we can inquire into the social context of the change of mentalities that preceded and accompanied it. First we have to determine the driving force behind the transformation of attitudes toward poverty and marginality. Obviously, it formed part of a process of secularization. The new mentality was more secular because it substituted a repressive and public order-oriented view of the poor for the image of holy poverty. Beggars were no longer following Jesus's footsteps; rather, the explanation for their condition was much more mundane. An entire social group, that had been considered originally from a religious point of view, was now considered primarily in terms of the worldly trouble its members might cause to the society around them. This secularization was only an episode in a larger movement. It constituted an early phase in a process that was to go on for centuries while everyone still entertained religious convictions. The moral campaigns accompanying the rise of imprisonment and the initiatives taken by churchmen were not incompatible with the changed attitude toward marginals. Only by adopting a longer-term perspective, do we see that a degree of secularization was involved in these campaigns and initiatives. Both Protestantism and Tridentine Catholicism were more worldly-oriented than medieval Christianity. The early modern churches insisted on a sharper distinction of the sacred from the profane, whereby the latter domain was 'left to the world.'

A parallel development took place in the institutional sphere. Supervision and relief of the poor, which had been almost exclusively a concern of the church, came to be controlled to a greater degree by laymen, magistrates as well as private persons. This was a long-term process, too. The struggle for control of hospitals between ecclesiastics on the one hand and private citizens and urban authorities on the other dates back to the thirteenth century.[81] To a certain extent, the dissolution of the medieval church accelerated this development. The crucial reform movement of the first half of the sixteenth century had a complicated relationship with the emergence of Protestantism. In some towns the coming of the Reformation was the major impulse behind it. When Hamburg turned Lutheran in the 1520s, for example, lay control increased over education, poor relief, and the choice of pastors. Lay deacons began to administer the charity boxes in each of the four parishes.[82] In Bremen, where the Reformation started in 1522, a similar arrangement was soon effected.[83] The Aumône Générale of Genève, on the other hand, was in place when Calvin arrived in the city and he did not basically change it.[84] It had been instituted on the model of Lyon. The reform of poor relief in the latter town was effected by a coalition consisting of a majority who remained Catholic and a few who later became Huguenots.

In Lyon the reform drew its principal inspiration from humanism.[85] Throughout Europe that was important, too. A broad intellectual movement was involved, with humanism rather than Protestantism at its center. It has been noted that Erasmus and More were in favor of the new system. Vives, the humanist who always remained a convinced Catholic, provided a program for it. His *De subventione pauperum* inspired a number of Flemish cities to reorganize charity in the 1520s.[86] In 1527–1528 the Estates of Holland discussed plans to imitate Flanders, but this did not result in provincial measures. Amsterdam issued ordinances against idleness in 1527 and 1529. For Holland as a whole, Charles V's placard putting severe restrictions on begging followed in 1531.[87] The prominent role played by humanists is compatible with my conclusion that the transformation of attitudes was an expression of processes of secularization. Humanism itself implied a temporary breakthrough of a more secular and bourgeois culture, and the rebirth of antiquity was also a reaction against the dominance of the Christian ecclesiastical tradition. Hence, it is understandable that humanists would champion the laicization of poor relief.

In one respect Protestant towns and countries could go further. Civil authorities confiscated monasteries and often turned them into asylums.[88] This is a clear case of secularization at the institutional level. This confiscation movement continued into the period when the first prisons appeared, which were sometimes established in former monasteries. The idea was that prisons were a sort of charitable institutions, too, and that the buildings in question continued in their basic function as places of assistance. This is a crucial point that I will return to in subsequent chapters. Contemporaries considered the introduction of prisons as an innovation in poor relief. In the Netherlands the medieval charitable institutions, collectively called *godshuizen* and *tuchthuizen*, were included in this category. The London bridewell was usually called a hospital during its early years. These observations, however, imply that a residue of the old notions of charity survived in Protestant countries, too. In France, where these notions lingered on longer, the term 'hospital' was retained for an even longer time. In the second half of the eighteenth century the *dépôts de mendicité* were the first prisons in France to bear a public order-oriented name.

To conclude, the transformation of attitudes toward poverty, marginality, and labor was a manifestation of processes of secularization. The Reformation, although not causing the transformation served as an accelerator within these processes. Protestants emphasized the principle that everyone should work, but this idea reached Catholic countries, too. The advice on confinement of marginals presented to the bishop of Paris in 1617 paraphrased a Biblical statement: "You will earn your living by your labor and eat your bread with the sweat on your face."[89] Since the late sixteenth century, Catholic as well as Protestant moralists were equally avid to proclaim the positive benefits of hard work.[90] It is now generally agreed that Max Weber overestimated the Reformation's role in forging a new mentality leading to a capitalistic outlook, methodical labor practices, and a stricter sense of time and punctuality. The wave of secularization discussed here was related to that forging, but it was relatively independent of the denominational struggle. Its links with economic and social processes were characterized by interdependence and mutual interaction rather than simple cause and effect relationships.

However, in relating the reform of poor relief to the work of Max Weber, another theme comes to mind: the progressive rationalization of administration from the sixteenth century onward. The new system of charity adopted in many European towns was a relatively rational one. Whatever those caught in its net may have felt about it, the dual principles of restricted almsgiving and repression of begging were based on a few simple presuppositions. The inhabitants of a town were to find employment in trades practiced there. Widows, the old, the infirm, and children were to be cared for by their families, but if they had none or that was otherwise impossible, organized charity provided for them. Since charity was based locally, people who were unable to work and sought relief should remain in or return to their place of birth. Residents who were temporarily unemployed could also claim some assistance in their home town. It followed that any healthy adult who was roaming around and begging was simply lazy and unwilling to work. Such people were chased away, or after prisons had been established, confined and sentenced to hard labor. The argumentation included only one premise which modern historians recognize as unrealistic: that the economy could accommodate everyone who was physically able to work. The authorities implicitly assumed that finding employment was easy if one wanted it, and vagrants were not seen as economically disadvantaged. They were considered lazy and idle, and their presence was considered to constitute a moral problem that justified their punishment.[91] The historian cannot assume that every healthy beggar was lazy. Even with regard to those who might have been, such an ethical judgment after four centuries would be completely irrelevant. Instead, we must explain why some people might have preferred to live a life of begging.

Pacification and Integration   It is not enough to argue that the transformation of attitudes about poverty and marginality formed part of a process of secularization. The argument connects specific and general developments in the area of mentalities. The next step is to inquire into the interrelationships of these cultural developments with other social processes. To what extent were they reinforced by such phenomena as urbanization, state formation, or economic differentiation?

A very old presupposition is that the negative attitude toward marginals followed upon an actual increase in their numbers. Earlier historians took at face value statements to this regard in legal texts from the fifteenth to the eighteenth centuries. It is unlikely that marginalization became continually more common during that long period. We want an exact count, but it is hard to tell how many beggars and vagrants were around at a particular time and place. Increases in their numbers have been deduced from demographic data. Notably, a population growth around 1500 is supposed to have led to an increase in migration, which in turn contributed to the breakthrough of the new mentality.[92] Thomas Fischer undertook a systematic evaluation of this argument and had to reject it. In the upper Rhineland there was no chronological connection between the rise of a money economy and demographic changes on the one hand, and the reorganization of charity on the other. The reform of poor relief in the sixteenth century antedated the most conspicuous wave of population growth.[93]

If this argument is to have any explanatory value, it would probably be in terms of a very loose connection between the new mentality and a greater visibility of marginality. That visibility was primarily a result of the rise of towns, which leads us to the process of urbanization. The rise of towns also was an impetus to secularization generally. Medieval urban culture, although intensely Christian, nevertheless constituted the first challenge to the church and the clergy. The burghers destroyed the church's monopoly over means of orientation.[94] This explains why the new mentality initially found a more favorable response in the cities. Urbanization, complemented by the rise of stronger states in Europe, also served as a precondition for the emergence of imprisonment, in that the relative pacification that resulted from these developments contributed to the new attitude toward marginality. From the twelfth to the fifteenth centuries, Western Europe witnessed the gradual development of a justice from above. It was related at first to the rise of territorial principalities and later to the consolidation of urban communities into more highly stratified and hierarchically governed towns.[95] But the idea of confinement did not arise in that period because in the larger society the pacification was not as apparent. A higher degree of pacification was reached in the course of the sixteenth century, when stronger states appeared on the European scene and towns were integrated into large networks. These developments reinforced the new mentality concerning marginals, culminating in the emergence of imprisonment.

It might be objected that some of the regions where the earliest prisons were established were not noted for centralization. The response to this is that the rise of stronger states led to a relative pacification in Western Europe as a whole that influenced the smaller territories and city-republics.[96] The thesis holds when we look at the chronology in a little more detail. There was a delay between the publication of books such as the *Liber Vagatorum* and the introduction of a more restricted system of charity on the one hand, and the foundation of prison workhouses on the other. The first event took place at the beginning of the sixteenth century and the second around 1600. This means that the movement had two separate phases. The first coincided with the rise of the New Monarchies in Western Europe. A period of civil wars and armed conflicts over religious and political issues followed. During that period the repression of marginals abated. The second phase of the movement was again one of relative peace. The Hanseatic prisons were founded in the period between the wars of religion and the Thirty Years' War. During the latter conflict Hamburg and Bremen had a hard time, but they managed to keep military operations outside their walls.[97] The Dutch prison system was established when the struggle against the Spanish went to an offensive stage and the Republic was consolidated. Thereupon, no foreign armies entered the Republic's territory until the French invasion of 1672. Although not centralized, most of the united provinces were certainly pacified.

It is easy to see why pacification served as a precondition for the rise of confinement. The foundation of prison workhouses implied at least two changes of policy. In the first place, the institutions served as concrete symbols of repression, testifying to the desire of magistrates to deal with new categories of offenders, namely, beggars and vagrants, whom the simultaneous change of attitude toward poverty and idleness had put into an unfavorable position. In a relatively pacified society, where private warfare and vendettas have been subdued, authorities have the opportunity to tackle new public order problems. When armed knights disappeared from the scene, beggars entered the picture. In 1473 the Parlement of Paris still linked the two groups by defining vagabonds primarily as armed persons who had falsely stated they were in the service of some *seigneur*.[98]

The second change of policy is implied by the fact that prisons constituted a new option for dealing with people who in an earlier period would also have been treated as offenders. Formerly they might have been banished. Within the penal system, imprisonment began as an alternative to banishment more than anything else. This is attested by Dutch terminology, in which, for most of the seventeenth century, imprisonment was referred to as a special form of exile. Magistrates spoke of banishing people into *tuchthuizen*. Only later were the notions of not being allowed to enter a place and being forbidden to leave a place differentiated and termed banishment and confinement, respectively.[99] The idea that unwanted strangers might be kept off the roads rather than chased away is more likely to arise in a relatively pacified society. In earlier times, when banishment was the rule, the problems of the neighboring town or territory that might receive the banished vagrant failed to bother local judges. The idea of keeping undesirables under custody was realized in the prison workhouse, which was a spatial solution to public order problems. Other types of penal bondage were spatial solutions, too. Convicted oarsmen could not leave the galley, or when ashore, the port area. Transported convicts were removed from an entire kingdom. Banishment remained a standard penal option until the early nineteenth century, but it functioned primarily as a police measure to facilitate procedures if and when the culprit had to be dealt with again.

This does not complete the story, however. Pacification alone was an insufficient precondition to dissuade local judges from merely chasing troublesome people away. In adopting the spatial solution, they had to identify with their neighbors' problems. A remark by the Leiden council, when they were reflecting upon the uses of imprisonment and planning to introduce it in their city, indicates the larger, spatial frame of reference. Prisons, it was said, "should also hold those persons whom we used to punish less than physically, *banishing them upon each other's backs.*"[100] Because the towns in Holland constituted an integrated urban system, concern about public order transcended the local level. Around 1600 the magistrates of Amsterdam, Leiden, and elsewhere decided to cooperate instead of sloughing off their problems on each other. That implied a major change in attitude. In the Republic supra-local cooperation was very common, in contrast to what it had been in the Northern Netherlands in the later Middle Ages. The changed nature of preindustrial labor protest is another illustration of the shift in attitude. In the fourteenth and fifteenth centuries discontented cloth workers often threatened to leave town, knowing that they could count on a sympathetic welcome in the next town. The cities were competitors. By the early seventeenth century, on the other hand, urban magistrates acted in consort to suppress labor unrest. Employers in the textile industry also cooperated nationally.[101] Thus, the republican political structure did not preclude supra-local integration.

In some rural areas, on the other hand, such a sense of belonging to a wider structure was much slower to develop. English villagers in the early seventeenth century, for example, had no special concern for the confinement of marginals, despite the availability of houses of correction. Local constables were often prepared to let vagrants pass on to the next village.[102] Urban and national authorities may have strived toward greater control, but visions at the community level were not that broad. These observations make it possible to avoid the traditional opposition of political versus economic causation. Merchants in medieval cities may have thought substantially in the same way as these seventeenth-century villagers. Medieval merchants were hard-working men who spent their day in a manner quite different from the marginals. Some of the marginals may have bothered them occasionally, but they were probably satisfied if the troublesome were banished from town. The difference between the medieval and seventeenth-century situation is that the merchant or entrepreneur of the latter period probably thought there was more at stake. He viewed the problem from a national perspective, exemplified by the mutual cooperation among Dutch cloth employers. Historians who state that those in charge of the economy wanted the confinement of marginals and hence favored the establishment of prison workhouses are certainly right. However, the implicit change of attitude involved a process that was only partly economic. It included economic and political integration. When urban magistrates founded prisons, they did so because they were aware that their city belonged to an integrated urban network. In like manner, the economic leaders were conscious of operating within a supra-local economic network. Integration is the key word. Imprisonment began in regions which had become relatively integrated, politically and economically. Those two aspects were interrelated: pacification was a precondition for economic integration and vice versa, and the general level of integration reached around 1600 affected the decisions of territorial rulers and urban elites alike.

Thus, the relationships among long-term historical processes should be seen as interactions, rather than as one the cause of the other. The rise of imprisonment was a result of such interaction. From the fourteenth century on, urbanization made marginality increasingly more visible, which led to the emergence of a relatively secularized view of the poor. An acceleration in state formation processes around 1500 led to greater pacification that affected less centralized areas, too. This reinforced the new mentality with regard to marginals, which increasingly included the notion that they should be forced to work. The spatial solution, the principle of confining undesirables instead of chasing them away, formed the link between the cultural and social developments. Its concrete implementation was different in Northern and Southern Europe. While the southern monarchies subjected marginals to galley servitude, the autonomous and semiautonomous cities of the North developed the model of the prison workhouse.

The Sequel   This chapter focused on the origins of imprisonment. A brief anticipation of later developments may conclude it. The discussion of economic and political integration is a starting point. During the early years numerous initiatives toward creation of prisons were taken by supervisors of the poor and other prominent members of the urban bourgeoisie. This occurred in the Netherlands and Germany. At that time the founding fathers still had hopes that prisons might finance themselves. As time went on it became clear that this was only a dream. During the later waves of prison foundations the authorities increasingly took the initiative. Their problem was crime and they knew that its repression always costs money. Rich citizens only took the initiative when the concern was private confinement of family members, but this would often be in private institutions, which were not financed with tax money. This leads us to two major themes that will be pursued in the following chapters. The first centers around forced labor and the policies of the authorities. Prison workhouses, which were mixed institutions of discipline and charity when they were inaugurated, were increasingly associated with the penal system. The second major theme revolves around the balance between tendencies toward concentration and differentiation within the prison system. Various categories of deviants were often concentrated in one institution, but there were countervailing tendencies, too. Notably, imprisonment in private institutions at the request of families implied a degree of differentiation. The eighteenth century, the heyday of this practice, was a period of transition with respect to family honor. Sensitivity concerning one's reputation was greater than before and representatives of the state still found they had tasks to perform in this area. That phase in the history of family honor is inextricably tied to the history of imprisonment.

PART TWO:

PRISONERS AND
FORCED LABOR

3

THE PERIOD OF EXPERIMENTATION
Prison Workhouses on the Continent, 1588–1650

It all began with a young man of sixteen named Evert Jans. At a loss what to do with him, Amsterdam's *schepenen,* the town judges, consulted the burgomasters and suggested that a house be built to keep such persons in custody. The advice set a chain of events in motion which ultimately led to the opening of a prison early in 1596. In turn, this triggered a confinement movement in other towns of the Northern and Southern Netherlands and the Holy Roman Empire. Amsterdam was the starting point for the movement in Continental Europe, and the workhouse model was developed more fully there than in England. Consequently, the early years in the Dutch metropolis will receive much attention. Although the Amsterdam rasphouse records have been lost, enough bits and pieces of data are extant in other archives to tell its story. The first section deals with Amsterdam and the second with its imitators elsewhere in Holland and in the Hanseatic towns up to about 1650.

Amsterdam: Starting from Scratch

Evert Jans was arrested near the end of 1588. He appears in the judicial records on 22 December of that year, the day of his first interrogation. The court clerk introduced Evert's case, noting that he had been born in the city and was sixteen years of age, and stating that he had been employed in cloth workers' shops. His latest master, Joost Jacobsz, had apparently turned him in. When questioned, Evert replied that toward evening the previous Thursday he had had himself locked in at the latter's workshop. He confessed to having stolen a few items there. He said he did this with one of his workmates. They sold the items, along with two tin plates he had taken from his master earlier, in a tavern frequented by rogues. In addition, he confessed to a theft from a warehouse. The judges were not satisfied with this confession, however, since they also suspected him of burglary. On 21 January 1589 the *schout* received permission to torture Evert. After he had been beaten with rods, he confessed to having broken into the house of an apothecary with two mates named Maarten and Geurt.[1]

So far it would appear to be a normal court case, thousands of which were conducted throughout the early modern period. For some reason, however, the judges were frightened by the prospect that a young adolescent apparently from a respectable family was entering upon a career of crime. They postponed their judgment for almost two months and even then, on 17 March, they merely pronounced an intermediate sentence. It was decided to bring the case to the attention of burgomasters. The latter were to request the town council to look for "some appropriate means to provide such citizens' children with steady labor, and thus dissociate them from their bad habits, so that an improvement of their way of life can be expected."[2] Since there is no record of the council's discussions, we only know about its final decision on 19 July 1589. It is indicated by the marginal notation "the house for the chastisement of malefactors," which suggests that the matter had been talked about before. The magistrates, the record said, had been informed that malefactors were apprehended daily, most of them very young and citizens of Amsterdam. Because of their youth, the *schepenen* felt uneasy and objected to capital or corporal punishments. Therefore, they requested that the burgomasters and council establish "a house where all vagabonds, malefactors, rogues and the like might be kept for chastisement." They should be obliged to work there and to stay as long as the *schepenen* found it necessary to keep them. The council agreed to erect such an institution and designated the Clara convent as its site.[3] Although no reference to the case of Evert Jans was made, it is clear that his intermediate sentence was the immediate cause for the magistrates' actions. The council referred to the initiative of the judiciary and in both the March and July proceedings there was talk of labor as a penalty for young citizens to make them mend their ways. The inclusion of the word 'vagabonds' in the July decision, on the other hand, suggests that the magistrates also thought of noncitizens.

It is unclear whether action was taken immediately. The original idea seems to have been to set up the house in just a part of the convent, so that the nuns could remain there, too. That would not have been very practical, however, and a pretext to expel them was soon found. Earlier that year the Reformed consistory had reproached a church member for taking his sick child to the Clarissians, which may have caused the consistory to complain to the magistrates.[4] In November the council accused the nuns of "superstitious practices," and noted that they had also unlawfully installed iron locks and a fence. They were ordered to leave the convent by May 1590.[5] Meanwhile, Evert Jans's case was not allowed to wait on the establishment of the prison. He had been condemned on 12 August for his thefts and especially his burglary by night with two accomplices. The judges took into consideration that he was a first offender and still young and that an improvement of his behavior might be expected. For this reason they sentenced him to be whipped indoors and be employed at the city's public works for six years. If he escaped and was apprehended again, he was to be whipped and his term of labor renewed.[6]

This final sentence is revealing. The judges apparently considered employment at public works a reasonable alternative to the form of confinement which they were planning but could not yet put into effect. This proves that the two forms of punishment were seen as alternatives. Nor was bondage incompatible with physical punishment. Evert Jans was whipped as well as bound into public works service, but indoors, that is, not on the scaffold, so that he retained his honor. The case as a whole makes clear that the decision to build a house of chastisement was perceived primarily as an action in the penal sphere. The house was for persons who had committed acts which, in principle, were matters for a criminal court. However, chastisement by labor was seen as very different from traditional punishments. It should offer the opportunity for resocialization, in the sense that it was to prevent those subjected to it from association with hardened rogues, the type of people who frequented the tavern where Evert Jans and his mate had sold their first stolen goods.

The Founding Fathers When Amsterdam magistrates began to reflect upon the purposes and the regime of the house, it soon acquired a name, the *tuchthuis*. It is difficult to evaluate the precise meaning and connotations of the word *tucht* at the end of the sixteenth century. It probably was halfway between discipline and punishment, while it also connoted coaching into better habits. It was the opposite of *ontucht* (vice). The word also appears in the title of a treatise published in 1587, Coornhert's *Boeventucht*, which might be translated "the discipline of rogues."

Dirk Volkertsz Coornhert (1522–1590), writer and engraver, was employed as a city secretary at Haarlem and Gouda. Working in the service of urban magistrates, he did not belong to the patrician elite himself. His treatise contains the only systematic discussion of criminality and punishment published at the time. According to Coornhert, idleness lay at the root of both poverty and crime, the prevention of which should begin with the supervision of poor households. His main concern, however, was with professional criminals. They were not afraid of the ineluctable 'bad morning,' when they had to end their life on a scaffold. The remedy was to find a penalty more bitter than death. Hard work, the opposite of the criminals' life of leisure, was the obvious candidate. They feared it more than anything else. Coornhert mentioned three possible options: galley servitude, public works, and the practice of several trades in prisons, which had to be constructed in each town and rural district. His third proposal may have been influential in the planning for the Amsterdam institution.[7]

The original founding fathers in Amsterdam were of course the *schepenen* of 1589.[8] From a more general perspective, it was the dominant faction in urban politics, one of whose leaders was Cornelis Pietersz Hooft (1547–1626). He referred to the *tuchthuis*, then in operation for two years, in a speech delivered to his fellow magistrates in January 1598. While Coornhert had spoken of a penalty more bitter than death, Hooft described imprisonment using terms like prudence, mildness, and toleration. The speech served to clarify his position in a controversial case. The Reformed consistory, which had banned one Goossen Vogelzang for opinions considered heretical or blasphemous, also urged the secular authorities to prosecute him. Hooft advised the court to drop the case, conceding that blasphemy was a punishable offense, but denying the consistory's right to determine its substance. Although the Old Testament prescribed the death penalty for blasphemy and adultery, he argued, such severity was no longer practiced. Concluding that times had changed, Hooft went on to emphasize that trials of even ordinary criminals were now characterized by prudence on the part of the magistrates.

> We all know with what great concern the gentlemen are used to proceed in various criminal, and especially in capital cases. . . . Yes from the beginning of this government, some of the gentlemen have always been very hesitant and reluctant to condemn some thieves, even though they had grossly gone astray, to death, notwithstanding the laws of this country. . . . The reluctance of the gentlemen who objected to such penalties, was based, I believe, upon the following: the Old Testament does not prescribe the death penalty for theft, an argument which I do not want to belittle. I know very well that the deliberations made on such matters for many years and several times are the principal cause for the foundation of the *tuchthuis* within this city, in order to keep delinquents there without cost for the republic if their misdeeds were not too exorbitant.[9]

Although Hooft considered imprisonment a milder sanction than capital punishment and Coornhert argued the reverse, they agreed to the extent that they reserved a prison primarily for delinquents. This is in line with our observation that the case of Evert Jans constituted the immediate cause for the decision to build the *tuchthuis*. The arguments Hooft ascribed to the gentlemen of the court are very similar to the motivation expressed by the town council. Was the institution thought of as a criminal prison from the start? Other opinions were voiced, too.

In the years between the council's decision to erect a prison and its actual opening, two reports were written, copies of which luckily survive in the Leiden archive.[10] The first, by Jan Laurensz Spiegel, is entitled "reflections upon the foundation of the *tuchthuis.*" He was unmistakably one of the founding fathers, since he was a *schepen* in 1589.[11] He must have written his text within a year of the council's decision, since he died on 13 July 1590. Spiegel dealt with all possible provisions for building and maintaining the house, but his main concerns were twofold. They centered on the way the inmates spent their days and the consequences of a stay. The purpose of the institution, he said, is to discipline the inmates. That the aims of this discipline included such things as health, industrious habits and piety does not surprise us. However, Spiegel's primary aims were to protect inmates from the taint of infamy. This is the earliest reference to the problem of the honor of prisoners, which was to become especially crucial in the history of German institutions. Spiegel's method of avoiding infamy essentially consisted of secrecy. Prison sentences should be pronounced indoors and those receiving them preferably brought in at night. The personnel of the institution were to swear an oath to remain silent on the identity of those under their custody. No one else was to see them. Spiegel went on to discuss how the inmates had to be occupied with labor. They could learn a trade in the house and would be allowed a part of the profits. Those unwilling to learn or practice a trade should be disciplined by more severe labor, such as rasping wood, beating hemp, or turning a wheel. As normal occupations Spiegel mentioned no less than twenty-six possibilities. The prisoners could be shoemakers, chair, lantern, wheel, and glass makers, various sorts of cloth workers, carpenters, and even locksmiths or sculptors. It appears that what he had in mind was an enormous school of labor. Holidays might be spent in "some pleasant exercises" to promote bodily health and conditioning. A few curious exercises are mentioned, such as fencing, throwing stones, and even shooting with a rifle for prizes.

If we take Spiegel's suggestions seriously, we can only conclude that he did not envisage that the institution would contain the sort of people who might consider breaking out. He spoke of discipline, but he must have had in mind a kind of fatherly discipline toward young adolescents. His *tuchthuis* was a school of trades for young men whose parents or masters had difficulties training and educating them. Spiegel never thought of hard-core delinquents. The inmates were to be children of good families. The reputations of their parents should not suffer any stains, which was the reason for secrecy. And yet Spiegel had been a member of the court and was familiar with the kind of delinquents and criminals who were brought before the court. The apparent contradiction is resolved if we assume that he had in mind the imprisonment of youths who had not yet committed an offense. This is suggested by his reference to preventing 'shamelessness.' The judges who were said to be hesitant to impose scaffold punishments on young offenders did so because they thought the infamy of the scaffold would take away the offenders' shame and thereby contribute to making them professional criminals. Spiegel's honorable prison was intended to ensure that children from respectable families would not become delinquents.

The second report was written by Sebastiaan Egberts, possibly in 1593, when he was a *schepen*.[12] Although his text was intended primarily as a reaction to Spiegel's, it opened with an admonition to his fellow magistrates: "This matter [i.e., the foundation of the *tuchthuis*] is of the utmost necessity and could easily be stopped nevertheless." To prevent that, Egberts anticipated the objections which might be raised, and proposed playing down the costs. These ought to be debated as little as possible at the council's meeting. The need for a starting capital should even be concealed, and the council was to be impressed instead with the small loss or even profitability which might be expected later. Once the matter had been decided upon favorably, he argued, those who were always eager to avoid costs would agree, too. He must have recommended this strategy either to the *schepenen* who advised burgomasters or to burgomasters themselves, who were leading the council's discussions. It amounts to no less than a proposal to mislead the council.

Egberts's ideas about the inmates' honor and the trades to be practiced were different from Spiegel's. His argumentation betrays a relatively modern view, in which 'honorable' and 'honest' were more or less synonymous. Those who felt they had become tainted with infamy, he said, should try to wash it away by doing good and living an honest life. This is a rationalist view according to which the stains of dishonor can be eliminated and do not leave a permanent mark. Egberts realized that not everyone thought that way. Consequently, he recommended that released prisoners go to live somewhere else. The obligation for the house personnel not to disclose their identity, on the other hand, was unnecessary. Most inmates would be anonymous, and if well-known children of citizens were confined, people would know or speculate about it anyway. On the daily occupations of the inmates, Egberts was practical, rejecting the bodily exercises proposed by Spiegel. Fencing and shooting were entirely out of the question. Exercises would only be allowed to some of the younger inmates and "those already most domesticated," while the constitution of the other inmates would be served best by steady labor. Egberts emphasized that the inmates would not be "free and unspoiled youths." The variety of trades proposed by Spiegel was unpractical, he argued. The majority of inmates would be thieves who had stolen out of ignorance, lack of shame, or laziness. It was best to employ them in a few simple occupations, which would also be most profitable for the house. The selection of trades would be dependent on the fact that the inmates had to be locked up securely. Working with knives, axes, or heavy hammers could not be allowed. Egberts went on to propose two regimes, dividing the prisoners either according to their propensity for escape or according to the seriousness of their misdeeds.

At the end Egberts returned to the matter of the anticipated opposition of the magistrates bent on economizing: "The money-devil, who is just another murderer to begin with and prefers the sight of many gallows with dead corpses to the prospect of a town with a good citizenry, will no doubt seek to prevent the foundation and maintenance of this *tuchthuis*, which is so harmful to him, by various means. But this will only encourage those who were requested to take up the matter to proceed, because no effort will be so great as not to be sweetened and remunerated by the thought of saving a few souls." Two further passages in a similar vein are noteworthy. The first urges the administrators of the prison to realize that they are saving souls: the souls of malefactors, but nonetheless people created in God's image and redeemed by the blood of His Son. Otherwise, they would have been "created to be lost forever." The second passage contrasts the prisoners' stay in the house to the life of their fellows outside. The latter are "naked, hungry, unhealthy and in fear for their lives; they roam around in rain and cold as heaven gives it and they sleep on sidewalks, in ships or, if they are lucky, in barns or haystacks; and thus they spend their days lazily and idly and finally die as the devil's martyrs because of some stolen goods of minor value."

Taken all together, Coornhert's and Hooft's views and the reports by Spiegel and Egberts provide a perfect illustration of the social and cultural climate in which the initiatives were taken toward Amsterdam's prison. The fact that the Amsterdam model had so many imitators justifies the amount of attention paid to these four writers. I will begin the evaluation of the work of these founding fathers with a comment on their social identity. It has been noted that they belonged to the liberal current in Dutch society. Coornhert championed religious tolerance. Hooft dominated Amsterdam politics until the ascendancy of a Calvinist faction in the 1610s. Both he and Egberts were removed from office by stadholder Maurice in 1618, a fate which they shared with the very first prison regent, IJsbrand Ben. Spiegel, a Protestant, was married to a woman from the pre-1578 Catholic patriciate. Clearly, the establishment of the *tuchthuis* was associated with the liberal element, while representatives of the church, liberal or moderate, were not involved at all. However, there are no indications that the Calvinist faction did not go along with the project. Purely theological arguments simply did not play a major role. Hellmuth von Weber's theory that a peculiarly Calvinist predilection for the Old Testament underlay the emergence of prisons is disproved. Hooft, for example, was selective in his references to Old Testament legal rules. He agreed with the rule that thieves should not always be punished by death, but he refused to go along with biblical penalties for blasphemy and adultery. The positions he took were determined by his own views on appropriate punishment rather than by formal religious prescriptions. Egberts, who stated that a nonimprisoned offender is "created to be lost for ever," somehow managed to reconcile the idea of moral improvement with the doctrine of predestination: if a soul is so unlucky as not to be saved, that is what was determined for him in the first place.

It is not surprising that several founding fathers were magistrates. Still, the group did not simply represent the top of the social hierarchy. Coornhert must be reckoned a member of the middle class, as must his literary friend, Leiden's secretary, Jan van Hout, who was to become the champion of imprisonment in that city. Even Sebastiaan Egberts was far from the top at the time. He was a new man, a physician who was suddenly appointed into the college of *schepenen* in 1593. He failed to be reelected to any office until he became a member of the council in 1602. In 1606 and 1608 he was a burgomaster. The involvement of people from the patrician elite as well as from the middle classes suggests a relatively broad ideological base for the establishment of prisons. Nevertheless, Egberts's remarks reveal the existence of an opposition group among the magistrates. The opponents' main argument was that the project would be too expensive. There is no reason to assume that this was only a Calvinist position. Indeed, were it not for the uniform allegiance of the founding fathers to the other faction, we would be tempted to link the economizing opposition with the merchant elite, who were mostly liberals. The reality was probably quite simple: some of the magistrates were more hesitant than others to spend money. It is revealing that Egberts was not a merchant but a physician. With the only known counterarguments of a financial nature, we may conclude that the introduction of imprisonment met with no opposition in principle within the upper and middle classes in Holland. Among these groups a relatively broad consensus existed.

The work of the founding fathers reflects longer-term processes. Evidently, there was no general agreement on what a prison should be like and the purposes of imprisonment. What was the purpose of a *tuchthuis*? Was it an institution of repression or of charity? While some envisaged an institution that would provide strict control over offenders, others spoke of relatively mild punishments. Control and compassion are interwoven in Egberts's formulations. On the one hand he gave practical advice on securely locking up rogues, while on the other he emphasized the house's character as a refuge for vagrants and petty thieves. We are in fact dealing with countervailing tendencies toward compassion and repressiveness and the latter would only come to predominate by the end of the eighteenth century. Neither were there uniform ideas on the character of the house and its potential inmates. Coornhert's advocacy of penal bondage, Spiegel's vision of a secret institution where recalcitrant children of respectable families were trained, and Egberts's sober advice on a prison for thieves and vagrants met at a decisive point in time. The result was the Amsterdam *tuchthuis*. It had been planned by neither of the three. Its emergence and further development were blind processes. Of course, there was something in the air at the end of the sixteenth century. The association of idleness, immorality, marginalized groups, and crime haunted people's minds in diverse manifestations. Coornhert, Spiegel, and Egberts each worked out their own version of the general ideas of their time. Coornhert considered hard work a severe form of punishment, while others may have thought of it as a kind of medicine for unwilling beggars. When Dutch and German towns imitated Amsterdam, they did not always adopt Spiegel's or Egberts's ideas. Various combinations of ideas resulted in various sorts of institutions, or sometimes in quite identical ones. In the long run, however, a few basic types of institutions evolved. This evolution was the effect of impersonal social forces and blind processes that created a context within which individual actors operated. Social processes consist of the actions of individual people, yet become relatively autonomous of personal intentions and conscious policies.[13] Thus, the analysis of the work of the founding fathers indirectly confirms the thesis advanced in the previous chapter: the introduction and further development of imprisonment all over Western Europe require an explanation in terms of impersonal social forces rather than in terms of plans and arguments of individual founders.

Developing the House Rules   The dossier on Amsterdam's prison in the Leiden archive contains two more papers, both listing internal rules and the penalties for infractions of them. The first was composed by Sebastiaan Egberts and dated 21 November 1595. He probably wrote it as a concept for the newly appointed board of regents, the administrators of the institution. Most of its clauses reappear in the second paper: the regents' proposal to the magistrates with regard to the internal order of the house.

In both concepts the possible infractions of the rules include frivolous cursing, swearing, failing to recite one's prayers on command, speaking licentious words, and lying. This testifies to the importance attached to the religious and moral component of prison discipline. The first concept opens with the recommendation that the "indoor father," instructed by a preacher, every Sunday morning collects those inmates who are "a little domesticated" to recite the Bible. Next, he may read a few "histories admonishing toward piety." The inmates will learn reading and religion at once from the Wisdom of Solomon, Ecclesiastes, or Jesus Sirach. Other infractions refer to more mundane affairs. They are disobedience to and attacking the house's personnel; insults and fights among the inmates themselves; refusal to work; damaging the house's property; attempting to escape; and sharing food with a fellow inmate who has been punished with a bread and water diet. Both concepts agree on the penalties with only minor variations. Five types of penalties are proposed, depending on the nature of the infraction. Minor offenders are put on a bread and water diet, with terms varying from one day to three months. They have to continue to work during that period. An aggravated form of this punishment is to be put on bread and water in a dark pit. Newcomers are automatically subjected to this regime for two weeks. Other sanctions are to be chained more securely, to be whipped and to be formally tried by the court. A trial would be held if, for instance, an inmate inflicted physical injury on a member of the personnel. Although burgomasters and council failed to ratify the proposal, these rules must have represented the house order during the early years. Another set of rules, from the early seventeenth century, is not basically different.[14]

The *tuchthuis* was opened at the beginning of 1596. According to Wagenaar, who still had the entry books at his disposal, the first twelve inmates arrived on 3 February of that year.[15] Faber recently discovered a source revealing that at least six of them were delinquents condemned by the court.[16] It was soon found that some inmates were dangerous and in March 1597 the house's personnel was guaranteed that they would never be prosecuted for injuring or killing a prisoner.[17] In November of that year three categories of prisoners were enumerated: unemployed vagrants; condemned delinquents, usually property offenders; and persons committed at the request of their families. The last category, remarkably, were said to be the most troublesome inmates, while thieves were among the more quiet prisoners.[18] Since this clearly contrasts with later evidence, it is probable that only very young thieves were condemned to confinement at this time.

Women in Prison   Although it was never stated explicitly, the prison planned between 1589 and 1596 was for male adolescents and adults only. This may be taken as an indication that the founding fathers were ignorant of English bridewells, which kept women as well as men. The Amsterdam plans were not without precedent in this regard. Some traditional asylums were unisexual, too. There were separate orphanages for boys and girls, and old men's and women's homes. But it was more common to have separate wards only. The sources do not reveal whether the Amsterdam magistrates at first thought that imprisonment did not suit women. In any case, if they had ever entertained that opinion, they soon changed their mind, and an entirely new institution for women was envisaged.

The decision to found the new institution was recorded on 13 November 1596. Upon a proposal of burgomasters, the council agreed to erect a *spinhuis* in town. In it "young girls and others, who are used to begging and idleness, could be trained in spinning wool and earning their living, so that they would stop begging and going about idly." Some Amsterdam merchants had offered to provide them with work under reasonable conditions. The supervisors of the poor were also in favor of the project and had promised a subsidy for it.[19] The house was built in the former convent of St. Ursula, and the first inmates arrived during 1597.[20] The information contained in the council's decision suggests reasons why the new spinhouse was not connected to the *tuchthuis*. The institution for women was associated with charity to a greater extent. No initiatives by the court were recorded. The supervisors of the poor played a role, instead. More so than in the case of the male institution, the magistrates had the reduction of begging in mind. The foundation of the spinhouse was connected more firmly with the changing attitudes toward poverty.

That the spinhouse originally resembled a traditional asylum rather than a prison is confirmed by the first ordinance that has been discovered with regard to it, dated 3 March 1599. The institution's purpose was formulated as follows: "to bring those women who have gone astray or who are unable to earn a living, to the fear of God and back to honor and to purge the city from beggary and unchastity as far as possible."[21] The house was managed by the supervisors of the poor, who acquired a right of punishment over three categories of inmates: women who worked in the house but went home at night; women whose bed and board were paid for by relatives and who were locked away; women 'banished' into the house by the court. A fourth category consisted of women who not only slept outside the house but apparently worked for an external master as well. Their employers had to hand over their wages to the institution each Saturday. If these women did not earn enough for their living, they received an alms, consisting of bread, stockings, shoes, and underwear. Two female supervisors, who had the additional task of caring for poor pregnant women and giving them permission to beg 'in a street or two," were also associated with the house. On Sundays all women belonging to the spinhouse assembled there to go to church. Next to the charitable character of the institution, the penal aspect stands out. The supervisors were authorized to look for women who engaged in prostitution in inns and taverns and arrest them and make them work in the spinhouse. Everyone opening a new inn had to pledge that he would not allow women to be abused there. If the supervisors learned that a married man had a relationship with an unmarried woman—one associated with the spinhouse, presumably—they were allowed to summon him, and might then attempt to make him pay an indemnity to the institution.

Because of the association of the spinhouse with charity, it is not surprising to hear that two citizens who favored the project donated 1000 guilders to it.[22] Still, its penal character soon came to dominate over the charitable character. The change is symbolized by two legends that were successively placed above the entrance. The first spoke of poor girls and women who were prevented from begging and going astray. It was replaced by the second when a new gate was constructed in 1607.[23] Pieter Cornelisz Hooft, the son of the founding father of the *tuchthuis*, composed it and it referred to the punishment of malefactors (see Chapter Five). The changed character of the institution was confirmed by Pontanus, writing in 1611. He mentioned three categories of inmates: girls roaming in the streets; women arrested in whorehouses; and daughters committed at the request of their parents. There is no talk of pregnant women any longer, nor of sleeping or working outside.[24] Presumably, the imprisonment of prostitutes was largely responsible for an increasing association of the spinhouse with the judicial domain. Its new penal character was fully compatible with the principle that the inmates were recruited primarily from among marginals and the poor. While unemployed young men had the choice between stealing and asking for alms, unemployed young women had a third option in the form of prostitution.

Thus, the two institutions became complements. In official terminology both were referred to as *tuchthuizen*, one for men and one for women. In popular parlance, the oldest prison was soon called the *rasphuis*, because rasping wood was its main form of labor. Thus, I will refer to it from here on as the rasphouse. However, some of its inmates were exempt from the labor program. Although Spiegel's initial recommendation of extreme secrecy had not been followed, his concern for the honor of the inmates lived on. The mixing of disobedient children from resident families with vagrants continued to be seen as a problem. In November 1600 the regents requested funds from the council for a reconstruction project to allow a separation of children of honorable parents from rogues and malefactors. The council agreed, and the reconstruction was completed in 1603. From then on the house had two courtyards, a public and a private one. The latter was appropriately denoted as 'the secret courtyard,' and the rooms around it as the separate or secret *tuchthuis*. Those staying there could not be seen by visitors and neither did they have to work. Their relatives paid for their board, which precluded the use of the secret ward by poor families. The prisoners in the sequestered part were popularly called the white bread children, while the secret ward itself was called the *tuchthuis* for the rich.[25] It was described in 1620 as a place for the domestication of disobedient and profligate persons committed at the request of parents, wardens, or other relatives. Their identity was kept secret, as Spiegel had proposed, so that their honor might be maintained as far as possible. When asked where they were, their relatives used to say they had left for Guinea or the Indies.[26] After their stay in the rasphouse, some did indeed go to one of those places. A standard protocol of release from the 1620s has been preserved. In it the prisoner promised to behave well in the future. He agreed to depart for the West on the first ship available and to remain there for as long as the Company wished. The prisoner declared that he had been confined with good reason and cherished no grudge against his relatives. Should his behavior become reproachable again, he could be imprisoned anew.[27]

The tale of Amsterdam's prisons became a standard subject in urban histories. Already in 1598 an anonymous German described the rasphouse and spinhouse in a booklet praising the system of poor relief and repression of begging in Amsterdam.[28] The first native account was by Pontanus. His idea of the rasphouse origins underlines my argument that the institution was the unplanned result of the actions of participants with different motives. Pontanus was apparently ignorant of the fact that the decision to establish a prison had been made in 1589. Instead, he referred to the provincial placard against begging of December 1595, which, according to him, had inspired the town to found both the rasphouse and the spinhouse.[29] Thus, he saw these institutions primarily as places for the confinement of marginals, male and female. For a number of decades the typical inmates of the rasphouse were beggars and vagrants arrested in the streets. This emerges clearly from a 1612 pamphlet about the 'miracles' performed in the house. Willem Baudaart, writing in the 1620s, likewise discussed the rasphouse in the context of the campaign against begging. On the other hand, both he and Pontanus emphasized that many beggars had committed thefts and other crimes. Delinquents still were confined along with marginals, and Baudaart shared Coornhert's view that the former feared prison discipline more than they did the gallows.[30] The association of the rasphouse with marginals ended in 1654, when a separate institution was opened.

Political Prisoners   One more feature of Amsterdam's early years should be discussed. As if the city wanted to pioneer in everything connected with imprisonment, it was the first to keep political prisoners. These were not condemned by its court, though. They were remonstrants and a few other religious dissidents. Various rulers had kept political opponents in jails throughout the Middle Ages, but this was the first time that the new *tuchthuizen* had them as inmates. Whatever the Calvinists may have thought about the rasphouse in the founding period, they were enthusiastically using it now. The episode sheds further light on the attitudes toward imprisonment in general. Our information on it, however, Geeraert Brandt's *History of the Reformation,* has to be viewed cautiously, since Brandt is favorable to the remonstrant cause.

After the Synod of Dordt and Maurice's coup d'état, the adherents of Arminius's doctrines went underground. For a time, the new ruling faction in Holland was very keen on detecting secret remonstrant meetings, and adopted a repressive policy toward ministers preaching there. A few were arrested in 1620. They included Johannes Grevius, who later became the author of the first treatise devoted to the abolition of judicial torture.[31]

Grevius was tried by a special committee of the Estates General. They condemned him to a life term in Amsterdam's secret ward, where he arrived on 4 July. He enjoyed the company of his colleague Samuel Prince eleven days later. The sentences of other remonstrant preachers were kept secret. A third, Bernherus Vezekius, refused the committee any answers and was taken to the prison at Haarlem to be questioned. The commissioners threatened that he would have to rasp wood all his life if he remained silent. Although aware of the "infamous and bloody" nature of this form of labor, Brandt says, he declared he was ready to perform it. Suddenly, however, the commissioners were content with a few replies he gave. They found it improper to use rasping as a form of torture. Vezekius remained in prison, apparently in close proximity to the regular inmates. All day long he could hear the "continuous and awful noise" they made.[32]

In the secret ward at Amsterdam Grevius and Prince were joined by "two protestants of another sort," about whom we have no further information, and the Jesuit Levinus Wouters, provisionally confined after an accusation that he had conspired to kill the stadholder.[33] The indoor father and the regents, convinced Calvinists, were said to have provoked these men frequently. Sometimes they were denied candles and writing material, while books on the doctrine of predestination were forbidden to them. On several occasions the officials threatened them with transfer to the public ward and even with the prospect of rasping wood. The harsh treatment was alleviated later on. Grevius, who had a basic knowledge of law, was allowed to read juridical books, and wrote the manuscript for his *Tribunal Reformatum*. Wouters devoted himself to Canon Law. One day the group had visitors: the exiled king of Bohemia, the English envoy, and a few other gentlemen and ladies of quality, who were escorted by the Amsterdam *schout*. The status of these visitors apparently made it possible for them to visit even the secret ward.[34]

The pro-Calvinist magistrates soon were unhappy with the form of repression they had adopted. Perhaps they became convinced that the new prisons were places unfit for people of such high social status as preachers. We may infer this from the easy escape of all of the political prisoners from Haarlem and Amsterdam in the autumn of 1621. An alternative or complementary explanation would be that anyone could escape who had sufficient assistance, and that most ordinary convicts simply could not marshal enough help from outside. It is unlikely, though, that the large company of sympathizers, remonstrants and a few Catholics, that stood outside the prison wall in Amsterdam with black ladders, ropes, and false keys the night of 12 to 13 October could have done so and then succeeded without the silent acquiescence of at least some of the magistrates. Only one passerby was reported, who thought the conspirators were aiming at the poor box in the nearby charity office. He kept his mouth shut, though, when he was told the preachers were going to be liberated.[35] Grevius fled to Hamburg, which also had a prison, though this may not have determined his choice. He published his book against torture there in 1624, with a remark on the title page that it had been written in the Amsterdam *tuchthuis*.[36] The entire episode demonstrates that the sequestered character of the secret ward not only served to maintain the honor of persons admitted on request, but could also be used to hide away prisoners whose identity would otherwise cause commotion among the visiting public.

The Imitators

With Grevius in Hamburg, the focus shifts to the towns that imitated Amsterdam. Among them, Hamburg and Bremen must get special attention, to allow comparison of the Hanseatic and Holland experiences. The name for a prison did not differ. The Hanseatic towns adopted the word *tuchthuis*, which sounded the same in their local speech and became *zuchthaus* in High German, the language that soon came to be preferred by their top strata. This section will begin with an overview of the first series of foundations in Continental Europe generally, and proceed to a discussion of the early years in three towns on which more-detailed information is available: Haarlem, Bremen, and Hamburg.

The First Wave   Prison workhouses spread over the Dutch Republic and the Holy Roman Empire in three successive waves, the first lasting until about 1620. Imitation of Amsterdam began in Leiden in 1598–1599. Leiden was the second largest town in Holland then, with a population of some 40,000, so it is not surprising that it also became the second town with a prison. Although its *tuchthuis* was built next to the old jail, this does not mean that it was seen primarily as a penal institution. The building, which was reconstructed to become a prison, had been an old women's asylum and belonged to St. Cathrin's hospital since 1389. The women were ordered to move. From the fact that the founder's testament and a few other documents relating to the asylum were included in the dossier on the construction of the *tuchthuis*, we may infer that the new institution was thought of as continuing the charitable purposes of the old.[37]

Besides Amsterdam and Leiden, prison workhouses were established in four other cities represented in the Estates of Holland: Haarlem (1609), Gouda (1610), Alkmaar (1613), and Delft (c. 1620). Outside Holland they were opened in Leeuwarden (1598), Groningen (1609), Utrecht (c. 1616), and Middelburg (1642). Although the provincial Estates were involved in some of the latter cases, urban elites were the most active initiators.[38] A major difference between Amsterdam and its imitators was that the latter each built just one prison, usually with separate wards for men and women. Plans were made in other cities as well. The magistrates of Hoorn acquired permission to hold a lottery to contribute to the foundation costs in 1614, and those of Dordrecht did so the next year.[39] Possibly, such plans were briefly put into practice.

The evidence on Haarlem and Delft documents the link between imprisonment and charity. In the first town the supervisors of the poor had taken the initiative and its prison was combined with an almshouse. The influence of the founding fathers is visible in the house's ordinance of 1612, which mentioned a special category of potential inmates: heads of households who enjoy relief but who use it for other purposes than supporting their families.[40] In Delft a "public workhouse for the prevention of begging" was planned in 1614, but it was only in the early 1620s that a spinhouse was opened.[41] It received a financial injection in 1628. The document in question tells us that a school for poor children had been started in the 1590s from a bequest by Maria Duijst. This school was not a success. The testator's daughter, widow of an ex-burgomaster, proposed to close it and divert its capital to the orphanage and the spinhouse. The Court of Holland gave its consent, and the Delft magistrates added that, if the spinhouse would cease to exist, the money should be used for the benefit of another asylum.[42] Despite this association with charity, the spinhouse had its penal aspect, too. It received seven women condemned by the court during the 1620s and 1630s.[43]

In the Hanseatic towns, as elsewhere in the Empire, the Dutch institutions were known immediately.[44] Bremen, Hamburg, Lübeck, and Danzig (1629–1630) belonged to the first wave. I have noted that the Bremen senate requested a copy of Amsterdam's prison ordinance in 1604. No answer has been preserved in the archives of either city, and Bremen's prison was not opened until four years later.[45] The earliest initiatives in Hamburg were taken in the first decade of the seventeenth century. In 1604 the *bürgerschaft* proposed to employ beggars at public works and to found a new orphanage for poor children. Five years later it was suggested for the first time to erect a prison workhouse. Several plans were proposed by the magistrates, the citizenry, the administrators of the orphanage, and the deacons supervising poor relief. The latter referred to the example of Amsterdam. The matter dragged on for a couple of years in negotiations between the senate and the *bürgerschaft*. The first patrons of the house were appointed in 1615, but it was not opened until three years later.[46] It differed from its Amsterdam example, and resembled the Haarlem prison, in one important respect: it was combined with an almshouse. In Lübeck the convent of St. Anne, built in 1502, was made into an almshouse in 1601.[47] Twelve years later its provisors and the *bürgerschaft* took the initiative to provide for a *zuchthaus* there. An adjacent building, a private old women's home owned by Jochim Wetken, was confiscated and the women were ordered to leave. Wetken did not acquiesce in the confiscation of his house and even took the case to the Imperial Court, but in 1621 he signed an agreement with the magistrates. He acquired the right to designate five honorable women to be maintained in the almshouse, but his own former home was now to function as a *zuchthaus*.[48] This first prison ward must have been a provisional one only. After another reconstruction project in 1632, the *zuchthaus* was formally opened as a separate ward of the almshouse. An inscription denoting that year could still be seen in the courtyard in the eighteenth century.[49]

No more prison workhouses were established in the Empire until the late 1660s, although a few were planned. An abortive project was reported in Berlin. In 1608 the Elector of Brandenburg decided to erect a *zuchthaus* for children and adult beggars. Artisans from Hamburg and Holland, who were to instruct the prisoners in a trade, had already been summoned. However, the elector's sudden death caused the project to be discontinued.[50] Had it been realized, it would have been one more example of princely initiative in starting a prison. A few other towns also cherished plans which were not put into effect. The council of Cologne discussed the possible erection of a *zuchthaus* in 1612; Münster did the same in 1619.[51] Two years later the Osnabrück magistrates approached the Bremen senate for permission to sell lots for the start of a prison workhouse.[52] Thus, the idea of imprisonment was certainly current.

The institutions established during the first wave were not always an immediate success. Prisons were closed in Leiden (1612), Leeuwarden (1615), Groningen (1623), Bremen (1627), Utrecht (1633), and Delft (1645). Sometimes this was because of financial difficulties, but on the whole, little information is available on why the prisons failed. In Delft it was said that the spinhouse was no longer useful to the urban community. There were practical problems, too. The religious instructor quit and a competent substitute was hard to find. The house's kitchen would have to be subsidized by the city. Despite these troubles, Maria Duijst's legacy still amounted to a capital of 6,646 guilders. Burgomasters decided to use the interest to keep two women who had stayed in the spinhouse in the madhouse for life.[53] All these institutions were reopened around or after the middle of the seventeenth century.

Two conclusions can be drawn from the data on the first wave. One concerns the firm connection of imprisonment with poor relief. In Amsterdam this was less obvious in the case of the rasphouse, but clear in the foundation of the spinhouse. Although Leiden erected its prison next to the old jail, the building in which it was housed had been an old women's asylum. In Delft a charitable fund was put to other than its original uses and employed to give the spinhouse a sound financial base. The supervisors of the poor took the initiative in Haarlem and the prison was combined with a voluntary workhouse. The same combination was effected in

Lübeck and Hamburg, where the deacons for the poor also contributed to the planning. Such a setup was not peculiar to the Continent. The London bridewell, too, had a training school for indigent boys attached to it.[54] In Catholic Antwerp, finally, the poor relief board was also involved. Three of its members temporarily assumed responsibility in 1619, when the first work boss was dismissed after a protracted conflict.[55] Thus, the establishment of prison workhouses was partly seen as charity work. But it was charity according to the code of the new mentality: relief for the deserving poor and a repressive policy toward the undeserving.

The second conclusion relates to the degree of support for the introduction of imprisonment. The groups involved were the administrators of charity and urban magistrates and officials. Their cooperation underlines my argument that the prison movement was endorsed by a broad spectrum of elite and middle class groups. This thesis is further supported when we realize that the ruling groups of the towns in question differed in one important respect. In the Dutch Republic urban historians distinguish two models of city government, the Western and the Eastern. In the first, the magistrates, that is, the burgomasters and judicial authorities, held sway in urban affairs. In the second, the magistrates shared power to a large extent with representatives of the citizenry. The latter model was employed, among other places, in Groningen.[56] The situation in Hamburg was similar to this model. In Hamburg, unlike in the other Hanseatic towns, the patricians had to share political power with the organized *bürgerschaft*. Negotiations between the two groups caused a delay in the completion of the project for a *zuchthaus*, though the two groups were in agreement on the principle. Apparently, with respect to the decision to establish a prison, it made no difference which system of government a town had. The 'Eastern' towns of Hamburg and Groningen built one, as did Amsterdam and other 'Western' towns.

Apart from the geographical locations of the prisons, the history of a particular literary work illustrates my thesis. The book in question is Theodor Reinking's *Tractatus de Regimine Seculari et Ecclesiastico*. It went through six editions between 1619 and 1659. The author was no stranger to Bremen, whose magistrates had founded a prison. In the 1640s he was the chancellor of Bremen's bishop, Christian IV of Denmark. At the Westphalian peace negotiations, Reinking defended the bishop's sovereign rights over the town. If ever the urban patriciate had an unequivocal political opponent, it was Reinking. Still, he found prison workhouses a very useful tool of policy. He devoted a separate section of his work to them, specifically praising the institutions at Amsterdam and Bremen. His learned opponents saw no reason to attack him on this point. Reinking thoroughly revised and extended his work in 1651, to reply to counterarguments by Hippolythus à Lapide. Although the text became more than twice as long, the passage on prison workhouses remained unchanged.[57]

Apparently, the antagonism between the two writers did not extend to their appreciation of these institutions. Whatever tore them apart, the elites shared Reinking's estimate of the usefulness of imprisonment.

To illustrate the early history of imprisonment outside Amsterdam, I will concentrate on three examples: Haarlem, Bremen, and Hamburg. I chose Haarlem because the opportunity existed to trace its convicts in the archival sources, and Bremen and Hamburg are important because their experience supplements the Dutch.

Haarlem: Convicts in Prison   The first condemned delinquent entered Haarlem's prison on 6 January 1611. The register in which his and other sentences were recorded stops at the end of 1615, and no criminal sentences were preserved for the next sixty-some years.[58] It is the period 1611–1615, therefore, which concerns us. The Haarlem court judged 167 cases in those years and imposed the following penalties: banishment (96); corporal punishment (35); death (6); imprisonment (22); and other (8). Thus, banishment was overwhelmingly predominant, even more so than the above numbers indicate, since all but one of the corporally punished delinquents were banished as well. Two of the six persons subjected to the death penalty were former prisoners, while the category 'other' includes two cases of dead persons judged suicides.

Prison sentences could be combined with banishment or corporal punishment or both. Prison sentences were imposed somewhat irregularly: in about 20 percent of the cases in the years 1611–1613; not at all in 1614; and in about 6 percent of cases in 1615. Clearly, the judges were ambivalent toward the new penal option. The inauguration of a *tuchthuis* did not immediately lead to a massive shift away from banishment. Moreover, the figures for imprisonment are inflated to a certain extent, because they include nine cases of people who were already in prison. In these cases, inmates were formally punished for escape attempts and riots serious enough to be handled by the court. Thus, the prison itself generated other crimes. Only four of the nine subversive prisoners had an earlier entry in the court's register, which means that five had entered the house originally as marginals or upon a request by their families. Within the house, convicts seem to have been a minority. Penal imprisonment was considered an extraordinary measure. This is revealed in the formulation of the prison sentences. They stipulated that the convict had deserved a more rigorous punishment, but that for the time being he would be put in prison. This was called a provisional sentence. The convict had to work in prison until the court reached a decision on his eventual punishment or his release. Since no further decisions upon such sentences were recorded, imprisonment was the actual final punishment. Its provisional nature was also reflected in the absence of specific terms in exactly half of the cases. In the others, terms varied from half a year to three years.

Although penal imprisonment was not a very significant disposition in quantitative terms, the convicts subjected to it certainly were not all special cases or minor offenders. A relatively high number were male. Only two women (9%) were condemned to imprisonment. Women made up 17 percent of the total population of convicts. If we subtract the subversives from the condemned prisoners, though, the percentage of woman prisoners approaches their percentage in the total population. The number of male prisoners not punished for escape or riot was eleven. They were 'normal' delinquents, tried for theft (4), violence (4), and miscellaneous crimes (3). The relative seriousness of their cases follows from the fact that nine were recidivists. Their sentences emphasized that they led a dissolute life, had been wandering about from youth on, and had committed offenses in various places. A number of them had been confined earlier, in Haarlem, Amsterdam, or elsewhere, some as vagabonds, others as convicts, while a few had served on the provincial galleys. Several had been corporally punished by the executioner. Almost all had been banished, either from Haarlem or elsewhere. Thus, the Haarlem court used imprisonment as a last resort rather than as a preventive measure. This is a far cry from the practice in Amsterdam with regard to juvenile offenders who were not real criminals, and who should therefore have been prevented from associating with criminals. On the contrary, the Haarlem convicts were frequently said to have previously associated with professional thieves and burglars. We can conclude that the town's *schepenen* found that delinquents ought to be banished first, and if they came back and committed further offenses, imprisonment might be tried. This is in line with Coornhert's arguments about hard work as the ultimate penalty for incorrigible rogues.

The Haarlem court, then, was not afraid to associate its *tuchthuis* with serious crime and the executioner's business. The case of the very first prisoner confirms this. Jan Gillissen's name appears in the register five times. He was a linen weaver by training who embarked upon the career of self-appointed preacher, but his religious opinions are not revealed. He was banished three times and did not receive a prison sentence until his fourth arrest. In the *tuchthuis* he behaved quietly for almost two years, but toward the end of 1612 he decided to work no longer and severely damaged his weaving loom. In January of the next year, when the judges visited the house to determine penalties for the obstinate, he had obtained a knife and stabbed a court servant in the neck. In addition, he declared later, he intended to do the same to a gentleman of the court. The judges condemned Jan Gillissen to death. He was hanged and his body was taken from the gallows and exposed in the *tuchthuis* for a time "as a spectacle to other prisoners" before being buried.[59]

Bremen: Patriarchal Discipline   The Bremen prison ordinance, dated 26 January 1609, designated the house for persons who were begging, leading an obnoxious life, or engaging in *böverie*.[60] The latter word referred to minor offenses bordering on the criminal.[61] Those guilty of it were imprisoned and released upon the orders of the *kämmerer* or the senate, exercising low and high jurisdiction, respectively.[62] The house administrators could release the others, who had been taken in by the beggar catchers or were given over by relatives. Only resident beggars, however, were to be taken to prison. Nonresidents were given a penny and led outside the city gate, and if they returned were put on bread and water in jail or flogged. From this it can be concluded that the other two categories of inmates—those confined on request of relatives, whose stay was paid for, but also those imprisoned by the *kämmerer* or the council—might include nonresidents.

Prisoners from outside the city were found among the inmates from the beginning, as evidenced by a dossier of requests from foreign rulers, the five oldest dating from the 1610s.[63] Three of them concerned more or less criminal cases. In 1612 a young man from nearby Vörde was confined who had previously been made to work on the walls in Vörde, from where he had attempted an escape. The administrators had objected at first to having him in the prison, arguing that this young man was too big and strong and that they did not really want to have such persons who were bent on breaking out. They agreed to keep him in prison, however, on the condition that he be taken through the city gate and into the *zuchthaus* "very quietly." The administrators were also reluctant in the case of a request in 1615 to imprison an offender who, it was stated, could have been subjected to severe justice. The senate replied that until now a prison stay had been denied to "such persons who have forfeited their life." They were willing to take him, however, if a handsome sum was paid. The third case was a request from the bishop of Minden in 1619. He related that his people at Wintheim had been terrorized by a group of arsonists who had almost burned down the entire village. After the culprits had been caught and tried, the court was left wondering what to do with a boy about ten years old. His stepfather, mother, and brother had been executed, and he himself had known of the conspiracy but had not actually participated in it. It was feared that, if left to himself, he would drift into bad company, especially since "he was not descended from a good sort of people and also clearly had the physiognomy for it." If nothing else, the bishop demonstrated that there were precedents to Lombroso.[64] Again, the prison administrators at Bremen only accepted the inmate reluctantly. The house was almost filled up, they said, and it was not meant for such boys. Still, they did not deny that they could discipline the boy in such a way that, if God granted it, he would set his mind to other pursuits. Surely, it was thought, in Bremen, God could beat Lombroso.

These cases show that the Bremen magistrates were not particularly keen on having criminal offenders in their prison. Presumably, residents of Bremen, who were imprisoned through a decree of the *kämmerer* or the senate, were not serious delinquents. A detailed study of the *kämmerei* records could reveal this, but such a study is not available.[65] The prison records up to about 1670 contain just a handful of documents referring to inmates from the city itself and all of these were committals by relatives. The first in this series is a request for release by Johan Wickboldt, dated 26 October 1611. It must be the oldest document in any Continental archive in which an inmate of a prison workhouse speaks in his own words. Wickboldt directed himself to burgomasters and senate, requesting them to intervene on his behalf with his relatives. It was apparently up to the latter to determine if he had stayed long enough. They had turned a deaf ear, he said, to his expressions of regret for his misdeeds and his repeated pleas for release. No answer has been preserved.[66]

This supplication suggests that the Bremen magistrates conceived of private confinement as an extension of patriarchal or family discipline, with which they did not think it necessary to interfere. The same impression can be derived from the only other interesting case in the early years: that of Harmen Hilcken. He may have been the first person in history to have seen the inside of prison workhouses in two different countries. On 3 May 1616 the senate wrote to the burgomasters and council of Amsterdam about him. The letter related how Jürgen Hilcken, a citizen of Hildesheim, had obtained the imprisonment of his son Harmen at Bremen. Harmen had been there for two and a half years, but toward the end of 1615 he had managed to escape, together with four other inmates. Afterwards, his father learned that he had arrived in the Dutch metropolis, where he had been arrested for some offense. The Bremen magistrates agreed with the Hilcken family that their honor was best served if their black sheep was brought back to the *zuchthaus* as soon as possible, without receiving a formal punishment in Amsterdam. They requested their colleagues in Amsterdam to send him with another member of the family who had gone to get him and would pay the cost of the removal.[67] The implicit idea of the Bremen magistrates is clear. They considered the prison a nonpenal institution, where malefactors who had broken no formal law were disciplined. In the case of children of respectable families, a stay there might have the function of preventing them from committing a criminal offense and consequently from being punished for it. Hence, they wanted Harmen Hilcken back in the disciplinary institution, and by implication, under the indirect control of his father, before it was too late.

The magistrates of Amsterdam had a different view. Although no correspondence between this city and Bremen on the case had been preserved, we know the sequence of Harmen's history, since his name turns up several times in Amsterdam judicial records. This can be taken as a denial of the request, if we assume that Bremen's letter at least arrived in Holland. Harmen's first interrogation at Amsterdam took place three days after the letter had been written. The court clerk recorded his age as "about seventeen." The suspect stated that making bombazine was his trade and that he had practiced it in Bremen until about a year ago. Bombazine weaving was indeed done in this city's prison, but Harmen did not mention that that is where he had been employed. He claimed he had stayed with his father afterwards. On 9 June he was whipped indoors and banished from Amsterdam for three years for stealing from his landlady.[68] This started off precisely the career his father had feared. Harmen was whipped in Amsterdam three more times, on the scaffold now, between November 1616 and January 1618. In the meantime, he roamed through the Northern provinces of the Netherlands and East-Frisia and was branded twice in that region. Only after he had infringed his Amsterdam banishment for the fourth time was he imprisoned there.[69] In April 1618, when he had been in the rasphouse for just a few weeks, he participated in a conspiracy. He and two other inmates confessed that they had resolved either to get out of prison or out of the world altogether. Harmen even begged the judges with folded hands to condemn him to death.[70] His actual punishment was not recorded, but the *schepenen* refused to honor his plea to be executed. He turns up once more, in November 1618, as one of twenty-two prisoners who were whipped in view of the rest for refusing to work.[71] Thereafter, his name disappears from the records. This case shows that the cultural identity of the Netherlands and the Northern parts of the Empire was manifested at the top of society as well as at the bottom. Not only did contacts between elites contribute to the establishment of prisons, there was also a reservoir of potential prisoners wandering throughout the area.[72]

Hamburg: Paid or Set Free   Moving to the larger of the two Hanseatic towns, our attention is drawn to a prison ordinance promulgated 8 March 1622.[73] Its preface explains that the institution is a combined prison and poorhouse. It is intended to alleviate the misery of the poor, it says, but there are a number of goats among the sheep, who ought to be approached with severity. Whereas the sheep are the deserving poor of the almshouse, the goats are the inmates of the prison proper. The motto of the house, *labore nutrior, labore plector,* is meant to refer to these groups, respectively. It was translated into German thus: "I am one who makes my subsistence through labor, and I am one who is disciplined by labor." The group to be disciplined is subdivided into the more manageable beggars, who were just lazy, and a mixed lot of more serious malefactors, also including beggars. With regard to the latter subgroup, the ordinance's authors reveal themselves to be masters of stereotyping.

There are also many strong, lazy, impertinent, lustful, godless, wanton and disobedient drunks filled with beer and booze, men as well as women, who grow up in vice, whoredom, roguery and all kinds of sin and shame. . . . These people are inclined by nature toward every evil and vice; they do no good of their own free will and they manage to get away masterly with cursing, swearing, unholy words, blasphemy, lying and cheating.[74]

And so on. The expressions lose force in an English translation; however, the intention of the words is clear.

Despite the stereotypical ideas of the founders, the actual divisions within the house were more practical and based on financial considerations. The logbook, begun in 1625, reveals this. From a financial viewpoint, there were three official categories of inmates. The *oeconomus,* who had to care for their food and board, received thirty-six ss. for each male prisoner, thirty for each female prisoner, and twenty for each poor person.[75] These were the rates up to January 1632. They were changed several times, but their ratio remained the same. Apart from these three categories, there was a fourth group of rich prisoners who remained outside this system altogether. Thus, a separate agreement was made with the *oeconomus* in 1626 on the provisions for Peter Heintzen, for whom board money was paid amounting to 300 Lübeck marks a year in 1628.[76] In 1633, when the sums for the *oeconomus* were revised again, four inmates were listed in a separate category.[77] They were housed in so-called *losamenten* and they were allowed lighter work or no work at all. Their rooms must have constituted a separate ward comparable to the one in Amsterdam. As a rule, this group remained very small, but a large part of the logbook is filled with correspondence on their board money.

The group of prisoners admitted at the request of their families was composed of the rich persons staying in the *losamenten* and others from a less affluent milieu, who had to work but for whom additional board money was often paid by their relatives. Sometimes relatives were unwilling to pay a sufficient amount or were late with it. These cases reveal the attitudes toward private confinement cherished by the provisors, as the administrators were called. On several occasions they threatened to release a prisoner. The stepfather of Margret Groten, for example, who chose not to reply upon a request to renew his contract, was given two weeks to do so. Even though Margret had been working diligently, she would be set free if no money was forthcoming.[78] Comparable cases were frequently recorded.[79] Clearly, it was up to the relatives of private prisoners to determine if and when they went in and out. No policy of the authorities was involved. The provisors, although they refused to admit some persons who could not work, agreed to take in others as long as a large enough sum was paid to prevent a deficit for the house. In this sense, the *zuchthaus* functioned as an asylum for some. On the other hand, it was evidently also a prison. This is revealed by the terminology of the provisors. The threat to unwilling relatives was always to "set the inmate free" (*auf freien Füssen*).

The logbook, then, enables us to tell what sort of people entered the Hamburg *zuchthaus*. They included the two extremes: poor and rich. The rich, lodged in the separate ward, were in prison because their families felt they had to be chastized or at least kept in custody. The poor, those considered unable to earn a living, were not locked up.[80] They were lodged in the almshouse part. In between were the male and female prisoners for which the *oeconomus* received a sum. A number of them were also admitted at the request of families who were not rich enough to place them in the separate ward. Beggars constituted the only other category in the middle group. This suggests that, unlike in Haarlem or Bremen, in Hamburg offenders imprisoned upon an order of the magistrates made up a negligible minority at most. Indeed, the only such case found in the logbook involves a rather unusual offender:

Anno 1639, 27 September, our lord patron, burgomaster Johannes Brant, Licent., ordered a man from Braunschweig, named Hanss Engebreht, to be taken into the *Werck und Zuchthaus* here, who claimed that he had been dead for several hours, that he had been in front of hell and in heaven where he had seen the holy and highly praised Trinity with his bodily eyes and that through an angel he had received an order from our beloved God to awaken the people to do penance.[81]

This man can be compared to the earliest inmate at Haarlem, although the latter had been tried by a court and the former was admitted on an administrative order. People like Engebreht, whom Beier calls "transient visionaries with no clear sectarian affinities," were imprisoned in England, too.[82] The Hamburg magistrates probably feared that Engebreht would cause popular disturbances. Originally, he had left town already when another angel appeared to him saying that he should abstain from eating and drinking for three weeks and would suffer no hunger or thirst. Thereupon he returned to Hamburg and was imprisoned. After five days in the *zuchthaus*, however, the angel ordered him to ask for water. During the next nine days his heavenly companion visited him in prison each morning and changed the water into wine. Engebreht also took two copious meals before his release on 11 October. Only God knows what really happened, the provisors added, leaving the impression that they did not preclude that an angel had really been in their institution.

The case is interesting for its own sake, and if we had more information on it, it would deserve a deeper analysis. Failing that, it nonetheless confirms my impression that the imprisonment of offenders upon an order of the magistrates occurred only in exceptional circumstances in Hamburg during the early years. Because of this situation and the fact that the prison was combined with an almshouse, the entire complex was seen as a charitable institution—more readily so than in most other towns. This is also suggested by the many pious gifts and legacies bestowed upon the house. They were offered to the institution as such, but the donors were usually motivated by the presence of the poor in it. Thus, Jürgen von der Fechte gave 300 Lübeck marks "for the poor of the *Werck und Zuchthaus*," and stated that he did so out of a Christian compassion for those suffering from poverty.[83] Gifts sometimes came from magistrates or members of patrician families, for instance from burgomaster Joachim Claen in 1630.[84] In 1639 all administrators pledged that, if one would become a member of the senate, he would seal his election with a gift of 500 Lübeck marks.[85] Ordinary citizens contributed, too; Hans Eggers even did so twice in his lifetime. In 1614 he bought a ticket in the lottery held to raise money for building the house and drew number 152, which won him an annuity of two and a half Lübeck marks a year. In 1633 he offered the total annuity as a gift to the house.[86]

Conclusion: The Early Years   A note in the Hamburg prison logbook in October 1648 lacks a direct relationship with the house: bells are tolling and festivities are going on in the city to celebrate the treaties of Münster and Osnabrück.[87] Apparently, the provisors were so delighted with these events that they felt they had to record them. They might also have thought that the peace would be beneficial to their institution, but on this they kept silent. The note reminds us that the *zuchthaus* was founded on the eve of the Thirty Years' War and had continued operations throughout it. While Hamburg's rulers steered a course of neutrality with regard to the political situation, they managed to occupy themselves with problems of poverty and marginality as well. The presence of private prisoners, some of whom came from as far away as Leipzig and Copenhagen, proves that communications were not severed altogether.

In Bremen the situation was different. The *zuchthaus* was closed in 1627 and it is uncertain whether this was due to financial difficulties only. Although the institution had debts, it also left a capital of 7,000 Bremen marks.[88] The chronicler Peter Koster says that the *zuchthaus* was closed "because of the German disturbances," but he only remembers that this happened "around 1629."[89] If Koster's statement is even partially correct, it suggests that the Bremen magistrates found it harder to run a prison in times of war. Whatever the case, they decided to reestablish it in 1645, but the second *zuchthaus* was destroyed by lightning even before the Westphalian peace. In 1650, finally, the third *zuchthaus* was built, which functioned into the nineteenth century.

The Dutch had less trouble with military activities. They waged an offensive war against Spain from 1621 onward and continued their internal affairs as usual. The fact that the Empire, unlike the Republic, was the scene of military operations explains why fewer prisons were founded there.

Regional characteristics were not a major determinant of the type of prison established. In Bremen it was decided to admit only resident marginals, while there is no trace of such a policy in Hamburg. Like their Bremen colleagues, the Haarlem magistrates seem to have been reluctant to imprison nonnatives. With regard to institutional arrangements, on the other hand, Haarlem resembled Hamburg: both towns had a combined prison and almshouse. Except in the case of Lübeck, there is no talk of such an arrangement in the other towns studied, but everywhere imprisonment was associated with charity. This did not prevent the Haarlem court from sentencing a number of recidivists to prison terms. Imprisonment of delinquents was a common practice in Amsterdam. In Bremen minor offenders could be committed upon an order of the senate or the *kämmerer*, but we do not know how many actually were. In Hamburg this seems to have been an exceptional practice. It looks as though the admittance of convicts was the major difference distinguishing Holland from the Hanse region in the early years. The Dutch were to make imprisonment of convicts normal practice after 1650 and the German territories only followed hesitatingly and after some delay.

An intriguing question remains: did the novelty of imprisonment give rise to any principled opposition? I already have noted that support for the new system seems to have been widespread among the upper and middle classes. Prudence in the financial sphere cannot be considered principled opposition. The next chapter will show that voices were raised against the custom of chasing marginals, but the opponents of this practice did not criticize the prison per se. Potential inmates themselves may have been discontent with aspects of the prison institution or system, but they were unable to articulate a protest which had a chance of coming down to us. I found only one piece of indirect evidence, and even this was a little ambiguous. We have to read between the lines. It concerns an event in Bremen, a town for which there was other proof of a consensus among the elites.

Bremen's second prison was blown to pieces 5 August 1647 when lightning struck a nearby arsenal tower. Although other adjacent buildings were damaged, too, only the *zuchthaus* was completely destroyed. The master of discipline, his wife, and four or five inmates perished and many prisoners stumbled through the streets with impediment blocks still fastened to their legs. As usual, such an event caused much anxiety and made the inhabitants wonder what God might have meant by it. Three contemporary chroniclers, who report on the thunderstorm, speak of a divine punishment.[90] "Everyone thought that heaven and earth fell upon each other," Koster writes, "and that the last day had come." The second author remembers that, before the storm, a boy in the house dreamt that it was raining fire from heaven, which killed everyone. This boy was the only person who had not been hurt at all. The crucial thing is that all three chroniclers stress that God's rage was aimed at the entire city, which, by implication, meant at no target in particular. They report that the senate announced a fast and prayer day. In addition, weddings in the city were to be celebrated soberly, without music, for the duration of the war, according to one of the authors.[91] Obviously, the weddings had nothing to do with the *zuchthaus*; this measure pertained to the city in general. The third chronicler says the senate feared further punishment from God, "because of the unrestrained luxuries and sins of the inhabitants."[92] By ensuring that supplication and atonement were distributed equally among all sectors of the population, the authorities proclaimed that the divine punishment had been meant for the entire city. They took this position anew when they advertised a lottery for the benefit of the house's reconstruction in 1649. They noted that the house had been struck by "an inscrutable fate determined by God."[93]

The only explanation for the senate's persistent statements to the effect that the *zuchthaus* had not been singled out for destruction is that there were people who held the opposite view: that God had purposely destroyed the *zuchthaus* to underline that such an institution did not enjoy his favor. To contemporaries this would have been an equally logical conclusion.[94] The only problem is that the parties supposedly drawing it left no traces in the records. It cannot have been the supporters of Bremen's bishop, which is obvious from my remarks on Reinking's work.[95] The most likely hypothesis is that the town's guilds contested the senate's interpretation of the fate of the *zuchthaus*. The *rass* makers in particular, who considered the prison workhouse an infamous institution, were engaged in a struggle with the authorities. This story will be told in Chapter Seven.

4

IN THE MARGINS OF
SETTLED LIFE
Imprisonment and the Repression
of Begging and Vagrancy

Throughout the seventeenth century the troubles beggars and vagrants caused to the settled population were mentioned most often as the major motivation for the erection of prison workhouses. This was especially so during the wave of reopenings and new foundations in the Dutch Republic around 1660. It comes as no surprise. A change of attitudes toward marginal people lay behind the emergence of prison workhouses in Europe. Consequently, marginals were a major category of inmates during the early years and continued to be present throughout the Ancien Régime. Several recent studies inform us about the way these people lived at large: their habits, the conditions of their existence, the confrontation with the settled population.[1] Discussion of this matter is not the purpose of this chapter. Nor will I discuss the entire apparatus of repression which sought to keep beggars and vagrants within acceptable bounds. For the present study, the crucial questions refer to the experience of marginals with imprisonment: the fate of some and the threat to all. The paucity of sources for this subject sets limits to the discussion. The arrest and incarceration of marginals went on almost unrecorded. There was seldom a formal trial and only special cases were recorded in logbooks or related sources. As a consequence, this chapter is less exhaustive than the importance of marginals as a category of inmates warrants.

Central figures on the repression side were the beggar catchers. It should be emphasized that the creation of this office usually antedated the establishment of a prison. In 1598, for example, the Haarlem magistrates appointed four men to this office following complaints about an increase in the number of marginals in 1590 and 1597.[2] The Aumône Générale of Lyon had made use of beggar catchers from its inception. This law enforcement apparatus was introduced in several European towns with the reform of poor relief in the first half of the sixteenth century. The appearance of beggar catchers was an earlier effect of the change of mentality with regard to poverty and marginality than the foundation of prisons.

Originally, the repressive measures taken against arrested beggars or vagrants primarily consisted of banishment. In towns with a prison the apparatus for rounding up marginals was usually linked to the prison institution.[3] From the late sixteenth century on, confinement was a new tool of the beggar catchers, and the association between the two was reconfirmed time and again. Even small towns that established a prison in the eighteenth century simultaneously issued decrees against beggary and appointed a team of catchers.[4] It was, of course, impossible to put everyone into prison: the beggar catchers accomplished the first round in a selection process.

The Tale of Legal Prohibitions   Our first task is to inquire in what way the opening of a prison workhouse shaped the policies of the authorities vis-à-vis marginals and influenced attitudes among the populace. The best way to do this is to consider the succession of legal measures and city ordinances in Amsterdam. Although these documents do not refer to individual cases, they are suggestive of and enable us to make inferences about concrete practices.

Implementation of the 1595 provincial law against beggary was left to local authorities. Amsterdam reacted on 25 January 1596, nine days before the first prisoners arrived in the rasphouse, with the publication of an ordinance laying down rules for licensed begging. Two commissioners were to issue tickets in each of the two sections into which the town was divided then. The ordinance as well as the provincial placard were a little vague on who could get permission to beg, but both referred to at least one specific category: persons in search of work. This implies some attempt to distinguish between professional beggars and migrant laborers. While looking for employment, the latter were allowed to ask for bread for two or three days, and if they found no work, they were to leave the town, again with a permit. No one was allowed to beg without a ticket.[5] This ordinance does not mention imprisonment as a possible sanction. The earliest source referring to it is the instruction for the provosts, as the beggar catchers were called in Amsterdam, dated 27 April 1597. These were to arrest unlicensed beggars and take them to their superiors, who were to decide whether they were to be imprisoned or otherwise dealt with.[6]

The ordinance dated 11 November 1597 is a revealing document. It denounced practices which must have been common in the city, warning four groups of possible saboteurs. The first consisted of poor parents who encouraged their children to beg or sent them to Amsterdam when they were too young to learn a trade. Innkeepers were the second group. Providing lodging to marginals depended on the consent of the supervisors of the poor. Landlords and ladies were told not to allow their guests to spend the money acquired through begging for food or accommodations above subsistence need; neither should they tell them how to evade the provosts. The third group, boatmen, were prohibited from taking marginals into town unnoticed. Finally, the ordinance warned masters and mistresses. Many were said to employ up to six 'artisanal children' and to send them out to beg instead of teaching them a trade. Any apprentice who ran away had to be reported immediately to the supervisors of the poor. If caught, he was to be whipped in the rasphouse in view of all prisoners and his master or mistress if he or she wished to be present. If apprentices ran away and were caught for the second time, they were to be imprisoned in the rasphouse.[7]

   This ordinance provides a look inside the mind of its authors. In their view, supervision of the poor, repression of begging, and imprisonment as the ultimate remedy were clearly connected. Professional beggars, they thought, merely tried to find a place to sleep and to evade the provosts. These beggars were potential inmates of the rasphouse in their own right. Children from artisanal families might drift on the road to marginality if their parents let them or if they fell into the hands of unscrupulous masters. When they took this road themselves, by running away, their guilt earned them a first acquaintance with the prison. The ordinance enabled the authorities to take over tasks formerly considered to belong to the head of a household, for which the presence of exploitative parents or surrogate parents may have served for legitimation. When an apprentice ran away from a bona fide surrogate parent, the latter also was deprived of his right of disciplinary punishment. The invitation to be present at the beating in prison served as a compensation. Finally, an inconsistency in the ordinance's approach to marginals should be noted. Its authors warned innkeepers not to inform their guests about the ways of the provosts. Logically, these guests must have been unlicensed beggars, and it would follow that all the money they possessed had been acquired illegally. Still, the innkeepers were only prohibited from serving them above subsistence level. The implicit idea is that marginals have a right to eat and sleep, too, but that beggary is an easy way of life which many use as a basis for prodigality. This stereotype of beggars affording themselves a hedonistic lifestyle, which religion denied even to those who earned their living by work, contributed to a negative view of all marginals.

   A reorganization of poor relief in 1613 led to greater repression of unlicensed begging. A new ordinance repeated most of the warnings of 1597 and added a new element: official collectors were appointed. They were to go from house to house to collect alms for the deserving poor. Consequently, no citizen was allowed to give anything whatsoever to a beggar coming to his door or approaching him in the street. The illegal almsgiver could be fined; a task also entrusted to the provosts, who received one third of each fine.[8] Not everyone was satisfied with the centralization of almsgiving and it is no surprise that references to opposition, a subject discussed below, appear a year later. In 1617 a new clause was added to the ordinance of 1613. Some people, it was said, evaded the prohibition of almsgiving by inviting into their homes beggars who came to their door. This practice could now be fined, too.[9] Later ordinances added no substantially new elements. In 1626 it was said to be common practice of the provosts to surprise illegal beggars and vagabonds in their lodgings and sleeping places. The lawfulness of this method was confirmed. An ordinance of 1648 repeated the old prohibitions such as the warning to boatmen and coach drivers not to take marginals into the city. However, 'artisanal children' were no longer mentioned.[10] This ordinance set the pattern for legal measures throughout the seventeenth and eighteenth centuries. Similar prohibitions were constantly repeated and the texts concentrated on vagrants and professional beggars who had no roots in the community. The repression of marginality had been separated more or less from the supervision of the poor.

Undecisive Policies   Two conclusions can be drawn from the analysis of legal measures in Amsterdam. First, the repression of begging was intensified in connection with the coming of prison workhouses. Imprisonment, as the fate of some and a threat to others, and the chase after marginals generally were associated in an integrated system. Second, there were groups of people who refused to welcome this and had to be forced to accept the new system. The same conditions prevailed in other towns as well. Opposition to the chase after marginals is documented all over Europe. Let us first consider the policies and attitudes of the authorities.

The archival sources and a number of historical monographs leave no doubt that legal measures comparable to those just discussed were taken throughout the Netherlands and the Empire in the seventeenth and eighteenth centuries. In Antwerp also, the rounding up of marginals was closely associated with the prison. Its first work boss was obliged to keep three beggar catchers as private assistants of a sort. He was to pay them from the proceeds of forced labor and the profits from the board money received for private prisoners.[11] Beggar catchers in Delft, on the other hand, worked under a deputy-*schout*, who faced complaints about ineffective repression in 1692.[12] In Bremen, at the beginning only resident beggars were threatened with imprisonment. An ordinance from the early seventeenth century fixed their terms at no less than one year.[13] Confinement disappeared as an option after the closure of the prison in 1627, but the *vögte*, whose task it had been to deal with beggars, remained active nevertheless. A document of 1640 tells us that the officials accompanied a procession of licensed beggars that crossed the town three days a week to collect money, food, and drink. The gifts were divided among the recipients by the *vögte* and the deacons. The document closed with the advice to erect the *zuchthaus* anew.[14] In 1645, when the institution was reopened, a new ordinance for the poor was issued. All beggary was now prohibited and imprisonment was no longer reserved for resident beggars. The resident poor were supposed to receive relief or to be cared for in hospitals. The foreign poor were either to be led outside the gate or imprisoned.[15]

The combination of beggars, *vögte,* and deacons suggests that the repression of begging was viewed as complementary to organized charity. The same linkage is seen in the other Hanseatic towns. Beggar catchers were associated with the Lübeck almshouse even before the erection of a separate *zuchthaus.*[16] In Hamburg representatives of the four parish churches met with the prison administrators in March 1626 and agreed on the appointment of four *vögte.* Their duty was to go about the streets and take all beggars "to the places where they belonged." Presumably, the *zuchthaus* was one of these places. The institution and the churches together paid the *vögte,* who were to change parishes each three months.[17] On Christmas day of the same year the parties resolved to prolong the agreement during 1627.[18] No further prolongations were recorded, which may be taken as a sign that the office was continued automatically. It was only in 1735 that the parishes no longer participated and the *vögte* came to work for the *zuchthaus* alone.[19]

We can conclude that the measures taken in Holland and the Hanseatic towns did not differ significantly, but there is little information on how the system worked in practice. Really tight control was probably an exception. A number of complaints about ineffective repression were heard in Haarlem.[20] In that town innkeepers were also identified as a counterforce. As early as 1615 one Deius Huibrechts, landlord at the Vergulde Vlies, was fined because he had hindered the beggar catchers as they were performing their duties and had encouraged the crowd to throw stones at them. It is likely, though not stated explicitly, that the law enforcement agents had been arresting visitors of the Vergulde Vlies.[21] Clearly, the motives of innkeepers might have been self-interested. In Hamburg authorities were confronted with similar problems. The first page of the prison logbook informs us that in 1625 "lord Ulrich Winckell, burgomaster and patron of this house, has summoned the following lodgers of beggars to the *tuchthuss* and has warned them seriously, in the presence of the provisors, to refrain from lodging beggars altogether." Six landlords and one landlady whose names and addresses were listed had been summoned. They were threatened with fines and even with the prospect, if found guilty a third time, of being punished in the *tuchthuss* themselves.[22] The most explicit statement about innkeepers acting from self-interested motives comes from France. In connection with the Parisian imprisonment project of 1611–1617 it was said that the hosts of taverns in areas that used to be frequented by marginals were protesting heavily. One of them complained that he served two barrels less of wine each evening.[23] An inn was also central in a Hamburg case which happens to be well-documented.

The Case of Claus Knopf   The provisors' story went as follows: in May 1629 our men inspected suspect places and beggars' lodgings. All kinds of idle people gathered at an inn named the Pulver Mühlen. Among them were Claus Knopf and his wife, and a maid who had been imprisoned for beggary before. The three were taken to the *zuchthaus*. The items found upon them included silver pennies and clothes with gold buttons. As we examined each item separately and inquired into its origin, Knopf finally confessed to having acquired these things through begging. He had hired the maid for that purpose, and his wife also went from door to door. For the rest, his answers were evasive and contradictory. Knopf offered to buy his freedom with fifty Reichsthaler out of a total of 193 which he claimed to have hidden in a drawer in the inn, but upon inspection of his room nothing was found. A few days later he suggested searching it again, whereupon we discovered 114 Reichsthaler. From this we concluded that a whole company of beggars was out there, whose members daily brought in new bounties. No doubt, Knopf was their leader. We held the three prisoners for nine weeks, and upon their release they caused us trouble again. We wanted compensation for feeding them and other expenses of their stay. Some of us wished to keep all the money, but we gave them back twenty Reichsthaler as well as the clothes and other goods.[24]

This episode would not have been recorded if Claus Knopf had acquiesced in the loss of most of his money or lacked resources to mobilize support. His marginality, however, did have its limits. He was a native of Salzwedel in Brandenburg, or at least the magistrates of that town acknowledged him as one of theirs. The Salzwedel council wrote to Hamburg in October 1629, endorsing his complaint that money had been taken from him under false pretexts.[25] Hamburg's reply was not recorded, but it must have been unfavorable to Knopf. Two more requests from the Salzwedel magistrates to their Hanseatic colleagues early in 1630 were of no avail.[26] Four and a half years later the question came up anew, when Knopf directed himself to the Elector of Brandenburg.

In the request he submitted to the prince we hear his story for the first time, thus: the war has uprooted many people including myself. I am a glazier but have been unable to earn a living by my trade. With my wife and children I moved from Salzwedel to Hamburg in the hope of employment, but only further misfortune awaited me there. Three of my children succumbed to the plague. A kind man, who had suffered from the plague, too, took me into his house, the Pulver Mühlen. Out of utter desperation my wife asked for alms from good people in Hamburg. After noticing this, the *vögte* suspected me and my companions of beggary, too. They took us all from our beds in the early morning and off to prison. For nine weeks we received nothing but a little bread and a meager portion of beans. Upon our release, 110 Reichsthaler were taken from me under the pretext that I had not acquired them lawfully.[27]

In Hamburg this request started off a new round of accusations and efforts by the provisors to save face. The elector could not simply be ignored, especially in a time of war. Knopf had requested him to seize goods belonging to the Hanseatic town until the money was restored. The prince did not go that far, but he informed the senate that he was convinced of Knopf's honest character and the truthfulness of his assertions. The senate was kindly requested to make the provisors pay back the money, but the provisors refused to yield so easily. In their report to the magistrates they stated that it was generally known that there had been a veritable beggars' nest, frequented by all kinds of *lumpen gesindlein*, in one of the city's quarters in 1629. The neighbors had complained, whereupon the matter had been investigated and the culprits arrested. Having reviewed the events anew, the provisors concluded that the Imperial laws would have allowed an even more severe punishment. They added the testimony of a witness, Hans Geger, whose occupation was not stated. Geger declared that he had known Claus Knopf very well. According to Geger, about six years before, Knopf was living in a room in the Pulver Mühlen, where he gathered with other idle fellows. They ate and drank excessively and often fought among themselves, while Knopf's wife begged from the early morning until the late evening. The couple kept a maid and a number of children not their own. They lived from the gifts received by the maid and put aside what was collected by the woman and the children. And Knopf loved the maid more than he did his wife. That was enough for the magistrates. In February of 1635 they replied to the elector that they were convinced Knopf had been guilty of wanton beggary and other vices. The prince was advised to ignore his request. Quite to the contrary, he sent another letter that was somewhat less friendly than the previous. The confiscation of Knopf's money, he claimed, was based on mere suspicion, not factual evidence. The laws against wanton and able-bodied beggars were laudable, but when applied in this fashion, their brightness would soon fade.[28]

That settled the matter. The pressure exerted on the Hamburg magistrates forced them to order the prison administrators to give way. One can imagine the sense of victory with which Claus Knopf returned to the *zuchthaus* on 14 April 1635 to pick up his money. The provisors restricted themselves to recording the two official documents which confirmed the 'agreement' between both parties. Knopf declared he had no further claims on the institution, now that the money kept there because of a misunderstanding had been restored. He made his mark on the document by drawing an arrow with a bar through it and an M underneath, "because I cannot write." Two of the provisors wrote their signature. The second document served to confirm Knopf's honorable status. It explained that inspecting inns was a normal task of the *vögte* in their combat of beggary and that the inspection had nothing to do with a criminal investigation. Knopf and his companions had stayed in prison for beggary; thieves were not admitted to the *zuchthaus*.[29]

Although the documents relating to the case do not allow us to decide what in reality Claus Knopf might have been guilty of, they do permit a few conclusions on the standard practices of the beggar catchers and stereotypical conceptions about beggars. Inns and other places of lodging were focal points for repressive activities. The victims were taken there by surprise, preferably in the early morning. It is understandable that the *vögte* thought they would have greater success in this way than if they simply patrolled the streets. But it was more than just a matter of convenience to focus on taverns and inns. Expressions such as 'beggars' nest' suggest that the deviance the *vögte* were after was concentrated in specific places. Taverns and inns where many marginals gathered were considered hotbeds of vice. Reports of sexual promiscuity and fights contributed to this picture. The stereotype included the notion that beggars were better off materially than hard-working people. Some were thought to have set up whole companies of organized begging. Anyone caught in a suspect lodging place was a candidate for prison and would have a hard time convincing the officials of his innocence. There must have been scores of imprisoned marginals who considered themselves innocent but lacked the determination and the resources Claus Knopf had been able to marshall. For the historian, the hardest part is to determine how much truth the stereotype contained. Knopf's possession of valuable clothes and money may have been exceptional. Beggars sometimes did operate in companies and preferred to employ children. This is confirmed by several historical studies. Beggars' feasts were a recurrent motif in picaresque novels and related literary genres as well as a favorite subject for painters.[30] It is impossible to tell, though, how many marginals actually were able to live comfortably. We can be sure that not all of them could afford to pay for lodging, even in 'beggars' nests', which no doubt were among the cheapest hostels. Marginals sleeping in the street may not have been arrested for the trivial reason that the beggar catchers did not work at night. We are left with the irony of contemporary policies. To the extent that the law enforcement agents concentrated on inns and taverns, imprisonment hit the beggar elite rather than the group's lowest stratum.

Resistance   The stereotypes cherished by the beggar catchers and their superiors were not necessarily shared by all the people. Some citizens must have agreed with the new policy of chasing and imprisoning marginals, judging from the complaints of the neighbors of the Pulver Mühlen. On the other hand, other people resented the new policy, based on evidence of hostility and resistance to the beggar catchers. This resistance was an international phenomenon.

We must first assess the beggar catchers' vulnerability. Their numerical strength always remained modest, a problem they shared with other law enforcement agents at the time. We saw that Hamburg employed four *vögte*, and that only two provosts were sworn in by the Amsterdam magistrates in 1597. Toward the middle of the seventeenth century Amsterdam had ten of them, led by one head-provost.[31] Additionally, the servants of the *schout* were authorized to arrest marginals after 1623.[32] According to their oath, the provosts had to refuse any gifts from beggars and to be polite to citizens.[33] This suggests that the magistrates did not automatically trust them to be polite. The reputation of the beggar catchers may have contributed to a predisposition to view them with hostility. The Hamburg provisors insisted on a right of disciplinary punishment over the *vögte*. In 1638 they admonished them to refrain from drinking and set penalties on coming on duty late or staying away altogether.[34] The Amsterdam provosts were reproached several times for drunkenness or fighting among themselves. In 1649 their superiors drew up a list of provosts who were said to be of no use because of their alcoholism or old age.[35] Similar reproaches, however, were made of nightwatchmen, against whom no particular public hostility was recorded.

The specter of hostility haunted the beggar catchers since the institution of the office. Amsterdam sources enable us to reconstruct the story from the beginning. The ordinance of November 1597 concluded with a general warning not to hinder the activities of anyone associated with the repression of unlicensed begging. In the early seventeenth century, together with the warnings against illegal almsgiving, more aggressive practices were denounced. An ordinance of 1614 accused "many people" of sabotaging the repression of unlicensed begging "from misplaced compassion or envy and also from wantonness and disobedience." It listed an all-too-visible escalation of events: refusing assistance to the provosts, yelling at them, walking in their way, throwing objects, snatching arrested persons from their hands, and attacking and injuring them. When a hostile crowd was so numerous that the provosts were unable to identify those who actually liberated beggars, a reward of 100 guilders was promised to informers.[36] The first serious incident was recorded in 1627. On 28 February a crowd gathered around the provosts, abused them verbally, threw stones, and managed to liberate two arrested vagabonds. The embattled agents defended themselves and in the process one of the provosts killed one of the crowd's leaders, a Scotsman named Jan Smith. Thereupon, the provost who did it was seriously injured by the crowd. Four days later the court issued a printed notification of the incident, promising a reward for information and assuring that the informant's name would be kept secret.[37]

Consecutive urban legislation repeated the prohibitions of the early seventeenth century. Resistance to the provosts and other officials who arrested marginals was referred to in ordinances published in 1654, 1655, 1670, 1682, 1685, 1693, 1713, and 1745.[38] Fresh incidents were sometimes noted as the basis for the repetitions. The ordinances generally copied the wording of earlier ones, including the imputed motives for hostility quoted above. The court was probably not very successful in laying hands on the aggressors, since few of them were actually tried.[39] The statement of a beggar in 1712 also suggests a relative helplessness of law enforcement agents in the face of the public's hostility. Hendrik Aarse, who was questioned because of other charges, additionally confessed to having evaded an earlier arrest. The previous winter, he said, he and his companion knocked on citizens' doors, telling them they had just arrived after migrating because of a bankruptcy. Hendrik was apprehended, but in a side street he managed to overpower his catcher and take his hat and wig from him. He said he did this because someone had screamed: "Do you let yourself be taken to prison by a provost so easily?"[40]

A systematic search in the court records of other towns and districts would no doubt produce supplementary evidence of resistance to beggar catchers. A large number of cases are cited in several historical studies. France, for example, witnessed the phenomenon from the beginning. The anonymous author describing the Paris project of 1611–1617 formulated it in this way:

> It [i.e., the policing of the poor] has also been obstructed by a number of persons without judgment or reason, such as *pages,* lackeys, *pallefreniers,* kitchen servants, poor artisans and workers, who beat and outraged the *sergens* of the said police, saying it was an offense to God to chase away the poor and that the Savior of the world, in reply to Judas who was envious of the unguents spent on our said Lord by the sinning woman, told him that we would always have the poor with us.[41]

The attitudes of the complainants are clear, though the passage in the New Testament they refer to seems a little inappropriate. The author's counterargument was equally ambivalent. First, he denied that the poor were chased away, claiming that their bodies and souls were well cared for. He then proceeded to argue that those arrested and imprisoned were not representatives of the poverty recommended by Christ. Rather, they were the impertinent ones who made such a noise that all the alms ended up with them.[42] The author also pointed out what kind of people attacked the beggar catchers, a specification seldom found in Amsterdam. In Lyon, where instances of resistance were recorded throughout the seventeenth and eighteenth centuries, the aggressors were mostly artisans and working people, but soldiers, domestic servants, and even nobles were involved as well. Aristocratic and bourgeois masters usually backed their servants in such instances. By contrast, the inhabitants of the countryside refrained from hostile behavior; the farmers only protected *contrebandiers.*[43] Resistance to beggar catchers was also recorded elsewhere in eighteenth century France.[44]

In England, on the other hand, where most of the research has been done on the seventeenth century, there are many records of vagrants who opposed their own arrest, without any help from the populace.[45] The situation in the Empire resembled that in the Netherlands and France, and there we have some information on the identity of the aggressors. During the third quarter of the eighteenth century the Hamburg magistrates made threats of more severe punishments for resistance.[46] In 1755 a *vogt* took a soldier to the *zuchthaus*, for snatching away the beggar whom the agent had arrested originally.[47] In Potsdam it was soldiers, too, together with orphan boys, who were accused of resisting the *vögte*.[48] A Nürnberg commentator in 1787, somewhat mysteriously, called resisters a "mob of lower or higher status."[49] In Liège, in the Southern Netherlands, officials who had to take mendicant girls to prison were often attacked by people from the lower-class Outre-Meuse district.[50]

Thus, internationally, we are confronted by a rather variegated array of aggressors. Some, particularly those denoted by the sources as being of the vulgar sort, may have acted out of a feeling of solidarity with the beggars. They were close in socioeconomic status to the victims of arrest. Soldiers, who were often recruited from the marginal population and became marginals again upon desertion or disbandment of the army, can be included in this group. Remarkably, members of the clergy do not seem to have been involved at all. It might be supposed that many of the clergy condemned the novel attitudes and policies with regard to marginals and charity, but few seem to have raised their voice about them. Presumably, because the change in mentalities was so gradual and the new approach was presented as a Christian one, too, most of the clergy accepted it as such. Their loyalty to the secular authorities made them acquiesce in confinement as a policy and certainly prevented them from participating in attempts to liberate beggars. That leaves us with the socially broad spectrum of the settled population, lay and urban, who viewed beggar catchers with hostility. Gutton argues that this group acted out of indirect solidarity, and that this means that traditional ideas about charity lived on.[51] This is a likely possibility, but it is also possible to be more precise.

A sociohistorical analysis begins with an identification of the groups who had a material interest in sabotaging the chase after marginals. We have met them already. The keepers of inns and taverns saw their earnings rise as beggars collected more alms from private citizens. Boatmen and coach drivers were happy to sell seats to vagrants, too. Since they were on their way again after their customers had arrived in town, we do not find them among the crowds attacking catchers. The rest of the settled population may have been motivated by attitudes persisting from an earlier period, but in this case, too, we must differentiate. The repression of unlicensed begging had two sides. One was the chase after marginals, the other the centralization of charity, or from the public's point of view, the expropriation of private almsgiving. The collectors appointed by the

Table 4.1

Decisions on Foreign Beggars in Amsterdam, 1597–1599

Decision	Men	Women	Total
Incarceration	2.7%	3.7%	3.1%
Ordered to leave town	65.4	57.9	62.7
Given permission to beg for some days	20	31.8	24.3
Other decision	11.9	6.5	9.9

magistrates did not accept gifts for themselves, so that the direct contact between almsgiver and receiver was lost. I would hypothesize that, while some among the settled population may have disliked both the chase after marginals and the expropriation of private charity, the majority resented the second. They were the citizens who invited beggars quickly and secretly into their house. At the same time they may have been in agreement with attempts to keep down the number of vagrants in the city. The established artisan classes also may have agreed to this policy in times of dearth or plague. If these suppositions are correct, it follows that a degree of ambivalence characterized the public's attitude toward the policies of the authorities especially in the case of the elites and possibly also among 're-spectable' working people, who did not wish to be identified with marginals.

Imprisonment and Quantitative Evidence   How many arrested beggars and vagrants were actually put to forced labor? Some scattered evidence, mainly from Amsterdam, provides an indication. By sheer luck one relatively old register, listing every stranger found in Amsterdam without work, has been preserved. It must have belonged to the archive of the commissioners appointed in January 1596 to deal with licensed begging. The register covers the period from 7 October 1597 to 27 October 1598 (with a few marginal listings of 'recidivists' in 1599).[52] In my study I examined every fifth entry, recidivists included. This resulted in exactly 400 cases. Men outnumbered women by 55 percent to 45 percent; their mean ages were 33.6 and 36.1, respectively. The major conclusion to be drawn from my study was that very few of the persons who reported themselves to the commissioners or were summoned by them were imprisoned. Table 4.1 presents the decisions made about them (27 percent missing).

Thus, the sample contained only nine cases of imprisonment—five men and four women. This indicates an incarceration rate of forty-four beggars per year. Five of the nine persons imprisoned were kept in a 'dungeon'; three were sent to the rasphouse; and in one case the place of incarceration was not mentioned. It is, of course, possible that persons picked up by the beggar catchers were not reported to the commissioners, but taken to the rasphouse directly. None of those imprisoned was in their twenties, but otherwise all age groups were represented. One-fifth of all beggars, including a few men, had children with them, and none of this group went to prison. Significantly, none of the nine prisoners was previously mentioned; repeat offending was apparently not a criterion for selection for incarceration. This suggests that an estimation of a beggar's character, possibly based on stereotypical notions, influenced the commissioners' decision of whether or not to commit him or her to prison.

Because imprisonment played only a marginal role in this source, I will not push the analysis further. It is possible that the number of beggars and vagrants sent to the rasphouse increased by the early seventeenth century; at least, that is suggested by literary sources such as Pontanus. Occasionally, marginals appear in the court records of this period because they had participated in acts of insubordination in the rasphouse and were taken to jail and tried for these offenses. This is discussed in Chapter Eight. But one conclusion may be anticipated: it looks as though beggars and convicts did not see themselves as separate categories within the rasphouse. The two groups freely interacted and participated in escape conspiracies together. There is no evidence for a hierarchy. The more serious escape attempts had the unintended consequence of further integration of the two categories. Conspirators from both groups received the same penalty, based on the current offense rather than the initial reason for their stay in prison. They were interrogated, formally tried, and punished, sometimes on the scaffold. In this way, beggars became convicts. The net result was to reinforce a tendency toward the formation of a professional criminal group. After their release these beggars had few options but to confirm the stereotype that many vagrants were also thieves.

In 1650 the Amsterdam magistrates decided to erect a third prison, which was designated at its opening in 1654 as the new home for marginals. People picked up in the streets by the provosts were henceforth taken to this (new) workhouse.[53] The institution's entry books, a series suddenly ending when it was exactly a hundred years old, have been preserved. In 1942 Oldewelt published figures on the annual numbers of entries.[54] Although delinquents were imprisoned there, too, these figures provide an indication of the number of marginals arrested in the city. They fluctuated between extremes of 522 in 1670 and fifty-seven in 1706. No correlation with such factors as years of high prices or the aftermath of war is apparent.[55] The number of arrested marginals must have depended on shifting preferences by the agents of repression. The nature of these preferences remains largely unknown. For a further analysis, I took a sample of entries in three periods of two years, at the beginning, the middle, and the end of the period covered by the records. Unfortunately, it turned out that marginals, as opposed to delinquents sentenced by the court, could only be identified for the first period, when "for begging" was added to their name. The following figures, therefore, refer to the years 1655–1656 only (including a few marginal entries of recidivists in 1657–1660). The marginals arrested in those years numbered 318—53 percent men and 20 percent recidivists. The mean age of the men was 32.9, that of the women 40.4. Terms were set for 53.8 percent of the men (mean: 11.2 months), while another 19.3 percent had to stay until they were ready to go to the Indies. No shortening of terms was recorded. The average real length of stay for men was 97 days, but this figure includes twenty men who were taken to the workhouse by the provosts and sent away immediately. Only 0.6 percent died in captivity, while 9.4 percent escaped. The corresponding figures for the women were: term set for 48 percent; 28.3 percent to the Indies; mean term of 8.4 months; average real length of stay was 138 days; twenty-two were sent away; 2 percent died; 1.3 percent escaped.

A minority of marginals were formally tried rather than committed to the workhouse directly. Faber's and my own investigations in the Amsterdam court records, though not complete, provide an indication in this regard. After 1614 the legal rule was that persons picked up by the provosts for the first, second, or third time were imprisoned without interference by the court. If arrested a fourth time, they were to be tried as criminals.[56] This happened to just a few, which was probably a result of the high degree of geographic mobility of marginals. Among the prisoners of 1655–1660 only four women were committed a fourth time or more. Only during two brief periods in the middle of the eighteenth century were relatively large numbers of beggars suddenly processed through the court instead of being imprisoned without a trial. In normal times criminal sentences for beggary or vagrancy were imposed in two types of situations. The first was when beggars were considered especially impertinent or threatening. The second was when they had been arrested under suspicion of theft or other crimes and these could not be proved. In such cases they were condemned for beggary or vagrancy nonetheless. The court's involvement with marginals did not lead to a reinforcement of the imprisonment solution. In the majority of cases the criminal sanction for begging or vagrancy was banishment, while occasionally a public corporal penalty was imposed. In the case of gypsies, too, the court imposed imprisonment in a minority of cases. In France, on the other hand, confinement of gypsies became more frequent around 1700. Gypsies were a distinct category of marginals who were increasingly criminalized in Continental Europe during the early modern period.[57]

Outside Amsterdam the possibilities for quantification are very limited. A few prisoners in the Delft entry books were listed as vagrants admitted upon an order of the *landdrost* of Delfland, but in this case registration was probably not complete.[58] The Bremen prison archive contains two series of petty notes indicating cases in which relatives of released beggars provided bail for them, in case they had to be imprisoned anew. For the years 1684–1687 there are twenty-five such notes, fifteen signed and ten underwritten with a mark. For the months August–October 1693 there are nine signatures and eight marks, but this series does not identify the released inmates as beggars. In all cases the guarantors were inhabitants of the city.[59] Clearly, these notes only relate to beggars who still had connections in the community. When large numbers of marginals were arrested in 1743, the Bremen *zuchthaus* faced capacity problems.[60] Everywhere outside Amsterdam persons picked up by the beggar catchers continued to be imprisoned with the condemned. Since the court was not involved, they were usually not registered. Because the Dutch metropolis had a separate workhouse, marginals could be identified more easily.

Criminalization of the Poor?   The data of this chapter confirm and elaborate on the findings of other historians: supervision of the poor and judicial repression were associated, especially with the emergence of prison workhouses; beggars and vagabonds were chased and some were confined; during the course of the early modern period the authorities increasingly defined crime as associated with persons steeped in poverty. Such observations led to the notion of 'the criminalization of the poor.'[61] But it is necessary to raise the question whether this phrase might be too all-inclusive. The sources referring to imprisonment contain a few clues in this regard.

The uneasy balance between charity and repression is nowhere depicted more cogently than in a popular play written by Abraham de Koning in 1616. It is one of the few examples of a nongovernmental source revealing the ideology behind the imprisonment of beggars and the centralization of relief. The occasion for which it was composed was governmental, though: a lottery organized for the benefit of the hospitals for old men and women at Amsterdam. The piece is a morality play, with abstract concepts such as "paternal supervision" appearing on the scene, though most of these characters are repersonified again. A central figure is "the useless beggar," which sets the tone of the play. De Koning adheres to the distinction between the undeserving and the true poor, one of the pillars of the new mentality. The useless beggar of course belongs to the group who do not deserve the gifts and assistance of the rich. However, the provosts also are tagged with a negative epithet. They are called "louse catchers," which may have been the popular name for them. They frighten the useless beggar, who complains that nowadays he gets no rest. Some of his mates have been whipped already and he himself has been imprisoned. The louse catchers had seized him on the blue bridge and he had been put to rasping in the *tuchthuis* for three months. When released, he goes to Dam square, where he meets some compatriots arriving from Bremen. He chides them because they solicit for work, and then he has to run away from another louse catcher. This completes the stereotype: the useless beggar is too lazy to work, some of his mates are delinquents, and he has wandered in from Northern Germany; he is imprisoned with good reason. Nevertheless, he is allowed to defend his way of life: begging requires as much dedicated effort as ordinary work and the profits are meager; beggars do not waste their money on prostitutes, as the white bread children confined in the secret ward have. This touching defense, however, turns out to have been hypocritical. When the useless beggar decides to try his luck elsewhere, he is stopped at the town gate because he is wearing a beautiful coat. He claims he inherited it, but the louse catcher does not believe him, searches his pockets, and finds no less than 700 guilders. That seals the beggar's fate. The louse catcher directs himself to the audience and proclaims: "Those people, bold and strong, play for beggar/ What else are they doing but stealing from the true poor/ And those paying gifts to them engage in the wrong kind of charity."[62] The overall lesson is that the true kind of charity is to buy a lottery ticket for the benefit of the old men's and women's asylums. The exhortation to contribute to organized charity is complemented by propaganda against private almsgiving and for the repression of unlicensed begging. These are two sides of the same coin, and the play's mission is to propagate this twofold message.

We can also view the connection from another angle. The distinction between nauseating and misbehaving marginals on the one hand and the deserving poor on the other also meant that the latter were washed clean. Shifting the focus of our question a little, we ask: "to what extent were the deserving poor criminalized, too?" We note that the earliest ordinances against marginals dealt with the recipients of relief as well. However, it should not be forgotten that in the beginning prison workhouses were seen as charitable institutions of a sort. At that point, then, both marginals and the deserving poor were criminalized, but only incompletely. From the later seventeenth century onward, prisons were increasingly associated with the judicial system. This meant that the criminalization of beggars and vagabonds was confirmed or even intensified. It also meant that the gulf between prisons and hospitals or almshouses had widened and that the deserving poor stayed within the sphere of charity.

The Haarlem *tuchthuis* is of special importance in this regard, since it remained combined with an almshouse until 1786. This suggests that Haarlem did not notice that widening gulf. There are indeed indications that asylum functions and repression were linked in that town. The almshouse, for example, also provided lodging to passing migrants when other hospitals were full. They could stay for one night and received some rye bread. But if one of them was unmasked as a beggar, he forfeited his bread, and if he was found to have cheated, too, he was arrested. The instruction for the institution's [head-]provost is revealing. Article 7 obliged him to visit the recipients of relief every year and to search their houses to look for hidden candies, liquor, or other "improper stuff." Article 9 recommended him to acquaint himself personally with them all, so that he could enter suspect taverns by surprise and see if one was there. This tactic was to be used "especially on Mondays or other days when people are working less."[63] Thus, the provost had authority with regard to injunctions toward soberness, enforcement of labor discipline, and combat of Saint Monday. Another crucial feature of the institution was the admittance of heads of households abusing relief.[64] The supervisors of the poor maintained that they were entitled to arrest and imprison unworthy recipients of relief on their own account and to put them to rasping. In 1634 the regents of the *tuchthuis* contested this privilege and burgomasters reacted with a Solomon's judgment: the supervisors were allowed to imprison their people, but if they wished them to rasp, they should notify the regents.[65] The burgomasters reconfirmed the supervisors' privilege in 1640, 1649, 1679, and 1684, restricting the term in prison to three months.[66] Thus, the supervisors used the *tuchthuis* for their own disciplinary purposes. The result was, on the one hand, that those imprisoned in the *tuchthuis* were no longer reckoned among the deserving poor; on the other hand, the new usage implied that abuse of relief was no criminal offense.

This situation at Haarlem should not deceive us. The distinction between the undeserving and the true poor was adhered to in Haarlem within the institution. The almshouse part was separated from the prison and its inmates could come and go. Despite the physical proximity of the two wards, they were clearly distinct in the minds of contemporaries. In 1679 the statue of a woman representing both charity and chastisement was erected above the institution's main gate. The attributes carried by her and the reliefs underneath symbolized both characteristics. For example, a collection box was featured in opposition to locks and chains. One attribute was a basket for collecting bread, with a snake wrapped around it to symbolize the necessity of caution to ensure that the alms ended up with those really indigent. In 1755 the town's historian, Pieter Langendijk, composed a poem on the statue and explained the dual function of the house: an asylum for the common poor and abandoned children and a place of punishment for thieves, rioters, and persons living an irregular life. He grouped the last category, persons committed by their families, some of whom enjoyed a reasonably high social status, with delinquents rather than with the poor. A verse which could be read in the regents' room stressed that "he who does well to the poor obtains the kingdom of heaven."[67]

Hence, in the eighteenth century caring for the miserable was still considered a work pleasing to God. The main difference from the thirteenth century was that the group entitled to this care was defined more strictly. Once defined, its members were unequivocally considered as worthy of compassion. With regard to the true poor, even to those who worked in physical proximity to delinquents, older attitudes largely persisted, alongside the newer attitude of criminalization of the undeserving poor. To conclude, the undifferentiated phrase 'the criminalization of the poor' is a misleading concept. It was beggars and vagrants who bore the main burden of the intensification of repression that accompanied the emergence of prison workhouses.

5

PRISONS AND THE IMAGINATION
The Public Image, the Miracles of St. Raspinus, and the Pumping Myth

The purpose of this book is to study mentalities, and in this chapter they are particularly central. Its aim is to penetrate into the areas of representation, ideology, and imagination in an attempt to reconstruct the imprint imprisonment made on people's minds. I will start with a general discussion of the way prisons were presented to the public. Next, with reference to the Amsterdam rasphouse, I will present two imaginative constructions—in the form of a propaganda pamphlet and the myth of pumping or drowning—the influence of which extended far beyond the Dutch Republic.

The Display of Justice Justice had to be visible in the early modern period. This applied most of all to the execution of capital and corporal penalties on the scaffold, which was the theater of justice par excellence. Imprisonment, although decidedly less public, had an audience, too. Its theatrical or display qualities were expressed in various ways, starting with architecture. These buildings were meant to impress. Modern prisons may also make an impression on the public by virtue of their solid structures, surveillance towers, or barbed wire. The institutions of the seventeenth and eighteenth centuries primarily reflected the power and dignity of the magistrates. These houses of punishment were adorned with ornamental façades just like other public buildings, as well as sculptures and inscriptions explaining the purpose of the institution. Again, it is the Amsterdam rasphouse, whose gate can still be seen today in its original location, which stands out as a model. The entrance was constructed in successive phases. When Baudaart described it in 1624 there was a relief representing a chariot loaded with Brazil redwood driven by a man with a whip and drawn by four lions, a wild swine, and a wolf. The animals symbolized 'cruel dissoluteness,' gluttony, and 'useless devouring.' The inscription relating to them, a line from Seneca's *Hercules Furens,* read: *"virtutis est domare quae cuncti pavent"* (it is virtuous to tame those whom all fear). Contemporaries referring to this line variously translated the term *virtus* as 'virtue' or 'braveness,' the latter translation suggesting the *virtù* of the Italian humanists.[1] The entrance was made more monumental a few decades later. It came to consist of two gates, one behind the other, the second adorned with stone lions and a statue of two rasping inmates.[2] Later still, a statue of a female *castigatio* with two chained prisoners was constructed above the first gate.

The architect Hendrik de Keizer designed a new entrance for the Amsterdam spinhouse in 1607. It also had a woman symbolizing *castigatio* on top. De Keizer requested Pieter Cornelisz Hooft to compose the motto to be inscribed underneath. Hooft translated the Latin word as *"straffe"* (punishment), which proves that he knew he was dealing with a punitive institution. Hooft claimed to have written the motto immediately after receiving the request: "Do not be frightened; I am not avenging wrong but forcing to do good; my hand is severe, but my mind is compassionate."[3] The spinhouse was destroyed by fire in 1643, but apparently its gate was saved. It remained at the same spot and became the entrance to the rebuilt institution, which, according to Dapper, was even more beautiful than the original one.[4] The beauty of the spinhouse was commented on again and again. Von Zesen, a German immigrant, stated that it had been "built with such splendor that one would be more likely to consider it an inn for princesses than a residence for such detestable and ugly maids."[5] Later writers praised it in similar terms. In 1693 it was described as "looking more like a palace than a house of coercion."[6] A French eighteenth-century guide to the city described it as "a house which resembles a palace more than it does a place of correction." In the 1753 edition this was changed to "this house has a very beautiful appearance and resembles a place of pleasure rather than a prison."[7] Apparently in the spinhouse's architecture the balance between the display of pride of the magistrates and the display of justice was tipped too far toward the former.

Prison facades in other towns were designed with similar care. The interplay between sculpture and text in Haarlem has been discussed already. The *tuchthuis* at Delft had a relief above the main gate showing two rasping prisoners and the city's arms.[8] The entrance to the Bremen *zuchthaus* was apparently inspired by the one at Amsterdam. A couple of wild animals with rods, sticks, and thorns were represented, and the inscription read: "If lions and bears can be tamed, why not wanton youngsters?"[9] The emphasis on recalcitrant youths instead of more common types of malefactors was, of course, characteristic in Germany at the time.

Inside the gate the decoration became more sober. In the Amsterdam rasphouse two paintings depicting fruit hung "in a room downstairs," which suggests that they might have been visible to the inmates. They were the work of one Ernst Stuven, who was sentenced there twice around 1700 and left them upon his release. Other paintings were all hung in regents' rooms. For the spinhouse, anonymous artists had depicted an old man, a procuress, and a weeping prostitute. The workhouse had a piece by the well-known painter Gerard de Lairesse. It showed an allegorical theme that in the eighteenth century was interpreted as "Discipline taking a man to prison."[10] The subject most frequently represented in these rooms, however, was the board of regents themselves. Arnoldus Boonen completed four different pictures of the spinhouse board around 1700. It was said that these pictures could be seen in the institution, which suggests that visitors were allowed in regents' rooms, too.[11] In this way, the administrators displayed their own dignity.

They shared this desire for public display with the boards that administered hospitals, orphanages, and other charitable institutions. Regents' portraits in the Dutch Republic constituted a specific genre, which has been studied by art historian Sheila Muller. She argues that the artists continued a sixteenth-century Italian tradition of representing the *vita activa*. Thus, the logbooks and other attributes displayed by the regents were meant to show that they were competent financial administrators. Most of all, the active life meant involvement in organized charity. This apparent similarity with regard to portraits and other public displays between the prison officials and officials of other charitable institutions would suggest that prison workhouses were not considered separate, punitive institutions. However, Muller's views are incorrect on this point. Her argument revolves around the interpretation of the oldest picture of the rasphouse regents, by Cornelis van der Voort (1618). She admits that the statue of *castigatio*, that appears at the center of the painting is an element specific to this piece, but she interprets it rather vaguely as expressing a humanist ethic. More likely the painter was inspired by the statue of *castigatio*, translated as punishment, that adorned the gate of the spinhouse at that time. If so, the painter would have been emphasizing the difference between a prison and a traditional asylum. A second factor makes this even more clear. Coins, which appeared on many paintings of this genre, are lacking among the attributes of the rasphouse regents. Again Muller's explanation is flawed, because she views the coins as symbols of *vanitas*. She supposes they were left out because their connotation of vanity was incompatible with the notion of charity.[12] This would mean that vanity was indeed represented on other portraits such as that by Frans Hals of the regents of St. Elisabeth's hospital at Haarlem. It seems odd that the regents, who commissioned these pieces themselves, would have agreed to be pictured as vain. A more adequate interpretation is that the coins represented charitable gifts.[13] That explains why they were included among the attributes of the regents of hospitals and left out of the picture of the rasphouse board. The conclusion must be that, while the unity of the genre suggests that prisons were ranked with asylums, within the genre painters differentiated and represented the prisons as punitive institutions.

The commonest way in which the prisons were displayed was through the admission of visitors. This practice occurred in prisons, hospitals, and madhouses. Some visitors even came from abroad. The Amsterdam institutions attracted more foreign visitors than those of any other town, which is one proof of their status as models. During the seventeenth century almost one half of the travelers from outside the Republic saw one or more of the city's prisons. During the eighteenth century about a third did so.[14] These visitors were especially attracted to the rasphouse. The peculiar type of labor performed there exerted a fascination for them that was expressed, to give but one example, by Edward Brown, a London physician. Brown saw the institution in 1668. He described how rasping wood produced a red dust which filled the air and covered the skins of the bare-chested convicts. The spectacle stimulated his imagination, reminding him of a story by the marquess of Newcastle about a nation where the people had an orange complexion and the king a purple one.[15] Others who came to see the inmates likened them to American Indians.

The majority of visitors were, of course, local residents and people living in the area. Thus, they left no travel accounts, which makes it harder to ascertain their impressions. We must start, then, from a few quantitative data. A text of 1659 states that every visitor to the rasphouse had to put two *stuivers* in a closed box, which was emptied each Saturday. The total amount per year was said to be "about 800 guilders, but usually more than that."[16] If all visitors paid the specified amount, they must have numbered eight thousand or more, which is about 5 percent of the city's population at the time. The same calculation can be made for Leiden. The money collected is specified in an account for 1671, and a 1699 source fixes the entrance fee at one *stuiver*. We have to assume that the fee had remained unchanged since 1671. The income from the box that year was 620.66 guilders, only six and a half guilders less than the income from the sales tax on liquor and tobacco. This amount translates into 12,413 visitors, or some 17 percent of the town's population. If these calculations are correct, the differences in numbers of visitors and number of visitors as a percentage of local population at Amsterdam and Leiden might be explained by two factors. First, the metropolis offered more possibilities for attractive pastimes than a town such as Leiden. Second, Leiden had a particular occasion when visits were especially popular. The work boss received an annual perquisite "for his troubles with the people coming to see the prisoners in the week of the fair." The popularity of this time for visiting is reflected in the 1671 account. It specifies that the box was emptied on 13 April, 17 May, and 29 December, and that it contained the largest amount (over 279 guilders) the second time. This means that 5,593 people saw the *tuchthuis* during the month that included the fair. We should take into account that this festival attracted a fair number of visitors from neighboring villages.[17] Thus, while Amsterdam's prisons were admired by representatives of the upper and middle classes from all over Europe, the prison at Leiden attracted a larger percentage of the local populace.

The identity of local visitors remains largely hidden. It is impossible to tell whether or not the percentages just established refer to a specific social group in the urban population. Neither do we know whether the same persons bought a ticket every year during the fair or different people did so each year. On a few occasions the sources reveal a particular detail with regard to the identity of visitors. The Amsterdam patrician Hans Bontemantel related that he saw the rasphouse as a visitor and not in any official capacity on 28 December 1663. It was a veritable family visit, because he was accompanied by his wife, children, and maids.[18] We only know the name and date of birth (1652) of a daughter of Bontemantel.[19] Assuming that she was with him, too, we may conclude that it was not uncommon to take eleven-year-old girls to see a prison. This conclusion is supported by a rule issued at Hamburg in 1683: no more than six visitors were admitted simultaneously, "not including little children."[20] The contemporary custom to expose youths to the sight of executions offers a parallel.

Family and friends of prisoners were among the regular visitors. No ordinance specifically mentioned that the inmates had a right to see relatives, and the sources hardly distinguished between them and the curious public. Administrators knew that people acquainted with inmates or just interested in them visited the institutions.[21] While the officials welcomed the money from entrance tickets, they distrusted the personal contacts the visitations allowed between prisoners and the public. Restrictive rules pertaining to visits were usually motivated by the inherent security risks. Such rules, issued in the last quarter of the seventeenth century, have been preserved in Haarlem, Bremen, and Leiden. Their main objective was to prevent individual inmates from being approached by visitors, and especially to prevent objects like knives from being passed from visitors to inmates.[22] In the course of the eighteenth century, relatives were gradually distinguished from the general public. In Delft it was determined in 1717 that the wives and friends of male prisoners could only come to see them on Saturdays at 2:30 P.M.[23] By the middle of the eighteenth century separate visiting hours for family and friends were common at Delft.[24]

Significantly, the sources fail to mention serious disorder in the institutions owing to visits before the second half of the eighteenth century. When they began to do so, the disorders were usually associated with the massive visits on special days. The popularity of prisons during festival periods, which has been noted at Leiden, occurred elsewhere, too. In Utrecht this was recorded as early as the 1620s.[25] Delft had its *spinhuiskermis*—the name probably going back to the early seventeenth century when the town had a spinhouse—on Women's Day (2 February). On 17 January 1767 the president of the board of regents reminded his colleagues that the prison had been particularly crowded the previous year, which had led to all kinds of troubles and danger. He proposed to abolish the *spinhuiskermis* and to let the prisoners spend the day with each other "in proper enjoyment." The proposal was accepted, but visits were not banned entirely.[26] In Hamburg a crowd used to visit the prison on Shrove Tuesday and complaints about disorders were first heard in 1771. The *jahrverwalter* drew up an elaborate proposal restricting admission to thirty persons at a time who had to follow a prescribed route through the institution.[27] Apparently, it did not help, and a new order was drawn up in 1790. The "carnival feast" in the Hamburg *zuchthaus* was abolished in 1807.[28]

It can hardly be a coincidence that these complaints and attempts at suppression date from the late eighteenth century. Comparable disorders must have occurred earlier, apparently without the officials bothering too much about them. Around 1800 a trend toward privatization of carceral institutions accelerated. Admitting the curious public into institutional homes gradually came to be viewed with distaste. This changing mentality was also manifested with regard to madhouses.[29] Nineteenth-century prisons and lunatic asylums would be closed to the general public.

Miraculous Cures   From the beginning, the fame of the new institutions was also spread in print. A sixteen-page booklet praising the Bremen *zuchthaus* was published in 1616. It is in the form of a dialogue between the author, Sebastian Mumen, and his friend Friderich. Sebastian has just been released from the *zuchthaus* and he is grateful because his stay has improved his life. He is from a good family and has been a clerk to distinguished gentlemen, but the desire for women and wine has ruined his career. His mother, who died during his stay in the *zuchthaus,* had obtained an order for his imprisonment. Again, the model inmate at Bremen is a recalcitrant youth, although Sebastian already has a wife and children. Friderich implicitly refers to the inscription at the gate, as he wonders if lions and bears can be tamed. His friend assures him that he has pondered his sins in prison and has been cured of his laziness. At the end the two friends recommend the *zuchthaus* administrators to God and call on all young people to stay off the wrong road.[30]

Our attention, however, must be directed at another pamphlet, about the Amsterdam rasphouse. This pamphlet has been particularly influential, and as a source for the history of mentalities deserves to be discussed in detail. It is also of interest as one of the clearest examples of an association of the policy of imprisonment with Protestantism, or at least anti-Catholicism. The title of the pamphlet, published anonymously by the printer Marten Gerbrantsz in 1612, can be translated *History of the amaz-*

ing miracles which have happened by the score and are still happening daily within the famous commercial town of Amsterdam, in a place called the tuchthuis, *situated at Holy Road.*[31] The preface introduces the background and contents. Many authors, it says, have described the miracles of just as many saints, but no one, so far, has written about the miracles of St. Raspinus.[32] The author promises to remedy that situation, whereby his veracity will compensate for his lack of a learned style. These miracles, he stresses, in contrast to those of the papists, have really happened. This sets the tone. It is a satirical pamphlet, simultaneously mocking the cult of saints and proclaiming the success of the policy of imprisonment and forced labor. The street on which the rasphouse was situated was indeed called *heilige weg* (holy road). It had carried that name from the Middle Ages, when a number of convents were established there, of which the Clara convent was one.

The pamphlet then cites thirteen individual cases of miraculous cures. The persons in question had all been unable to work because of an illness or handicap, and were cured during a pilgrimage to the rasphouse. These religious and medical metaphors are used consistently. The pilgrims make offerings to St. Raspinus not in Flemish pounds, coins used in the city at that time, but in Amsterdam pounds, which represent the weight of rasped wood. St. Labor and St. Ponus are also worshiped in the sanctuary at the rasphouse. Those devotees who are still unconvinced of St. Raspinus's power, and as a consequence are lacking in pilgrim zeal, receive a medical treatment. The most recalcitrant among them, notably those trying to break out, are dealt with by the Haarlem surgeon—the executioner lived in Haarlem. He smears their backs with birch oil, whereupon their zeal increases and they happily dance the *gaillarde*. Dancing the Spanish *gaillarde* was a picaresque expression for being flogged. Calling the executioner a surgeon may have come readily to mind since in reality he used to perform medical services. Most pilgrims do not require such serious treatment, however: the rasphouse chaplain merely smears their backs with daily oil. We also learn what the inmates were incarcerated for. Two have been imprisoned at the request of relatives; the others were all deceitful beggars. One of them has a snake in his body from which he could not be freed at other sanctuaries such as Our Lady of Halle near Brussels. St. Raspinus is able to free him of the snake. He cures all beggars, in fact, and they gratefully leave their crutches as an *ex voto* offering. An illustration shows the rasphouse courtyard with these objects exhibited against the wall. In one case, the sanctuary obtains nothing but an *ex voto* offering, because St. Raspinus even manages to cure someone outside. A crippled beggar, who hears the people scream that the provosts are coming to get him, suddenly throws away his crutches and runs to the Haarlem gate so fast that the provosts are unable to catch up with him.

The cases are presented as historic. Except for the first, the names of the devotees and the month of their arrest are mentioned. The dates fall between February 1604 and February 1605, except for the last two cases, which are dated 1607 and 1610. Since the rasphouse entry books are not extant, the historicity of the cases is hard to check. One of the pilgrims, however, turns up in the court records. According to the pamphlet, a certain Frans Roos, born in Antwerp, about forty years of age and a shoemaker by trade, had received back his strength from St. Raspinus, but used it in the wrong way by attempting to break out. In the margin his arrest is dated December 1604. The interrogation books mention a Frans Fransz from Antwerp, about thirty-seven years old and a shoemaker by trade, who must be the same man. He was questioned about an escape attempt on 13 January 1605. To the *schepenen* he explained that he had stayed in the rasphouse for three weeks. The beggar catchers had arrested him when he was sitting somewhere in the street, weeping from pain.[33] The pamphlet credits him with simulation of melancholy and phrenesis, which is not incompatible with his own account of his arrest. We may conclude that, despite its satirical content, the pamphlet has a recognizably realistic dimension. Of course, we should not take its suggestion that all marginals picked up from the streets were frauds with fake handicaps at face value.

The concluding passage of the case histories again explains that Catholic miracles are all pious frauds. This is followed by a sort of appendix describing a miracle by St. Justitia. It is the story of a possessed woman, Anna Arents, who had attracted a considerable crowd and thrown stones at servants who came to arrest her. The patient was cured and the devil exorcized from her through a whipping and branding on the scaffold. The Amsterdam court records confirm the historicity of this case.[34]

The stereotypical tales of vagrants with fake illnesses and beggars arousing pity by simulating handicaps are not novel. Nor is the thesis of the pamphlet that repression rather than charity was the appropriate reaction to this type of fraud, and by implication, to problems of beggary and vagrancy in general. This had all been part of the new cluster of attitudes about marginal people. Comparable stories about false beggars had been the stuff of books such as the *Liber Vagatorum*. The Flemish jurist De Damhoudere had included a few such cases in his legal works and Pontanus referred to these when he discussed the imprisonment of beggars.[35] The novelty of the *History of amazing miracles* was twofold: the idea of the prison workhouse as a remedy, and its association with an attack on the cult of saints. This lends credence to the hypothesis that Protestantism constituted an accelerating force in the emergence of prison workhouses. It was not Protestantism per se, though. The force derived from those currents within the Reformation that functioned as accelerators in the process of disenchantment of the world generally. The pamphlet's appendix, with its skepticism regarding possession, makes this clear. In this same period English Puritans and French Catholics were publicizing and exploiting cases of possession.[36] On the other hand, a critical attitude toward superlative claims with respect to the cures obtained at holy shrines and related propaganda had been a tradition within the Catholic church since the later Middle Ages. Thus, the 'Protestant' treatment of St. Raspinus's pilgrims was an expression of a general secularization of attitudes about poverty and marginality. The author of the *History of amazing miracles* may have believed that traditional charity held full sway in Catholic countries, but in reality it had been undermined there, too.

The sources which must have inspired the author can be identified. In 1604, Justus Lipsius published his *Diva Virgo Hallensis*, substantiating the miracles performed by Our Lady of Halle near Brussels. Lipsius, reconverted to the Catholic faith and living in the Spanish Netherlands again, was not especially liked by the Protestants of the North. A parody on his book appeared at Delft in 1605. It presented a Dutch translation of the original along with marginal comments such as "this is not the Holy Virgin but a trunk of wood." It opened with a verse by one P.v.B., explaining that mothers who used to treat their children to tales of brother rooster and sister fox now have another "miracle-book."[37] It is likely that the author of the *History of amazing miracles* got the idea for his book from this work. He specifically referred to Halle and other sanctuaries in the Southern Netherlands. His introductory remark about his lack of a learned style became "a Ciceronian or Lipsian style" in the preface to the French edition. The idea of secular miracles happening in the rasphouse may have been current, too. A year before the pamphlet was published, Pontanus had spoken of the miracles performed on beggars who claimed to be mutes, lunatics, or demoniacs. He also confirms that false crutches, that is, crutches that had been used as props by beggars shamming disabilities, were exhibited against the wall of the prison courtyard.[38] Alternatively, the author of the *History of amazing miracles* might have invented the theme of worldly miracles. It is possible that there had been an earlier edition, all copies of which have been lost. That is suggested by the concentration of eleven case histories in a one-year period ending in February 1605. The first version may have consisted of these eleven cases and been published shortly after the parody on Lipsius, and the two later cases and the appendix would have been added in the second edition.

Although we are uncertain about other Dutch editions, I was able to locate one French and three or four German translations. The French edition, dated 1612, appeared in Leiden. It omits one of the case histories and explains a few puns which would be incomprehensible otherwise, but for the rest it is true to the Dutch original. That holds true as well for two German editions, one of which is dated 1613; they merely Germanize the inmates' names.[39] Another German edition, of 1617, however, combines our pamphlet with Sebastian Mumen's dialogue on the Bremen *zuchthaus,* with a new title page referring to both.[40] In between the two works there are a proclamation denouncing beggary and four entirely new cases. The latter will be discussed below.

The frequent references to St. Raspinus in Amsterdam testify to his popularity. He turns up, for example, in Abraham de Koning's play, discussed in the previous chapter. The useless beggar admits that, while in the rasphouse, he refused to honor the saint, for which he was disciplined with daily oil on his back. The louse catcher boasts that once he arrested a beggar who claimed to have a snake in his body, which was exorcized through the power of St. Labor.[41] In Baudaart's contemporary history (1624) the rasphouse is mentioned just in passing, but this is followed by a paraphrase of most of the miracles. The tone is less humorous and more moralistic than in the *History of amazing miracles*, which is understandable since Baudaart was writing for a learned public.[42] Fokkens (1662) embellishes his description of the rasphouse with a verse on the false crutches displayed there, and St. Raspinus figures in it.[43] The poet Vondel, a Catholic but still very popular in Amsterdam, also referred to St. Raspinus on two occasions. He conferred the name, secularized into "Raspijn," upon the chariot driver figuring in the relief above the main gate, though. This shift in interpretation may have been due to his Catholicism.[44] After about 1665 we no longer hear of St. Raspinus or his miracles in the Republic. The novelty of imprisonment and the public's fascination with it had faded.

Abroad, the St. Raspinus and his miracles theme lived on even longer. In France the anti-Catholic element may have prevented widespread proliferation of the theme, but Antoyne de Montchrétien, recommending the Amsterdam prison model to his government, stated that "labor performs a new miracle there every day."[45] It is possible that the miracle topos was an independent tradition in France. In the 1610s an area between the St. Denis gate and Montmartre—then outside Paris—was popularly called the "Cour des Miracles." Beggars and vagrants assembled there at night for merriment, walking the last mile with their crutches on their shoulders. The place bore that name because its visitors who were ordinarily crippled or ulcerous were not so afflicted in that place.[46] Around the same time, this theme appeared in literary works devoted to beggars' feasts.[47] St. Raspinus's sanctuary was, of course, an involuntary and more sober cour des miracles.

The greatest proliferation of the theme occurred in the Empire. The number of German editions and the association of the rasphouse's miracles with Sebastian Mumen's admonitions indicate active propaganda for imprisonment. Philipp Hainhofer, who visited Berlin in 1617 and reported on the abortive project for a *zuchthaus* there, said that, had the project materialized, the prisoners would have been obliged to make offerings to St. Raspinus.[48] The anti-Catholic implications of the theme, that is, the parodistic aspect, were not forgotten in the Empire. That is attested by

two broadsheet depictions of the expulsion of the Jesuits—very temporary, as it turned out—from Bohemia and Hungary in 1620. The first is a
single page with a plate and a verse underneath it.[49] Its headline informs
us that the Jesuits are traveling to the Amsterdam *zuchthaus* on a pilgrimage to St. Raspinus and St. Ponus. The verse is serious rather than humorous. It ends with a recommendation to the pilgrims to carry out the
tasks which the saints will impose on them, while praising the miracles
they have wrought already. The second broadsheet is a comic strip consisting of eleven acts, and incorporating the theme of the first broadsheet.[50] It relates the vicissitudes of the Jesuits in detail, but their
pilgrimage is the central motif. Since they are on the road anyway, the
expelled fathers decide to take course to Amsterdam. St. Raspinus and St.
Ponus welcome them at the gate. They are prepared to act as mediators,
but since the Jesuits show symptoms of the "heresy of *pigritia*," this can
only be done effectively with heavy doses of daily oil and birch oil. A
'welcome' in the form of an automatic beating would indeed be practiced
in many German prisons. The saints, a little overzealous perhaps, offer to
treat the Pope as well. That introduces the next act, in which a courier
arrives in Rome who informs the Holy Father of the Jesuits' predicament.
The Pope promises to redress events with Spanish help. After this episode
there are no more references to St. Raspinus. Our attention is drawn to
the strip's central plate, picturing the saints when they welcome their
devotees at the gate. Directly behind it is the institution's courtyard, with
one inmate rasping and another being whipped. The saints carry a
rasping-saw and a rod. Both on this plate and the one from the single-
page broadsheet the city gate at which the travelers arrive is simultaneously the entrance to the rasphouse. The town and its prison are identified as one and the same. Amsterdam *is* the rasphouse.

We may wonder if the authors later learned that a Jesuit was imprisoned
at Amsterdam, although not in the forced labor ward, and that the Winter
King, expelled in his turn, visited this man and his remonstrant companions there. The theme of St. Raspinus was put to more directly anti-
Catholic uses in the Empire. Remembering that the German *zuchthäuser*
of this period were all in the North, we may conclude that in the Empire
the emergence of imprisonment was more closely associated with Protestantism than it was elsewhere. On the other hand, we also find plain propaganda for imprisonment in southern Germany in the same period. A
broadsheet printed at Augsburg in 1630 depicts the rasphouse courtyard.
It recommends Amsterdam as a health resort where parents should take
their disobedient children to be cured. Thus, it focuses on imprisonment
at the request of families rather than on the discipline of beggars and political opponents.[51] It implies a cure motif, but not one of miracles. The
miracle motif lived on in Germany longer than it did in the Netherlands.
St. Raspinus became another name for imprisonment at hard labor

generally. Friedrich Krausold, writing in 1698, once more praised the saint in the title of his book. In his preface he immediately stated that the miracles in question were not supernatural, and the rest of his work is a learned tract advocating the utility of prisons. It focuses on German towns such as Hamburg, rather than on Amsterdam.[52] In Krausold's book the theme of St. Raspinus is completely secularized and devoid of any polemic content other than the advocacy of a specific form of punishment.

Work or Drown   In addition to generating satirical and propaganda literature, imprisonment at Amsterdam gave rise to popular mythology. Or to be more precise, there were many stories and one great myth. Stories have probably been told about the rasphouse from the beginning. Gerrit Schaap informs us that "it is said that the first prisoner was the father of that notorious painter and idler Torrentius of Haarlem."[53] Johannes Simonsz van de Beek (1589–1644), called Torrentius, was known as a pornographic painter. In 1627 the Haarlem court summoned him on charges of blasphemy and licentious living.[54] Apparently, Torrentius's notoriety led to the belief that his father had been no good either, and thus to the tale, probably fictional, that he had been the rasphouse's first inmate. Other tales involved speculation about the identity of the prisoners in the secret wards and the reasons why they were kept from public view. The spinhouse had such a ward, too. Fokkens thought that the women who stayed there were "too beautiful little Venuses to be seen by everybody." In some cases, he said, their families feared that if the prisoners were kept in the public ward they would be abducted. He contrasted them with the women who had been corporally punished before entering the house: you would as readily fall in love with one of them as the dog does with the club. Once the Ursula convent counted eleven thousand virgins, Fokkens commented, but now it was difficult to find half a dozen in the whole city.[55]

The story that concerns us here has wider ramifications. A myth that persisted throughout the seventeenth and eighteenth centuries held that the most recalcitrant inmates of the rasphouse were disciplined in a rather drastic manner: by placing them in a cell into which water was allowed to flow, and the prisoner had the option either to pump out the water or drown. This myth fascinated later historians no less than it did contemporaries, and some actually believed it. Recently, Simon Schama began an essay on Dutch seventeenth-century culture with a discussion of "the mystery of the drowning cell." Even Schama does not entirely preclude the possibility of nonfiction, but he is mainly interested in the story as something people wished to believe. He considers a mythology connected with water typical of the Dutch mentality. This view, however, cannot stand the test of a closer look at the available sources, some of which Schama refers to apparently without having consulted them.[56] The pumping myth was not characteristic of Dutch culture, since it had been fabricated in Germany.

Its international spread and its importance for our understanding of the cultural climate in which imprisonment originated, justify an attempt to unravel the myth as far as possible. Its literal sense constitutes the smaller part of the story and I will begin with it. Next, I will demonstrate once and for all that the drain-or-drown tale was indeed a myth. Finally, I will attempt to trace the origins of the story, and conclude with a tentative explanation of why it originated.

The story recurs, with minor variations, in travel accounts from the 1660s onward. Edward Brown, for example, saw the rasphouse in 1668. He was told, he said, that prisoners refusing to work were placed in a large cistern where water was let in. There they had to pump or drown. The author went on to discuss the imprisonment of children of rich citizens, and in this connection he added another myth: "long ago in Cologne such youths were locked up in the white tower; they received no food, but a piece of bread was placed high above them; if they climbed up there they broke their neck." [57] With Maximilien Misson (1688) the cistern had become a cellar, which could be filled with water in a quarter of an hour. [58] William Mountague (1695) spoke of a "close dark vault," Thomas Bowrey (1698) of a "cellar into which the water runs," and Johann Zetzner (1699) of a "full reservoir." [59] In all cases the prisoner had to pump to save himself. Zetzner did not consider this to be a disciplinary punishment for refusing to work but a sentence imposed on the most serious offenders. Assuming that these writers really had been in Amsterdam, they still may have read and been copying the accounts of their predecessors. Blainville, who saw the rasphouse in 1705 but published his book in the 1740s, commented on a remark in Misson's second edition that the custom had been abolished. Blainville claimed he knew the reason it had been abolished: because an inmate under a life sentence had chosen to drown rather than pump. [60] A Hamburg citizen (1752) evidently had not read this and thereby showed that the myth was still alive. He wrote that "a separate cellar is the greatest [disciplinary] punishment, because it always gets full with water; those sitting in it must pump or drown." [61] These are a few of the myth's manifestations; no doubt there are more travel accounts with the story.

The first author who explicitly denounced the story as false was the historian Jan Wagenaar, writing in the 1760s when the rasphouse was still in full operation. Discussing disciplinary punishments, he said: "One also tells people that the prisoners are put into a water cellar, where they have to pump day and night if they do not want to drown. But such a water cellar is not there and, in all probability, has never been there." [62] He did not specify who "one" was and only referred to a tourist guide. As we will see, Amsterdamers themselves never said the myth was true. In the 1780s

John Howard was the first foreign author to regard it as fictional. He confirmed that he had heard the story before he came to Amsterdam, but his inquiries made him conclude that it was false.[63] Subsequently, the water cellar still had its partisans, despite Wagenaar's judgment. Von Hippel, the pioneer in the comparative study of the origins of imprisonment, believed in it.[64] In the Netherlands Hallema even thought he had found a contemporary illustration.[65] The American scholar Thorsten Sellin convincingly argued that the plate in question, located in Rome, anyway, did not depict the pumping or drowning punishment at all. Nevertheless, he argued that this punishment had actually been practiced in the rasphouse until the end of the seventeenth century. He even found Wagenaar's and Howard's "willingness to regard it as pure fiction" hard to explain.[66] To the contrary, I would comment, it is odd that Von Hippel, Hallema, and Sellin, who viewed the rise of imprisonment as an important and positive change in the treatment of deviant persons, were willing to believe that it was accompanied by such a drastic discipline. Perhaps their gullibility is connected to the fact that none of the three was a professional historian. Von Hippel was a lawyer, Hallema an amateur researcher, and Sellin a criminologist.

Why does a closer historical analysis inescapably lead to the conclusion that the punishment of pumping or drowning was a myth? First, the argument from silence applies: the archival sources have no reference to it whatsoever. Admittedly, the records of the rasphouse itself have been lost almost entirely. But the only historian who made use of them, Wagenaar, discredited the story. In the Amsterdam court records there are numerous cases of prisoners who had misbehaved, but we never hear of the punishment in question. On the contrary, these records make it quite clear that the most serious offenses in the rasphouse were dealt with by the *schepenen,* who selected from their regular repertoire of punishments, which included public corporal penalties. Other sources, from the earliest house rules until Wagenaar's work, confirm this right of the *schepenen.* We also know for certain which punishments the regents could impose of their own authority. The most severe was to be put into a dark pit on bread and water, a treatment which newcomers received automatically. These pits were constructed in 1595, as revealed in the earliest set of rules, which also explicitly forbade other prisoners from giving food to those undergoing the bread and water treatment. Hence, they must have had access to the pits. Dapper does not speak of this as a disciplinary punishment, but he confirms that newcomers were put for two or three days in what he calls "a moist and subterranean cellar, which is so low that no man can stand there upright."[67] Wagenaar only refers to penalties for recalcitrant inmates again, and he speaks neutrally of a "prisoner's cellar."[68] All of our sources leave no doubt that the persons staying in the pits just sat there, and had bread to eat and water to drink. There is no reference to any pump or pumping. The possibility of being drowned would have been viewed as a sort of capital punishment, and according to the prevalent conceptions of justice, its imposition would certainly have been reserved to the magistrates. Since the influence of ocean tides sometimes caused cellars to be flooded in Amsterdam around 1600—but usually only a few inches—it is possible that a few inmates who were put into the pits got wet feet. But if the water rose too high, it is likely the prisoners would have been removed from the pits. Of course, such events could well have been the source of the pumping myth.

The silence of the archives is complemented by the silence of residents who published a description of Amsterdam and its institutions in the seventeenth century. Pontanus, Fokkens, Dapper, Von Zesen, and Commelin all devoted a few pages to the rasphouse, but none of them referred to the water punishment. The only Dutch source claiming it existed is an anonymous architectural guide, published in Haarlem in 1736. Most of its text is derived from Dapper, including his passage on the low cellar. The guide adds that it "continuously has to be kept dry by pumping and they [i.e., the prisoners] have to stay there for a while as a punishment."[69] The anonymous author did not say that the prisoners had to pump, nor that they were in danger of drowning. That was only claimed by foreign visitors. Their published travel accounts, a number of which have just been cited, are the only sources referring to the pumping myth as something that existed in reality. Needless to say, their testimony is highly suspect. Most authors who reported the pumping myth did not claim to have seen a prisoner pumping or the place where this was supposedly done. They formulated it: "I was told that . . ." Nevertheless, Sellin thought that travelers in the seventeenth century presented a realistic account of the pumping and that the custom was abandoned in the 1690s. His argument was based on a remark in Misson's work, in French but published in The Hague. The first edition (1691) just mentioned the pumping story, but in the second (1698) it added that the custom had been abolished a few years ago.[70] However, this was one of a number of marginal remarks that were probably inserted by a local editor. He also inserted the Dutch words *rasphuis* and *spinhuis*. Apparently, he wished to play down the notion of the water cellar, but he could not contradict the book he was editing. To conclude, the travel accounts testify to the imagination of their authors rather than to the realities of disciplinary punishment in Amsterdam's prisons.

How then did the pumping myth originate? Except for one, the travel accounts which include it are not earlier than the 1650s or 1660s.[71] The German Johan Wilhelm Neumayr, for example, who visited Amsterdam in 1614 and described the disciplinary beatings in the rasphouse, did not refer to it. The myth was apparently unknown to him.[72] The earliest travel account which did mention it is a curious one. Martin Csombor, a Hungarian schoolmaster, wrote about a journey through Germany, Denmark, the Republic, England, France, and Poland undertaken from 1616 until 1619. He published his book in Hungarian in 1620.[73] Csombor presents a highly imaginative version of the water punishment. Lazy inmates, he explains, are taken to a little house resembling those which can be seen in Heidelberg and Prague. In the middle is a copper fountain and there is only one window, so high that a man can't reach it. The prisoner is given a bucket. As soon as he has entered, water pours out of the fountain with such force that no corner remains dry. The prisoner has no choice but to throw the water out the window with his bucket. Some finish by swimming around in desperation and are taken out half dead. It is a kind of purgatory, Csombor says, but he has more surprises for us. According to him, some inmates were trained to be goldsmiths, others to be carpenters. Newcomers had to drag heavy stones from one place to another for days. Others were made to lie in the burning sun. When a group of inmates conspired to escape, one of them warned his fellows citing two Latin lines from Virgil. There is no need to go on. Csombor had never even been in Amsterdam. The entire passage on the rasphouse is fictional and especially his remark about the burning sun betrays an ignorance of the Dutch climate. He was probably one of those authors who had only traveled in their study. His account may have been meant as a textbook lesson for his schoolboys, who must certainly have been frightened by the prospect of a stay in the rasphouse. Csombor adapted a story which he had read and it is possible to tell where he read it.

The very first reference to the pumping myth is to be found in the 1617 German edition of the *History of amazing miracles*. As I made clear, four new case histories were included in that edition and only in that one. They appear after the appendix and have obviously been invented by the German editor. He probably came from the Strasbourg area: the proclamation denouncing beggary, which he also added, includes a story situated in that town and the new prisoners have to reach their destination by going down the Rhine.[74] There is a change of style too. Where names and places of birth were mentioned in the original case histories, we now hear of Lamprecht N. from N. and other anonymous inmates. The fourth case history prisoner is not imprisoned in Amsterdam but in the Bremen *zuchthaus*. Neither does the third arrive in Holland. He is also a German, whom his father merely threatens to take to the rasphouse. The institution is likened to purgatory. It is Lamprecht N. from N. who is subjected to the water punishment. In the hallway behind the entrance there is running water, the editor says, without wondering how this is possible. The water is pumped into a nearby room, presumably through a window. This means that the prison personnel or others assisting would have been obliged to toil as heavily as the prisoner did. The latter is locked into the room and also has a pump at his disposal. Lamprecht lets the water come to his neck and then starts to drain it fanatically. Thereafter, he works industriously in prison for three years and upon his release his parents offer the institution a sum of money.[75]

This completes our search. The popularity of St. Raspinus in the Empire assured that the pumping story would catch on. We may wonder if the anonymous editor who originated the story had any idea that one small fantasy would trigger a myth that would haunt Europe for two centuries. In any case, we can now say with confidence that the myth was not specifically Dutch. The order of events must have been as follows. As more German readers acquired copies of the 1617 edition of the *History of amazing miracles,* the pumping story became a special object of interest. It caught on throughout the Empire and it may even have been considered a form of punishment worth trying. Article 29 of the Danzig prison ordinance of 1639 threatened lazy inmates with pumping or drowning in a well.[76] In the meantime, readers visited Amsterdam and inquired about the water room. At first, the personnel of the rasphouse must have been astonished by the Germans asking them about something they had never heard of. Later, when the questions persisted, the house personnel may have stopped contradicting them and regarded the story instead as one more attraction increasing sales of entrance tickets. From then on the myth became ineradicable and spread to countries such as France and England.

Were it not for Amsterdam's position as a European model of the prison movement and the international proliferation of the pumping myth, the theme would not have deserved the attention I have paid it. The success of the myth needs an explanation. I resist the temptation to call it specifically German, although it is true that in German prisons a greater emphasis was laid on disciplinary physical punishment. But it is in that direction that we should look for an answer. The success of the pumping myth was due to the novelty of imprisonment as a judicial sanction. Apparently, in the early years, it was hard to imagine that forced labor and the deprivation of liberty alone would be sufficient to cause prospective lawbreakers and other deviant persons to reform. There had to be something more. Many people did not quite understand or agree with the changing conceptions of punishment. They continued to associate the treatment of offenders with at least the threat of physical pain or the loss of life. The pumping story satisfied their expectations. It made the rasphouse both a sensational novelty and a bastion of cherished conceptions about the severity of punishment. That the myth failed to catch on in the Republic may simply be explained by the proximity of the inhabitants to the rasphouse. They knew well enough what was happening there. We may turn this argument into a positive one. By the middle of the seventeenth century the Dutch were the only European nation with a more than superficial familiarity with imprisonment. Contemporary houses of correction in England often existed in name only. To the population of the Republic the novelty of the new form of sanction had worn off to a great extent. As merchants and artisans, whether Calvinists or not, thought that God had imposed on them a life of hard work as their destiny, they found that forced labor was a suitable punishment for malefactors. Consequently, they had no need for a particular myth associated with the execution of this punishment. Contrary to Schama's theory, it can be argued that the *failure* of the pumping myth in the Republic was an expression of Dutch national character.

6

THE PRISON AS A
HOUSEHOLD
Management, Forced Labor, and
the Economy

From mythology and representation we return to the concrete realities of daily routine. We will continue to view the institutions from the outside, though; internal life is the subject of chapter eight. This chapter deals with the administrative and economic management of prison workhouses. Such a vast topic requires limitations. Two major problems will structure the discussion: one situated within the realm of mentalities, and the other resulting from the necessity to relate this realm to the development of society generally. The first problem regards the management of prisons— the assignment of management roles and what this tells us about perceptions about these institutions. The second regards forced labor—the uses made of it and its possible links with capitalist production.

Because a number of historians have argued that the spread of prison workhouses was due primarily to the need to have training schools for the unemployed, instead of a concern to punish offenders, it is necessary to consider that thesis. However, there are a few things the reader should not expect in this regard. I have declined to do a detailed prosopographic study of the managers, not because such a study would be uninteresting, but because its results would add up to the social and economic history of an occupational group rather than increase our understanding of the evolution of imprisonment. Neither did I attempt a microeconomic analysis of the finances of various institutions and the fluctuations they underwent during the two centuries under review. Finally, I have not provided technical details on the trades practiced in the institutions, except in the crucial case of rasping wood. The two general problems raised above can be solved, nevertheless. Section one deals with the first. It discusses administrative management and the view of prisons which can be deduced from this. The second and third sections treat economic issues. They discuss, respectively, the expedients devised to finance these houses, and the labor program, with special attention paid to rasping. The overall conclusion is implicit in the chapter's title: prisons did not resemble manufactories and contemporaries saw them primarily as a sort of enlarged household.[1]

The Supervisors: The Family Illusion

Our base is simply a list of functions. Although there was local variation in the rank-order of officials and the titles conferred on them, it is possible to generalize. The overview is based on my information from Holland and the Hanseatic towns and is probably representative of the situation in the Republic and the Empire as a whole. It does, of course, refer to prisons founded and controlled by urban patriciates.

A Four-Level Hierarchy

At the top were the magistrates themselves. They had founded the town's prison and continued to supervise it, but they only intervened in the daily life of prisoners or the institution's internal affairs in very exceptional circumstances. Of course, they appointed the administrators, the second level. In the Netherlands the latter were almost always called *regenten* (regents).[2] They were called *vorsteher* in Bremen and *provisoren* (provisors) in Hamburg.[3] In that town the provisor who was about to abdicate at the end of the year acted as *jahrverwalter* or daily supervisor. He kept the log book, decided cases that could not wait until the complete board met, and hence was more intimately involved in the institution's internal affairs than his colleagues. As a rule, the administrators met once every few weeks and they did not really intervene in daily life and routine affairs of the institution. A close involvement in the labor process or other forms of contact with individual prisoners would certainly have been considered below their dignity. Their principal task inside was sentencing. They were notified of serious cases—severe insubordination and escape attempts, notably—whereupon they usually convened immediately. The main purpose of such an extra meeting was to judge and punish the culprits as soon as possible. Less serious cases they judged during their regular meetings.[4] For the rest, the board's tasks were largely external. They were responsible for the institution's financial management and had to report on it to the magistrates. They also represented the institution to third parties, if necessary.

A Haarlem document of 1733 is explicit on the qualifications required of administrators. They should have a good reputation and a quiet temperament and lead an irreproachable life; they should have ample means at their disposal and be 'well in their middle age.' To be sure, the three candidates it lists for a vacancy are 38, 35, and 30 years old.[5] All three are said to be merchants. Indeed, from the outset, regents had usually been businessmen. When Jan van Hout arrived in Amsterdam on the morning of 22 November 1597, he was unable to contact a member of the board until the afternoon because it was a market day.[6] The oath sworn by the Haarlem administrators forbade them to deliver any goods to the prison themselves.[7] At Delft this seems to have been the rule, too, judging from the fact that an exception was explicitly recorded.[8] Regents had to be relatively rich, because their function was not a paid job but an honorary office. Clearly, the members of prison boards were merchants or entrepreneurs, belonging to the socioeconomic stratum just below the patriciate. It was also necessary for them to enjoy a relatively elevated status inasmuch as they were the superiors of the persons at the third level.

A peculiar feature of Holland not recorded for the Empire was the existence of female regents. They were not appointed in every town, and where they were, they constituted a separate board. In Haarlem they had even been equal in number to their male colleagues for some time, though by the middle of the seventeenth century they were in the minority again.[9] The appointment of regentesses was not dependent on the presence of female prisoners. The combined prison and madhouse at Delft, where both sexes were admitted, had an all-male board. The Amsterdam rasphouse, on the other hand, had two or three regentesses (along with four regents) from 1607 until 1747. The task of the regentesses was to supervise the supply of food and clothes to the inmates. When the supply system was altered in 1747, they resigned and no successors were appointed. The spinhouse had six male and four female regents, who, since its foundation, also administered the workhouse.[10] Regentesses were involved in the administration of several other institutional homes in the Netherlands, a subject in women's history which has received little attention up to now. There is less information on the identity of these regentesses than on that of their male colleagues.

Another difference between Holland and the Hanseatic towns lay in the social position of the administrators. Although in both regions the boards consisted of representatives of the upper-middle class, in the latter they were closer to the ruling group. In Hamburg appointment as a prison official could be a first or second step in a *cursus honorum* ultimately leading to the magistracy. That this was not uncommon is suggested by an agreement in 1639 to which the provisors of the *zuchthaus* bound themselves and their future colleagues. If any of them would be elected into the senate, he would pay a tribute of 500 Lübeck marks to the house. On the day of his inauguration the inmates were excused from work. Instead, they prayed to thank God that "one of their fathers had been elevated into the ranks of the government."[11] In 1644 a double event was recorded:

provisors Peter Sijllm and Lücas Beckman were simultaneously elected senators.[12] The boards administering the spinhouse established at Hamburg in 1669 regularly counted members bearing names of patrician families. In Holland such a *cursus honorum* was exceptional. It may not have made much difference in smaller towns, where little social distance existed between magistrates and the group of merchants and entrepreneurs outside the government. It made a difference in Amsterdam. In 1659 it was said that the rasphouse regents were appointed for life or until they obtained a function of higher dignity.[13] The latter alternative was apparently the less common and it did not necessarily imply a seat in the government. A comparison of Wagenaar's list of rasphouse regents (1595–1764) with J. E. Elias's repertory of council members and their genealogies yields the following information: nine out of seventy-five regents were elected into the council and four were close relatives of council members. Another four belonged to a family who would boast a magistrate one or two generations later. Sixteen are listed as distant relatives or in-laws, including five cases in which it is uncertain that we are dealing with the right person. The remaining forty-two do not appear in the repertory index. The regents who became council members were concentrated in the early years; the last one was appointed in 1660. Among the regents appointed in the eighteenth century was just one distant relative.

The third level of the hierarchy consists of personnel paid by the institution. They were the ones who directed the internal and routine affairs of prisons and the highest level that had direct contact with the inmates. There were local variations with respect to division of tasks as well as the rank-order within this group. In Haarlem the indoor father and his wife occupied a superior position. The 'mother' of female prisoners, for example, had to report acts of disobedience by her women to either one of them. But the indoor father was just the first among his peers. In the early eighteenth century it was specified that he was not entitled to give orders to his colleagues. If a difference of opinion arose, he should try to prevail by mild persuasion, and if the others remained unconvinced, the case was to be judged by the regents.[14] At the Amsterdam rasphouse the indoor father was assisted by a 'master of discipline.'[15] In Delft the leader of personnel, officially denoted the *concherge,* was the central figure controlling all the institution's internal affairs.[16] The Hanseatic towns adhered to a tripartite division of tasks, with no member specifically designated as the head of personnel. One kept the inmates at work, another provided them with food and other necessities, while the third took care of maintenance of discipline. In Hamburg they were respectively called *werkmeister, oeconomus,* and *zuchtmeister;* in Bremen *fabriqueur, speisemeister,* and *zuchtvogt.* Sometimes, however, the Bremen sources refer to work bosses for separate trades.[17]

The sources occasionally disclose the ages of personnel. The *oeconomus* serving the Hamburg spinhouse was fifty-three in 1709. His colleague Henning Wend was fifty-eight then; he had been contracted in 1700.[18] Metje Füken, mother of the Bremen *zuchthaus* was fifty-five in 1726. Her daughter Gebke, who also worked there, was twenty-six. The wife of Gottfried Goldstein, a master of discipline, was forty-six when he was murdered in 1754.[19] In Amsterdam two widely contrasting ages were recorded. Jan de Lange resigned as master of discipline because he was eighty-four and "very weak."[20] The indoor father who was dismissed in 1704 was twenty-nine.[21] These two, also the younger one, must have been exceptional. Dutch as well as Hanseatic sources frequently refer to sons and daughters of personnel members who are assisting them. It is likely that most of these fathers and mothers were in their forties or fifties.

The fourth and lowest level of the hierarchy, that of the minor personnel, was directly dependent on the third level. As a crucial feature, this group as such was not employed by the regents. It was also subdivided internally. There were journeymen assisting the work boss, servants of the master of discipline, kitchen maids, and washing women. Individual members of the higher personnel were their superiors and the latter hired and fired them as they thought fit. As a rule, their employers also paid them. When a servant was paid directly by the institution, this formed part of his boss's contract. In Bremen in 1748, for example, the *speisemeister* Hans Köhler and his wife were allowed to hire a maid at the house's expense if they needed one.[22] There was no specific category of guards, as in today's prisons. Also, the lower personnel were few in number. Prisoners sometimes acted as servants, too, a subject discussed in chapter eight. The four-level hierarchy as a whole testifies to the preindustrial concern, more marked than today, for a careful demarcation of status positions.

Fathers and Mothers   A paternalistic terminology was the most notorious element in the hierarchy of functions. At the very beginning in the Netherlands it had been applied to the second level as well as the third, administrators being called 'outdoor fathers.' But that term soon became obsolete. The administrators must have found it beneath their dignity and thereupon began to style themselves regents, in imitation of their colleagues of other institutions. 'Outdoor mother,' on the other hand, remained a synonym for regentess, testifying to the lower status of that function.[23] In the Republic the terms 'father' and 'mother' were applied most notably to the leading couples among the personnel. In informal speech these terms may have been even more common. Official documents in Delft always refer to the work boss as the *concherge*, but the sources make it clear that the prisoners used to call him father.[24] In the Empire this kind of terminology was recorded on several occasions; we saw that the Hamburg provisors were once called the inmates' fathers. But in German prisons, too, these terms were mainly reserved for the personnel at the third level and probably were widely used informally. The Hamburg *oeconomus* was admonished to act as a good *hausvater* and the Bremen *speisemeister* and his wife were referred to once as the *speisevater* and *mutter*.[25] These words were also used in Danzig in 1669.[26] In the eighteenth century, paternalistic titles for the higher personnel were recorded in München, Waldheim, Halle, Magdeburg, Berlin-Spandau, and in several places in Middle- and East-Prussia and the Habsburg lands.[27]

Quite another situation prevailed in France. A number of female religious orders had been founded expressly to assist in the management of *hôpitaux généraux*. They were not active everywhere, but only where the administrators felt they needed their services. Celibate women who had pledged to devote themselves to the poor sometimes joined the nuns. The task of these nuns and laywomen was to control the institution's daily routine, which makes their position comparable to the third level in Dutch and German prisons. The literature does not reveal whether, within the hospital system, they were connected only to almshouses or also to closed wards.[28] Their presence on the scene is significant, nevertheless. Where the Republic and the Empire had fathers and mothers, the French had sisters. Could this possibly be a reflection of religious differences? However, the alternative, paternalistic model also manifested itself in Catholic Austria and Bavaria.

The history of religion and the family together provide a solution to the problem. To explain why the paternalistic imagery arose, we have to go back to one of the roots of imprisonment, monasticism. Since about the ninth century, settlement patterns in Western Europe were fairly uniform. Apart from the *familiae* of a few great lords, the agrarian society was almost exclusively composed of households, most of them with two generations under one roof. Monastic institutions were the major exception within this pattern. Monks and nuns did not live as families. A paternalistic terminology, admittedly, also characterized their pattern, though the words abbot and abbess were no longer seen as paternalistic or familial by the populace in Western Europe in the later Middle Ages. These titles were also conferred upon heads of other nonfamilial groups living together— notably on the keepers of brothels.[29] Brothels shared the relatively closed character seen in the religious institutions. As one author states, governmental regulation in fifteenth-century Languedoc caused prostitutes to live "virtually cloistered."[30] Thus, monasteries constituted a model for the cohabitation of a large number of people outside a normal household. Hospitals, on the other hand, with their transitory population, could hardly be viewed as models in this sense.

In the late sixteenth century, prison workhouses emerged as a new type of institution where a large group lived together. Originally, however, most were established in Protestant regions, where religious orders had been suppressed and their buildings often confiscated. Moreover, Protestant theologians as well as worldly leaders advocated marriage for everyone and extolled the patriarchal nuclear family. Monasteries and convents having disappeared from the scene, the family rather than the monastery became the model for prison institutional life.

This change of models was facilitated by another feature of preindustrial society. Servants, apprentices, and journeymen were seen as also belonging to the nuclear group, with their employers acting as surrogate fathers. There was little separation between working space and living space, between the shop and the household. It is understandable, therefore, that prison workhouses came to be viewed as households that were just a little more complex. The first inmates of the rasphouse were regularly referred to as journeymen. The earliest preserved contract with a work boss, dated January 1598, allowed him to bring along "some of his former journeymen."[31] Clearly, they contrasted with the inmates, his new journeymen. That word indicates the position of the prisoners in this system. They are not considered pseudochildren. Note that the word master, too, was not uncommon. The work bosses and other members of the higher personnel acted as surrogate fathers over male and female inmates, just as employers in the world outside did over their journeymen and maids. Their wives were surrogate mothers. The parallel only becomes somewhat strained when we realize that the system included lower personnel, too. They were servants as well, but they occupied a position superior to that of the prisoners. It might be objected that prison life was much tougher than an existence in the bosom of the family, so that the two cannot have been mentally associated. Historians disagree on the extent to which early modern family life was characterized by affection and consideration, but they conclude that households were more patriarchal and authoritarian than in the twentieth century. Even revisionist historians concede that surrogate fathers might exercise a relatively tough regimen over their journeymen.[32] This suggests that for noninmates the paternalistic and familial parallels were more than just semantic. We might still wonder what they were to the inmates themselves, especially to marginals, many of whom hardly knew the experience of living in a family.

The authorities' preference for the family model is implicit in their concern always to have at least one couple conducting the prison's affairs. Fathers were only fathers if they were assisted by mothers, and vice versa. When the Hamburg work boss Casper Seehmans died in 1626, his widow was granted a 'mercy-fee' of three months' salary and a partial reimbursement of the cost of burial. Thereafter, she apparently had to leave the house and later the same year a new couple was appointed.[33] An episode in the 1640s is revealing. On 16 December 1643 it was said that the prisoners and the poor of the house would henceforth be fed by an *oeconome*, Gesche Heimb. Presumably, the previous *oeconomus* had quit or died. A detailed inventory of furniture and victuals was taken, and the total value was almost 5,000 Lübeck marks. The exceptional situation of a woman in charge lasted for nine months. On 9 September 1644, Gesche Heimb married Jacob Schumacher, who took the oath as *oeconomus* on 17 October. Unfortunately, Jacob died on 27 February 1645. Gesche Heimb was allowed to exercise her function alone again for twenty-one months. On 3 December 1646 Jürgen Johansen was appointed as *oeconomus,* assisted by his wife. Gesche was bought off with an annuity of fifty Lübeck marks, beginning in 1647. The provisors recorded the considerations which had led to this decision: she has always performed her function in an excellent manner and has even burdened herself with expenses on behalf of the house. However, the house should be served by an *oeconomus,* and she "has no desire to marry again." It is better for both parties, since Gesche is getting older and longs for a deserved rest.[34] In eighteenth-century Delft the administrators also used paternalistic selection criteria, though their recruitment method was based on modern communication techniques. Several times, beginning in 1736, they advertised the post of indoor father in newspapers. When the board met to choose between the two applicants who merited serious attention, they explicitly considered the personalities of the candidates and of their wives.[35]

Total Institutions?   The final question is to what extent the four-level hierarchy and the paternalistic model shaped the character of the institutions. Erving Goffman's work may be taken as a point of departure. He lists five types of "total institutions," in Western societies in the twentieth century, but his analysis is based especially on insane asylums and prisons. The primary characteristic of a total institution is a distinction between inmates and staff. "Inmates typically live in the institution and have restricted contact with the world outside the walls; staff often operate on an eight-hour day and are socially integrated into the outside world."[36]

In the present study the word 'staff' has been deliberately avoided, and the analysis of the prison hierarchy shows why. Who would constitute the staff: the regents or the fathers and mothers? The regents were the directors; they controlled the institution's finances and they punished offending inmates. They were closer to the institution than mere external inspectors, but they assembled in prison no more than about once a week. On other days only their portraits were there. Their contacts with inmates were too transitory for them to be 'the other party.' The personnel, the third party, on the other hand, were too close to the inmates. Precisely Goffman's criterion of going home at night does not apply here. Just as other preindustrial employers, the indoor father lived in his shop, which happened to be a prison. In Amsterdam both the indoor father and the master of discipline had their homes in the rasphouse. When the aged master of discipline Jan de Lange was succeeded by Jacobus ter Horst, the latter moved in and the former was allowed to stay in one of the rooms of the indoor father, who happened to be his son-in-law.[37] Living quarters for these personnel were considered part and parcel of the institution as a whole. Because the institution enjoyed freedom from urban and provincial taxes, the indoor father did so likewise.[38] Goffman's "often" with reference to the eight-hour day is an important caveat, but it does not apply to his second qualification. The fathers of the early modern period and their families were integrated into prison life to a greater extent than a twentieth-century staff, even when they are residential.

An Amsterdam case illustrates the problems inherent in the personnel's close integration into the world of the prison. In 1704 Willem Boons and Maria de Vlieger, indoor father and mother of the rasphouse, and their maid were accused of negligence or even complicity in a prisoner's escape from the secret ward. The crucial point was that the act had been facilitated by Willem's absence from the house that night. The case was submitted to the court. The *schepenen* first reminded him of his instructions forbidding him to leave the house unnecessarily. Quite to the contrary, they noted, he had been out during the white-bread children's dinner time. Willem defended himself with the argument that the secret ward counted only three inmates then. When he had some administrative business or was out, his wife and the maid had often brought them dinner. That night he had bought a hat and had visited a tavern afterward. The *schepenen* banished Willem and Maria from Holland for twenty-five years and disqualified Willem for any office in the city. The maid was judged not guilty. The judges seem to have thought that the rich inmate who had escaped had bribed the couple.[39] This may have been true. All the same, the urge to stroll around town and visit taverns occasionally might be thought of as a subconscious reaction to the feeling of being imprisoned oneself. In doing so, Willem Boons emphasized that he was not an inmate, but fit into Goffman's definition of staff. The perception that the personnel somehow belonged to the institution is perhaps best illustrated in a Bremen document of 1764. Arnold Schönhülde calculated the expenses for all prisoners, referring to them as "persons." He expressly noted that he did not count the *speisevater* and the master of discipline and their wives among the "persons."[40]

In addition to maintaining a distance from the internal world of the prison, the higher personnel wished to maintain a relatively independent position vis-à-vis the board of administrators, their superiors. In eighteenth-century Delft this resulted in a series of conflicts, which were particularly sharp owing to the fact that the indoor father occupied an extremely powerful position. To counteract that situation, the board had appointed their own "private servant" in prison in 1736. He had the special task of detecting escape conspiracies, against which the personnel apparently were thought to have made too little effort, and he was not allowed to assist in employing the inmates.[41] Two months later, Leendert van den Heuvel, who may have been annoyed with this competitor from the outset, assumed the office of indoor father. His contract expired without being renewed, and on another occasion we learn that the regents found he had misbehaved in office.[42] His successor, Jan van Steenvoorden, had a list of critical remarks appended to his contract, the purpose of which was to delineate his area of competence more strictly than it had been delineated for his predecessor, and especially to minimize the range of occasions when he could punish inmates on his own authority.[43] In 1757 tensions escalated around an apparently trivial event. Van Steenvoorden had refused to convey a message of the board to a newly appointed member on 21 February. He claimed that his contract did not oblige him to act as a messenger. Both parties remained obstinate and three weeks later the magistrates formally demanded that the indoor father apologize for his disobedience to the president of the board at the latter's house within twenty-four hours. A week later it was recorded that Van Steenvoorden had accomplished his journey to Canossa. A committee was ordered to investigate the affair. The committee came up with a four-page report stating that the indoor father had treated the board disrespectfully and that he was too severe toward the inmates.[44] Van Steenvoorden remained in office until 1760, and apparently the conflict continued all this time. His successor, Pieter Maas, inherited the conflict and continued it, but this time the other party withdrew. The president of the board, Van der Sleijden, announced his resignation in December 1762. He was no longer willing, he said, to bear Maas's "constant impertinence and improper behavior" during their meetings, and he chose "to prostitute himself to this no longer." Two of his colleagues resigned with him, and a fourth regent had recently died. Faced with four vacancies, the burgomasters appointed two magistrates and the city secretary to the board. This emergency situation lasted for several years.[45]

Clearly, the Delft indoor father regarded himself as the real prison director and the administrators as unwelcome meddlers into his business. The unspecified supposedly impertinent remarks no doubt helped him maintain his psychological independence from the regents, who summoned him to their meetings to report on the prisoners and who treated him as an inferior. The board regarded these protestations of independence as signs of disrespect. They saw themselves as the representatives of the magistrates, and therefore expected an attitude of reverence. The board finally found an obedient indoor father, in the person of Willem Maas, possibly a relative of Pieter. When this man died in 1794 they recorded how sorry they were, because he had performed his function so well.[46] The troubles in Delft originated from a certain incongruence between formal status hierarchies and informal power relationships. To some extent, this incongruence existed everywhere and structural tensions between administrators and higher personnel must have been ubiquitous. The dualism inherent in the prison management system accounted for it.

This leads to a conclusion on the four-level hierarchy, with an answer to the question of whether early modern prisons were total institutions. The household model with its familial imagery was incompatible with Goffman's neat distinction between inmates and staff. At the first level, the magistrates were of course mere external supervisors. The dualistic system especially involved levels two and three. There was not just one party confronting the inmates, in permanent contact with them and yet keeping aloof from them. The administrators were too far away from the prisoners; they stood outside the institution as a household, though they were ultimately responsible for it. At the third level, the personnel were too close to the prisoners; they were integrated into institutional life and a part of the household. Both groups performed 'traditional' roles: the higher personnel as surrogate fathers and mothers in a preindustrial pseudofamily; the administrators as the occupants of an unpaid, honorary office, entangled in a web of status expectations. The fourth group, the lower personnel, were too few in number to carry much weight. With respect to the prisoners, finally, Goffman's concept is valid to the extent that staying in the institution totally determined the way they lived. Still, they had a relatively large measure of contact with the world outside because of the prevailing custom of admitting visitors.

Prison Profits

With the family its model, the prison community of the early modern period was considered a household. The personnel and the inmates worked together to earn a living. But did they really earn their living, or did these complex households require financial assistance? In Amsterdam in 1595 Sebastiaan Egberts already thought the prison would require assistance, when he expected opposition from council members who would think too much of the city's money would be spent. The profitability or unprofitability of prisons was debated from the outset. What further complicates this problem is that the profits of such institutions might be reckoned in other than cash values. Questions on these matters are often raised in the literature on the subject, which makes it imperative to discuss them.

The economic approach to the history of prison workhouses focuses on the idea that their emergence and proliferation was due primarily to the material profits they brought to their owners or to a more widely conceived community. First, I will define the term 'economic approach.' It is obvious that every human activity, from punishing offenders to sailing to the Indies, has an economic aspect. A modern economist defines his subject in terms of the management of scarce resources and their application to various ends, including the maintenance of nonprofit organizations. Historians, on the other hand, often adhere to a less inclusive terminology.

When I speak of economic motives or economic considerations in connection with imprisonment, I am referring to a supposed prevalence of the expectation of material gains over other useful purposes that contemporaries might attribute to the institutions in question.

The thesis that prison labor was meant to "bring a very specific economic profit" was defended in a learned but strongly polemical tract by Max Adler in 1924.[47] Georg Rusche elaborated a comparable type of argument in a more scholarly fashion. The influence of the bourgeoisie, which increased in the later Middle Ages and the sixteenth century, he argues, led to a renewed interest in the potential value of manpower. A result was the development of the idea that people withholding their labor power from the market—beggars and thieves, for example—might be forced to become profitable. This idea was associated with the rise of mercantilism. Especially in the seventeenth century authorities were concerned about the coincidence of a scarcity of labor with widespread local poverty and a low level of production. If the marginal poor were forced to work, they hoped, production would increase and poverty would diminish. This caused the spread of prison workhouses in that century, according to Rusche.[48] However, his empirical base is relatively small. He only refers to two German theorists who actually advocated employment of the marginal poor, which they did, moreover, in the second half of the eighteenth century. By that time, prisons had evolved into penal institutions and the poor were employed in new types of establishments.[49] Rusche's argument implies that prison workhouses generated financial profits for their exploiters. He raises the question himself, and although he is not really sure, he claims that many institutions produced profits in hard cash. If nothing else, the expectation of material gains is supposed to have been a decisive motive for the founding fathers. More or less as a subsidiary matter, Rusche argues that the training unskilled workers received in prison was a major contribution to the rise of capitalist production.[50]

Cash Revenues?   The study of economic history has greatly progressed since Rusche put forward his thesis. Still, the problem of the profitability of prisons has not been solved satisfactorily. To begin, it may be reduced to the simple question of whether income exceeded expenditure. An answer is particularly hard to obtain for the seventeenth century, for which few sources on the financial administration of prison institutions have been preserved. Only for Haarlem is a series of random data available, starting from the early seventeenth century. Hence, that town will receive special attention. That Haarlem's prison was combined with an almshouse makes no difference, since the documents usually distinguish the two facilities.

The earliest financial document which unequivocally deals with the prison alone is dated 20 October 1614. The institution has to pay a total amount of 10,330 guilders for wood logs, rye, and beer. It is due to receive 3,000 for sales of rasped wood and 1,800 for board money, which makes a total of 4,800 guilders. Further, there is a stock of unsold rasped wood and yarn to be woven, valued at 2,000 and 1,500 guilders, respectively. This amounts to a deficit of slightly over 2,000 guilders. In addition, an appendix specifies a number of debts, totaling 6,210 guilders, which have to be paid in the near future. There is no information on the exact period over which this has been calculated.[51]

A year account with specifications has been preserved for 1635; the values are in Flemish pounds this time. It also deals with the prison alone and there are no items which can be associated with the poor; it specifically refers to the alimentation of prisoners. The biggest item on the revenues side is the board money for private prisoners (1,491.18 pounds). Others include sales of rasped wood and interest and rent on houses. The total income is 3,263.14.7 pounds. On the expenditures side there are, among other things, butter and cheese and wood logs. Total expenditures are 3,301.19.12 pounds. Although the deficit is not considerable, there is certainly no profit. It is especially striking that, when we consider rasping separately, the amount paid for raw material (628.17 pounds) exceeds the amount received for the end product (617.6.7 pounds).[52]

Later accounts, which have been preserved, are less specific. In 1657 a profit is recorded for the first time: an income of 10,012 guilders, including 4,251 for sales of rasped wood, and expenditures totaling 9,027 guilders. Among the expenditures, however, there are no major purchases of logs, so this year may be unrepresentative. An appendix lists the value of the institution's capital at the beginning of 1658. It is estimated at 18,312 guilders, of which 15,900 represent the value of the houses it owns. The income from the rents of these houses is 671 guilders.[53] Although there is a profit in 1657, seven years later the regents are obliged to request a subsidy of 3,000 guilders to buy wood logs.[54]

A fourth account, dated 7 September 1666, is called a summary account. It probably refers to just a part of the year. It includes revenues of of 2,420 guilders and expenditures of 3,100, and there is no mention of wood having been rasped.[55]

In the late 1670s the financial administrations of the prison and almshouse were merged. This seems to have ameliorated the material position of the institution as a whole. A document referring to the merger says that "during the last three years" income has exceeded expenditures by 45,000 to 30,000 guilders. A calculation is made for future years, specifically 1681–1700. The profits will be converted into capital, which will amount to 363,932 guilders (including interest) in 1700. Among the annual income, however, a city subsidy of 19,000 is figured. It is calculated that this subsidy may be withdrawn in 1700. Even without it, the profits, mainly from interest, are expected to amount to more than 10,000 guilders a year.[56]

The extant accounts for the eighteenth century are less relevant for our purposes, because they deal with prison and almshouse together. In any case, the rosy expectations of 1681 do not seem to have come true. The institution is in trouble again in 1710–1711. The regents are authorized to negotiate a loan of 22,000 guilders, of which 13,000 is spent immediately for the payment of debts. The rest is meant "for use in these expensive times."[57] The city still pays annual subsidies to the institution from 1710 until 1740, usually of 13,000 guilders.[58] Specific accounts are extant for the years 1733–1741. They show an annual deficit of about 10,000 guilders until 1739 and almost 30,000 over the last two years in this sequence. The latter deficit, however, is mainly caused by great amounts spent on relief. Subsidies and gifts figure on the income side.[59]

A document dealing with the period from October 1762 to September 1763 may refer to the prison alone, judging from the small amounts involved: an income of 35,563 guilders (still including subsidies) and expenditures of 37,138.[60] Conditions in the 1780s are no better. The city provides the institution with an annual loan of 3,000 guilders without interest and still its finances are said to be in a bad state.[61] The almshouse and the prison are finally separated in 1786. The prison receives a starting capital of 4,000 guilders, and the city guarantees to pay the annual deficit. The institution remains in possession of eight houses.[62]

The conclusion must be that, except for a few years, the Haarlem prison workhouse was financially unprofitable throughout the seventeenth and eighteenth centuries. Information on other towns does not conflict with the Haarlem data. In Bremen, individual administrators were originally responsible for the *zuchthaus* finances. As early as 1610 it was stated that several *vorsteher* of that year and the previous year still had claims on the institution. An account over 1612 lists a deficit of over 80 Reichsthaler, due mostly to claims, because of inferior deliveries, by the English merchant Robert Edwards at Hamburg. In January 1613 there is again talk of *vorsteher* with claims on the house. An account dated 4 January 1622 indicates a profit, but it deals with the finances of one administrator only.[63] The first prison at Groningen had an annual deficit of over 2,000 guilders between 1616 and 1623.[64] In an account of Leiden's prison over 1671, income and expenditures were only equalized because the first included payments by the *schout* for prisoners sentenced by the court.[65] At Delft the regents were asked in 1682 to specify who among the prisoners were able to earn their living and who were not. Such a distinction was impossible, they replied, but all prisoners together could never earn as much as they consumed.[66] The Amsterdam workhouse was operating at a loss in the second year of its existence and thereupon continued to have annual deficits of several thousands of guilders.[67]

Table 6.1

Cost of Maintaining and Incomes from Prisoners at Bremen, 1748–1757 (all amounts in reichsthaler)

Year	A	B	C	D
1748	1,771.56	320.69	308.30	629.27
1749	1,844.44	468.52	257.71	726.51
1750	1,556.49	703.19	204.23	907.42
1751	1,552.23	467.07	299.58	766.65
1752	1,675.44	322.44	362.61	685.33
1753	1,454.43	298.71	393.38	692.37
1754	1,603.37	269.55	398.15	667.70
1755	1,684.41	329.46	427.11	756.57
1756	1,682.71	355.29	300.48	656.05
1757	1,622.13	441.41	288.20	729.61
TOTAL	16,447.61	3,978.01	3,241.15	7,219.16

Key

A: Expenditure (including the salaries of the *speisevater* and the *zuchtvogt*, but excluding that of the preacher; also excluding repair costs)
B: Income from the manufacture of blankets
C: Income from rasping and spinning
D: Total income

These data referred to the seventeenth century and comparable information is available for the eighteenth. The financial situation of Delft's prison was said to be deteriorating in 1704, the regents having to negotiate a loan. Throughout the eighteenth century they were obliged to request subsidies from the town.[68] A similar situation prevailed in Amsterdam. In the 1740s the rasphouse regents complained about the institution's deteriorating financial situation. The amounts of the city subsidies they received fluctuated between 8,000 and 17,000 guilders during the period 1740–1747. After a financial reorganization they were lowered to about 4,000 guilders, but in 1751–1752 they rose again. This caused the commissioners of the city's treasury to complain; they proposed a reduction in the personnel wages, to which the regents objected.[69] Finally, an eighteenth-century Bremen source is quite detailed. It concerns the calculations made by the *vorsteher* Arnold Schönhülde in 1764, referring to the period 1748–1757 (see table 6.1).[70] Based in these data, Schönhülde calculated that, with an average of sixty-five inmates, each prisoner would cost 5 guilders a day and would earn 2.2 guilders. This was without taking into account a board money totaling 2,324 Reichsthaler received during the years in question. Considering that income, too, he arrived at a deficit of slightly over two guilders per inmate per day.

No plan to ameliorate the house's financial situation accompanied these calculations, or at least none was recorded. If one was proposed, it had little success. During the 1780s and 1790s several committees were charged with the task of improving the institution's financial picture.[71] In 1799 one of them inquired into the finances of neighboring *zuchthäuser.* The committee found at Braunschweig, Kassel, Copenhagen, Hamburg, Hannover, Lübeck, and Celle that prisoners cost money, although the amounts differed.[72] Thus, prison workhouses were also expensive elsewhere in the Empire and in neighboring kingdoms. The scarce financial data mentioned in historical literature confirm this. Deficits, debts, and the necessity of subsidies were recorded for Danzig (seventeenth and eighteenth centuries), Arnhem (eighteenth century), Magdeburg (1727), Pforzheim (1732–1802), Münster (1730s and 1774), Potsdam (1779) and several towns in Franken (second half of eighteenth century).[73]

Sales, Taxes, and Lotteries   By themselves, then, prisons were not economically viable as manufactories. Qualitative information tends to confirm this. The sale of the products of forced labor, for example, was usually problematic. Potential buyers considered them of inferior quality. An expedient to promote sales frequently tried in Holland was to oblige sister-institutions in the town to buy goods produced in the town's prison. A resolution to that effect was passed in Delft in 1686 and had to be repeated in 1693, 1713, 1715, and 1761. Thus, even these sales were problematic. The resolution of 1693 followed upon a complaint by the indoor father. Several boards of other institutions, he claimed, did not fulfill their obligation in this regard. They refused to buy his cloth and worsted, arguing that it was priced too high. Upon inquiry, only the regents of the orphanage admitted that they refused to buy the cloth, because of its inferior quality, they said. The other boards claimed they never evaded the council's resolution. After the directors of the cloth hall had estimated the quality of the goods, the authorities ordered the regents of the orphanage to purchase their cloth and worsted from the prison in the future.[74] Magistrates of other towns issued similar orders. In 1760, Haarlem's prison had recently begun production of linen. Burgomasters requested all boards of regents to see whether they could use it and to buy as much as possible.[75] In Amsterdam this kind of interinstitutional recycling could even be practiced within the prison system. The inmates of the workhouse wove canvas from which sacks were fabricated to pack the rasped wood produced in the rasphouse.[76]

The necessity of sales promotion—though even this tactic was usually ineffective—accords with the conclusion that prisons had difficulties operating in the market. Part of the deficits must have resulted from inability to sell or the necessity to sell at too low a price. Attempts to reduce the deficit consisted of the organization of lotteries and the institution of special taxes. The first expedient was recorded primarily during imprisonment's early years, together with the charitable gifts referred to in previous chapters. That is understandable, because the success of lotteries depended on the perception of *tuchthuizen* as partly belonging to the sphere of charity. Lotteries for the benefit of all kinds of asylums were very common in the Dutch Republic in the late sixteenth and early seventeenth centuries.[77] In 1612, when the Hamburg senate asked permission from their colleagues in Amsterdam to sell lots there for the benefit of their *zuchthaus*, they received a negative reply. So many lotteries had been held recently, the burgomasters explained, that they had been obliged to ignore similar requests from neighboring towns.[78] We know about the lotteries in Dutch cities because they were authorized by the Estates of Holland. Some were apparently not very successful. Delft obtained permission for the foundation of a *tuchthuis* and the organization of a lottery for this purpose in 1614, but its spinhouse was only opened around 1620.[79] In 1615 Dordrecht obtained a similar permission, but following this no prison was established.[80] In Gouda, on the other hand, a lottery was instituted in 1611, a year after the opening of a prison. In Hamburg the lottery was instituted, despite Amsterdam's refusal to allow tickets to be sold there, in 1614; the delay in the opening of the Hamburg institution was caused by other factors.[81] The same expedient to raise money, called *glückshaven* or *glückspott*, was especially popular in Bremen. The magistrates of that town used it for all kinds of purposes besides financing the prison.[82] The first lottery for the benefit of the *zuchthaus* was held in 1618. Another was organized in October 1645 to finance the second *zuchthaus*. Gold and silver kitchen utensils could be won, as well as pictures, clothes, closets, foils, and pistols, together worth a few thousand reichsthaler. In 1647 and again in 1650, the third *zuchthaus* was financed by the same method.[83] Around 1700, lotteries were again held for the benefit of the Hamburg *zuchthaus*.[84] In Prussia and München this method of reducing the deficit was being used in the eighteenth century still.[85]

The second expedient, levying special taxes, was more common throughout the seventeenth and eighteenth centuries. From the beginning the Amsterdam spinhouse was largely financed in this way. In October 1597 its regents were entrusted with the task of licensing wine and beer houses. The keepers had to renew their permits every three months, which cost them two *stuivers* for serving wine and five for serving beer. Unlicensed keepers could be fined.[86] Problems with the income from just this tax were recorded in 1628. The regents complained that their income had decreased considerably, while ever more poor women who were unable to earn their living were imprisoned. In addition to the tax mentioned, they claimed to be entitled to revenues from comedies, lotteries, fencing tournaments, and other plays. The magistrates merely repeated the original stipulation of the tax on selling beer and wine. They ordered a few servants of the court to accompany the regents through town to look for new taverns and to collect fines from unlicensed ones.[87] The prohibition on serving without permission from the spinhouse regents was repeated in 1655 and again in 1675. The tax amounts were fixed anew and sales of brandy, tobacco, and certain types of food were included in the system.[88] Such permits were sold throughout the early modern period.[89] Taxes were reported in several other Dutch towns, such as Delft.[90] Tavern keepers in Leiden had to make contributions similar to those of their Amsterdam colleagues. During the years 1703–1713, the first decade for which information is available, an average of 618.65 guilders was collected annually, about two years' salary of a hired laborer.[91] Taxes were also instituted in German towns such as Hamburg and Danzig.[92]

The data presented so far permit a firm conclusion on the market value of prison workhouses. If their income ever exceeded expenditures, this was not because of the value of the labor performed there, but in spite of its unprofitability. By itself the work program always resulted in a deficit, and the institutions had to be supported by other means. At the beginning, this was made possible by their association with poor relief, which induced the public to pay charity contributions and participate in lotteries. Some institutions remained in possession of the capital of the hospitals or religious establishments from which they had originated, and this enabled them to profit from the interest on houses and rural estates. Since the middle of the seventeenth century the authorities regularly contributed to the institutions through special taxes or directly from the public treasury. Another important source of income consisted of board money paid by private persons who had a family member imprisoned at their request. The amount of their contribution in excess of the amount necessary for the prisoner's subsistence served to maintain the entire institution. In addition, a handsome sum was usually requested from neighboring jurisdictions that wanted to accomodate prisoners.[93] In the early years, as we saw, the unprofitability of the work program induced the magistrates of some towns to conclude that prisons were too expensive and had to be closed. From the 1660s on, European rulers increasingly found that forced labor, although failing to produce financial gains, was a desirable instrument of discipline and punishment.

A Training School?   A more crude version of this conclusion has been drawn already by some historians. Others still cherish an economic approach to the subject. To them, prisons were established out of general and diffuse economic needs. The transient population of marginals and deviants had to be disciplined, in order to serve as a reserve army of potential laborers. In prison workhouses they were taught the skills in demand in the world outside, or at least were made accustomed to continuous heavy labor. To nondeviant workers, the institutions stood as a permanent warning to persist in their voluntary career of selling their labor at a low price. Or in other words, by disciplining the unruly in prisons, the authorities ensured that the majority of the population was willing to work for entrepreneurs in large manufactories. All this, it is concluded, was the real economic significance of prison workhouses.[94] According to this argument, financial contributions to the institutions could be seen as investments that paid off to the community as a whole.

The authors who present this type of argument probably overestimate the disciplinary potential of prison workhouses within society. Far too few people were ever committed for the institutions to make a serious contribution to disciplining the work force. Their function as visible symbols of repression—in a way comparable to but not quite the same as public executions—was more important. The notion that the authorities made an investment for the general economic benefit has been derived mainly from the evidence on some late eighteenth-century German foundations by territorial princes. These were large-scale institutions, but as a rule, most inmates were committed to a 'voluntary' workhouse section. The only prisons which came near to being run as factories were those entirely farmed out to private entrepreneurs, but such a practice was not recorded very often.

There were three types of arrangements defining the formal position of members of the higher personnel. They might simply be employees paid by the administrators. That was the system prevailing in Amsterdam until 1747. In another, mixed arrangement, a part of the prison's business was farmed out. That part more often involved feeding the inmates than employing them. The contractor received a specified sum for each prisoner. The indoor father of the rasphouse had such a contract since 1747. In Hamburg the *oeconomus* functioned in the same manner from the beginning. The amounts accorded to him for various categories of inmates were regularly revised, depending on the prices of rye and other foodstuffs.[95] In Hamburg and Bremen the work boss did not usually have his own business, although his earnings might partly depend on output. Individual agreements stipulated what was to be paid by the work boss and what by the institution.[96] Delft adhered to the mixed system from the last quarter of the seventeenth century, the regents contracting with the indoor father every three or four years. He received fixed amounts per inmate and fed the prisoners as well as the insane. But he also acted as work boss. If a forced laborer produced more than what was expected from him, the extra revenues were shared between the prisoner and his employer. The latter regularly requested a revision of the fixed amounts when prices were high.[97]

Not everyone was enthusiastic about the mixed system. In Delft it reinforced the conflicts between the regents and the indoor father. When the board accused him of too much initiative in punishing inmates, it was not just a question of authority and status. He punished them "in their bellies," it was said. The contract system made it advantageous for him to provide as little food as possible and doing so by way of punishment was a convenient rationalization. It might cause discontent among the inmates and hence disorder in prison, which the administrators would try to prevent. In 1746 the regents explained that the prisoners' sentences required them to perform heavy labor. If strong men received too little food, they did not work hard enough, so that the intention of the sentences was not fulfilled.[98] In other words, heavy labor was a penal requirement and not an economic one. The indoor father's economic interests actually ran counter to it, because although he could make a profit on the provision of food to the inmates, he could not do so on their work. The Amsterdam regents had reservations in this regard after 1747. The new system, they argued, invested the indoor father with too much power vis-à-vis the inmates—while the maintenance of his authority still required that the board could not lightly disagree with him. They also feared that he would provide inferior and too little food. In 1751 he was actually suspected of this. The *schout* and some of the *schepenen* visited the rasphouse by surprise, but they found the suspicions untrue. They only requested the indoor father to provide a little more meat and syrup once a week.[99]

The third system, the farming out of the entire prison to a private entrepreneur, has been recorded in a few German states, notably Prussia, from the middle of the eighteenth century. In such cases, the labor of voluntary inmates of poorhouses was usually exploited alongside that of the involuntary inmates. The Nürnberg magistrates negotiated with potential candidate entrepreneurs in 1698–1699, but without success. The masters of the weavers' guild found the yarn which had been made under such systems of inferior quality and the canvas makers would not entrust their equipment to a *zuchthaus* or a poorhouse. The stocking manufacturer Daniel Grisel pledged his willingness to employ children, but he insisted on a right to dismiss those found to be unfit, who should then be cared for by the supervisors of the poor.[100] In Paderborn in the 1740s the authorities were equally unsuccessful in their attempts to contract with private entrepreneurs to start a canvas manufactory in prison.[101] In Potsdam, on the other hand, the textile entrepreneur Lange, who employed some 12,000 free laborers, also farmed the workhouse between 1774 and 1786. He was succeeded by the brothers Hesse. This workhouse, however, hardly seems to have been a prison at all.[102] Where convicts were involved, the authorities normally distrusted this type of arrangement. They feared that a private contractor would attempt to influence the court's decisions as to what kind of people were sentenced to imprisonment. In Münster, where plans for farming out the prison were discussed in 1778, they formulated their misgivings thus: there is no adequate punishment, "when the nature and the length of a term are not a function of the condition and the circumstances of the perpetrator, his act and his crime, but of the convenience and the profit or loss of an entrepreneur."[103] Penal considerations conflicted with economic ones, and the former prevailed.

An emphasis on gaining material profits from convict labor and the leasing of prisoners to private contractors were rather a feature of nineteenth-century America. According to several authors, economic considerations seem to have been more prevalent there.[104] In preindustrial Europe forced labor, if not introduced for penal reasons in the first place, was soon put to penal uses. A discussion of the type of work performed, and especially an analysis of the significance of rasping wood, will make up the final element in my study of the relationship between early modern prisons and the market.

The Labor Program:
The Success and Failure of Rasping Wood

Whatever the financial considerations of the authorities, the administrators, and the personnel, for the inmates the economy of the prison household meant forced labor. Work was a major element of their daily experience and we will consider the subject from another point of view in chapter eight. This section deals with the labor program from a macroeconomic viewpoint. Briefly, it inquires into the trades practiced in prisons. Then, it focuses on the early modern prison trade par excellence: rasping wood.

The Trades   Although rasping was the most conspicuous prison trade, various sorts of cloth work were also very common. Even in the rasphouse weaving was practiced alongside rasping until the 1660s.[105] Since rasping was a heavy job compared to weaving, the combination made it possible to differentiate tasks for stronger and weaker inmates or serious and less serious offenders. In Haarlem, for example, the raspers were considered the most infamous group of inmates. Women and minor offenders were put to work spinning, weaving, or sewing. From the 1730s on, prison production concentrated on linen and 'ribbons.'[106] The inmates of the Amsterdam spinhouse honored its name at first, but by the eighteenth century most of them were sewing linen.[107] Workhouse jobs were weaving coarse linen and canvas, beating hemp, and knitting nets.[108] In Leiden there is no information on the labor program of the first *tuchthuis*, but when the second was opened in the 1660s, cloth work soon came to dominate.[109] In the combined prison and madhouse that was opened at Delft in 1677, rasping seems to have been practiced for a very brief period only.[110] During the eighteenth century, too, the labor program centered around the textile industry. The Hanseatic towns followed the example of

Amsterdam in the early years, with a combination of rasping as heavy work and cloth trades as light work. In Bremen the production of *rass* (or *rasch*), a light woolen material, was predominant in the seventeenth century. Weaving bombazine and rasping brazil wood came second, as the officials explained in 1669.[111] During the eighteenth century the production of *rass* and bombazine continued, supplemented by manufacture of stockings in the first half and blankets in the second. In 1782 most inmates were making blankets or spinning *rass* yarn; others were spinning yarn for stockings; just one inmate was occupied with each of the following tasks: knitting, picking wool, beating hemp, and rasping.[112] In the early decades of the Hamburg *zuchthaus,* rasping was combined with the production of bombazine, mock velvet, linen, or wool.[113] At the end of the seventeenth century canvas succeeded bombazine as the predominant product. After canvas and bombazine, the next most prominent products in the eighteenth century were stockings and blankets, just like the situation in Bremen. Rasping was continued in Hamburg at least until 1750. The spinhouse opened at Hamburg in 1669 always concentrated on cloth production, usually wool.[114]

Various cloth industries are mentioned most frequently in the literature on other prisons. In the Dutch Republic they included, besides those already referred to, knitting and repairing clothes, spooling silk, carding and dying wool, hackling, twining, fulling, and picking oakum. Nontextile trades included beating tuff, repairing shoes and sorting coffee beans.[115] In the German countries cloth production, usually in combination with rasping, is mentioned for the *zuchthäuser* at Danzig, Spandau, Königsberg, München, and Nürnberg in the seventeenth century.[116] In the eighteenth there was more variety. In Münster and Paderborn, for example, canvas was made, while marble work was performed in Bayreuth.[117] A wide array of trades was recorded for the Prussian *zuchthäuser* of the second half of the eighteenth century. Next to cloth production and in some cases rasping, these included molding sausages, stamping gunpowder, tailoring, and shoemaking.[118] A particularly unhealthy job was performed at Nürnberg, where one of the *zuchthaus* wards was set up as a glass-polishing workshop. It was notoriously difficult to get free workers to do this. The cheapest method, dry polishing, was used, which resulted in fine glass dust being breathed into the lungs of the workers. Many prisoners died, according to Sothmann, who studied the Nürnberg *zuchthaus* but who presents no concrete figures.[119]

It is understandable that cloth production occupied the first place among the labor programs of Dutch and German prisons. Jan de Vries calls the textile industry the largest and most widespread of the 'traditional' economy. In the early modern period this industry was organized on a commercial and entrepreneurial basis, but that observation does not necessarily conflict with it being practiced in the prisons. Cloth production in prisons remained separate from the economic mainstream in two important respects. First, prisons almost always were located in towns, while in the putting out system labor was usually performed in the countryside. The earliest attempts at concentration of production, in a protoindustrial form, occurred in rural areas, too. Institutional labor contributed to this concentration in the second half of the eighteenth century, but large almshouses and voluntary workhouses were involved rather than prisons. The urban pseudohouseholds were unable to compete with the cheap work force of rural real households. The second major deviation from the mainstream consisted in the near absence of references to cotton among prison labor programs. It was only mentioned frequently with reference to the mixed product bombazine.[120] Cotton was the booming new product in Europe in the course of the eighteenth century, in England especially, but also on the Continent.[121] Thus, where the textile industry at large was starting on the road toward innovation and growth, prison cloth production remained tied to the economic system of past centuries.

Rasping: Why and How   The job most closely associated with prisons, rasping, requires our special attention. The original considerations which prompted its adoption were both penal and practical. It was such hard work, it was punishment by itself. Whether it was also unhealthy because of the dust, as the glass-polishing in Nürnberg was, is hard to say. This is not discussed in the available sources. A practical consideration was that it involved unskilled labor; anyone, if strong enough, could perform it. Moreover, very little equipment was needed for it: just a rasp saw and a bench to lay the wood logs on. Finally, it required little movement, so that the workers' feet might be chained. For these reasons, rasping proved an ideal prison labor. To the extent that the Amsterdam prison was considered a model in Europe, imitation notably took the form of adopting rasping as at least one of the program activities. Well into the eighteenth century, authorities and administrators expressed their faith in it. It became the most conspicuous and notorious prison activity, so that its economic status, that is, its profitability or nonprofitability, indicates the economic status of early modern prisons generally. If we find this job to be unprofitable from the market point of view, too, then imprisonment as a whole must definitely be considered a noncommercial enterprise.

The economic history of rasping is the economic history of the production of coloring materials. That this history is largely unwritten may be related to the association of rasping with carceral institutions. In fact, a study of early modern imprisonment sheds more light on the economic history of dye production than vice versa. Production of coloring materials was also associated indirectly with the other major prison business, since it was mainly cloth which was impregnated with the dye produced from rasped wood. What follows is an attempt to piece together an outline of the history of the rasping business, based on prison sources and a few scraps of literature.

Originally, dying and painting were just two different techniques for producing splendor. Before the Renaissance, painters did not have the status of creative artists, and well into the fifteenth century, pictures were mainly valued for the quality of their colors.[122] There was no basic difference between the splendor of a dress represented on a painting and that of one actually worn. Painters as well as dyers produced their coloring material themselves, and both groups did so within an artisanal context. That is apparent from Carolus Battus's *Secret Book of Arts*. Battus (c.1540– c.1617) presented a compilation of traditional knowledge, including such subjects as the preparation of medicines and forecasting weather. His recipe for making dye from rasped wood unambiguously raises the image of an individual master who has procured a small quantity of the raw material.[123] Wood-powder was never the only coloring material source. Other vegetable stuff and minerals were its main competitors before the period of the chemical industry. But redwood was important as a raw material at least from the twelfth century, when its use was first recorded in Spain. It produced a brighter color than that which could be derived from roots. This 'glow of fire,' *braza* in Spanish, gave its name to the origin of the redwood, brazil trees, and the active element in the wood, brasiline. These trees did not grow in Europe, which explains why redwood dye remained a luxury article throughout the medieval period.[124] Coloring clothes— with vegetable or mineral matter—was a subsidiary activity of the textile industry in the Middle Ages. In Holland a tendency toward specialization between weavers and dyers became visible, and by the sixteenth century the latter formed a separate guild.[125] They were still working in an artisanal fashion. When they used redwood, they chopped it into pieces as small as possible, put them into a cistern and exposed the solution to the air. After a few weeks the cloth could be put into the cistern too.

In the sixteenth century two factors facilitated the production of dye from wood on a larger scale. The first lay on the supply side. Massive forests of redwood trees grew in the New World, in particular along the coast in the country named after them, Brazil. In addition, a new raw material, bluewood or Campeche wood, was discovered in Mexico. Great quantities were shipped to Europe.[126] The second factor was an improvement in the production process itself. The quality of the end product, dyed cloth, as well as the quantity that could be handled at one time, depended on the fineness of the particles prepared for oxydation. It was discovered that grating the logs with a many-bladed saw produced much better results than chopping them. That was the origin of rasping. The problem then became one of manpower. If the production of colored cloth was to be increased, the dyers could not make the raw product themselves. It would take too much time and effort: rasping was very hard work and very labor-intensive. There are no references to free workers being hired to do this work, so it seems that the foundation of the Amsterdam *tuchthuis*, at the end of the sixteenth century came as a *deus ex machina* for the dyers. They themselves may have suggested having prisoners do rasping; among the founding fathers only Spiegel referred to such work in passing. The earliest reference I found to an inmate having it imposed on him was dated 9 October 1597.[127] Rasping continued to be reserved exclusively for convicts as long as it was performed.

This sounds like a success story about prisons. Their appearance on the scene paved the way for the mass production of colored cloth, so it seems. Of course, demand would have to increase, too. In the sixteenth century practically everyone wore black clothes, and black dye was produced from mineral sources. Demand for vegetable coloring matter, especially from the newly discovered bluewood, increased as fashions changed in the course of the seventeenth century. Of course, the change in fashions was at least in part due to the availability of new dyes and colored cloth. All this made the proliferation of rasping programs in prisons possible.

The economic modernity of this enterprise is attested by its dependence on supply and demand, but also by its operation outside the guild system. The first dyers exploiting convict labor must have been free entrepreneurs; at least, the official guilds originally refused to go along. It is a commonplace of economic history that capitalistic mass-manufacture goods are often cheaper but of less quality than those made in an artisanal fashion. As a rule, the guilds aimed their protests at the inferior quality. In Leiden in the first half of the seventeenth century, they managed to obtain legal prohibitions of certain new techniques, and the assayers were determined to track down offenders.[128] The dyers had to give up their struggle in the 1660s, when the town itself introduced convict rasping. The traditional system simply persisted longer there because of the dominance of the old textile trades, which were in league with the dyer's guild. Elsewhere, the guild system had already been superseded. Coloring cloth had become a traffic industry, unconnected with weaving.[129] The trade in dye-powder also became an independent function. The records often refer to dealers whose business it was to buy wood logs, have them rasped in prison, and then sell the powder. From a conflict over payments in Haarlem we learn that the trade in convict-produced dye from wood was international as early as the 1610s.[130]

Men and Machines   That is not the whole story. The apparent economic modernity of rasping rested on a noneconomic base. To illustrate this, I have to go back to the late sixteenth century. On 30 January 1589, a half year before the decision to found the Amsterdam *tuchthuis*, Albert de Veer, a citizen of that town, obtained a patent from the Estates General for a machine he had invented. It concerned "a certain instrument, driven by a horse going round, with which it is possible to break all kind of wood, brazil and other, in a better way than with the means used heretofore."[131] This invention was probably not successful, because we do not hear of the use of horsepower again. Other technicians tried other means, though. In 1601 two men were granted a patent on a machine for "breaking and milling" all sorts of dyewood and driven "by wind power or otherwise." A third patent of this type was requested two years later by Frederick L'hermite, a resident of Amsterdam. He had invented a multipurpose mill for the preparation of dyewood and other products. In this case, the Estates General granted the patent on the condition that the instrument would not be used to prepare dyewood in Holland.[132] In other words, the rasping method had become technologically obsolete from the very moment when it was introduced in prisons.

At first, the construction of mills using mechanical technologies was both threatening and beneficial to the rasphouse. The work of convicts left a residue of chips, which could now be dealt with mechanically. But the threat was obvious, too. An ordinance of January 1599 prohibited rasping in the city by anyone other than prisoners.[133] Thereupon, one Pieter Jansz erected a mill in the Zaan region, just outside Amsterdam's jurisdiction. In April 1602 the regents concluded an agreement with this miller, who promised to handle only chips and *fiset*-wood (of a yellow color), which were unfit for the convict program.[134] Probably, Pieter Jansz agreed only because he knew that the matter had been discussed at the provincial level. Two weeks later the Estates granted the Amsterdam *tuchthuis* a monopoly on the production of dye powder throughout Holland.[135] Since there are no indications that rasping on a large scale was ever done by free workers, it is clear that this privilege was directed against the new technique of milling wood. The text explicitly referred to the agreement with Pieter Jansz and immediately went on to express the fear that others would compete with the rasphouse in a similar manner. The Estates of Holland granted the monopoly because they agreed with the Amsterdam magistrates that without a supply of work for the inmates the house could not subsist. That the Estates General shared this opinion can be inferred from the clause they attached to Frederick L'hermite's patent a year later. The desirability of maintaining a penal institution justified the discouragement of technological innovation.[136]

Amsterdam's privilege was probably encroached upon from the start. In 1646 it was admitted that rasped and milled wood had been imported from outside the city, and new fines were set on this practice. Moreover, the ordinance was reissued, in almost identical words, in 1657 and 1660.[137] Local authorities in the Zaan region did not bother about Amsterdam's privilege. They permitted one Adriaan Gerritsz to erect a mill for the preparation of dyewood in 1643. Meanwhile Pieter Jansz and his successors had continued to interact with the rasphouse, milling the chips left over there. However, in 1656 the Amsterdam magistrates unilaterally terminated the agreement and authorized the regents to build their own mill within the town's jurisdiction. The Zaan millers continued their operations for a time, claiming that the privilege of 1602 allowed them to do so. Toward the end of the 1660s they seem to have been bought off.[138]

In the 1660s and 1670s competition came from another direction. In 1660, Leiden followed Amsterdam's example in combining convict rasping with the processing of harder pieces by a mill. The same thing was done somewhat later in Rotterdam. The result was a protracted conflict between these two cities and Amsterdam.[139] Amsterdam's representatives in the Estates argued against authorization of Leiden's mill, even pretending that their own was to be dismantled again.[140] The provincial authorities denied Leiden an authorization, but that did not prevent that town from pursuing its project anyway. In November 1662 the Amsterdam magistrates twice complained about this.[141] Leiden then changed its strategy and contracted clandestinely with a private miller. He pretended to have only house painters as his clients, where in fact he processed the chips left over from prison and packed the product into sacks "not resembling ordinary dye powder sacks." This was found out by two Amsterdam undercover agents who had successfully offered some brazil wood to be milled in December 1664. Apparently, their superiors failed to put a stop to the illegal milling activities and even had to tolerate it in Rotterdam around 1670. Thereupon, Amsterdam claimed that although the millers in both towns did not work for the prison, under this pretext, the magistrates there condoned encroachments upon the monopoly by private entrepreneurs. During a surprise visit to the Rotterdam prison in January 1672, the agents found only two inmates rasping. The conflict continued for some years.[142] Its resolution was not recorded, but Amsterdam apparently had to give in. A 1677 document reveals that the Leiden mill was openly serving the prison and the town's cloth dyers, now broken away from guild restrictions.[143]

The severity of the conflict resulted from Amsterdam's defensive position with regard to the whole matter of rasping as the economic basis for its prison. If the mills were simply catering to a demand which the rasphouse could not meet, the city might have waived its objections. Quite to the contrary, it is clear already by the middle of the seventeenth century that in a free market rasped wood would have been unable to compete with milled wood. Mechanical production was not only cheaper, the end product was of superior quality. In the 1677 document the Leiden dyers made no secret of their preferences. Their method was to boil the powder, packed in permeable sacks, in large kettles together with the textiles to be colored. Rasped wood had to boil for a longer time than mechanically prepared wood, and it contained splinters which might damage the textile. No wonder, then, that dyewood mills continued to be built. At least three were in operation in the Zaan region during the period 1671–1690.[144] For the prison historian the difficulty is that the records usually refer to these mills simply as preparing coloring matter, which might include the milling of minerals. Indeed, the way of evading the prohibitions of the 1602 privilege seems to have been to state officially that only minerals were milled, though wood was being prepared clandestinely. The Gekroonde Visser, built by the dye trading house Vis around 1725, was situated in a meadow a few miles from the road. When the rasphouse agents came to inspect it, they had to take a little boat from Zaandam. They were noticed from afar, so any compromising materials could be removed in time.[145] Windmill counts in the Zaan region in 1731, 1795, and 1801 listed twenty, nineteen, and twenty-four, respectively, as dye mills.[146] Despite the silence about illegal milling activities, notarial acts and related sources contain references proving that a number of these mills also processed wood. A ledger of the Vis house covering the years 1767–1772 referred to several Amsterdam merchants who traded with the rasphouse and also had wood milled in the Zaan region.[147]

These developments explain why a number of prisons stopped the rasping program around 1700. Although it was still considered the most suitable job for serious offenders, it was no longer economically feasible. In eighteenth-century Rotterdam prisoners merely chopped wood, which was then processed mechanically.[148] Haarlem attempted to hold out for a while. Between 1685 and 1712 the regents regularly concluded an agreement with the dyers. The former took care of purchases, supplying quantities and colors according to the latter's needs. The dyers promised to use nothing but rasped wood from the Haarlem prison. In 1712, finally, it was admitted that they preferred milled wood and they were allowed to choose the one or the other.[149] That sealed the fate of convict rasping in Haarlem. Amsterdam held out for a longer time. A new agreement between the rasphouse and a group of dye traders was concluded in 1736. The institution's mill would produce the same amount of milled wood as the inmates produced rasped wood, whereupon the two were mixed.[150] This agreement did not really help, since cloth dying as a traffic industry tended to concentrate in Rotterdam.[151] Consequently, the trade in dyewood was deflected there too, as evidenced by the complaints of Amsterdam merchants in 1760.[152]

A series of documents from the 1760s illustrate the difficult position of Amsterdam dye traders, torn between a legal obligation to have their material prepared in the town's prison and a proliferation of mills producing a preferable dyewood.[153] The rasphouse failed to meet their demands, they claimed, because of a lack of prisoners. But they did not mean that there were too few inmates to ensure sufficient production. The crucial point was that their short-term demands of large quantities could not be met immediately, while millers were able to meet such demands. As a remedy, the traders suggested that the rasphouse keep an enormous stock, from which deliveries to clients could be made at any time. The regents supported this proposal in a request to the magistrates to change their sentencing policy. They suggested that strong persons who formerly had been committed to the workhouse and whose offenses, they claimed, were no less than those of ordinary criminals, would henceforth be condemned to the rasphouse. There is no indication that the court adopted this suggestion. It would have raised the same objections as those formulated in Münster: that if this were done, penal considerations would have been subordinated to economic ones. In addition, once sufficient stock had been produced, the number of inmates would have to be reduced again. There was simply no way to satisfy the merchants. Thus, the legal obligation for residents of Amsterdam to have dyewood prepared in the rasphouse in the end contributed to a shift of the dye trade to other places.

After the middle of the eighteenth century the Amsterdam rasphouse, once a model for the entire Continent, was the only prison which stuck to rasping as its main business. Everywhere else it had been discontinued or relegated to secondary importance. Even in the mother-city what were previously secondary activities were gaining in prominence. Except in peak demand periods, there were too many inmates for the work that needed to be done. The younger ones had always chopped wood, but originally there were few other subsidiary tasks.[154] In the 1760s, on the other hand, besides the woodchoppers, we hear of two or three prisoners who assisted with weighing, one or two who gathered chips, two who assisted serving meals, two who supervised the choppers, and two or more who swept the courtyard. Finally, there was a kettle-scourer and a cobbler.[155] In 1776 only ten or twelve inmates out of fifty-four actually performed rasping; in 1783 almost no one was reported to do it.[156] Convict rasping disappeared entirely from the Dutch scene when Amsterdam closed its first prison at the beginning of the nineteenth century.[157] Milling dyewood, on the other hand, remained a profitable business during the larger part of that century.[158]

In the Empire and Denmark the story was slightly different. An attempt was made to save rasping as convict labor by combining it with mechanical processing. The origins of this strategy are revealed in a Bremen document of 1749. A Hamburg engineer had invented a treadmill for the preparation of dyewood. Apparently, he failed to interest the authorities in his home town and sent his drawings to Bremen. The idea was that prisoners would walk the treadmill, causing movement in a water reservoir, which was the source of energy for milling the wood. Based on an advice signed by forty-four Dutch master mill-makers, the Bremen council decided to support the project, but it does not seem to have been carried out there.[159] According to Wagnitz, such a treadmill was in use in a few German *zuchthäuser* around 1790, notably at Magdeburg, where a thriving dying business existed. But it was operated by only two inmates at a time; there were plans to construct another one which would be operated by four.[160] The historical significance of this method is that it links the originally productive work of rasping with the use of treadmills in nineteenth-century British prisons, which has generally been denounced as unproductive. It did not give a new life to convict rasping, though. In the 1790s rasping was reportedly performed in six German prisons and in Copenhagen, but it was usually imposed on only a few inmates.[161]

The Functions of Prison Labor   The history of convict rasping definitely proves that the spread of prisons had nothing to do with the promotion of a capitalistic system of production. Quite to the contrary, in the seventeenth century imprisonment functioned as a counterforce to economic modernization, and this was especially visible in the Republic. In every other respect the Dutch economy was "a thoroughly commercialized economy that had pushed preindustrial technology and organization to its limits."[162] The development of industrial windmills was one of the hallmarks of this technological innovation. They were used to saw wood for construction and to prepare tobacco and a number of other articles. During the first half of the seventeenth century the entire area North of Haarlem and Amsterdam was turned into one great windmill park. Within this area the Zaan region, the same region where the first recorded dyewood miller operated, was most important.[163] The rasphouse's privilege prevented the dye sector from immediately partaking of these developments. From an economic viewpoint, Amsterdam's prison represented state-supported stagnation.

Thus, the labor program was never meant as a conscious investment in economic development. The function of prison labor in the early modern period was twofold. First, it formed part of the prisoners' disciplinary regime: an essential characteristic of prisons, as I defined them, in contrast to jails. The obligation to work served to punish and help correct the inmates, as well as help ensure order within the institution.[164] Its second function was to keep costs within acceptable limits. The concern to avoid excessive expenses reflected traditional prudence rather than any mercantilistic policy. Preindustrial rural and artisanal families normally expected children to make an economic contribution from the age of six or eight onward.[165] Similarly, the inmates of the paternalistic institutions were expected to contribute to their subsistence. Just as these families could hardly be considered protocapitalistic training schools, neither could the prison workhouses. This brings us back to the subject with which this chapter began. Against the thesis of material profitability, I am arguing for the importance of the household model.

7

THIEVES, PROSTITUTES, AND AGGRESSORS

The Evolution of Imprisonment as a Penal Sanction

According to the household model, labor served as punishment within a paternalistic context. Economic considerations were subordinate to penal ones. This chapter will demonstrate that prison workhouses increasingly acquired the character of judicial institutions. Though the creation of a disciplined work force in the interest of economic growth was not their principal function, they served to keep troublesome persons from the streets. Originally, the prison policies focused on beggars and vagrants especially, although in the Republic criminal offenders were among the inmates from an early date. This has been discussed in previous chapters. We now have to inquire into the subsequent evolution of imprisonment in reaction to crime. Section one discusses the spread of prisons, traces the supralocal network that was woven around them, and demonstrates that they increasingly housed delinquents. Section two deals with the emergence of the first truly criminal prisons in history: institutions whose inmate population consisted entirely of condemned offenders. Even before 1700 the Amsterdam rasphouse and the Hamburg spinhouse were criminal prisons. Section three presents quantitative data on these institutions, supplemented by figures from elsewhere. The final section deals with a mentalities theme again. It discusses attitudes toward honor in the German countries and the ways in which the authorities confronted these attitudes in order to promote penal imprisonment.

The Network

Prisons began as local institutions. They did so as a matter of course in city-states such as Bremen and Hamburg, but also in monarchical countries the earliest initiatives were taken by urban authorities. That was the case with the foundation of the London Bridewell and the projects in Lyon and Paris. In Holland the cities enjoyed a large measure of autonomy. In the judicial and institutional sphere they were practically independent from whatever provincial bodies existed. Urban magistrates established prisons and decided whom to commit there. Yet it would be wrong to consider these towns and the prisons within them as isolated places in a turbulent world unaffected by their presence. I have argued that increased pacification around the towns contributed to the emergence of the carceral idea. In the Dutch Republic, and especially in Holland, absence of a strong central authority did not prevent local rulers from acting together in affairs of mutual interest. Throughout the seventeenth century the spread of prisons remained a local phenomenon, in the Dutch Republic as well as in the Empire. The crucial point is that this localism was quite compatible with cooperation among localities. Cities not only imitated each other, but exchanged plans as well, and, finally, admitted prisoners sentenced by courts without an institution of their own.

The Spread of Prisons   From the later seventeenth century onward the number of prisons steadily increased. In the German-speaking countries the Hanseatic towns finally acquired company. About a dozen *zuchthäuser* were founded between 1668 and 1691, in most cases by urban authorities. With the exception of Königsberg, the towns in question were situated in inland areas.[1] In other countries this period also witnessed a spurt in the building of carceral institutions. In France, for example, the spread of *hôpitaux généraux* followed upon a royal decree of 1662. In the Republic, foundations in inland regions occurred after 1700, beginning with the first *tuchthuis* in conquered territory. The city and the barony of Breda had jointly petitioned the Estates General in 1706, and after an affirmative reply, the house was built the next year.[2] The province of Gelre established a prison at Arnhem in 1710.[3] The provincial *tuchthuis* of Overyssel, opened at Zwolle in 1740, was a joint project of the cities and the gentry.[4] Thus, supralocal authorities were increasingly involved in the Netherlands. After 1700, the same tendency was visible in the Empire and the Prussian and Austrian dominions bordering it. During that period the involvement of territorial authorities became very common. In the Electorate of Hannover, for example, the Lüneburg quarter took the initiative in 1707. Three years later, four quarters and some of the towns jointly adopted the project. Final authority for the project, however, came to lie with the Hannoverian government. It took some time yet to build the house, which was opened at Celle in 1731.[5] In the second half of the eighteenth century there were some seventy prison workhouses in the German-speaking countries.[6] By 1740 the Dutch Republic counted about twenty.[7]

By itself, the proliferation of prisons is an insufficient reason to speak of a network. That word becomes more appropriate when we realize that the spread took place within a context of frequent mutual contact and exchanges of plans. This began as early as the 1590s with Jan Van Hout's visits to the rasphouse. Such visits are referred to in Dutch sources throughout the seventeenth century. In October 1677, for example, two regents of the recently combined prison and madhouse at Delft went on a tour to Leiden and Amsterdam, "to inquire into the situation of similar houses."[8] Of course, the distances between the cities in Holland were small, but contact also crossed national boundaries. The early lines of influence from Holland to the Hanseatic towns on one side and Antwerp on the other have been discussed already. In 1653 the Ghent magistrates requested the text of prison ordinances from Amsterdam, Antwerp, and Malines.[9] Word about the Amsterdam institutions spread as far as Venice. The ambassadors Donato in 1618 and Contarini in 1626 reported on the practice of justice in the Netherlands, and in particular, recommended the imprisonment of beggars as an example to their own republic.[10] Within the Empire and from there to its borderlands a lively exchange of information was carried on, too. Bremen received requests for information from Nürnberg in 1669, Regensburg in 1688, and Celle in 1718. In 1735–1736 the Bremen magistrates corresponded with the duke of Schlesswig-Holstein, also king of Denmark, who wished to erect a *zuchthaus* at Rendsburg. In their own prison archive they kept copies of the ordinances of the Hamburg spinhouse of 1669 and the Cassel *zuchthaus* of 1720.[11] Johann Fresse, *jahrverwalter* at Hamburg, visited the Amsterdam institutions in 1670 and returned with new plans.[12] Besides asking information from Bremen, the founders of Celle's prison directed themselves to Hamburg, Geneva, and London.[13] When Warsaw considered building a prison in 1732, Danzig was approached.[14] In 1769 the Hamburg senate received a letter from the municipal authorities at Metz, who intended to establish a *maison de retraite forcée* and wished to know about the situation in Hamburg. The senate returned a copy of its spinhouse ordinance, then exactly 100 years old, but added that it was no longer up to date and advised Metz to make inquiries in Amsterdam, too.[15] When the Berlin judge Schmidt was preparing a proposal for the reform of the town's prison in 1772, he wrote to Amsterdam, London, and Copenhagen.[16]

Contracts   These are a few examples; more correspondence of this sort can be found in the archives, no doubt. The records confirm that the officials involved wished to learn from each other, but the evidence is still not sufficient to speak of integration. An integrated network of prisons was built up, finally, when offenders from foreign jurisdictions were also admitted. There is widespread Dutch evidence for this practice and it was in use elsewhere, too. Amsterdam seems to have accepted 'foreign' prisoners from the beginning, always on the condition of payment by the court that sentenced them. A thief condemned at Hoorn was in the rasphouse in 1617.[17] A list of 1658 mentioned three inmates committed by the *baljuw* of Amstelland and one by the admiralty.[18] From then on Amsterdam court records regularly referred to criminal prisoners sentenced in neighboring districts. In the second half of the eighteenth century they were admitted as a matter of course, also arriving from far-away jurisdictions of Zeeland and Brabant.[19] The rasphouse was certainly not the only 'hospitable' institution. A thief condemned to two years in prison by the court of Mijdrecht had served his full term at Utrecht in 1624, while another one from Montfoort was awaiting his release.[20] Convicts sentenced by the court of Kennemerland were committed to the Haarlem *tuchthuis* beginning in the middle of the seventeenth century. An agreement to accept prisoners between Haarlem and the *baljuw* of Blois and Beverwijk was concluded in 1766.[21] The final cancellation of the plans for a provincial prison in Holland, which had been discussed repeatedly from the middle of the seventeenth century until the 1720s, probably caused a proliferation of such agreements.

For reasons unknown, Delft became *the* prison town in Holland. In the 1650s its court had still been obliged to confine some offenders at Gouda. Later, the institution at Delft became a veritable supralocal prison. The magistrates concluded an agreement with the neighboring district of Delfland in 1714, enabling its court to send prisoners to Delft.[22] They reached similar agreements with the town of Zierikzee a year later, the island town of Tholen in 1721, and the Supreme Court-martial and the court for the Generality Lands of Brabant and Overmaze in 1750.[23] Contracts for individual prisoners have been preserved, too. In 1720 three female gypsies from the Heusden district were confined for twenty-five years.[24] Since 1739 Delft used printed standard forms for individual contracts, where just the prisoner's name, the condemning court, and financial details had to be filled out.[25] No general agreements with the Court of Holland or the court of The Hague have survived. The former had its imprisonment sentences executed at Delft throughout the eighteenth century, while the latter started to do so toward the end of the century. Several times the Court of Holland was obliged to accept a raise in the payments due for its prisoners who were unable to work. In 1760 it agreed to Delft's proposal that it would pay proportionately for the religious instruction of its inmates.[26]

The cited examples prove that a true prison network existed in eighteenth-century Netherlands, making it possible for every court to pronounce confinement sentences. That does not mean that they all did. In 1809 the Court of Holland requested every jurisdiction in the province to present a list of its criminal prisoners. Ninety out of 146 replied they had none at the moment. The remaining fifty-six still represent a considerable number, because many jurisdictions consisted of just one or two villages where almost no criminal sentences were pronounced at all.[27] The Dutch data can be supplemented with evidence from the Empire. Chapter three showed that Bremen accepted prisoners from neighboring places in the early seventeenth century, although the delinquent status of some of these prisoners was a little ambivalent. Before the Hannoverian *zuchthaus* at Celle was completed, offenders condemned by its court were occasionally imprisoned at Hamburg. The first time this occurred, in 1699, the condemned consisted of a group of three women who were sentenced to two years each. They were the wives of a company of thieves who were all capitally executed at Celle. These sentences were followed by that of a thirty-six-year-old man, whose offense was not recorded, in 1702.[28] Throughout the Empire, agreements on committing prisoners must have been common by then. In 1711 the Osnabrück authorities resisted their overlord's plans to establish a *zuchthaus* in the town, arguing that offenders could easily be confined elsewhere.[29] That was not entirely true, as it turned out, for Bremen refused to admit an Osnabrück academician six years later, on the grounds that its prison was too crowded. But such a refusal was not standard practice in the Hanseatic town. In 1725 three women condemned by the court at Stade were accepted. After that, a number of foreign delinquents were imprisoned at Bremen, the thief Gerd Hörmann, for example, condemned as a result of an inquisitorial procedure in the small town of Varel in 1788.[30] It should be noted that as territorial governments increasingly became involved in imprisonment, the need to call upon neighboring urban magistrates lessened. The prisons in question might be situated in small places, but they served every court in their territory.

Prisons and Crime   In the eighteenth century, then, the Continental core-area was saturated with carceral workhouses. Imprisonment had become a sanction available to every court. Noncriminal offenders, on the other hand, continued to be admitted into most of these institutions. We may ask, therefore, to what extent they were associated with the realm of criminality and the penal system. That question can only be answered with the help of quantitative data, which will be provided in subsequent sections. Nevertheless, the evolving perception of contemporaries in this regard is revealing, too.

There are three indications of an evolution in the direction of a closer association of prisons and crime. The first is a change of tone in contemporary descriptions. Around 1600 the general public in Holland always thought of beggars, first, when they considered the inmates of *tuchthuizen*. A century later criminals had taken their place. The Rotterdam baker and popular author Gerrit van Spaan, writing in 1698, listed twelve sorts of people who were committed to his town's prison. He began with criminals who had also been whipped and branded, and continued with various types of property offenders. Persons committed at the request of their families were only mentioned after aggressors, prostitutes and procurers.[31] Another description simply said that Leiden's prison housed criminals condemned by the town and by Rijnland.[32] Although The Hague later sent its convicts to Delft, its own *tuchthuis* was said in 1730 to admit an increasing percentage of delinquents.[33] It is also instructive to consider the debates in the Estates of Holland about plans for a provincial prison, although these plans never materialized. The question came up in the late 1640s and again at the beginning of the eighteenth century. In the first period the discussions followed in the wake of new legislation against marginals, while the combat of crime by wandering bands was a major motive during the second.[34] Outside Holland the same tendency was visible. The founders of the provincial *tuchthuizen* of Gelre and Overijssel explained that these were meant primarily for delinquents. Groningen's prison almost exclusively had condemned offenders as inmates after about 1720.[35]

The second indication is that the perception of prison workhouses as charitable institutions of a sort gradually disappeared. It was a significant change when Caspar Commelin, publishing a description of Amsterdam in 1693, separated them from the category of *godshuizen* and called them "houses of justice," instead. He specified that the rasphouse and spinhouse were "subordinate to the court."[36] In two other towns with early foundations the original association with charity received a more concrete blow. The institution at Alkmaar had been opened as a combined prison workhouse and almshouse, just as in Haarlem. In 1616 the council had even prohibited thieves or other notorious criminals from being committed there. The combination of two houses lasted until 1683. From then on the voluntary poor were accommodated in a ward of the orphanage, so that the prison workhouse became a judicial institution only.[37] In Haarlem a comparable change took place somewhat later. Well into the eighteenth century, the combination of the two types of institutions had raised no objections. Between 1679 and 1682 there had not even been any prison regents, supervisors of the poor directing the entire institution. The wish to separate the two facilities became more pronounced in the course of the eighteenth century. In 1737–1738 there were plans to build a new almshouse, but they were not implemented. Discussions started anew in the late 1770s. Finally, in 1786–1787, the urban poor and the reformed poor were lodged together in a new almshouse. From then on the original workhouse was solely a criminal prison, though the regents were allowed to keep four poor men and two women to assist in providing the prisoners with food and equipment.[38] The transformation in the perception of *tuchthuizen* was reflected in a change of policy after the Batavian Revolution of 1795. The new government continued the traditional tax freedom of charitable institutions, but it excluded prisons from this category. Delft protested in vain in favor of its combined *tuchthuis* and madhouse.[39]

The evidence for the first two indications of a closer association of prisons and crime is confined to the Netherlands; the third indication was visible in the Empire as well. Because they were perceived as judicial institutions in the eighteenth century, prison workhouses stood almost completely apart from renewed attempts to put the poor to work in an institutional setting. The prison movement around 1600 had never led to any disappearance of the able-bodied unemployed, and new commercial projects were discussed repeatedly. Significantly, the first attempts at employment of the poor outside the system of prison workhouses were recorded in Amsterdam, Bremen, and Hamburg, where the evolution of the criminal prison had set in relatively early. Since 1682, Amsterdam had a workhouse for poor girls, who had their meals outside and went home at night. Around 1700 some 500 girls were employed there.[40] A Bremen report, dated 30 December 1675, advocated building an almshouse next to the prison, but it was not opened until 1698, as a separate institution with a capacity of 300.[41] The Hamburg senate proposed a large-scale project for the employment of the poor to the *bürgerschaft* in 1725. Poor persons still worked in the *zuchthaus,* it was said, but changed circumstances had made it necessary that the old institutions were supplemented by new ones. Some poor people refused to enter the *zuchthaus* because they found it an infamous place. The senate wished to occupy 30,000 to 50,000 of the unemployed with making stockings. However, the number of people whom the initiators thought they were able to employ steadily decreased. In 1732 only 142 were employed.[42] For our purposes the degree of success of these projects is less important than the observation that prison workhouses, because they were judicial institutions, were not involved.

In the second half of the eighteenth century new voluntary workhouses were established in a number of countries. In the Republic they were called *pauperfabrieken* and they had nothing to do with the earlier prisons. Their historian counted thirty-nine foundations, which resulted from a combination of traditional notions of charity with utilitarian views influenced by Enlightened philosophies.[43] Projects in the Southern Netherlands provided for semiforced labor of the poor in the 1770s. Simultaneously, and apart from these projects, new prisons for serious criminals were opened in the provinces of Flanders and Brabant.[44] A related development of establishing separate voluntary workhouses can be traced in the Habsburg lands since the late eighteenth century.[45] Elsewhere in the Empire the picture was more variegated. A number of prisons were still combined with orphanages, almshouses or madhouses, but others were not. At Gotha, for example, the prison was separated from the widows and orphans' home around 1790 and moved to a new building.

At Ludwigsburg, on the other hand, a prison was opened in 1736 and charitable institutions were annexed to it later. Quite a different association, finally, was that of prisons and public works. In some places, male delinquents condemned to imprisonment were actually employed in the streets or at the ramparts, only being kept within prison walls at night.[46] The effect of the association of prisons and public works was to link the prison system to the sphere of crime again.

The total number of prisoners staying in these institutions at any one time remained relatively small compared with the numbers of prisoners today. Few exact figures can be found in the literature or even in the archival sources, especially for the period before the end of the eighteenth century. Moreover, in the case of combined institutions, prisoners were not always differentiated from the voluntary poor or the needy seeking asylum. Where excessively high numbers were reported, this was always due to the presence of the latter categories. The Hamburg *zuchthaus* counted some 500 inmates at the end of the seventeenth century and an average of 443 at the end of the eighteenth, but that included the poor of the almshouse ward.[47] The largest institution of early modern Europe was the *Salpêtrière* at Paris, with a population of about 8,000 at the end of the eighteenth century. But only a minority of these were actually imprisoned.[48]

Prisons that were simply prisons in the early modern period seldom had more than about a hundred inmates. The closed ward of the London Bridewell is reported usually to have counted less than 150.[49] In the Utrecht *tuchthuis* there were 42 men and 22 women in September 1624.[50] The Amsterdam spinhouse counted only 15 inmates in 1611, 34 in 1643–1645, 70 to 80 in the 1660s, about 80 in 1698, 60 in 1765, and between 32 and 46 during the years 1776–1781. The workhouse had 114 inmates, 87 women and 27 men, in 1765, and 25 men and 120 women in 1781. The new combined spinhouse and workhouse that opened in 1782 had a greater capacity. It counted more than 390 inmates in 1787.[51] The number of prisoners at Pforzheim in the second half of the eighteenth century fluctuated between 25 and 116.[52] In Bremen, in annual counts during the period 1748–1757, the average was 65; the highest number during those years was 80 and the lowest 54. In 1776 the number of inmates had declined to 39, while 28 were reported in 1781 and 24 in 1782. Around 1790 the average was about 40.[53] A 1799 Bremen report on prison workhouses in neighboring towns, gives the following numbers of inmates: an average of 100 at Braunschweig, without specification of categories; 20 male and 22 female prisoners at Kassel; 106 criminal offenders (45 of whom were pardoned from the death penalty) at Copenhagen, and another 374 in the *verbesserungshaus* there; almost 100, without specification, at Hannover; about 20 criminal offenders and 400 to 450 inmates of the workhouse/poorhouse at Lübeck; an average of 333, without specification, at Celle.[54] Numbers for the two purely criminal prisons at Amsterdam and Hamburg are discussed in the next section.

The Appearance of Criminal Prisons:
Amsterdam and Hamburg in the Second Half
of the Seventeenth Century

The previous section showed that carceral workhouses spread over various countries beginning in the late seventeenth century, and that they were increasingly associated with the penal system. Still, many remained multipurpose institutions, also admitting nondelinquents such as persons expelled by their families or beggars taken from the streets. Those houses were not criminal prisons in the sense of being meant for convicts only. It might be argued that their association with the penal system was rather tenuous. Such an argument would be inappropriate, because delinquents put a considerable imprint upon prison workhouses, and judicial control over nonconvicts was increased, too. Moreover, purely criminal prisons also existed in the early modern period. As a result of a differentiation process, two were in full operation before 1700 already. Amsterdam and Hamburg were the pioneers. Thus, the birth of the criminal prison must be situated in Amsterdam and Hamburg in the second half of the seventeenth century.

Differentiation in Amsterdam   In the case of the Dutch metropolis, since there are no entry books for the rasphouse, we have to be content with indirect sources. The rasphouse had always been thought of as a suitable place for delinquents: the condemnation of a young thief was the immediate cause for its foundation.[55] But in the first half of the seventeenth century beggars and private prisoners made their mark on the institution, too. The transformation of the rasphouse into a purely criminal prison was a result of the erection of new institutions for the other categories of deviants. The workhouse, opened in 1654, was destined for male and female beggars and minor offenders. From then on, delinquents made up the great majority of inmates in the rasphouse's public part. Nothing illustrates the transformation better than the fact that Dapper (1663) referred to convicts only and even refused to believe that simple marginals had ever been inmates at all. He criticized Pontanus for stating that the combat of beggary had led to the foundation of the rasphouse. Dapper thought "that the principal cause was perhaps that *schepenen* were forced to hang many young thieves, who were not frightened by physical punishment." Marginals were of another kind: "it seems rather hard and almost inhuman to put beggars (though some used to steal under that guise) to such heavy labor."[56] Dapper's use of the word "perhaps" is crucial. It betrays that he was not sure about the past, but he took it as a matter of course that the heavy labor of rasping wood was performed by convicts.

From about 1650 on there are no references to persons committed on request to the rasphouse's public part. The *schepen* Bontemantel is very plain about it: men and women imprisoned by their relatives stayed in the secret wards of the rasphouse and spinhouse, respectively. They were accompanied by a few of the condemned who were privileged because of their high status. The rasphouse's public ward housed condemned offenders only.[57] Since the secret part never held a very significant number of inmates, it is fair to call the rasphouse a criminal prison from the middle of the seventeenth century. This explains why weaving was discontinued there: because this job had always been reserved for less serious offenders. The rasphouse was unequivocally a criminal prison since the end of the century, when the secret ward in its turn underwent a change. It probably began in Bontemantel's time already. For one thing, a relative who was able to pay a nice sum did not necessarily have to lodge the prisoner in his home town. In this period a number of private institutions appeared in Holland, and one was opened in Amsterdam in 1694. That completed the differentiation process. According to Wagenaar, few private prisoners were lodged in the rasphouse's secret ward after that time.[58] In November 1704 there were only three inmates.[59] This depopulation of the secret ward paved the way for other uses. Reviving the precedent of 1620, the court reserved it for political prisoners and others whom they did not want to be seen by the public. In the second half of the eighteenth century most were persons convicted of sodomy and spared the death penalty.[60] Their number never rose very high, though. In 1765 the secret ward counted seven inmates; in 1777, eight.[61]

Our information on the total number of inmates covers most of the eighteenth century. In contrast to the figures presented at the end of the previous section, these figures are for delinquents only. In 1698 and again in 1743–1744 there were over a hundred inmates. Then the number declined rapidly to a low point of fifty in 1765. In 1809 it had risen again to 115.[62] Of course, the number of inmates lagged far behind the number in criminal prisons in the modern world. A much lower percentage of the population were tried for criminal offenses then, and a lower percentage ended up in prison. The rasphouse, and early modern *tuchthuizen* generally, were important primarily for their symbolic function. The presence of fifty to one hundred inmates made it possible for them to fulfill that function. There were about two to five times as many delinquents in the rasphouse as were punished on the scaffold on each 'justice day.'[63]

Reduction Amsterdam was the first European town with a criminal prison, and also the first to experiment with a system whereby a convict's behavior inside might influence his term. He could earn *afslag* (reduction), as it was called. The invention and elaboration of this system cast doubt on the supposition that the lengthening and shortening of prison terms were equally common. That is suggested by Rusche. "The length of confinement was, therefore, arbitrarily fixed by the administrators in all cases except those voluntarily committed by their relatives."[64] Based on scanty evidence, he thought that minor offenders were often kept for years, while more serious delinquents might be released after a few weeks. He made this interpretation within the context of his economic view of prison workhouses, arguing that the administrators were keen to retain strong inmates or those in whom an investment in the form of training had been made. In the Dutch Republic, however, it was rather the other way around. In the first place, it was precisely in the case of confinement at the request of relatives that a prolongation of the prisoner's term was common. Second, it was only in the case of marginals taken from the streets that the regents themselves were allowed to determine the length of a stay. In all other cases the court did so in advance, based on penal considerations, and only the court could change these terms. When it prolonged a person's stay, this was not simply the opposite of reduction, as a few authors incorrectly suggest.[65] Lengthening a prisoner's term required a process that involved sentencing him to a new imprisonment. This occurred only after serious misdeeds during his first stay that counted as punishable offenses in their own right. In such cases the prisoner was always formally tried for his new offense or offenses.[66] Thus, a lengthening of term constituted an additional punishment, whereas reduction was used as a tool to promote prison discipline. To the extent that these aspects pertain to internal life, they are further discussed in chapter eight.

The earliest recorded cases of reduction were in the form of conditional clauses in a sentence. An inmate in 1597 was condemned to twelve years with the provision that the last four would be remitted if he behaved well. A similar case was recorded in 1613. In November 1617 it was noted that the court of Hoorn had imposed a term of no less than 100 years on an imprisoned thief. On the advice of the regents, the Amsterdam *schepenen* reduced this to six.[67] Reduction as a means of rewarding prisoners in the course of their stay originated in connection with the wish to collect denunciations. If an inmate of the rasphouse accused a person under trial of a new offense and the defendant confessed to it, the accuser was granted a shortening of his term. A round of such denunciations, dated 18 September 1658, has been preserved.[68] Forty prisoners in the rasphouse each testified against one to eight other men. This resulted in 137 accusations, many of them overlapping. Some of the witnesses were themselves accused, while a few among the accused were not even on trial in Amsterdam but in The Hague and Amersfoort. What concerns us here are the prospects for the prisoners. The document records the term remaining for each; these varied from six weeks to fourteen years, while the average was three years and nine months. Fifteen prisoners received reductions, the amounts varying from one-ninth year to one year. The reductions depended on the effect of the denunciations, that is, the number of confessions that resulted, which did not correlate with the number of persons denounced. Neither was there a correlation between the inmate's remaining term and the amount of his reduction, although everyone who received a reduction received less than his time left. The mean reduction was about six months. The fifteen inmates who received reductions had to remain in the rasphouse, on average, another four years and two months. Their mean percentage of reduction was 14. The total amount of reduction granted in relation to the time left to all forty accusers comes to, on average, two months, or 6 percent.

Thus, the system of reduction was well-established in Amsterdam by the middle of the seventeenth century. If one round of denunciations resulted in a shortening of the terms of fifteen prisoners, we may assume that almost all eventually had the chance to obtain this. Court records of sentences from the 1650s and 1660s sometimes noted reduction amounts in the margin. Bontemantel listed "services to justice" as the principal reason for reductions, while good behavior in prison came second.[69] Throughout the period 1650–1750 the Amsterdam *schepenen* regularly tried recidivists who would still have been in prison for earlier offenses had they served their complete term. According to Faber, some ten to twelve prisoners testified against offenders under trial each year during the period 1732–1811.[70] This suggests that many received reductions.

A document dated 1 February 1777 offers further matter for quantification.[71] It lists the inmates of the rasphouse at that moment, their date of entry, term imposed, amount of reduction, and time left to serve. Of the forty-six prisoners in the public ward, twenty-nine had earned reductions. Of the remaining seventeen, twelve had arrived less than a year previously, and five had been condemned by courts other than that of Amsterdam. Hertog Salomon, for example, had been condemned to twenty-five years by the court of Amstelveen in 1765 and had received no reduction. Gerrit Jans, a prisoner of Purmerland, had been in the house since 1764 and received merely two years' reduction. The largest was earned by Willem de Groot: twenty-two years. He had been condemned to fifty years by Amsterdam's *schepenen* in 1765, and so had sixteen years left to serve. All the others had been confined in the 1770s. Since these prisoners had arrived at different times, the amounts they earned are not comparable. It is remarkable though, that reductions were counted in months and even days. This suggests that, except in the case of a few rural courts, reductions were extremely common. In Amsterdam there was one major exception. The inmates of the secret ward received no reductions at all. Incidentally, they were condemned to the longest terms: an average of

33 years. The inmates of the public ward were condemned to an average of 19 years. This is far above the figure for all prisoners sentenced by the Amsterdam court, and suggests that the rasphouse received only the most serious delinquents at this time.

Finally, the only remaining entry book of the rasphouse, begun in the 1780s, regularly listed amounts of reduction. Only prisoners condemned to a term of one year or less received no reductions at all. Those with the longest terms received up to 65 percent, and one even received 78 percent.[72]

The Hamburg Spinhouse   Whereas the rasphouse became a criminal prison because new institutions were inaugurated in Amsterdam for less serious offenders, in Hamburg it was the other way around. A new prison for delinquents, the *spinnhaus,* was opened in the town in 1669. Contrary to what its name suggests, men were admitted there, too. As discussed in chapter three, sentenced criminals had hardly been received by the *zuchthaus* at all. Still, at the time of its foundation, some people must have thought it would be used to house criminals. When a lottery was held to raise funds for the *zuchthaus* in 1614, a poem was published describing the purposes of the projected prison. One passage translates as follows: "so that the rope does not lead to so many bones of thieves being broken at the place of execution."[73] The idea to imprison thieves was realized with the foundation of the spinhouse. It became the second criminal prison in European history, after the Amsterdam rasphouse.

Reorganization plans had probably been around for some time. According to the spinhouse ordinance, it was the lawyer and patrician Peter Rentzel who had planned it during his lifetime. At his death, 13 November 1662, he left 10,000 marks destined for the project. Four years later the *zuchthaus* burnt to the ground. The accident made it possible to erect a new combined institution, but if this was ever considered, the idea was dropped. The *zuchthaus* was rebuilt on the same spot and reopened in 1670. A separate spinhouse was completed a year earlier.[74] As potential inmates, the spinhouse ordinance specifically mentioned whores and thieves, who previously might have been subjected to corporal punishment. Not daunted by this punishment nor even by sentences of banishment, it seemed, they continued their practices in town. That was all the ordinance said about spinhouse inmates.[75] The contrast with the pompous stereotypes in the *zuchthaus* ordinance is striking. It seems as if, in the earlier case, the incarceration of nondelinquents had to be justified with a list of negative epithets, while a brief, practical statement of purpose was sufficient in the case of the spinhouse, because it was for criminal offenders.

I studied the spinhouse's entry books systematically for the first four decades, 1669–1708 (the years refer to dates of entry; the last exit took place in 1736). During that period there were 829 entries, involving 679 different persons. There were 113 recidivists, some of whom were committed more than two times; one was in six times. This body of data almost seems to have been specially constituted for the scholar adopting a process-oriented approach to the history of penal systems. Even within these four decades the institution underwent an evolution. At the beginning it featured several elements which more or less contradicted the idea of a purely criminal prison, but by the early eighteenth century they had disappeared. The most conspicuous of these elements was that, originally the inmates included persons committed at the request of relatives. Apparently their families were undisturbed by its designation as a prison for whores and thieves. Two persons were committed at the request of the Reformed supervisors of the poor, and eight women were admitted on their own initiative; most of these had been in before. The above categories made up 9 percent of the entries during the period studied. The overwhelming majority of inmates were imprisoned on a judicial order. In Hamburg the senate acted as a criminal court in serious cases, while less serious cases were handled by a lower court consisting of two *gerichtsverwalter,* also called praetors. Throughout the period studied, 69 percent were imprisoned by this lower court and 21 percent by the senate. Private prisoners were concentrated in the earliest years. Between 1669 and 1675 they constituted 40.9 percent of the prison population, but during the years 1676–1686 private prisoners declined to 5.3 percent, and then disappeared altogether. After 1687 there were only two 'mixed' cases of women committed by their relatives and the lower court together, and a few in which the prisoner was committed on an order of burgomasters.[76]

A second variable revealing the spinhouse's evolution is the ratio of male to female inmates. It was no coincidence that the ordinance of 1669 referred to whores and thieves in this order. Although the institution was meant for both sexes, in practice it was predominantly a women's prison for several decades. During the period investigated, 91 percent of the entries were women. When private prisoners were no longer committed, the percentage of male entries even decreased for a time. Between 1669 and 1686 the male share was 10.2 percent of the total; this decreased to 7.4 percent in the period 1687–1708. Between 1700 and 1708, however, the male share rose to 11.7 percent. The percentage increased further in the eighteenth century. The annual counts of inmates made in each January enabled me to push the analysis beyond the period for which the entry book data were categorized. Because men received longer terms than women, their share of the annual counts was greater than their percentage of entries. Table 7.1 presents the average number of male and female inmates in five periods, which have been delineated in such a way that the caesuras represent conspicuous rises or falls (especially in the number of male inmates).[77]

The number of women fluctuated without a specific pattern, with a low

Table 7.1

Average Numbers of Male and Female Inmates in the Hamburg Spinhouse at the Annual Counts, 1671–1774

Period	Men	Women	Total
1671–1686	6.0	38.9	44.9
1687–1705	2.7	45.7	48.4
1706–1725	16.5	47.3	63.8
1726–1752	41.1	52.8	93.9
1753–1774	22.1	32.9	55.0

of twenty-eight in 1671 and again in 1762, and a high of sixty-nine in 1718. A rebuilding project started in 1723 greatly enlarged the spinhouse capacity.[78] We may conclude that it was meant to provide more room for men. That completed the bisexualization of the institution, although the average share of women remained greater. Men only outnumbered women in 1769 and 1770. The highest total number (112) occurred in 1748, and the lowest (22) in 1753. The depopulation was due to a massive release of prisoners who volunteered to be transported to America. No counts were recorded after 1774.[79] On the whole, these numbers are comparable to the more fragmentary data for the Amsterdam rasphouse.

The third element in the evolution of the spinhouse is closely related to its original association with women. To explain the change, we have to anticipate themes belonging to the next chapter. During the first three decades of the institution's existence a number of female inmates had small children with them. At the beginning, the provisors may simply have thought that most prisoners were to stay for such a short time, this didn't matter. The first childbirth in the spinhouse was recorded in 1671. Elisabeth Hinces was committed by relatives on 24 October 1670, without a term; she was released on 3 June of the next year with a child of seven weeks.[80] In October 1671, on the other hand, a prostitute, sentenced for five years, was taken to the spinhouse by the executioner, while her child of twenty-seven weeks went to the orphanage.[81] Another prostitute, imprisoned in June of that year, was delivered of a child in the house; it was baptized there and then taken to the orphanage.[82] In 1672, however, the orphanage refused a child whose mother was imprisoned for the second time, after a flogging by the executioner. The provisors of the orphanage now decided that they did not want to be burdened with infamous children. The case ended when mother and child, who were both infected with the French disease, were taken to the poxhouse and then ran away from there.[83] Since then, the provisors of both institutions were caught in a tug-of-war. Some children were still admitted to the orphanage, but others remained in the spinhouse. Sometimes, but not systematically, the latter were recorded in the annual counts, where their number varied from one to four. The age was given just once in 1683, when one child was counted, age three. Some of the children were in for quite some time; the longest four and a half years.[84] After 1698 no more children were recorded. Two major incidents ended the tug-of-war between spinhouse and orphanage. In 1694 and again in 1698 a child was murdered in prison. After the second incident the *jahrverwalter* concluded that it was "no good for this house that small children are in it." Provisors immediately met with burgomasters and requested that neither children nor pregnant women henceforth be committed. Part of the request was fulfilled. Thereafter, as a rule, children were taken to the orphanage, but childbirths in prison continued.[85]

One element ran counter to the observed trend. Despite its penal character, the spinhouse did not function entirely outside the sphere of charity. It was noted that the starting capital for the house was from a bequest by Peter Rentzel. The 1669 ordinance encouraged others to follow his example with gifts of money or materials. Gifts to the house were recorded throughout its history, even in the eighteenth century. There were annual collections for the spinhouse in the parishes, too, but in 1701 the proceeds were said to be too meager. To remedy this situation, provisors themselves henceforth went about as collectors.[86] Against this counterexample, the elements indicating the spinhouse's penal character clearly predominate. In the course of the eighteenth century, the evolution of imprisonment as a criminal sanction continued in Hamburg. The most conspicuous development was that even the *zuchthaus* came to admit presumably minor delinquents. Nonetheless, in 1713 the senate declared that the house was a place of "honest detention," unfit for rogues.[87] On the other hand, in 1744, it was established that, in addition to privately committed persons and the poor, it was to admit prisoners condemned by the senate and the lower court.[88] Inmates in the spinhouse were still mainly prostitutes and thieves, though the proportion of the latter increased as more men were committed.[89] In the 1780s there were plans to make room for the former in the *zuchthaus* and to reserve the spinhouse for thieves and murderers, but these were not put into effect.[90] In 1788, finally, after the promulgation of a new ordinance on the poor, the *zuchthaus* lost its ward for voluntary inmates, which became a separate institution. Since then the *zuchthaus* admitted beggars and minor delinquents only.[91]

Imprisonment as a Penal Option:
Terms and Sentences

Because for the overall thesis of this book the appearance of exclusively criminal prisons is such a crucial phenomenon, a separate section has been devoted to it. Some quantitative data were presented in connection with these institutions; we now continue the analysis of numbers.[92] Quantitative evidence on the status of imprisonment as a penal option can be derived from two types of sources: entry books and court records. The former list every inmate of an institution regardless of the court or agent that committed him or her, but they cannot tell us who were sentenced to noncarceral penalties. The latter sources do that, but they are silent on the prison's other inmates. In some cases, the two sources can be matched. For this chapter, I consulted entry books of the Delft *tuchthuis* and the Amsterdam and Hamburg spinhouses. Entry books are not extant for other prisons in the towns investigated (except for the Amsterdam workhouse, which was discussed in chapter four). For data from court records I depended on previous studies.

Entry Books   I am starting with the former. The entry books of the Hamburg spinhouse, broken down into categories for the first four decades of its existence, have been introduced already. Those of its Amsterdam namesake present no particular problems. It should be remembered that in Amsterdam they refer to women only. The series preserved begins in 1678; I studied the first book, which ends in 1725.[93] The combined *tuchthuis* and madhouse at Delft always remained a multipurpose institution, but its *tuchtelingen* were registered in separate entry books, which have been preserved for the period 1675–1752.[94] Since this chapter deals with imprisonment as a penal sanction, our attention must be focused primarily on delinquents. In the case of Hamburg, they are easily identified, making up 744 cases out of 829. The following quantitative discussion only refers to that group. The entry books of the Amsterdam spinhouse, including 1,510 entries, unfortunately, do not differentiate between women condemned by the court and private prisoners. Every woman was recorded to have been committed by the *schepenen,* but for a minority this must have referred to the college of *schepenen's* consent to a private request.[95] In the case of Delft, the population of convicts, totaling 229, including 159 men and seventy women, consists of those condemned by its *schepenen* and the courts of Delftand and other jurisdictions in the Republic. Only convicts were considered for the quantitative analysis.

In addition to distribution by sex, determined in part by the character of the institution, distribution by age group is the other major variable revealing the identity of prisoners. The mean age at entry of male and female convicts was 37.9 and 35.4, respectively, at Delft and 29.2 and 25.4 at Hamburg; at Amsterdam it was 28.4. In the Hamburg spinhouse 19 percent of the inmates were under twenty, while only 4 percent were under twenty at Delft. Although more than half of the ages were missing from the Delft entry books, this does not entirely explain the difference. The Delft logbook also conveys the impression that many convicts were committed there who already had had a long career of crime and had been sentenced to banishment several times. Apparently, this was the case less frequently in the two other houses. Distribution by age groups there was comparable to that for any population of preindustrial offenders.

The distribution of offenses in entry books is a function of the authorities' sentencing policies as well as the character of the prison. For this category the Amsterdam spinhouse can be disregarded, since the offenses are almost never mentioned. At Delft slightly over half of the offenses were missing. The data available suggest that no particular group of delinquents was singled out for imprisonment. Interestingly, more of the women (34.3%) than the men (24.1%) were condemned for a property crime. In Hamburg, on the other hand, no less than 68.3 percent of the inmates were condemned for a morals offense and 21.4 percent for a property crime (with only 6.3 percent missing data). These figures call for some comment. Court records are not available for Hamburg, and the information in the entry books is provided only summarily. Most prisoners were simply called *"eine hure"* or *"ein(e) dieb(inne),"* just as in the institution's ordinance. The group of morals offenders consists almost exclusively of women denoted as whores. It cannot be said with certainty whether they were all professional prostitutes. The sources leave the impression of some terminological confusion between promiscuous living, extramarital pregnancy, and prostitution, although distinctions with regard to these categories were sometimes explicitly adhered to. That many imprisoned women were indeed professional prostitutes is suggested by the fact that 36.3 percent were suffering from such advanced cases of syphilis that they were taken to the *pockenhaus* for a cure during their stay (making up 93 percent of all delinquents temporarily sent there). Those who had not been sent to the poxhouse had been condemned by the praetors or the senate, too. It is the contemporary authorities who define what activities are crimes, and the spinhouse was a criminal prison. The dominance of prostitution there indicates what type of offenders were selected for one possible penal sanction.

The criminal status of the property offenders in Hamburg is less ambiguous. Most of them were called thieves, while a few women were condemned for swindling. There was at least one organized band of thieves with two couples at the center and consisting of seven people, a few prisoners who were born in Hamburg and others from Danzig, Amsterdam, and Antwerp.[96] Another summary indication in the entry books provides an unambiguous picture of the prisoners' criminal status. Throughout the German-speaking world the mere touch of the executioner was considered a permanent mark of dishonor.[97] To receive a physical punishment from him was even more disgraceful. The identity of the person escorting the prisoner to the house and additional punishments to which she or he had been subjected were usually recorded. The overwhelming majority break down into three main categories: escorted by an honorable person, usually

Table 7.2

Term Imposed versus Actual Length of Stay in Prison (in Months)

	Hamburg spinhouse 1669–1708	Amsterdam spinhouse 1678–1725	Delft *tuchthuis* (1675–1752)	
			Men	Women
Average term imposed	46.3	27.1	138.6	101.9
Average actual stay	30.9	18.0	63.9	84.1

a court servant; escorted by the executioner or his servant; and escorted by the executioner and subjected to a corporal penalty by him. The latter two dishonorable categories included 34.2 percent of the women and 84.4 percent of the men. The difference was entirely due to the fact that male prisoners were more often subjected to a corporal penalty in addition to confinement. These figures confirm that the Hamburg spinhouse was an infamous institution.

In the Dutch Republic, where less symbolic value was laid on the mere touch of the hangman, prisoners were probably always escorted by a court servant.[98] But they often received a supplementary physical punishment. Among the offenders condemned to imprisonment in Amsterdam between 1650 and 1750 (to anticipate the discussion of court records), 1,323 were also subjected to a public corporal penalty. The corporal punishment did not precede the prison stay. The scaffold was only erected one to four times a year in Amsterdam, and on justice day offenders whose sentences included a corporal penalty were taken from the rasphouse or spinhouse, the penalty was administered on the scaffold, and they were returned to their respective house.

Entry books also tell us when and why a convict left prison. Some of this information, such as death rates and the data on escapes, is pertinent to the subject of internal life. With respect to imprisonment as a judicial sanction, it is more important to relate the original imposed to actual length of stay. Table 7.2 presents these data for the convicts in the respective institutions (inmates with life sentences, who were only a few everywhere, are excluded).

The differences between Delft and the spinhouses are marked again. They are largely due to the imprisonment of more serious convicts in Delft. The female convicts there had received relatively heavy sentences, too. The high incidence of escapes among the males (28.3%) further explains why the average stay of the women was longer. The few men imprisoned at Hamburg had an average term of 122 months, while the actual length of their stay averaged 54 months.

A comparison of imposed term and actual length enables us to test

Rusche's thesis about arbitrariness. This thesis was criticized in the previous section with reference to the Amsterdam system of reductions. In the Dutch Republic it was uncommon for prisoners sentenced to a specific term to be kept for a longer time. Only the stay of those committed at the request of relatives could be prolonged, following a request for renewal. In the Amsterdam spinhouse 3.9 percent stayed longer than their term, and these may have been private prisoners. That was certainly the case at Delft, where the 3.3 percent staying longer than their original term were all persons committed by relatives, except for three cases due to peculiar circumstances. As the system of reductions spread from the rasphouse to other Dutch institutions, shortened stays became common. The entry books of the Amsterdam spinhouse refer to a shortening of terms for 34.6 percent of the inmates. The total amount of reductions ranged from one to 170 months, but two-thirds of the women involved received reductions of a year or less. The corresponding figures at Delft are 10.1 percent for male convicts (with reductions ranging from four to 96 months) and only 1.4 percent for female convicts. Some underreporting may have occurred here. On the other hand, the fact that the magistrates were unwilling to hand over condemned prisoners to the military in 1696 suggests that they wanted them to serve their full term.[99] If so, they changed their minds forty years later, when they recommended the practice of reduction to other courts (see chapter eight). Since this was toward the end of the period covered by the entry books, the effect is hardly seen there. Systematic shortening of terms was not adopted in the Hanseatic towns. In the Hamburg entry books only two reductions were recorded. The senate determined in 1700 that a woman who had been condemned for life only had to stay for eight more years if she behaved well.[100] In 1715 David Steinauer was granted a reduction of five years, also upon a senate's decree.[101] There are no figures for Bremen, but at the end of the eighteenth century the magistrates expressly rejected a proposal to adopt the reductions system. While recognizing its advantages, they argued that orderly behavior in prison should be achievable without such concessions, and that making the penalty of imprisonment so light would be an injustice to convicts condemned to death.[102] In Pforzheim, on the other hand, delinquents were regularly released without having served their full term, sometimes because of overcrowding, but also for good behavior.[103]

In Hamburg a number of inmates of the spinhouse were kept beyond the expiration of their term. Since this may be taken as a confirmation of Rusche's thesis, the figures for this city must be considered in closer detail. In fact, it was all or nothing in Hamburg. A considerably larger number of prisoners also stayed for a shorter time than their term. Instead of reductions, pardons were common. In some cases, the pardons were granted for betraying escape conspiracies, but more frequently they were granted following a request. During the early years of the spinhouse some of these requests were recorded in the logbook, with comments such as "consented," "refused," "taken into consideration," or "has to stay" added without further explanation.[104] The entry books mention only pardons. No reasons are ever given for keeping prisoners longer than their original term.

Let us first look at the reasons given for pardons. When a pardon was requested by someone other than the prisoner, the petitioner usually stated his readiness to assume his responsibilities with regard to the transaction. Then it was "her husband / father / mother is prepared to take her back," or "his brother / uncle wants to take care of him," or "her previous master promises to supervise her better." In one case a woman was released to visit her mother at her deathbed and take care of her aged father.[105] In line with such reasons for pardons, it was often recorded whether the parents or the husband of an inmate were alive or dead. This provides a clue already. The Hamburg magistrates cherished the household model even more than their colleagues in Holland, both inside and outside of the prison. Since prison life constituted a surrogate family, the prison could only be left for a real family. On the other hand, financial considerations were involved, too. A couple of times, relatives pledged that they would pay a sum of money if the released convict returned to Hamburg.[106] The freedom of some prisoners was more or less bought. Monetary presents upon discharge by inmates or their relatives were recorded several times.[107] In a few cases it was said that the prisoner was set free because he or she was weak and unable to work; in one of these cases the prisoner had been bedridden for four years.[108] But these were in the minority. Thus far, the sources provide a suggestion as to what determined the length of a prisoner's stay: those who served their full term or even were kept after its expiration were unable to marshal the help of relatives or find other means of support.

It is possible to put the thesis of an economically determined arbitrariness versus my alternative hypothesis to a quantitative test. To do this, I will compare the group of convicts who were kept beyond the expiration of their term with the group released earlier than their term. Those whose stay ended by escape, death, or transfer to the pesthouse or jail were excluded from the comparison. Also, I did not want to quibble with the officials involved and granted them a margin of one month. 'Before expiration' and 'after expiration' were defined as differences between imposed term and actual term of more than 30.5 days. The terms, which were coded in months, were multiplied by 30.5. Using this definition, fifty-two prisoners (7 percent of the delinquent population) fell into the 'after expiration' group. There was a broad and relatively regular range of additional incarceration, with two of the inmates staying more than three years longer than their imposed terms. The mean in this group was 294 days. The 'before expiration' group consisted of 325 prisoners (43.7 percent of

Table 7.3

Hamburg Prisoners Released before or after Expiration of Their Imposed Term (1669–1708)

Characteristic	Before Expiration	After Expiration
Average imposed term	55.3 months	21.6 months
Average actual stay	26.6 months	31.2 months
Average age at entry	25.09 years	25.11 years
Percentage of men	7.7%	7.7
Percentage of recidivists	13.2	17.3
Percentage of thieves	18.8	27.7
Percentage condemned by the senate	27.1	9.6
Percentage escorted by honorable person	56.5	83.3
Percentage infected with syphilis	26.8	30.8

the delinquent population). The largest difference between imposed term and actual length was sixteen years, eight months. The mean was two years, 156 days.

If a prisoner's labor power influenced the outcome, we would expect the two groups to show marked differences with respect to other variables such as age and sex. As it turns out, this is not the case, as shown in table 7.3. There was a slight tendency to keep thieves for a longer period, but on the whole, the distribution of types of offenses in the 'before expiration' and 'after expiration' groups does not differ markedly. The only conspicuous difference was with respect to the average imposed term. This is perfectly understandable, since persons with relatively long sentences were unlikely to be kept longer still. Note that the mean imposed term for the 'after expiration' group was one and three-quarter years, which is far from Rusche's "few days." The 'before expiration' inmates cannot have been released because of severe unprofitability, since they remained in the house almost as long as their counterparts did. The figures with respect to imposed term correlate with those with respect to the person escorting the prisoner and the condemning agency. So far for the marked differences. Age and sex would have been significant factors if economic considerations determined early or late release. The similarity between the two groups in these areas, therefore, is highly significant. The differences with respect to recidivism and syphilis are too slight to be considered important. Moreover, with respect to syphilis, if the difference between the two groups was due to economic considerations, it should have been the other way around. Possibly some women who had stayed in the poxhouse had to make up for the time spent out of prison. In only two cases, however, was the duration of the cure longer than the 'after expiration' period served. One inmate, Maria Köhn, was sent to the poxhouse after her term had already expired, and then returned to the spinhouse afterwards.[109] The cases of Cathrin Elisabeth Wiebaus and Maria Brügmans illustrate that a stay in the poxhouse made no difference with respect to the 'after expiration' period. Both women were twenty-three; they were admitted together and also released on the same day, four months after the expiration of their one-year terms. In fact, their cases were similar in every respect except for Maria's stay in the poxhouse for thirty-eight days.[110]

These figures confirm my thesis. Whatever arbitrariness there was was not caused by the wish to keep strong persons in prison and get rid of weaker ones. Those who obtained a pardon were able to marshal the help of relatives or friends. The others had no one to care about them, and some may even have been ignorant of their imposed term. Keeping beyond the length of their imposed term may have been the result of carelessness or indifference.[111]

Court Records: Amsterdam   From the information in entry books, we cannot tell how important imprisonment was in the penal system as a whole. An answer to that question is to be found in court records only. We must inquire into the percentage of sentences including confinement as the only penalty or as one of several penalties in a combined sentence. Extensive sets of figures are available for Amsterdam and a few other towns. The data for the Dutch metropolis in particular were collected originally for quite different purposes.

At the beginning of the seventeenth century only about 4 to 5 percent of the sentences pronounced by the Amsterdam court included imprisonment.[112] By the middle of that century its role had become considerable. The figures for the period since 1650 are derived from Sjoerd Faber's project and my own investigation of executions in the city.[113] That is the reason why in table 7.4 the latter numbers will be presented split up into cases that involve a scaffold penalty and those that do not. The cases that do not involve a scaffold penally are usually combined sentences, too, in which imprisonment is supplemented by banishment, for example. In figure 7.1, however, to provide an overview of the percentage of prison sentences among the convictions by the Amsterdam court, 1651–1807, my numbers have been computed anew to include all cases.

The increasing importance of imprisonment within the penal system clearly emerges. Until the beginning of the eighteenth century, about one fifth of all sentences included confinement. Soon afterwards the percentage rose to about 35 to 45 percent, and from about 1760 it remained well above half. Significantly, the percentage of prison sentences among convicts who had also been subjected to a scaffold punishment far exceeded

Figure 7.1

Percentage of Prison Sentences among Convictions by the Amsterdam Court, 1651–1807

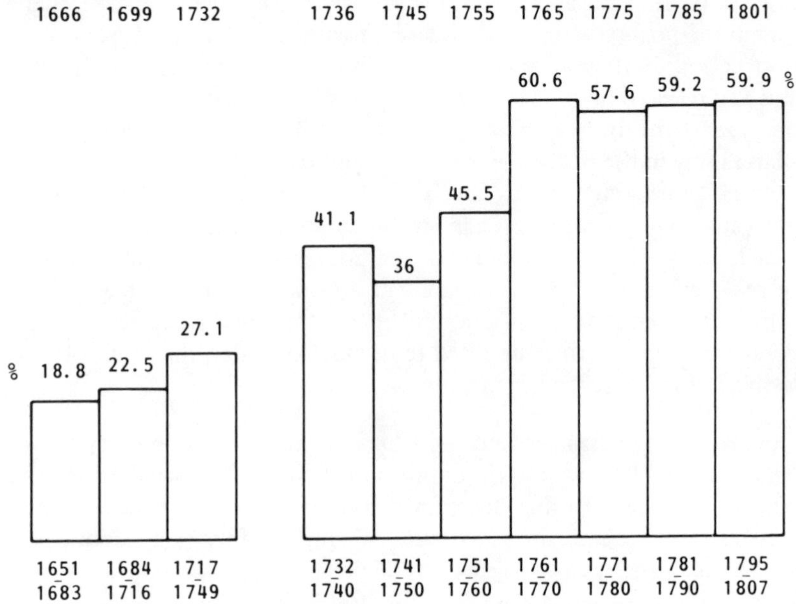

the percentage among all convicts. This means that imprisonment was not considered only appropriate for minor offenders, and it confirms the association of prisons with the penal system. Between 1650 and 1750 the percentage of sentences including confinement among convicts also subjected to scaffold punishment fluctuated between 34 and 54. Since the percentage of public sentences among all convictions rose at the beginning of the eighteenth century, the percentage of scaffold punishments among the prison population rose as well. In the rasphouse, from the 1720s through 1740s, inmates who had also been punished on the scaffold outnumbered those who had not.[114] Women who had been publicly punished were committed to the spinhouse. The workhouse received only an occasional offender from the group that had been punished on the scaffold.

Terms have been discussed with reference to the entry books, but of course they are mentioned in the present source, too. This aspect of judicial imprisonment is important for the long historical view. In so far as medieval jails had been used for penal purposes, the stay had usually been relatively short. Offenders who were put on bread and water in the Dutch Republic only stayed a few weeks or a few months at most. Numbers discussed earlier, such as those for Hamburg, showed that this was not the

Table 7.4

Average Terms for Amsterdam Convicts 1651–1806 (in Months)

Period	Sentences including Scaffold Punishment	Nonpublic Sentences	Total
1651–1683	—	12.7	—
1684–1716	—	22.2	—
1717–1749	—	47.2	—
1651–1660	60.1	—	—
1661–1670	48.6	—	—
1671–1680	47.3	—	—
1681–1690	76.8	—	—
1691–1700	84.1	—	—
1701–1710	75.2	—	—
1711–1720	108.1	—	—
1721–1730	121.3	—	—
1731–1740	161.8	—	83.9[a]
1741–1750	136.0	—	95.7
1751–1760	—	—	96.7
1761–1770	—	—	71.7
1771–1780	—	—	54.9
1781–1790	—	—	52.6
1795–1806	—	—	91.4

[a]1732–1740

case in prison workhouses, again confirming the important role of imprisonment in the penal system of the early modern period. Table 7.4 presents the terms for Amsterdam.

Clearly, the average term was on the rise from the moment when these sets of data begin until about the middle of the eighteenth century. In the three periods for nonpublic cases, terms went from about one year to almost two to almost four; for the scaffold set there was not a continuous rise, but a big leap around 1710. The 1730s were the high point, but Faber's figures, which combine nonpublic and scaffold cases, suggest that the rise continued into the 1750s. Thereafter, the average term declined, only to rise again around 1800. It never went below four years, though. The rise in the first half of the eighteenth century may have been a reaction to a simultaneous drop in the general number of offenders. In this way, the court apparently tried to ensure that the town's prisons would remain reasonably full. Life sentences, which could not be computed, were almost never imposed.[115]

The variable 'length of term' can be broken down for subgroups among prisoners. Not surprisingly, men received terms above the general average and women below it (except in the first period of the nonpublic cases, where it was the other way around, but the difference was insignificant). Both among the public and nonpublic cases, there is no significant relationship between the convict's age and length of term. In the three nonpublic sets, but most notably in the third, length of term correlated with the number of offenses committed, but in the scaffold sets there was no significant relationship. The pattern is less clear when we consider types of offenses. Among the scaffold sets, convicts sentenced for violent crimes received terms far above the average. This may have been because only the most serious cases involved the scaffold. Among the nonpublic sets, no significant relationship was found between length of term and type of offense.

The actual length of a prisoner's stay, of course, was usually shorter than the imposed term. The amounts of reduction for this population are not known.

Court Records: Elsewhere   To supplement the Amsterdam data, there is information from a few ongoing projects and a number of unpublished theses. It is a pity that German historians have not done this kind of work so far, so that comparable data for the Empire are lacking. For Delft, the excerpts from its court records, kept at the archive, permit general calculations.[116] Between 1675, when its prison was opened, and 1811, the end of the Ancien Régime, 445 out of 997 criminal sentences (44.6%) included imprisonment. In Haarlem (1740–1795) the corresponding figures were 112 out of 302 (37%).[117] Among property offenders condemned at Alkmaar (1680–1795) 16 percent of the men, 23 percent of the women and 45 percent of the juveniles had imprisonment as part of their sentence.[118] The court of Enkhuizen, on the other hand, having no *tuchthuis* of its own, imposed a stay in such an institution for the first time in 1792. From 1795 onward Enkhuizen regularly sent delinquents to the Amsterdam rasphouse.[119] These towns were situated in Holland, but *tuchthuizen* were used for penal purposes in other provinces, too. The Court of Gelre pronounced over 50 percent prison sentences in the years 1710–1735, although this declined to about 40 percent in the years 1750–1795.[120] Military judges also increasingly pronounced prison sentences, first for common crimes, later for military offenses as well. The court-martial at The Hague condemned about 400 deserters, out of a total of some 600 cases, between 1790 and 1811. Almost all deserters were imprisoned.[121]

More-detailed information is available for the courts of Leiden and Groningen-City. These data, presented in figure 7.2, show that the use of imprisonment as a penal option varied widely between towns.[122] Clearly, the Leiden judges were less willing to pronounce prison sentences than their Groningen colleagues. The latter even surpassed Amsterdam until about 1720. In both towns the lowest levels were reached at the beginning

Figure 7.2

Percentage of Prison Sentences among Convictions by the Courts of Leiden (1601–1811) and Groningen City (1665–1750)

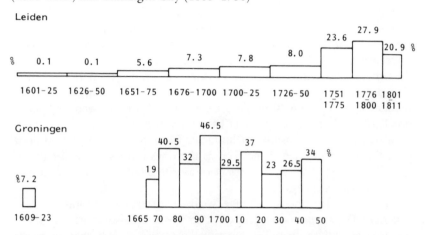

of the seventeenth century; during most of these years their *tuchthuizen* were closed. Groningen shows no particular pattern, but in Leiden there was a steady rise, which only became marked from the middle of the eighteenth century, however.

Honor and Crime:
The German Predicament

Although studies of court records and comparable quantitative investigations on alternative penal options do not exist for the Empire, some qualitative analysis of problems in this area is possible. The notions of honor and crime provide a starting point. We are now back into a mentalities type of study. Before imprisonment could become a common penal sanction in the Empire, a formidable obstacle had to be surmounted. This obstacle was *unehrlichkeit* or infamy. Infamy was a vaguely defined concept, but it had an intense emotional significance. The lines separating honor from its opposite were drawn differently by different groups of people. Ensuing conflicts over who was allowed to associate with whom put their mark upon the history of German prison workhouses. This chapter's final section treats two themes: attempts by the authorities to defeat or circumvent popular notions about the infamy of judicial institutions, and the concomitant association of imprisonment and criminality.

Infamy and the Guilds   In the German countries a broad spectrum of occupational and other social groups—but most notably skinners and executioners—were considered infamous. The origins of and possible explanations for this phenomenon have been discussed elsewhere.[123] During the period when ideas about marginality changed, the stigma of infamy was also imprinted on beggars and vagabonds. Moreover, the *vögte* who had to catch them received it, too. Possibly, marginals came to be considered *unehrlich* precisely because they were hunted by semijudicial agents. These were mostly popular perceptions and attitudes. The authorities, on the other hand, wished to consider only condemned criminals *unehrlich*. This difference in attitudes created an obstacle to the evolution of imprisonment as a penal sanction. As long as the magistrates were obliged to proclaim the honorable character of *zuchthäuser*, it was hard for them to imprison even an occasional delinquent. Consequently, more traditional punishments continued to be seen as the ones most suitable for thieves and their ilk. It was only as a result of a protracted struggle over infamy that these views changed.

To try to understand this change, we have to start with notions of honor generally. Four types of sources of infamy may be distinguished. First, it was associated with various occupational groups such as barbers or beggar catchers. In the case of the latter, the first source overlapped with the second: criminals and anyone connected with detecting and punishing them were infamous. Consequently, the public tended to consider any servant of authorities with policing tasks as *unehrlich*. The *untervogt* of Osterstade in the Bremen territory, for example, complained to the senate that the town's smiths would not let his son present his masterpiece, though he had been well-trained in Hamburg and was engaged to the daughter of a guild member.[124] Third, ethnic and religious minorities received the stigma of dishonor. These included Jews, gypsies, and in Baltic towns members of the native Wendic population. A fourth possible source was one's own behavior. Any deviant sexual act, and especially the birth of an illegitimate child, entailed infamy. A few Bremen examples may again serve as illustrations. In 1616–1617 the shoemaker J. Vischbeck was expelled from his guild because his child was born some twenty weeks after his wedding. The same thing happened to the baker Berent Cappelmann in 1623; his dismayed colleagues nailed boards to his windows. In both cases the expelled members were supported by the senate, which caused the guilds to appeal to the *reichskammergericht*. The Imperial court confirmed the senate's judgment that the persons concerned were to be readmitted after paying a fine. The guilds remained discontent with this solution. In 1647 the senate had to force the bakers to accept Berent Cappelmann's son Cord—the son born precipitately—as a master. In 1726, on the other hand, they confirmed the expulsion of the shoemaker Johann Drake for a similar offense to Berent Cappelmann's. But this confirmation was because he had insulted established masters, and the senate added that his children should be considered honorable.[125]

These examples show how deeply these matters were felt. Similar cases were recorded throughout the German-speaking world. Infamy descended from father to son and became attached to anyone associated with a dishonorable person. This was true for all four sources. Thus, bastards were *unehrlich,* as were the sons of skinners, beggar catchers, and condemned thieves. The crucial point is that these attitudes were felt most deeply and exclusively by the settled lower and lower-middle classes, notably by guild members. That explains the guilds' readiness to expel offenders. While everyone might suffer from sanctions such as moral disapproval and avoidance of social contact, a more concrete sanction threatened guild members. This exclusion threat had a geographic dimension, too. The Hamburg guilds, for example, supervised the behavior of colleagues in nearby Oldesloe. If the latter group accepted a bastard as a master, their whole guild became tainted and no apprentice or journeyman from Oldesloe would be accepted in Hamburg.[126] In this way, artisans of entire regions became antagonists because of real or imagined irregularities in the past. By 1700 all red-tanners in the Empire were divided into two parties, each calling the other *unredlich* (implying a slightly milder form of infamy). Both parties considered the tanners of Sweden, Denmark, and the Netherlands *unredlich,* because they accepted anyone who asked for work.[127]

Urban and territorial authorities were the guilds' active opponents in these matters. During the early modern period, governments continually tried to restrict the scope of infamy and to curb the degree to which it was applied, without entirely abolishing the notion. Understandably, the authorities were primarily concerned about the status of their own employees. Yet, the Bremen examples show that they were also keen on asserting their dominance over the guilds.[128] The guilds considered the persistent policies to make infamous groups into honorable craftsmen as attempts to downgrade the artisanate. Rather than giving way, their exclusiveness increased in reaction to this opposition: "the fervid moral preoccupation of the guilds, like their social and economic restrictiveness, seems mainly to have developed in the seventeenth and eighteenth centuries."[129]

This subject deserves a more elaborate study, but we have to focus here on the consequences for the history of prison workhouses. The magistrates of the first German towns with a *zuchthaus,* Bremen, Lübeck, Hamburg, and Danzig, did what seemed the most logical thing to them: they proclaimed these institutions to be *ehrlich.* Had they not done so, the houses would probably have been deprived of an income from charitable gifts as well as from board money for wealthy prisoners. The main argument to sustain the proclamation was that dishonor was only tied to crime. Persons to avoid were professional thieves and robbers, notably those who had been corporally punished by the executioner. Alcoholics and licentious youths might be unmannered and beggars obnoxious, but they were not infamous. Indeed, many journeymen themselves, roaming on their grand tour, upset public order. They gambled and quarreled and sometimes even begged.[130] As long as no more than an occasional minor offender was imprisoned upon a court order, the institutions retained their honorable status. The authorities' argument is reproduced by most German authors who write on the history of imprisonment. Being legal historians, they take it at face value. However, emotions cannot simply be legislated. The authors ignore the crucial fact that the authorities always had a hard time defending the idea of the honesty of *zuchthäuser*. Just as in other matters, the respectable working classes had a different estimation of the subject. To them, the stereotypically conceived way of life of beggars entailed infamy. In addition, many women and some men were committed to the *zuchthäuser* because of loose morals. They were suspected of the very behavior which, when exhibited by guild members, led to expulsion. Thus, a duality of attitudes developed. The authorities proclaimed the honesty of prison workhouses and families having someone inside wanted this to be so. But to the working population at large, the institutions were tainted with *unehrlichkeit*.

My idea of dual attitudes is perfectly compatible with Mack Walker's analysis. His is the most perceptive study of the imprint the guilds and their notions of honor made upon German society. According to Walker, *ehrlichkeit* was essentially the ethic of the geographically immobile urban artisans. They suspected everyone who moved about—merchants, nobles, and marginals—of sexual promiscuity, whereas they considered the peasants simply uncivilized. The influence of this ethic, and the power of guilds generally, was greatest in so-called 'home towns.' Walker defines them as towns with a maximum of ten to fifteen thousand inhabitants, and either independent or situated in a small territory. They differed from the bigger cities in terms of their relatively uncomplex social stratification, and from small towns in the larger territories inasmuch as the latter were subject to a tighter control from above. Only in the home towns, therefore, did the organized trades have a strong grip upon the government, which often caused guild prescriptions to attain the status of official administrative rules. The bigger cities witnessed a tripartite social division between patriciate, *bürgerschaft*, and noncitizens, and the urban government was usually in the hands of the wealthy. Such was the case in the Hanseatic towns; also in Hamburg, except in the years of political crisis at the end of the seventeenth century. Significantly, almost no home town had a prison workhouse.[131] It was, of course, to be expected that especially the larger towns would erect one, but in the eighteenth century territorial rulers also established them in small places. These rulers and their civil servants, together with the leading strata in the bigger towns, formed the group of movers-and-doers, as Walker calls them. Their mental world was the opposite of that of the home townspeople. The latter relied on community sanctions instead of judicial measures, relative to their fellow citizens, but as for marginals, they preferred the traditional method of chasing them away to imprisonment. In the mental world of the home townspersons, marginals belonged to the class of movers-and-doers, too. In this way, the administrators and the inmates of prison workhouses were linked: both stood apart from the small domain of purity.

All this meant that in cities with a prison workhouse in the seventeenth century patriciate and artisanate were caught in a cultural conflict. Respectable workers may have acquiesced in the foundation of *zuchthäuser*, but they refused to have anything to do with them. A series of incidents in Bremen testify to this. In 1646, during the brief period of the second *zuchthaus*, an agreement was concluded on *rass* making. The town contracted with Johan Schnakenborg to instruct the prisoners in this trade. Inmates who had completed a three-year training period would receive their certificate from the city's chancellery. It was stated explicitly that both the senate and the *bürgerschaft* had agreed to this procedure. The guilds were warned not to criticize Schnakenborg because of his birth, training, or present behavior, and the authorities promised to protect him against anyone who would hinder him in the practice of his trade.[132] He surely needed this help and protection, because the city's *rass* makers soon protested. It is difficult to reconstruct in detail the ensuing conflict, since the documents referring to it are damaged and incomplete.[133] It seems to have broken out in January 1648, when Bremen's prison actually lay in ruins. As I suggested in chapter three, the artisans in particular may have felt satisfaction with God's destruction of the second *zuchthaus*. Possibly, Schnakenborg continued to instruct a few prisoners in a provisional room. The guild called the employment of a journeyman *rass* maker from Hamburg as a servant in the institution a kidnapping from his actual master. Schnakenborg was accused of incompetence, interloping, and ruining the guild trade. The fear of unfair competition must have been involved, but as we have seen, prison labor could seldom compete with free labor. Psychological and economic motives were intertwined in the guild's objections. Several times its representatives referred to the infamous character of Schnakenborg's business. An exchange of journeymen would stain the guild and create the danger that Bremen artisans would be considered *unehrlich* elsewhere, which would imperil them economically.

The sequence of events is a little unclear. Immediately after hearing the guild's objections, in January 1648 the senate decided not to yield, even intending to punish certain *rass* makers by whom they felt insulted. In October 1651, however, both parties agreed that a guild master or an experienced journeyman would instruct the prisoners in *rass* making. The guilds were promised they would not be burdened with infamous journeymen.[134] But in September 1654 the Bremen magistrates and the *zuchthaus* administrators were requested to defend themselves at the

Imperial Court in an appeal case started by the *rass* makers. Neither the details of this case nor its resolution have been documented.[135] The next surviving record is an agreement of 1671, when another *rass* maker, Frerich Ludwig Freese, was contracted to live in the *zuchthaus* and instruct the prisoners. It was not stated whether he was also a member of the guild.[136]

In the first half of the eighteenth century, conflicts centered around the position of the master of discipline, or *zuchtvogt*. Since part of his duty was to administer physical punishments to the prisoners, his job was considered particularly infamous. Again, the magistrates reacted by constantly repeating that the office was *ehrlich* and that no infamy whatsoever was attached to it. Successive masters of discipline who came from outside Bremen were granted citizenship. On the other hand, on several occasions the senate refused them official certificates stating that their children were admissable into guilds. In individual cases the magistrates promised to intervene with a guild; for example, in 1724 on behalf of the master of discipline Johann Asendorp, who sought admission to the guild of boatmen.[137] The office continued to be viewed negatively in the second half of the eighteenth century.[138]

Delinquents in Prison   These examples illustrate the sensitivities involved. The authorities were never completely successful in asserting the honesty of prison workhouses. Confining thieves and similar delinquents there would make this task even more difficult. Still, the idea of imposing prison sentences on such offenders was being considered in the Empire in the second half of the seventeenth century. The Hamburg solution has been discussed. The magistrates erected a new and separate institution, the infamous character of which was flatly acknowledged. It seems as if Bremen intended to follow this example, but the extant sources are not conclusive on the subject. The need for two differentiated houses had apparently been felt from the beginning. In 1621–1622 there were plans for a separate workhouse, presumably for the less serious cases.[139] When the third *zuchthaus* was built, the senate decided it would consist of two separate institutions. This decision, however, was not put into effect: in 1656 there was talk of imprisoning strong beggars in towers, because there was no workhouse.[140] The question was raised anew in 1715. In May the senate had condemned one Johann Horn *ad ergastulum*, but there was no suitable room for offenders like him in prison. Thereupon, four senators were commissioned to report on the possibilities for reconstruction. In July it was decided to equip the town's prison in such a way "that criminals and those condemned by justice can be held there safely and that dangerous consortings of the inmates are prevented."[141] The project appears to have been too costly. Similar ideas were expressed a decade later. In 1726 there had been disturbances during the execution of corporal penalties and it was proposed to make room for flogged delinquents in prison. A year later there was talk of a separate workhouse for delinquents whose death sentence had been commuted.[142] In the end, no new institution was erected.

Yet, the Bremen prison became a place for the confinement of delinquents. The chronicler Koster mentions a few seventeenth-century cases, beginning in 1650 with a thief whose death sentence had been commuted. He was a minor and the son of a citizen. The other cases were special, too, such as that of a prostitute who had tied her four-year-old child to her body and jumped into the water. They were saved, whereupon the woman was committed to the *zuchthaus* and the child to the orphanage.[143] These persons had not been touched by the executioner. In 1694 the senate refused to accept a female thief, condemned by the court at Celle, who had twice been publicly whipped in Hannoverian territory. The Bremen house, they said, had no room for delinquents who had been punished on the scaffold. In 1727 the dismayed parents of a woman sentenced to prison for blasphemy requested that her penalty be commuted to a fine. A woman who had been committed at the request of the court at Stade in 1731 and who had escaped in 1734 was caught stealing in Bremen territory a year later and imprisoned anew. She was released in 1742.[144] In 1747–1748 and 1756 the earliest recorded *inquisiten* (persons subjected to a criminal investigation) were imprisoned upon a senate sentence. In 1756 the offender in question, Gesche Bringmans, had confessed a number of thefts.[145] Several documents from the 1760s also refer to imprisonment by the senate for theft. I. H. Schufert and his mother had additionally been exposed, with a sign reading "book-thief." Schufert was condemned for life.[146] At the end of the eighteenth century Wagnitz confirmed that most inmates of the Bremen *zuchthaus* were condemned for property offenses. Women who had stolen from their employer were first exposed for half an hour wearing a neck iron.[147]

The Bremen records include one counterexample. In 1774 the senate condemned a Jew to be whipped and branded and to perform forced labor for the rest of his life. Instead of imprisoning him, they requested the Hannoverian government to employ the man at their fortifications. The request was denied. Their garrison, Hannover replied, had no use for such publicly punished and consequently highly infamous persons. Only *ehrliche* peasants condemned for minor offenses at short terms worked at their fortifications, and it would be improper to expose them to the company of serious delinquents.[148] Was the combination of scaffold punishments and Jewish religion simply too infamous? It was not recorded what Bremen did with this convict following the negative reply to its request.

The evolution in Bremen was drawn out longer than in Hamburg, because Bremen never undertook to establish a second house. The Hamburg authorities had to struggle with the problem of infamy, nevertheless. The earliest references date from the period before the opening of the spinhouse. Already in 1626 the senate found it necessary to order the bombazine makers to accept ex-prisoners, if the latter had been industrious during their captivity and were of honorable birth and reputation. Three years later the provisors and the guild concluded an agreement, the text of which has not been preserved. In 1634 there were complaints that apprentices who had completed their training in the *zuchthaus* had been rejected by several masters. The representatives of the guild claimed ignorance and promised to investigate the matter. They confirmed the earlier agreement and declared that they would take the present work boss and his successors to be honorable masters of the bombazine makers.[149] Defending the honesty of the *zuchthaus,* the provisors took the familiar position that it could only be damaged when criminals were admitted. In 1655 they gave three reasons for rejecting persons who had been touched by the executioner: so that respectable people should not be reluctant to commit their relatives to the house; so that inmates who learned a trade there should not run into trouble later; and, actually the first reason, so that the provisors themselves should not be scoffed at "as if they ruled over thieves."[150] This quotation forms a perfect illustration of the mentality under scrutiny here. In the Netherlands it was never considered that the dishonor attached to prisoners could ascend upwards to the regents. In the Empire it was so considered. In the popular view, the administrators of a criminal prison were accessories of a sort: as if they ruled an independent sea robber town, where the magistrates, of course, were pirates, too.

When Hamburg opened the spinhouse, the older prison became more honorable by contrast, at least for a time. Even the inmates themselves were reported to be solicitous of its honorable character. In 1672 Maria Wageners was committed there for begging, but when it became known that she had been publicly whipped three years earlier, her fellow prisoners refused her company. She was transferred to the new institution.[151] From then on it became routine that people who were picked up as beggars but who had been touched by the executioner on an earlier occasion were taken to the spinhouse instead of the *zuchthaus.*[152] Neither did the latter institution accept persons who had already been inmates of the former, while it happened the other way around several times.[153] The general memory with regard to infamy must have been very acute, indeed. Dorothe Fritz stayed in the spinhouse from February 1687, when she was twenty-three, until March 1691. In 1705 when she was caught begging and delivered to the *zuchthaus,* she was immediately transferred to the spinhouse. She was recognized, in spite of the fact that she now called herself Anna Dorothe Berens.[154]

The Empire Follows   In the Baltic towns the triangle of prisons, honor, and crime led to similar problems. The Danzig authorities also stressed the institution's honorable character. Despite this, one group of inmates were imprisoned upon a court's sentence, but they were only minor offenders. An entry book covering the years 1630–1641, still extant in Von Hippel's time, listed the condemned inmates in a separate 'black' register. In the second half of the seventeenth century a few prisoners condemned by the town's supreme judicial body entered the house. In 1690–1691 a rasphouse for infamous criminals was opened, but it is unclear whether this was a separate ward of the original *zuchthaus* or an entirely new institution.[155] The East-Prussian town of Königsberg, which established a prison system in 1691, apparently imitated Danzig in founding one institution for beggars and minor offenders, and another for serious delinquents. In this case, too, it is unclear whether they were at separate locations.[156] Lübeck opened a prison before Danzig or Königsberg, but was the last of the three to solve the problem of infamy. Already in the first half of the seventeenth century the senate was prepared to commit delinquents to the *zuchthaus* at St. Anne's, but its provisors resisted. In 1631 they declined the committal of an unspecified jailed person, and in 1667 two "street robbers" who had been in jail for more than a year and a half.[157] In 1690, on the other hand, a thief condemned at Lüneburg was admitted. Still, in 1727, a delinquent from Lauenburg who had been in the hands of the executioner was refused.[158] In the meantime, plans to establish a second house had been contemplated. As early as 1686 the senate, apparently inspired by Hamburg, had decided to establish a separate spinhouse in the St. Anne institution. This decision was not implemented. In 1724–1725 there were plans to build a prison for "thieves and other delinquents" who had been "condemned to public works and not to death." From 1759 onward the planning became more serious. A special committee was set up, which appears to have solicited designs for a new prison from several architects. One of them proposed to build a tower with seven floors, each floor making up a separate ward. A main building at the base of the tower would consist of the two stories and contain the personnel quarters. This design might have become a competitor to Bentham's, but it was not realized. Lübeck finally acquired its separate prison for condemned delinquents in 1778 adjacent to the older institution.[159]

Echoes of a now familiar struggle were heard sometimes in the vast area south of the North Sea and Baltic coasts. Orders to admit former prisoners into guilds or prohibitions to call them dishonored were issued at Spandau in the 1710s, München in 1748, and repeatedly by the Austrian administration during the eighteenth century.[160] More research is needed to determine their context. The rest of the Empire did not simply have to repeat the Northern experience. In the course of the eighteenth century the structural conflict over imprisonment lost its sharpness. Governments followed a pattern of designating separate wards for delinquents, and generally increased their control over the artisanate. This paved the way for an influx of condemned offenders into prison workhouses. Still another factor may have been responsible for the original delay in this development. A significant difference between the Dutch and Hanseatic towns is that the latter had a large number of lawyers in their councils. That can partly explain why Germans found it more difficult at first to condemn delinquents into *zuchthäuser.* Lawyers cherished accepted legal rules, which did not refer to imprisonment as a penal sanction. Dutch *schepenen* were less scrupulous in this regard. From the end of the seventeenth century, an increasing number of German legal authors recommended the incarceration of thieves and their ilk.[161] Thus, imprisonment as a penal sanction acquired a legal base in the Empire. An issue with respect to the Celle *zuchthaus* is symptomatic of the change. The house's ordinance was to refer to prisoners who had been in the hands of the executioner and it was first proposed to add "as a rule this will not be the case." In the final draft this clause was omitted.[162]

In the second half of the eighteenth century, criminal offenders were mentioned as inmates of *zuchthäuser* in several places in the Empire.[163] To Carl Eberhard Wächter, who published an essay on prisons in 1786, this was a matter of course. He made a distinction between inmates committed for reasons of *polizey* and those committed through the exercise of criminal justice: "the frequent use of the *zuchthaus*-punishment in criminal cases makes *zuchthäuser* extremely necessary nowadays."[164] Wagnitz adopted his definition and used it to differentiate the Hamburg *zuchthaus* from the spinhouse. He visited most German institutions in the late 1780s, and found the inmates were often thieves, swindlers, and prostitutes. His report on the Silesian *zuchthaus* at Brieg, for example, listed 1,141 committals, including men and women, between 1779 and 1789; 678 of them were thieves.[165] In the survey undertaken by Bremen in 1799, several towns reported criminal offenders among inmates. At Copenhagen, for example, inmates included persons whose death sentence had been commuted and who had received infamous physical punishments instead, as well as minor offenders who had been subjected to 'honorable' penalties.[166]

Thus, by the end of the eighteenth century, imprisonment was a common penal sanction in the Empire, too. This development coincided with the spread of carceral institutions. The prison experience had become characteristic everywhere except in the small world of the home towns.

1. Rasphouse coin (Amsterdam Historical Museum; photo: J. Wit).

2. Token for licensed begging (Amsterdam Historical Museum; photo: J. Wit).

3.   Cornelis van der Voort, regents of the Amsterdam rasphouse, 1618 (Amsterdam Historical Museum).

4.   Philip van Dijk, regentesses of the Amsterdam spinhouse, 1728 (Amsterdam Historical Museum).

5. Two rasping prisoners (From Dapper, 1663; photo: University Library, Amsterdam).

6. Sts. Raspinus and Ponus welcome the Jesuits at the gate (From Scheible, 1850: drawing after the original broadsheet; photo: University Library, Amsterdam).

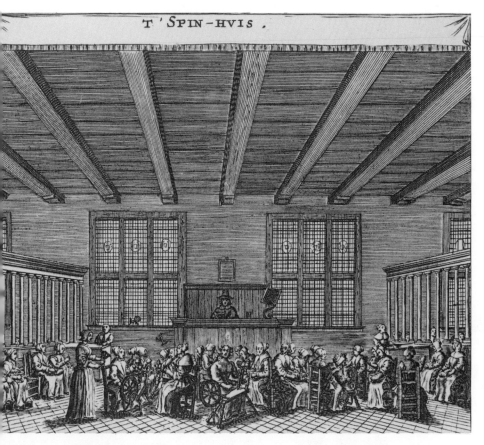

T 'SPIN-HVIS ,

7.   Interior of the Amsterdam spinhouse (From Von Zesen, 1664; photo: University Library, Amsterdam).

8.   Claus Knopf's mark (Staatsarchiv Hamburg).

10.　Gate of the Amsterdam rasphouse (Photo: Pieter Spierenburg).

(Left:) 9.　*Zucht-und spinnhaus* at Lübeck, opened 1778 (Photo: Pieter Spierenburg).

(overleaf): 11.　Gate of the combined almshouse and prison at Haarlem, presently in the Frans Hals Museum (Photo: *Monumentenzorg,* Haarlem).

8

THE PRISON EXPERIENCE
Internal Life from Above
and from Below

Internal life in prison deserves attention for at least two reasons. For a mentalities study such as the present one, it is a central subject. Historians have told us how preindustrial peasants lived and worked, what artisans thought and did, and in which way vagabonds at large spent their days. Comparable studies on prisoners are lacking. Second, the subject is equally relevant to the history of penal systems. Controlling the sequence of events within a prison is a form of enforcement of judicial sanctions, and that has always been somewhat problematic. Banished offenders may return and scaffolded delinquents may not behave as docilely as judges would like. With imprisonment, however, the problem acquired greater proportions. Courts had to ensure that their sentences were complied with day to day. Internal life being such a central theme, I was constantly on the lookout for whatever the records might disclose about it.

Prison life can be viewed from above and from below: from the angle of the ideal order which authorities, administrators, and personnel wished to impose on it, and from the angle of the activities of the inmates, who accommodated themselves to this order or revolted against it. The distinction serves an analytical purpose, though in reality the two aspects are inseparable. Disciplinary punishment, for example, originated from above, but as a rule it was a reaction to disobedience or insubordination. But, an acknowledgement that the two aspects are inextricably interwoven cannot do away with the necessity of imposing order on our data. That is the major purpose of the above-below dichotomy. Moreover, to moderate it, I am distinguishing an intermediate category: aspects of institutional life which were either influenced to an equal extent from above and from below, or which could hardly be influenced at all. An intriguing episode in which social tensions that originated in the outside world influenced the world of the prison completes this chapter.

References to internal life were not divided evenly through the extant sources for the towns studied. Scattered information is found in the sentences and interrogations of the Amsterdam court. The records of the

Hamburg spinhouse during the forty years studied were valuable, too. For the eighteenth century, I mainly relied on one particularly rich source: the logbooks of the Delft regents. The first begins in 1677, but for the first forty years or so, little was recorded. From then on there was a report on almost every meeting, except during the 1740's. These sources, together with a few findings in other archives, allowed me to construct a more or less coherent picture.

This chapter deals with the most neglected theme in prison history. On the world inside the detention centers of our own time we are better informed; through investigations by criminologists or journalists and through books by ex-convicts. In historical writing life inside prison has hardly been a subject at all. It is practically absent from the literature on early modern carceral institutions. Authors writing before 1970 simply lacked an interest in the theme, but the situation is not much better in the recent literature on nineteenth-century penitentiaries. Discipline and surveillance are central to Foucault's work, for example, but he primarily discusses the directives issued from above and programs developed in the world outside. Since he did no research in the archives, he is hardly able to tell what happened within the walls. In contrast to Foucault, Patricia O'Brien wanted to write a "history of the prison from the inside out."[1] Her study of French penal institutions in the nineteenth century provides the major point of comparison for the data and conclusions of this chapter. She discusses, among other things, the inmate subculture, sexual life in prisons, work and discipline, and the interaction between prisoners and guards. Even this rich study seldom penetrates into the experience of individual prisoners, though. O'Brien's reconstruction of the inmate subculture, for example, is basically the story of what the staff thought went on. Even the guards, who must have known quite well what really occurred, are rarely heard. O'Brien cannot be blamed for this; it is the result of shortcomings of her sources. Early modern documents, such as the logbooks of the Delft and Hamburg administrators, are much better resources. From a statistical point of view they may be less than satisfactory, but they inform us about actions and thoughts of individual prisoners.[2] Because there is almost no information to be gathered from the existing literature, this chapter is based for nearly 100 percent on archival records.

Prison Order

When historians confront a hierarchy, they are used to proceeding from the top down. I will follow that pattern here: in this case it is the most logical way to proceed. Generally, the more powerful are able to influence the actions of the less powerful to a much greater degree than vice versa.

This is especially so in the case of a prison, where the convicts are by far the weakest party in the game. Consequently, the ways in which the other parties tried to influence their behavior must get priority.

Prison builders are the first persons to influence the experience of the inmates, though it is an indirect influence. Nothing resembling the fervid debates on the architecture of prisons in later times has been recorded for the early modern period. Early modern arrangements represented a compromise between the demands of forced labor and the need for security. To subject the inmates to a regime was certainly considered important; the structure of the building mattered less. The architectural model adhered to in Holland differed somewhat from the Hanseatic model. The first made the courtyard central. It was surrounded by cells denoted as *hokken,* which may be translated as "cages." Their average size was about twenty to forty square meters and they housed from four to twelve inmates each.[3] Each one had a latrine. Only the most serious offenders stayed in these cages, and they almost never left them. They worked and slept there and received their meals through small openings in the doors or walls. Where rasping was done, this group of offenders made up the raspers. They were given a few logs at a time in their cages, while lighter work, such as weighing or chopping wood, was done in the courtyard.

Even horses saw the inside of early modern prisons, since they dragged the redwood trees through the gates into the courtyard.[4] The courtyard was also the location of the whipping post and for the inmates of adjacent cages it was the only source of fresh air—a major concern of reformers beginning in the late eighteenth century.[5] In addition to the cages and the courtyard, many prisons had large halls, separate for women and men, that were usually reserved for cloth work. Men condemned for lesser offenses and women performed their daily tasks there. As a rule, these prisoners slept in dormitories, each with a number of bedsteads, or 'cribs.' In the Amsterdam spinhouse most cribs were shared by three women.[6]

The custom of letting prisoners work and sleep in the same room was not adopted in the Hanseatic towns. There, during the day, men as well as women stayed in places called workshops. The women slept in dormitories, two per bedstead. In the Hamburg spinhouse every man was locked up in an individual cell for the night. The Bremen *zuchthaus* had such cells, too, but each one had two beds for four men. Neither in Hamburg nor in Dutch prisons did I find references to men sharing a bed.[7] Although the Hanseatic prisons had courtyards, too, they do not seem to have been as central as in Dutch prisons.

Prison Regimes   Everywhere the regime centered around forced labor. Next to the loss of one's freedom, the obligation to work was the second most important element of the prison experience, influenced from above. According to the ordinances, workdays could vary from about ten to twelve hours, which is comparable to what was required from free laborers. The idea was to subject the inmates to a regular and precise schedule. In addition to working hours, there were praying hours and periods devoted to meals. Most ordinances were as detailed and methodical about schedules as the nineteenth-century ones discussed by Foucault. We should not automatically assume, though, that these texts reflected reality.

Forced labor meant that a minimum output was required. From the extant sources it is hard to tell exactly what was demanded from spinsters or weavers, but we do know this in the case of rasping. The unit measured was always the output of two raspers, because they worked together with one rasp saw, which had a handle at both sides. The two had to synchronize their movements into a collective rhythm. In 1597 a pair of strong convicts in Amsterdam produced sixty pounds of rasped wood a day, while the least productive pair achieved forty. From the early seventeenth century until the end of the eighteenth, the output required from a pair of strong inmates was set at fifty pounds.[8] Comparable requirements were referred to in Bremen.[9] Prisoners producing more usually received a small sum of money, which could be spent to buy items from the indoor father. In Amsterdam special prison coins were used for this purpose.[10] We do not know how common it was to earn this money, since our only source is the Haarlem account of 1635. Payments for "over-rasping," varying from 13 stuivers and 8 pennies to 14 guilders and 19 stuivers, were listed seven times during that year. These were collective payments and it was not recorded how many prisoners shared them.[11] Payments for overwork were also mentioned in Bremen, Delft, Danzig, and Spandau.[12]

Some privileged prisoners were temporarily entrusted with special tasks, including assistance to the personnel or services to the court. The service to the court usually consisted of guarding a fellow convict in jail. As a rule, the latter was awaiting the execution of a death sentence and was suspected of suicide plans. The vigilance of the guard, who was temporarily transferred to the jail, earned him a shortening of his term. This practice was recorded in Delft as well as in Amsterdam. In both towns it was customary to select inmates for such service whose term was nearly over, so that they could be released immediately after finishing this job.[13] Assistance to the personnel was performed within the prisons. In most Dutch *tuchthuizen* the indoor father selected two or three inmates who helped him hand out equipment and serve meals and the like. A similar practice was used in the Hanseatic towns. In Bremen in 1748 it was determined that the work boss, the master of discipline, and the *speisevater* each might choose a prisoner to assist him.[14] An inmate of the Hamburg spinhouse who was employed as a kitchen maid in 1696 took advantage of the situation and fled. Of course, she lost her privileges when she was returned.[15]

Prisoners from rich families who lodged in separate rooms or wards, were exempt from work—from the regular labor program as well as privileged jobs. In the eighteenth century, when the secret ward in the Amsterdam rasphouse was reserved for men convicted of sodomy, they, too, were exempt from forced labor. They were the only delinquent prisoners outside the forced labor system.[16] I found no records explicitly telling why they were kept separately. Some historians assume that this was to prevent the 'infection' of other prisoners with homosexuality, but it is also possible that it was feared that, if they stayed with the latter, they would be heavily harassed, as sex offenders are often harassed in today's prisons. Around 1750 the regents complained that too many people had been committed to the secret ward during the previous twenty years. The administrators disliked this because it lessened the income of the house, but they also pretended to have a measure of empathy with the men staying there: "these unfortunate prisoners live separately in a gloomy dungeon, barred from access by anybody, without fire in winter and devoid of an occupation all year long. Many are committed for life and they have no other company but their conscience which accuses them."[17] Interestingly, the case of these sodomy convicts anticipated nineteenth-century solitary confinement, which was held to be particularly wholesome by so many reformers then. The exclusive confrontation with one's conscience, the cherished objective of the advocates of solitary confinement in the 1800s, was considered an extra punishment by the Amsterdam regents of 1750.

The monotony of the work program had interruptions. The Christian setting of these institutions dictated a respite from labor on Sundays and other holy days. In Delft secular festivities were recorded, too. In 1765 the prisoners petitioned to be free from work during the week of the fair. After a brief deliberation the regents granted them three days of the requested week.[18] A peculiar festivity took place in 1777. The board decided to celebrate the fact that the institution had formally started as a combined *tuchthuis* and madhouse a hundred years earlier. This seems to have been the earliest recorded centennial celebration in prison history. On September 20 the regents and their wives had supper in the house—in their own room, presumably—together with the indoor father, the steward, and their wives. The inmates were free from work that day and were treated to meat, wine, beer, and tobacco at noon and rice porridge in the evening. Afterwards, the regents recorded that "the day of jubilee" had been passed "in a becoming joy among the prisoners."[19]

Religion   The reason for placing religion in the category of aspects of prison life imposed from above is far from self-evident. Some people entered a prison with deeply felt religious convictions. That is obvious in the case of the remonstrants and Catholics who stayed in the rasphouse's secret ward in 1620–1621. But other delinquents may have felt a need for religious devotion too, as suggested by the admittedly ambivalent case discussed in section four. In that case, a Catholic prisoner insisted on seeing a priest, but, as we shall see, his motives may not have been genuinely religious. In general, personal religious feelings may have been expressed most often when they were opposed to the dominant faith in a particular institution.

The notion that the *tuchthuizen* were meant to save the souls of those gone astray must have contributed to their original image as charitable institutions. In the view of the founding fathers, attending a service or receiving any form of religious instruction was a bonus for a prisoner. As a disciplinary beating was a punishment, the opportunity for spiritual exercise was a present. But presents, too, arrive from above. In the end, so the authorities thought, the entire order to which the inmates were subjected was beneficial to them. This was true of disciplinary punishment, as well, which, though bitter, was a medicine for correcting an unwholesome way of life. Within prisons various kinds of deviants were to be taught obedience, humility, and the right form of behavior generally. Religion had a place in such a project as a matter of course. As long as crime, immoral conduct, and sin were hardly differentiated, the inmates were automatically viewed as ungodly. Inasmuch as they shared this view, contemporaries, too, thought of religion as something which had to be imposed from above.

It may be remembered that Sebastiaan Egberts found the proverbs of Solomon and the books of Ecclesiastes and Jesus Sirach especially suitable for reading in the rasphouse. Hence, it is not surprising that precisely these three texts, together with the book of Wisdom, were published in a separate edition. The first appeared in 1599, the title page specifying that it had been printed "for use in and for the benefit of the *tuchthuis* within the city of Amsterdam." It is no longer extant, but a copy of an edition of 1635 has been preserved.[20] The original owner signed and inscribed: "Dirck Molenwerf / In the year 1651, on June 27, I have arrived here / At La Rochelle."[21] Since no one under that name appears in the court records for 1651, I suppose that "here" does not refer to the rasphouse. Neither are there references in the sources which suggest that released prisoners were allowed to keep these books. Probably, Dirck Molenwerf had purchased it somewhere else and then emigrated to join his fellow Calvinists at La Rochelle. In that case, the three lines he wrote suggest that copies of the book were not only used in prison but also sold to the general public. The public may have bought them in support of the institution, which would explain the word "benefit" in the title.

It seems that the expectations concerning religious instruction were highest during the early years. By the middle of the seventeenth century it was acknowledged that certain groups in the population were lost anyway. In Amsterdam as well as Haarlem the raspers no longer attended Sunday services. The late seventeenth-century instructions for the personnel in Haarlem even suggest that they were not required to say morning and evening prayers. By the middle of the eighteenth century a solution had been found. The Sunday sermon was delivered in one of the cages, so that the inmates of adjacent ones could hear it, too. The weavers and the women were collected in the courtyard.[22] A *ziekentrooster,* a sort of deputy minister, usually took care of this sermon.[23] In the Hanseatic towns, on the other hand, regular ministers visited prisons and preached there. The magistrates placed a greater emphasis on religion in their institutions than the Dutch did. In Hamburg both houses had a separate room called the church, where the inmates assembled on Sundays. Services in the *zuchthaus* around 1630 were even accompanied by music from "students and instrumentalists."[24] Both in Hamburg and Bremen, depending on the period, a minister came to preach each Sunday, every two weeks, or every four. Two or four times a year there was an occasion for a communion.[25]

Religion formed a bridge from the prison to the world outside. The sale of pocket-bibles already suggested that. In Hamburg the general public was invited to attend services with the inmates in the spinhouse church. This practice had the additional advantage of providing another occasion for collections. In addition to the collections, some people paid for a permanent reserved seat. From the first *stellenbuch,* covering the years 1682–1692, we learn that a few seats were reserved for provisors and dignitaries. Others were rented, some for a short time, the majority over the whole period. Blanks indicate seats not rented. For a total of 267 seats there were 113 blanks.[26] Not everyone from outside attended the service from pious motives though. When two men had escaped in 1690, the provisors discussed possible improvements in security. It was noted that church visitors often crowded together during communion and some took this opportunity to hand objects to the inmates.[27] In the eighteenth century, successive *jahrverwalter* had special tickets printed for the invitation of important guests to the service. The date and the invitee's name were to be filled out by hand. Two tickets, for 1733 and 1750, have been preserved.[28] Elsewhere in the Empire this custom was recorded, too. At Celle the 'free community' sat in the middle of the church, between the male and female inmates.[29] In the Dutch Republic such a practice was less common. A public sermon, primarily meant to raise money, was delivered in the Haarlem *tuchthuis,* probably in the almshouse part, until 1614. Then it was decided to collect gifts during special services in two parish churches.[30] In 1701 the Delft regents decided to attend Sunday sermons in turns. They obliged themselves, on penalty of four stuivers, to stay until the hourglass was finished. There was no talk of the general public attending.[31] In 1781, however, John Howard and a small company attended a service in the Rotterdam prison.[32]

The services provided to prisoners were always those of the dominant religion alone. It was only in the course of the eighteenth century that this situation gradually began to change, in connection with a growth of tolerance in society at large. In 1670 the Hamburg senate allowed a Catholic priest to administer communion in the *zuchthaus*. In the case of the spinhouse, as we will see, such events could stir up emotions four decades later. Toward the end of the eighteenth century, however, Catholic clergymen could freely visit their coreligionists in both Hamburg prisons.[33] By that time, Lutheran ministers were allowed to do the same in the *zuchthaus* of Calvinist Bremen.[34] As a result of the religious geography of the Empire, almost everywhere people of different persuasions were incarcerated together. In Augsburg there had been separate prisons for Catholics and Lutherans until 1755. In that year both houses were combined into a new building with separate chapels for each group of inmates. At Pforzheim Catholic prisoners got their own chapel in the 1770s. According to Wagnitz, Lutheran, Reformed and Catholic services were held both there and in the *zuchthaus* at Mannheim.[35] Although the Dutch Republic was noted for its religious tolerance, there were no comparable references in the Dutch prison records I studied. This does not preclude that non-Reformed clergymen paid visits to the *tuchthuizen*.[36]

The religious facilities enjoyed by Christians at the end of the eighteenth century were extended to Jewish prisoners to a lesser degree. We never hear of rabbis visiting the institutions. Jewish inmates of the Hamburg spinhouse were regularly invited, though not forced, to attend Lutheran sermons. Those who refused had the additional advantage of an opportunity for escape while the personnel were at the service. During most of the eighteenth century, converts were baptized with great publicity in the churches of both Hamburg institutions. At the Purim celebration in 1754, on the other hand, the Jewish community were allowed to present kosher food to their brothers and sisters in the spinhouse. In 1781 the senate decreed that Jewish inmates would henceforth be left undisturbed on Sundays and allowed to say prayers on their own holy days.[37] Comparable privileges were recorded in a few other places. Upon a survey by the Münster authorities in 1794, Spandau, Brieg, and Wesel reported that Jewish prisoners were excused from work on Saturdays. Cologne was considering founding a separate *zuchthaus* for them.[38] Jewish inmates of the Amsterdam workhouse were also allowed to rest on the Sabbath, if they produced as much as the Christians during the remaining five days.[39] In the Rotterdam *tuchthuis* they were served mutton instead of pork.[40]

Food   Thus, religion leads to food. The pork problem cannot have been that acute, because meat was served very infrequently. This is not surprising. If meat had been a regular part of their daily meal, prisoners would have been better off than free workers. The earliest prison menu is from the Amsterdam rasphouse in 1659. The menu is given for each day of the week. Sunday: salted meat with carrots or cabbage; Monday: grey peas; Tuesday: green or yellow peas; Wednesday: groats; Thursday:

barley-porridge; Friday: stockfish or salted fish; Saturday: what the fish-market offers. These were the main dishes; it was added that the inmates received buttermilk each night.[41] A list of the food provided by the indoor father Nicolaas van Gelder in the 1740s specified the meals taken at different times of the day. The prisoners received bread and butter each morning. Main dishes were served at noon. They included meat on Sundays, and a little bacon was added. On weekdays the menu was more frugal than in 1659: fish was served only once and the rest of the days the main item was peas, beans, groats, or dry bread. A sauce made of water, fat and vinegar was used to make these items more palatable. No vegetables were mentioned. Evening meals were only served on Sunday and Wednesday. These consisted of warm buttermilk with groats. Another list, dated 1753, was basically the same, except that on Wednesday the prisoners now received beer over their groats.[42] The menus did not refer to drink. According to Wagenaar, every inmate of the rasphouse received two *mingelen* of light beer per day. He called this and their food a normal ship's diet.[43] Thus, a prisoner's diet was as unbalanced and unhealthy as that of contemporary sailors. It was acknowledged that the inmates needed calories in order to work. To achieve this, the officials relied heavily on pulse and corn, supplemented by butter and fat. Meat was a specialty and fresh vegetables were hardly served at all.

Data from other towns are not basically different. In eighteenth-century Delft bread and beans were equally preponderant, supplemented sometimes by cheese. There were no breakfasts at all, just noon and evening meals. Meat was served on Monday instead of Sunday.[44] Prisoners in 1775–1776 were particularly fortunate. In those years the Estates of Holland had provided a bonus of 500 guilders to every ship going out to catch herring and they recommended that all institutions serve as much herring as possible. The Delft magistrates ordered their indoor father to comply with this recommendation.[45] Here we finally have an example of a link between state economic policies and prison workhouses. The situation in the Hanseatic towns was comparable to that in the Dutch Republic. A major difference was that meat was even more of a specialty item. As a rule, it was only offered on a few feast days, such as Easter, together with white bread, which on such days took the place of rye. For the rest, things were pretty similar between the German and Dutch regions. Bremen menus, recorded since 1695, relied heavily on pulse, and cabbage was provided occasionally.[46] The regular diet for the Hamburg *zuchthaus*, recorded in 1749, consisted almost exclusively of groats, beans, and fat. Two minority categories among the inmates, however, received better food.[47]

That serves as a warning. These menus did not necessarily represent everything individual prisoners got. For one thing, wealthy inmates locked up in separate rooms were provided a different regimen altogether. But inmates of the regular wards also often received extra items that were

brought in by relatives or friends. And for everyone there was the possibility of earning some money with overwork. The indoor father or another member of the personnel kept a shop, and with their money,
prisoners could buy not only supplements to their meals but also extras
such as tobacco or candy. Institutional life had to remain frugal though.
In 1761 the Delft regents found it necessary to warn the new indoor father
not to sell in unnecessary quantities. They also told him to adhere to the
prices of the free society, after complaints that his predecessor had charged
his clients too much.[48] Later in the 1760s' it was decided that, as an en-
couragement, every woman would receive two *loot* of tea and every man
one pound of tobacco free every six months.[49]

Irregularities involving food or drink were recorded occasionally. In
Delft in 1775 three men found their bacon rancid and threw it out into
the courtyard, claiming they had fed it to the dogs.[50] A Bremen rule of
1695 stipulated that if sick or dying prisoners ate less than they received,
the leftovers should be returned instead of being divided among the others. This rule was not observed. In 1748 there was talk of leftovers being
sold or kept in a special "sick-basket."[51] Around the same time the Amsterdam regents complained that some inmates of the rasphouse kept a
shop in which they sold all kinds of food. Family or friends illegally
brought in liquor, and prisoners got drunk sometimes.[52]

Discipline: Prevention and Punishment   The possibility of infringe-
ment of the prison order was acknowledged from the beginning. Understandably, prison officials preferred prevention to punishment, and the
records occasionally speak of measures taken to that effect. The foremost
task for the officials was to anticipate conspiracies, and a favorite tactic to
prevent them was to have prisoners change cages regularly. This was recorded in Delft as well as Amsterdam, where changes were mandated
every fortnight.[53] The Delft records twice referred to a convict having
been recruited as a spy.[54] Other preventive measures were matters of routine. Several inspections into the state of repair of an institution were recorded.[55] Correspondence to and from prisoners was to be checked.[56]
Personnel were regularly told to be vigilant when equipment was used for
work that could also be used for breaking out. They were to take good
care that no one kept possession of such equipment overnight.[57] The records I studied contained no references to personnel carrying weapons,
certainly no references to firearms. The guards of the Pforzheim *zuchthaus*,
however, were authorized to carry pistols in 1754.[58]

Chains and blocks were used for security measures and for punishment.
They were sometimes fastened to dangerous convicts as a preventive measure, and sometimes to prisoners who had tried to break out. In Amsterdam it was stated explicitly that only obstinate inmates had to work in
chains.[59] Court records occasionally confirm this. An inmate in 1689

claimed to be innocent of an escape attempt; he said his chains had prevented him from reaching the hole his fellows were digging.[60] Similar
restrictions were imposed on a Delft prisoner, who was just able to reach
his bed, his place of work, and the latrine. Another wore his chain for
three years and four months, finally regaining his freedom of movement
because of good behavior.[61] In Haarlem such measures must have been
rarer. When a few men were to be bound by their feet in 1688, it was
remarked that "there are some very suitable chains in the house, which, in
all probability, have been used to that end in earlier times."[62] The ordinances of both Hamburg prisons determined that the men who spent the
night in cells had to do their daytime work with a block tied to their legs.[63]
Additionally, the spinhouse records mention prisoners who were chained
for punishment. These cases almost always involved men. In Dutch prison
records there were no references to chains or blocks for women, but this
happened once in the Hamburg spinhouse: a block was tied to Anna Marie Lorens's leg after an escape attempt in 1691.[64] Even such measures did
not always prevent convicts from escaping. On 14 November 1702, Hans
Hinrich Budeler and Christian Schröders broke through the wall between
their cells, and still wearing their blocks, fled the spinhouse with outside
help. The next day drums were beaten and a reward was set on the two
men, but it was not necessary. One of the praetors surprised them that
night in the house of Schröders's brother-in-law. As he burst in, they were
busy trying to free themselves from the blocks by burning them at the
fireside. Although these instruments did not prevent the prisoners from
walking, they were fastened securely.[65]

When prevention failed, punishment followed. Disciplinary penalties
were a feature of prison workhouses from the beginning. The ordinances
testifying to this. One of the earliest references to an actual punishment is
a Bremen protocol of 28 June 1616: "the four kaṁmerer and the vorsteher
of the tuchthus have visited the house and exercised justice there. Daniel
Harthwich and Johan Neding were flogged at the post and Snidewint and
the one from Luñeburg on the horse; all were seriously admonished.[66]
That is not to say that the Bremen officials would reach for the whip
immediately; in that town, too, withholding food was the first disciplinary
measure.[67]

There is no point in discussing the prescribed scale of disciplinary punishments in detail for every town. What matters, moreover, are actual penalties, rather than those prescribed in ordinances, and the context in which
they were meted out. Delft provides a good example. I noted that the
indoor father was allowed to administer punishments on his own authority. He seems to have done so notably when inmates were unwilling to
work or were too slow about it. If their dilatory tactics were not too prolonged, it was considered a minor infraction. The indoor father would
beat the prisoner with his hands or with a stick to make him work. In

more serious cases he would withhold food. The regents entered into the picture when inmates attempted to escape or committed other serious offenses. Their basic repertoire consisted of three penalties, often imposed in combinations: flogging, a few days on bread and water, and a stay on the so-called grating. When it was first mentioned, in 1714, the grating was also called "the water-hole." But we should not suppose there was any danger of drowning, which would be incompatible with the imposed sentence of five days. It must have been a pit with some water in it and a grid above the water on which the offender was obliged to sit. Five days was a long period for such a punishment; later in the century, most prisoners sentenced to the grating received two or three. Sometimes it was noted that a prisoner had to sit on the grating with his hands and feet tied.[68]

Comparable punishment regimes existed elsewhere. Both Hamburg institutions, for example, had a dark cell for recalcitrant inmates.[69] Flogging was the most universal means of enforcing discipline in serious cases. The Delft regents considered it a more severe punishment than the grating, and they often imposed it when escape attempts had been accompanied by some form of violence. In Delft and Haarlem, where there was no master of discipline, court servants were usually ordered to execute the sentence. Sometimes they objected to this; in Delft there were also conflicts over payments.[70] Although the Hamburg spinhouse had a master of discipline, its entry books regularly referred to one or two "masked persons" who administered whippings to prisoners. The logbook of the provisors, however, make it clear that these persons were in fact court servants.[71]

A special form of physical treatment was the 'welcome': a beating the prisoner received automatically upon his or her entry into the institution. This practice lay on the border between disciplinary punishment and penal measures. It was not practiced in the Dutch Republic, but several other countries, including England, were familiar with it.[72] It was most common in the Empire. The Bremen senate, for example, sentenced a few convicts to the *zuchthaus* in 1747 and prescribed that they were to be "received with the usual welcome." As if he sensed that future generations might forget the meaning of the word, the next year the clerk wrote "with the usual beating."[73] In these cases, clearly, the welcome was a part of the sentence, and hence a penal measure. This was also the case in Austrian *zuchthaüser.*[74] In other cases mentioned in German literature we often cannot tell which it was. In addition to a welcome, a few authors also refer to a 'leave.'[75]

The subject of physical discipline and punishment in prisons is central to the history of long-term developments in the field of repression. I have stressed that the latter were characterized by reduction in the elements of physical injury and publicity, over several centuries. Early modern prisons represented an intermediate phase with respect to both elements. At the moment we are more concerned with physical punishment. On the one hand, the prison buildings stood as symbols of a type of repression different from that practiced on the scaffold. On the other hand, physical treatment was the fate of many inside their walls. Indeed, the spectacle of the scaffold was often limited within the institutions. Fellow prisoners were required to watch an inmate being beaten. This is the main reason why the beating was administered in the courtyard. When the case was serious enough, the administrators, and sometimes even magistrates, were present, too. Such instances were recorded in Delft and Hamburg.[76] When magistrates were watching, it was usually because the offender's behavior had been dealt with as a court case. This happened as late as 1801 in Delft. Dirk Bijkerk, who had repeatedly tried to break out, was whipped and branded by the hangman in prison with a rope around his neck. When the executioner had finished, Dirk received an admonition, followed by a speech of the presiding *schepen* to all prisoners.[77]

Although in this case a few tickets of admission were handed out to persons of status, it is clear from the sources that normally the execution of disciplinary penalties in prison was private.[78] Illustrations showing visitors in the courtyard while someone was being whipped at the post simply were a means of portraying several possible prison scenes, which were not necessarily concurrent. The privateness of disciplinary punishment implies a paradox: visitors were admitted as a matter of course at other times, but when subversive inmates were solemnly flogged, the public at large was not invited to come and see. Actually, this procedure was perfectly logical. Disciplinary penalties were imposed for offenses such as escape attempts, which could only be committed within the context of prison life. They were breaches of the institution's normal order. Consequently, it was the inmates who were collected as the audience to be impressed. This was a case of 'general prevention' at the micro-level, and visitors would only constitute a disturbance factor. When the inmates complied with the normal order, on the other hand, this constituted punishment, too: for crimes committed in the outside world. Consequently, a demonstration of the institution's daily business was also a case of general prevention, this time at the macro-level. In that case, the public at large was welcome.

The Case of Frederik Krop   A case of disobedience and punishment in the Delft prison in 1778 reveals the limits of the maintenance of discipline. An exceptional feature of this case was that a refusal to work, normally not a concern for the regents in eighteenth-century Delft, constituted the offense. Questions of jurisdictional authority complicated the matter. Frederik Krop was serving a six-year term at Delft upon a sentence by the High Court-martial, and he may have considered it against his honor as a soldier to perform forced labor. In any case, he refused. For this he had been punished twice, the second time with the grating. The punishments had been of no avail. Thereupon, the regents informed the prosecutor of the Court-martial, J. G. van Oldenbarnevelt Tulling, who arrived at the Delft prison on June 1. Tulling seriously admonished the prisoner and told the regents that, should Krop's recalcitrance continue, he was to be whipped at the post. In that case the prosecutor himself wished to be present. Since Krop persisted in his refusal to work, the regents decided to have the whipping the next day and prepared to invite Tulling. The *schout*, however, objected, that it would seem as if a "foreign prosecutor" administered justice on Delft territory. The fracas caused Tulling to withdraw his request to attend.

The day of the whipping was 9 June. After a final admonition, Frederik Krop was put to the post. The regents watched from the windows of their room. After forty lashes the prisoner was asked if he was willing to work, and he replied "no." This same procedure was repeated after each twenty lashes. When the total had reached a hundred, Krop stated that he would work, but not for his board. This ambiguous answer satisfied the regents. Krop was untied, admonished once more, and taken back to his cage. But it had all been for nothing. On 27 June the regents were notified that the prisoner, whose wounds, presumably, were considered healed that day, still refused to work. They were amazed, because they had taken his loud screams as a sign that the penalty had made the required impression upon him. For the administrators, the limits of the maintenance of discipline had been reached. They decided that Krop was too obstinate to ever work for his board, and they now treated the case as a financial one. Since the prisoner earned nothing toward his board, they had a right to ask the High Court-martial for board money, they said. Tulling and the High Court-martial refused to pay. Since he had been refused admittance to the beating, Tulling triumphantly added, it was entirely up to the Delft court to decide what to do with the prisoner. Had he been present, he would have found a means to make the prisoner yield. Now the case had turned out to be a particularly bad example to the other inmates. Tulling said he would have ordered the servants to continue with flogging, "even if this fellow had dropped dead." He said he felt able to account for this decision with, in this order, the Supreme Being, his conscience, and the High Court-martial. It is difficult to say whether he really would have gone as far as he said. Disciplinary punishment carried to such extremes—which, for the most obstinate prisoners would make a sentence of forced labor the same as the death penalty—clearly was unacceptable to many. Interestingly, the use of the term 'Supreme Being' suggests that Tulling was influenced by Enlightenment notions, which however, did not prevent him from taking his extreme position.

As if he had just wanted to play with his antagonists, Frederik Krop seems to have complied after all. He was put on the grating for two days, with "a certain kind of squeezing shackle" provided by the indoor father. On 19 July it was reported that he had started working. Since then his name appeared in the logbook only once more. On 14 February 1782 he escaped along with three other men.[79]

INTERCONNECTIONS

Shifting the focus to the intermediate category between 'above' and 'below' forces I have to emphasize once more that, in reality, all elements of prison life were connected to each other. This section deals with three themes: term reduction (including pardon), sickness, and death. The shortening of a term depended on the magistrates' decision as well as on the inmate's behavior; to become ill or to die, although also related to institutional circumstances, ultimately was the result of natural forces beyond the control of either party.

Reduction: Hopes and Promises   Nothing linked the prison order, as dictated from above, more closely to the inmates' inner experience than the system of reductions which became commonplace in most Dutch prisons in the course of the eighteenth century. In the previous chapter reduction was considered from the perspective of evolution of penal policies; now we will see how it affected prison life. The system was instituted and operated by the authorities, but it was individual inmates who earned a shortening of their term through good behavior. Reduction was part of a complex network of interactions.

The authorities and the administrators were the most powerful party in the game; they determined the if, when, and how much. At times, they made a ceremony out of the granting of reductions. These ceremonies were recorded in Delft in 1765 and again at the occasion of the centennial celebration of 1777. In planning for that event, a few weeks prior to it the regents recommended reductions and pardons for several inmates. When the centennial day arrived, inmates from outside Delft were still awaiting approvals of the recommendations from their courts. However, three women and one man from Delft were pardoned, and two men and one woman received reductions. The regents walked in procession to the courtyard, where the four prisoners about to be released were also taken. The other inmates watched the scene from behind bars. The president of the board made a speech, praising the behavior of the beneficiaries and recommending it to their fellows. The ceremony ended dramatically.

When the president had finished, one of the pardoned women, Maria Wijmalen, requested a word with the board. Weeping bitter tears, she admitted that she was uncomfortable about her release. Her original sentence had included a banishment from the province for eight years. This part of the sentence she would still have to comply with. But as a young woman in a foreign land without family or friends, she feared she would be tempted into a bad life again. So she pleaded that her banishment could be commuted to confinement and that she would be allowed to stay in prison. Her request must have been granted; since the sources reveal that she was released six and a half months later.[80]

The system of reductions became a tool of prison discipline. This is evidenced by the correspondence of the Delft burgomasters with their colleagues elsewhere. They wrote to Zierikzee in February 1736 about three men and two women who had been committed by that town's court, which they noted had a habit of imposing life sentences. The prospect of a confinement until the end of their days made these prisoners desperate. They thought of nothing but breaking out. Delft pointed out that there had been no conspiracy in recent years without the involvement of Zierikzee prisoners. They were neither restrained by the fear of further punishment nor by the hope of obtaining a reduction. This positive sanction was said to be the best means to encourage prisoners to behave well and to make them more tractable. The Delft burgomasters found the case serious enough for a threat to annul the contract with Zierikzee. They gave their Zierikzee colleagues the options to pick up their convicts within four months or to shorten their terms and authorize the regents to promise them further reductions if they kept quiet and perhaps betrayed conspiracies by other inmates. In reply, Zierikzee denied that the present contract could be validly terminated, but promised to grant reductions in the future.[81]

In this case, the absence of the prospect of reduction was exacerbated by having to serve a life sentence. Gradually, more jurisdictions became accustomed to a routine application of the reduction system.[82] In 1782, however, there were problems again, because the court of Southern Holland did not go along with the system. The relationship between the absence of a prospect of reduction and a hardened attitude of prisoners was emphasized once more. In 1736 the regents had come to such a conclusion. This time the idea was voiced by an inmate himself. When Pieter Rietveld, a convict sentenced by the Southern Holland court, was questioned about his leadership in an escape conspiracy, he replied that, "since he had no hope of reduction, he would always attempt to find his way out, the more so to the extent that he was kept more securely and subjected to more discomfort." This suggests that the expectation of a shortened term had become a familiar one within the inmate subculture and that they discussed it among each other. Everyone may have weighed the pros and cons before deciding whether or not to break out. Faced with a hopeless—and in that regard exceptional—situation, Rietveld's choice was obvious. The court of Southern Holland, however, when confronted with the problem, argued that its convicts were blackmailing the Delft regents. Despite this, it had no choice but to yield.[83] If these prisoners had really attempted blackmail, they could only have done so because they knew that the regents, content with the system of reductions, were susceptible to pressure. Conspiracies were a problem of discipline and of no concern of the *baljuw* of Southern Holland, who simply stated that a very strict surveillance should be sufficient to insure order and discipline. As in the case of Frederik Krop, those who actually had to deal with the prisoners were inclined toward a more lenient attitude. They felt that solutions proposed by outsiders might be simplistic. The insiders had learned the lesson that the management of a prison was a complicated task and that discipline could not be maintained just by punishment, but depended on rewards as well.

Outside Delft there is little information on how the application of the system affected prison life. It was once stated in Amsterdam, as in Delft, that without the prospect of a shortening of their term, prisoners would become desperate.[84] Amsterdam is of importance, however, because of the counterexample of its secret ward. The sodomy convicts who were kept there in the eighteenth century received no reductions at all. Since they were also condemned to rather long terms, most of them died in captivity.[85] It may have been that the judges considered sodomy such a reprehensible offense that they denied reductions to these prisoners out of moral indignation. Alternatively, it is possible that the reason lay in the special nature of the secret ward. Because inmates there did not work, there was never the problem of making them work. Normally, making sure that everyone did their job must have been the routine business of discipline. Escape conspiracies, too, were less of a problem in the secret ward, since there were never more than two prisoners in one room. Thus, the counter-example makes it more clear how, elsewhere, the system of reductions was woven into the fabric of prison life. It encouraged inmates to perform their assigned tasks and discouraged breaking out. It guaranteed internal division when some inmates cherished escape plans nevertheless. By introducing a system of rewards, the managers of prison workhouses made these institutions resemble the manufactories in free society to a certain extent. Still, the differences between prisoners and free workers remained considerable, because the former earned something to which the latter would be indifferent. Ultimately, the motivation of inmates striving to collect their reward and those busy trying to break out was the same: to end their job sooner than originally expected.

A final point about reductions relates to an intriguing parallel with religious notions of punishment. To understand this, we must ask ourselves what makes one prison sentence more severe than another. It might be a heavier labor requirement. However, the severity of the imprisonment penalty was determined first of all by the length of the term imposed. Severity or mildness were expressed in time units. This was not an entirely new situation. Severity or mildness had long been expressed in time units in the penalty of banishment. The difference was that banished offenders went away; they had to. Their behavior was of no concern to the judges, and in a localistic world could not be ascertained anyway. The novelty of imprisonment lay in the fact that the original sentence could be changed. Imprisonment was historically the first judicial sanction that could be moderated while an offender was subjected to it. Now we can see the parallel with religious notions. The only precedent for a punishment that could be changed while the offender was undergoing it was the religious notion of purgatory. There, too, the intensity of a sinner's sufferings was expressed in time units, and God's original sentence was not irrevocable. It is strange that the managers of prisons in the Republic, who were all Protestants, invented the system of reductions. Moreover, in so far as it deviated from the idea of purgatory, it was still very Catholic. Not the prayers of friends outside helped to shorten a prisoner's term but his good behavior within. This reminds us of the doctrine of 'works', except that in this case, they can be performed during one's sojourn in the place of punishment rather than having to have been done before.[86]

In the Hamburg spinhouse reduction was hardly practiced, but inmates were often released long before the expiration of their term. This happened usually following a family request. Typically, it was written that the prisoner had been taken back by relatives upon their many pleas (*bitten*). This was a standard formula; we do not know whether there was a correlation between the number of pleas and the portion of time remitted. If we suppose there was, it amounts to still another parallel with the idea of purgatory. Was Lutheran Hamburg also influenced by Catholic notions?

However, from a different point of view the situation loses its paradoxical character. I emphasized that, although Protestantism was an accelerating factor in the emergence of prison workhouses, a broader process of secularization was one of its deeper causes. The Dutch Republic, whose dominant church rejected the religious doctrine of purgatory, invented a terrestrial purgatory. Catholic notions of divine punishment were not suppressed; they were transferred to an earthly setting. The model of punishment with the possibility of mitigation afterwards had been developed in a religious context, and it was imitated in the form of prison sentences with the possibility of reduction. As the prison was an earthly purgatory, reduction was a secular form of reward for good works. The original model was secularized.

Syphilis and Other Diseases   Originally, sickness had not presented significant problems. Since prisons were established to detain those who were a burden outside, the administrators expelled those who became a burden within. The Haarlem ordinance of 1612, for example, determined that seriously ill inmates were to be sent away and readmitted only if they recovered. This ordinance was aimed especially at persons committed on request, who had not received a formal sentence. When criminal convicts were or fell seriously ill, the judges somehow had to alter their original sentence. In Haarlem the problem presented itself in 1648. The *schepenen* had imposed a one-year prison term and a banishment for ten years on Cathalina Pieters, when it was discovered that she suffered from the Spanish pox. They commuted the prison sentence, so that she was banished for eleven years now.[87] We do not know what Amsterdam, the first town to imprison delinquents in significant numbers, did with diseased inmates then. Reference is only made to a few isolated cases of plague around the middle of the seventeenth century.[88] The plague, which inspired a particular fear of contagion, was a special case. Toward the end of the seventeenth century it largely disappeared from Northern Europe. None of the inmates of the Hamburg spinhouse who were transferred to the pesthouse were said to be infected with it. Concrete information was given on some of them, for example on three women who had suffered from a stroke and were paralyzed on one side of their bodies.[89] In general, it seems that Dutch and German prison workhouses remained free from the recurrent epidemics which are said to have characterized English jails.[90]

The real problem became that of syphilis, usually called by names such as the pox or the French disease. As an increasing number of delinquents were committed to prison and as the magistrates were unwilling to pardon them when they showed symptoms of the disease, some solution had to be found. Most patients, of course, were prostitutes, but other delinquents, female and male, suffered from syphilis, too. Our earliest information comes from the records of the Hamburg spinhouse. The solution adopted there was noted in the previous chapter: women suffering from the French disease were taken to the poxhouse, returning to serve the remainder of their term after their cure. Among this group of women 7 percent had been condemned for offenses other than prostitution. The cures usually took from three to six weeks, but a few lasted several months. About a dozen women were taken to the poxhouse twice during their imprisonment. One had to embark upon a third cure and was then taken to the pesthouse instead.[91] Not surprisingly, prisoners undergoing their first cure had recently entered the house. The poxhouse's *balbier* visited the spinhouse every three months to examine whores who had newly arrived.[92] In 1695, two women were said to have been infected during their stay, one of them by the child of another. A third woman entered the spinhouse in June 1697, had a miscarriage the next month, and went to the poxhouse in February 1699. Inmates were apparently afraid of being infected in the institution. When Liesebeth Peterssen from Lüneberg returned to the spinhouse after her second unsuccessful cure in 1708, the women who slept with her objected to having to do so for fear of contagion.

Liesebeth was released and sent to her home town.[93] The poxhouse was a female institution; syphilitic men in Hamburg were cured in St. Job's hospital. In 1696 its board of administrators refused admittance to Hans Hinrich Borges on the grounds that he was a thief who had been in the hands of the executioner. Not wanting to see the prisoner remain in agony, either, they found a compromise. Poxmaster Brambach came to the spinhouse and administered his cure to Borges in his cell. It was finished in three months, but in spite of this, Borges died within a year.[94] Another male prisoner suffering from the French disease was likewise treated in his cell in 1697.[95]

In eighteenth-century Haarlem, which formerly had sent syphilis patients away, the same solution as in Hamburg was adopted. A number of references, the earliest dated 1706, explain that prisoners suffering from what was there named the Spanish disease were temporarily transferred to St. Elisabeth's hospital. As a rule, the hospital paid two-thirds of the surgeon's bill and the prison one-third.[96] In the Amsterdam rasphouse, on the other hand, a special ward for syphilis patients was mentioned in 1710. A surgeon appointed by the regents treated the sufferers and reported it when they had recovered to the extent that they were able to rasp again.[97] A sick ward was also opened in the Hamburg *zuchthaus* in 1692, while Rotterdam's prison had one in the eighteenth century.[98] In Delft it was decided in 1767 that the house surgeon would examine newly arrived inmates condemned for prostitution or other offenses, but only if the latter were suspected of suffering from "the dirty disease." It was not mentioned where they were cured.[99] The choice for one method or the other was probably determined by the capacity of the institution rather than local preferences.

By the early eighteenth century it was accepted that delinquent inmates had periods of illness and that this constituted an extra burden on the house. The persons in question were kept in prison, nonetheless, because their sentence required it. This serves to underline once more that penal considerations prevailed over economic ones. The Delft entry book for the 1730s and 1740s mentions a number of prisoners for whom the court paid extra money because they were unable to work or were partially handicapped as a result of ill health or old age. A register covering the period 1759–1790 offers an opportunity for quantification.[100] It lists expenses on behalf of a group of about a dozen inmates each year, but we do not know the criterion or criteria for the grouping. They may have been all prisoners condemned by the Delft court or just those who were provided with clothes and shoes. Taken together, they make up 383 cases: 197 women, 179 men, and seven persons whose sex could not be ascertained. The register lists payments to the indoor father for each week that the inmates were sick or disabled. From these data it can be calculated that, on average, no less than 89.3 percent of the female prisoners and 80.4 percent of the males were temporarily ill each year. The average period during which these inmates were unable to work was 8.7 weeks: 7.9 weeks for the men and 9.3 weeks for the women. Female prisoners either were less healthy or they were more easily excused.

Natural Death and Suicide   Exact figures for prison deaths can be derived only from entry books. We have to include the cases in which a prisoner was taken to a hospital or pesthouse and never returned. Figures varied according to the institution. For the Delft *tuchthuis* (for all inmates) and the Hamburg spinhouse they amounted to 10 percent; for the Amsterdam workhouse 8 percent. Faber mentions a death rate of 5.8 percent for the rasphouse during the period 1781–1800, but he provides no figures for transfers to a hospital.[101] In the Amsterdam spinhouse, on the other hand, less than 2 percent died in captivity, and almost none were taken to a hospital. Were conditions so much healthier there? It is difficult to interpret the extent to which prison life influenced these figures. Moreover, death ratios were a function of the age and the state of health of prisoners upon entry and the terms imposed on them. Since in most cases we do not know the total number of inmates staying in the institutions in any one year, it is impossible to count death rates as a percentage of the population as a whole. If we assume the average number of inmates of the rasphouse from 1781 to 1800 to be sixty, and of its public ward to be fifty, we can calculate from Faber's figures that the annual death rate was 4.1 percent for the entire institution and 2.9 percent for the public ward. The latter figure is more or less comparable to those calculated for three orphanages in the city for the period 1800–1820: 3.2, 1.8, and 1.6 percent.[102]

Qualitative evidence on death in prison is scarce; causes of death, for example, are seldom mentioned. Considering the frequency of pregnancy in the Hamburg spinhouse, it is not surprising that two women died in childbirth there. The first was delivered of stillborn twins in 1675. The second was actually delivered while undergoing a cure in the poxhouse in 1696. She passed away after four hours, and her son, baptized Lüder Casper, died in the spinhouse two days later.[103] In a number of cases the house records mentioned the place of burial. Usually this was the Gertruden cemetery, sometimes the cemetery of the poor.[104] There was no talk of bodies being sent to the anatomy room. That must have been a common practice in Delft, as suggested by a rule issued in 1781. It determined that, when corpses of prisoners from foreign jurisdictions were given to the anatomy lecturer, permission of the regents was required. The bodies of the town's convicts were apparently given to the anatomy lecturer automatically.[105] The Delft records also contain the only reference to the theme of preparation for death. In 1765 there were complaints that dying inmates simply were allowed to lie in agony in the presence of their fellows in the cage where they had worked. This situation was not conducive to preparation for eternity. Expressing a wish to care for the souls as well as the bodies of their people, the regents determined that, henceforth, prisoners approaching death were to be taken to a separate room next to the chapel. The house deputy preacher was to visit them daily there.[106] This rule constitutes another example of the privatization of dying which took place in several European countries toward the end of the eighteenth century.

References to suicide are not very numerous. An excerpt from the Lübeck logbook has been preserved, reporting that a beggar had hanged himself with his scarf in 1701. After three days a skinner took his body from the *zuchthaus* and dragged it to the *schindergrube*.[107] In the Hamburg spinhouse two women were reported to have tried to kill themselves. One case was associated with a special matter that will be discussed in the next section. The other involved Catharin Rosenbrock, a woman who had been a soldier and a sailor in men's clothes. It is recorded that she "did a very sorrowful thing to herself" only twelve days after her arrival, whereupon she was immediately transferred to the pesthouse.[108] We should also take account of the possibility of indirect suicide by truthfully or falsely confessing to capital crimes. Margretha Schmits, for example, stated that she had killed her child in Glückstadt many years previously; she repeated this when a few magistrates interrogated her in prison, and she was taken to jail never to return.[109] The case of another woman is more ambiguous. She claimed to have killed both her children while in Holland. She told this eight days after her release, to the spinhouse preacher, who apparently did not scruple to make it public. Presumably, the court considered the case inconclusive, so she was sentenced to a new term.[110] Another indirect suicide attempt was reported from St. Gallen in 1781. A thief imprisoned there on a twenty-year term claimed to have committed "the *crimen bestialitatis* with cattle," but this was found to be a lie.[111] The Delft records do not refer to suicide until 1800. In October of that year there were two incidents, one shortly after the other but unconnected. Both inmates attempted to cut their throat. One was a man from the insane ward and it was found that it was no use trying to talk to him. The other, a woman from the *tuchthuis*, declared that she had felt unjustly punished. She was also attacked by some of the women in her room.[112]

The Making of a Subculture

After a series of turbulent events in the Hamburg spinhouse during the years 1698–1700, the next twelve months seemed like an oasis of peace to the *jahrverwalter*. In the logbook he recorded only a few financial details.

At the end of his period of administration he wrote: "thanks to God, nothing happened this year." [113] That serves as a warning at the beginning of this section. In Delft, too, there were periods when few events were recorded. We do not read in prison logbooks: "today he did his job obediently" or "she was very attentive during the sermon." The historian learns most even about the 'normal' aspects of prison life by reading between the lines of stories about misbehavior—which is why such stories figured in the previous sections as well. The reader should not get the impression that there was permanent chaos in early modern prisons; my emphasis on breaches of discipline is simply a reflection of the content of the sources.

Five subjects may be distinguished, each implying a contravention of the prison order in the eyes of the officials who recorded them. I will start with conflicts among inmates, notably those which resulted into violence. Next, I will inquire into the inmates' sexual lives. This will be followed by a discussion of the fate of female prisoners' children. Revolts and other expressions of disobedience or disrespect make up the fourth subject; escape constitutes the fifth.

Conflicts and Violence   Minor quarrels and simple fights must have been common. They were handled informally by the personnel and hence were seldom recorded. [114] It is not until the 1790s that we hear of preventive measures to protect inmates from each other. A prisoner from The Hague was placed in a cage all by himself at Delft, because the judges considered him a very dangerous person. They feared he might injure or even kill fellow inmates. In 1797, however, two men were placed with him, since he could no longer be exposed to the "horrible situation of complete and continuous solitude." [115] The exceptional character of the case implies that, normally, prisoners were not thought to be predisposed to hurt fellow inmates. This suggests that acts of violence that were recorded were a function of the dynamics of prison life rather than resulting from the aggressive character of individual convicts.

Some of these acts were probably committed out of desperation. That was clearly the case in the first instance of serious violence in the *zuchthaus* in Hamburg in 1635. One man hit another on the head with a heavy instrument. The attacker later declared that he had wanted to commit manslaughter in order to get into the hands of the court. [116] Similar, possibly unconscious, wishes may have played a role in two comparable incidents in the spinhouse; no motive was recorded in either case. In 1702 Christina Schrieberin hit her bedmate on the head with a big stone while the latter was asleep, and then hit her a second time. Two years later Maria Engel Wichmans pretended to be ill for two days in order to be alone with Cathrin Stehlmans while the rest of the women attended the Sunday sermon. Cathrin, who was apparently also excused from the sermon, was then severely beaten on the head with the base of a yarn winder. She recovered and eventually died in the spinhouse in 1712.[117] In Delft at the beginning of the eighteenth century a few men were reported to have hit fellow inmates on the head or broken their limbs. One of them obtained a knife with which he cut his fellow's arm.[118] An inmate of the Amsterdam rasphouse was stabbed and barely survived in 1664. His attacker confessed to have done it in a fit of rage when they had words.[119]

Knives were usually smuggled in for purposes of escaping, but when inmates quarrelled they sometimes used them on each other. Three casualties were reported in the sources studied. The first took place in Utrecht in November 1625. When the visitor's box was opened, the inmates used to be treated to beer. According to the regent Van Buchell, some men drank too much that night, which resulted in a fight in which one was killed.[120] A casualty in the Amsterdam rasphouse in May 1739 also followed upon a quarrel. The prisoners involved, Marten Gijsbertsz and Michiel Schoonheer, may have borne grudges against each other already before the event. The incident began on a Thursday night when Marten was sitting quietly on a redwood log and Michiel proposed to him: "if you were to sing a song, I will make a dance." A line of chalk was drawn on the floor, but Marten refused to sing, whereupon Michiel called him a "lice-noddle." That was the end of it for a while, but Marten stayed up all night in their cage and the next day after work told Michiel: "I can't catch my lice." This resulted in a fight in which Michiel was stabbed, while two fellow inmates tried to separate the contestants. With the knife in his back, Michiel dragged himself to the bars of the cage, crying out, "I am hurt," whereupon, he dropped dead in a sea of blood. Marten, who under threat of torture confessed that he had obtained the knife from the closet of the assistant work boss, was condemned to be hanged and his body taken to the gallows-field. At the last moment the judges revised their sentence and allowed him to be buried.[121]

The third casualty occurred at Delft. The perpetrator, a prisoner from Delfland, bore the name of Philip Heukenswagen. He had entered the *tuchthuis* in 1727, when he was twenty-five years old; exactly as many years as the term he was condemned to serve. In January 1736, indoor father Bolland claimed there was a conspiracy to overpower him, and he identified Philip as one of the leaders. Philip was supposed to have threatened to break Bolland's neck, which he denied.[122] This may be taken as a sign that Philip was an especially violent man, and his violent nature was a contributing factor in the later homicide. On the other hand, in March 1737 he received five years reduction for reasons which were not recorded. At any rate, in August 1740 Catharina Vermeulen, then thirty-four, who had been born in Antwerp and had been living in Delft, was condemned to five years by the town's *schepenen*. She met Philip in prison and their story illustrates the social life which could exist on the margins of forced labor. Despite the fact that Catharina already had a husband, she and Philip exchanged marriage vows in prison on 12 May 1742. He gave her a pair of golden earrings and she gave him a pair of silver clasps. They never quarrelled and she carefully kept the money he earned with over-work. On 15 June 1744, however, he demanded his pennies in order to buy drinks. She first refused and then handed them over, exclaiming: "Swallow as much as you want." After a little while Catharina also went to the prison kitchen. Twice she refused a drink from her lover, but she accepted one from another man. Philip went berserk, pursued her with a knife, and stabbed her in the breast and the belly. She died shortly after-wards. Two weeks later Philip was executed.[123]

Sex   This crime of passion assists the transition to the next theme—the sex lives of inmates—although the sources do not reveal whether Philip and Catharina had physically consummated their vows. In the early nineteenth century, reformers repeatedly expressed their concern about an insufficient separation of women and men in prisons. They considered it a primary cause of the 'corruption' supposedly reigning there. Already in 1793 the debate on this issue was anticipated when a Hamburg senator complained that the populace viewed the *zuchthaus* as a great brothel.[124] However, as we will see, extant sources hardly support such a view. It is not quite self-evident that sex should be considered one of the 'below' aspects of prison life, since most of the cases collected involved relations between prisoners and personnel, rather than among inmates. On the other hand, there can be no doubt that all these activities ran counter to the prison order as envisaged by the authorities.

Discussions about sex in today's prisons usually center around homo-sexual behavior; that is the unintended success of the nineteenth-century reformers. Early modern sources contain surprisingly few references to such contacts, either among men or among women. This is also true for Amsterdam, the only town with separate male and female institutions, although the loss of the rasphouse's archive may play a part here.[125] The magistrates were content to assign sodomy convicts to separate rooms in the secret ward and apparently thought that this prevented an 'infection' of other prisoners. In the Republic, the theoretician Van der Pauw argued that confining several men in one cage encouraged the *libido nefanda*.[126] On the French galley fleet, by contrast, homosexual activities seem to have been tolerated.[127] The theme of sodomy turned up in the Delft prison records once in a quite ambiguous sense. In 1778 two men had a quarrel because the one repeatedly called the other an informer. He retorted by calling his harasser a sodomite who deserved to be burnt, an accusation serious enough for a complaint to the regents. They merely ordered the two to stop insulting each other.[128] I found another reference, though not very detailed, to actual erotic contact between members of the same sex.

The commissioners of the court of Holland, visiting their prisoners at Delft in 1746, received an unfavorable report on Anna Maria Moitet. The indoor father declared that "from time to time she had engaged in many dirty lewdnesses with the other women in her cage."[129] Since she had also tried to break out, she had been chastised and transferred to another room (it remains unclear whether she was alone there). The commissioners agreed that she deserved no reduction at all and warned her that her fate would be worse if she persisted in her godless life.

Patricia O'Brien is the only historian so far who pays ample attention to sex in prisons, but her evidence on this subject is mostly indirect. In nineteenth-century France, estimates of the extent of homosexual behavior among male convicts ranged from 8 to 70 percent. Relationships between female prisoners, O'Brien claims, were characterized by intimacy and romance, even though she has to admit that her only sources, published collections of letters, may very well have been fabricated as a form of Victorian soft pornography. The only cases of actual intercourse she mentions were heterosexual, involving male guards and female inmates. They took place in 1818 and 1819, when no female personnel were employed yet in women's prisons.[130] The subject of heterosexual intercourse is practically absent from the literature on early modern institutions; until recently it was not considered a suitable historical topic. Mayer is the only author devoting a separate paragraph to it. He discusses two cases at St. Gallen, which are both special: one involved a married couple who had been committed together and the other a rich private prisoner.[131] Stier very briefly discusses a few cases at Pforzheim in the second half of the eighteenth century.[132] That is about all.[133]

My own evidence is restricted to Hamburg and Delft, whose prison records are generally the most informative about internal life. It is understandable that these sources refer almost exclusively to heterosexual behavior. As in the world at large, the discovery of pregnancies was the main reason sexual activities were recorded. The records do not speak of rape; in all cases, contacts were presented as voluntary on both sides. This was not merely a matter of the authorities' assumptions. It was the women who were questioned and whose views were recorded, so that the historian can be reasonably confident of their voluntary participation.

The story of a lover's homicide in Delft showed that the separation of the sexes was not quite complete. But the opportunities for actual intercourse among prisoners must have been few, since we hear so little of it. The earliest recorded case took place in the Hamburg zuchthaus in 1646, when the inmates Harmen Brave and Catrina Lahers confessed to having fornicated several times.[134] Four more cases in this institution were reported between 1696 and 1743, without any details being given.[135] The only incident in the spinhouse during the forty years studied, on the other hand, was recorded in such detail that it will be discussed separately below.

The Delft logbooks contain six cases, beginning in 1760. In one case, the father was also a prisoner. He had managed to escape before the pregnancy was discovered, and the escape was taken as a confirmation of his guilt.[136] Four pregnant women designated servants of the house as the begetters, and all these men had fled, too. One of them had at least pretended to love his partner. He and the prisoner, Sijtje Staalman, had agreed to get married as soon as she was released. Sijtje later told the regents that they had done it "because of the affection which they had acquired for each other."[137] But the context could also be more "traditional." For example, a pregnant inmate declared that she had committed the act twice—once during the spinhouse fair on 2 February, and once during the town fair—with a married wool worker who had assisted the indoor father.[138] From the literature on illegitimacy in preindustrial societies we know that conceptions often took place during festival periods, and, in this case illegitimate sex in prison conformed to that pattern. In another incident, two female inmates, one of whom was pregnant, accused the indoor father's son of having seduced them and several other women. He denied all accusations under oath and the records do not disclose what happened to him.[139]

The case of Johanna Dusseldorp, also at Delft, was different in that she was not pregnant. In the end the court decided that nothing had happened, but the documentation leaves room for some doubt. She was thirty-three and a widow when she was condemned to a term of four years for swindling in January 1769. In prison she assisted the indoor father and mother as a nurse. The troubles began in July 1770, when the mother was out of town for a few weeks. As Johanna later confessed to the court, she tied a handkerchief around her body in order to look pregnant. Returning on July 21, the indoor father's wife asked Johanna why she was so stout, whereupon she replied that she had had intercourse with the house surgeon. She also said she had miscarried during the night of 8–9 July; a claim incompatible with her swollen belly. Nothing further happened until August 10, when she was beaten by the indoor father for quarrelling with his wife. To her fellow prisoners she now declared that she had had intercourse with the indoor father, and that he had advised her to accuse the surgeon. Again she claimed to be pregnant. In addition, subsequently she spread accusations against other women. Her fellow prisoner Jaapje van het Hoff was said to possess an abortion potion, with which she had expelled the fruit of her sexual activities with several personnel members. All this caused Johanna to be summoned to the board's meeting on 17 August. There she repeated her accusations and now claimed to have miscarried during the night of 1–2 August. She also specified the places and times over the past year when she and the indoor father were supposed to have engaged in sex. It is these specifications which were left out of the court's sentence in the case, that convey the impression that her story was not entirely invented. Once, for example, she said she was washing clothes while his wife was out and he called her to pick up a dime which had fallen from his desk. When she bowed down, he lifted her skirt, saying, "it doesn't lie here," and closed the door. The regents, however, were inclined to believe their official, who immediately demanded complete satisfaction to maintain his reputation. Johanna persisted in her story and was taken to court, where at first she continued to stick to it. Since no interrogation protocols are extant, we do not know what kind of pressure the judges applied to make her confess that it was all a lie. The only motive she gave for her lies was that she had hoped to be released if she had been believed. The sentence was not pronounced until a month later. She was condemned to ten more years in prison and a banishment. In addition, she had to beg forgiveness from the indoor father, his wife, and Jaapje van het Hoff. She did so in the *tuchthuis,* in the presence of the court, the regents, and all prisoners.[140]

It is impossible to tell with certainty whether the indoor father was guilty after all, or if Johanna was consciously lying or simply the victim of her fantasies. A conclusion of sorts can be drawn, nevertheless. This case and the ones discussed above show that sex between imprisoned women and personnel was always a possibility. Within the community of prisoners it must have been viewed as an ever-present possibility, although as something which other women would do. There is no evidence for the use of physical force or threats by the men, but of course the inherent inequalities and potential for intimidation are obvious. For the women, potential advantages of a relationship with a personnel member are also obvious. They could earn several privileges, if only not to be punished. An unfounded claim of pregnancy could be a conscious or unconscious reaction against what was felt to be a denial of these privileges. The possibility of such a claim served as a permanent threat to the male partner to keep his promises. This mechanism certainly played a role in the next case to be reviewed.

The Case of the Women and Hans Jürgen Stange　　Hans Jürgen Stange, formerly a *balbier,* was chosen as master of discipline of the Hamburg spinhouse in August 1696 from among three candidates, one of whom was the brother of the *oeconomus.*[141] He left again three and a half years later under circumstances not very flattering to him. The story deserves to be told in detail, because it offers a unique inside view of a prison at the end of the seventeenth century and start of the eighteenth. Let us follow the events as they were recorded in the logbook virtually from day to day, by two successive *jahrverwalter.* The entry book confirms the main outline of our story and adds a few details.[142]

The story began on 23 March 1699, when the *jahrverwalter,* Claus Wilckens, noticed that something was "not right" with Cathrin Reders.

This woman, eighteen years old when she was condemned by the senate for prostitution and theft, had entered the spinhouse on September 10 of the previous year. When Wilckens persisted in his questions, Reders said that a hangman's son had made her pregnant during her stay in jail. The next day she repeated this statement to a praetor, but she refused to add further details. Nothing happened for some time. On July 1, however, after a quarrel with fellow inmates, she attempted to strangle herself with her garter. Thereupon she was transferred to the separate room occupied by the wife of the lawyer Stehnheuser, who had been committed there for killing her child in a fit of melancholy and who was the only one in the house not obliged to work. Another prisoner, Elisabeth Reumans, was lodged there, too, to keep an eye on her. Four days later Wilckens wrote in the logbook: "according to the testimony of the Reumansche, Hans Jürgen Stange is supposed to have approached the Redersche from behind the oven and to have asked her if she was alone. But when he learned that the Reumansche was with her, he said nothing more." This caused Reders to be questioned again, and on 10 July she voluntarily confessed that she had had sexual intercourse with the master of discipline twice. He had advised her to say that she had been made pregnant in jail. When asked whether she had received something in return, she replied that she had only enjoyed minor favors. The question was now whether her story should be believed. The provisors did nothing for the moment, but the 'greater college' of provisors and patrons at a meeting on 20 July decided that Stange should be interrogated by the praetors and forbidden to leave the house. The interrogation did not take place until 22 September. That was all the more remarkable, since a new accusation had been levelled a long time before then. On 29 July one of the women gave this statement: "once, when Hans Jürgen Stange thought that no one noticed him, he approached Gerdrut Prens on her bed. He touched her, saying 'aren't you my daughter?' and had intercourse with her." So now there were two eye-witnesses against the master of discipline, which, according to the contemporary law of proof, was enough to start a criminal trial. But, since the witnesses were prisoners, they may not have met the criterion of reliability. Stange's interrogation must have been inconclusive, since we do not hear of any follow-up measures as a result of it.

In early modern Europe generally a great symbolic value was laid on the statements of a woman at the moment of delivery. Such statements were recorded as special truths in the Delft prison, too. For this reason it is likely that the Hamburg magistrates awaited the day when Cathrin Reders would give birth before they took further steps. But she kept them in suspense. The spinhouse midwife, who had visited her regularly, declared on 21 October that she was not carrying a child at all. The senate midwife, who was called to give a second opinion, thought that, in any case, there was no living child. The uncertainty about Reders's condition encouraged Stange, who was said to have spoken with her on 15 November. Whatever he may have advised her, it did him no good. Two weeks later, when the senate midwife visited Reders anew, the prisoner gave a reason for her long expectancy. She claimed the current pregnancy was her second. She said she had aborted herself the first time and that she had sex with the master of discipline six times altogether. The midwife calculated that the child was due in January. The case grew more dramatic still. On 4 December Reders made a second suicide attempt in the same clumsy manner as the earlier one. Her two companions foiled the attempt. On 9 December Hans Jürgen Stange was suspended "for one or two months."

We are now in 1700. The leading role was suddenly taken over by Gerdrut Prens, the woman Stange was said to have called his daughter, and who had been entirely forgotten since. She had been condemned for swindling in December 1697, when she was twenty-three. Since her term was two years, she would normally have been out by now, but supposedly the suspicion against Stange had caused her to be kept longer. However, no one seems to have noticed that she was pregnant, too. But the begetter knew, and he was determined to keep the matter secret as long as possible. It may seem surprising that he remained active in the house while he was suspended. However, he lived there. Here we see one of the consequences of the paternalistic model of imprisonment. The master of discipline was suspended from his duties, but still present in the prison. Considering also that he called Gerdrut his daughter, the case is like a modern incest story. On Sunday, 28 January, Gerdrut complained about an aching belly, for which the house *balbier* gave her a potion. During the rest of the day she was only in the company of her fellow inmates Magdalena Schröders and Anna Glotz and the master of discipline and his wife. Did the latter believe her husband to be innocent? In any case, to accompany him then was probably the last thing she did for him. The two female prisoners secretly assisted Gerdrut in her labor that night, without calling the house midwife. The next morning rumors spread that Gerdrut's bed was 'impure.' Mrs. Bockelman, the wife of the *oeconomus,* inspected it, found much blood, and concluded that Gerdrut had had a miscarriage. Her husband had to go out for some business, but he promised the *jahrverwalter* to investigate the matter upon his return. Was this an unconscious attempt to offer his colleague a helpful delay? If it was, we must at least conclude that Bockelman held no grudge against Stange for beating his brother in the competition for the post in 1696. Using this time, Stange tried to persuade Mrs. Bockelman that there had been no miscarriage. The prisoners Schröders and Glotz argued with him, but when Bockelman returned at ten o'clock, they were accused of hiding something. Finally, the child was found, wrapped in blue cloth, dead.[143] A few provisors hurried to the spinhouse with shocked faces and immediately inquired into the whereabouts of Hans Jürgen Stange. They were too late. No one could find him; not even his wife knew where he was. Never again did his name turn up in the records.

The story does not quite end here, however. The magistrates considered the begetter in the pregnancies determined, but the culprit was gone. The circumstances under which Gerdrut Prens had been delivered presented a new problem. In most countries, secretly giving birth to a dead child without calling a midwife constituted a criminal offense. According to Hamburg custom, the child was 'decried' in front of the spinhouse on 1 February "because it has probably been killed." The next day the body was examined by physicians and buried in the cemetery that incidentally bore the mother's name. On 3 February the 'greater college' met to appoint a new master of discipline. Two candidates presented themselves, but it was decided to postpone the decision for a week and during that time to make careful inquiries into the reputation of both. At the meeting of 10 February the majority of votes went to one Henningh Went. Stange's wife was told to make room for him and to leave the house as soon as possible.

Meanwhile, probably the fake pregnancy of Cathrin Reders continued. But on 18 February she claimed to have "lost something, although only a stone was found," and the midwife and other experienced women declared that nothing had happened to her. Reders insisted, however, and, indeed, within a few weeks her body grew thin again. On 5 April she was placed back with the other prisoners and told to work again. Soon afterwards she made her third suicide attempt. To the new *jahrverwalter* she explained that she was obsessed day and night with the long term she still had to serve—in fact another five months—and that she would rather be dead. Her interrogator showed that there was no possibility of a cross-class empathy in such circumstances in 1700. He merely warned her that the place where suicides went to was much worse than a prison, but she refused to heed him. Thereupon, she was put into a dark cell on bread and water, and securely fastened so that she was unable to hurt herself. She was released from the dark cell in a few days on a promise to behave well and there were no more complaints about her.

The female actors in this drama had different fates, but they all left the spinhouse in 1700. On 5 April, when Reders was removed from her room, Elisabeth Reumans, who had been her guard for nine months, requested and received her freedom. She would have had one year to stay. Anna Glotz, a prostitute who was serving her third term in the institution, was transferred to the poxhouse on 24 May. "Her godless body was infected so much by the French pox that it broke open." She died at the age of forty-three on 5 June, after expressing regret and repentance over her sins. Cathrin Reders was set free on 21 July, "following the wish of the board and because her term is over and she has promised to improve her life." Gerdrut Prens was apparently found innocent of the death or stillbirth of her child. She was taken to jail on 20 August to testify in the trial of Magdalena Schröders in the matter of the death of Gerdrut's child. From there she must have been set free, because her term had expired months previously, and her name did not reappear in the records. No murder could be proved against Magdalena Schröders, but she was considered guilty enough to be flogged at the pillory and then banished from the city.

Children and Marriage   Two minor themes are closely related to the previous one. Since most of the evidence comes from Hamburg only, they will be given just a brief treatment. The presence of children, even past the stage of infancy, in the Hamburg spinhouse during the early decades appears to have occurred only in that institution. In the Dutch Republic we hardly hear of them at all. The entry books of the spinhouse or the workhouse at Amsterdam do not speak of any children being admitted. The Delft sources refer to a woman who gave birth in prison shortly after her entry in 1739 and another such occurrence in 1793.[144] In 1805, on the other hand, it was said as a matter of course that women were being delivered of babies in the house. Upon the advice of two physicians it was decided that newborn children would henceforth stay with the mother for four to six weeks.[145] Children past the stage of infancy were never admitted to the Delft prison during the seventeenth or eighteenth centuries. When there was no one to take care of them during their mother's imprisonment, they were temporarily lodged in the orphanage.[146]

In the case of the Hamburg spinhouse, we have to differentiate between a birth in the institution and a longer stay of a child. In the early years of the house, children, whether born in the institution or not, might stay there with their mother indefinitely. This practice generally ceased, however, after the second child murder of April 1698. Childbirth in the house, on the other hand was common throughout the institution's existence. In this case the child would stay with the mother for only a short period after birth. Because the house had a midwife of its own, deliveries must have been considered normal events. Pregnant women were sent there from other places of detention, such as the *zuchthaus* or the jail, to be delivered of their child.[147] In 1702, however, two pregnant women were released because their relatives were prepared to let them give birth at their home.[148] Clearly, the spinhouse also had the function of preventing delinquent women from having their child in the wrong place.

There were no apparent motives for the two murders of children in the spinhouse. In August 1694 a twenty-four-year-old woman cut the throat of her daughter, who had been born in the house seven weeks earlier.[149] This first murder gave the provisors second thoughts about allowing children to stay in the institution, and the next year a woman was set free, "because children are a burden to the house."[150] A permanent solution was not yet found, however, and in 1698 the child of Maria Fischers from Zerbst was the second victim. This woman had entered the house for the third time in June 1697, when she was thirty-two. In December of that year she gave birth to twins, baptized Hans Christoffer and Maria Elisabeth. The girl was killed by another prisoner, Anna Neuhauss, on 26 April of the next year. Significantly, this woman had been condemned for attempting to cut the throat of a child. Neuhaus had carried Fischer's daughter in her arms for half an hour and then she suddenly threw her into the latrine. Directly afterwards she cried out, admitting what she had done. Servants of the house immediately cut off the water supply to the latrine, but, when the child was recovered, it had drowned. Neuhaus gave no other reason than that she had been depressed because she had to stay for such a long time. She was executed on 16 May. Fischers and her son had already been released then. In December 1712 she briefly stayed in the house for a fourth time, after being caught begging.[151] She was transferred there from the *zuchthaus*.

The provisors were only half content with the solutions decided on in the wake of the murders. They had wanted to ban not only children but also pregnant women. Childbirths they argued, could only take place "at the common dormitory in the presence of all the whores," which caused many inconveniences. They suggested that pregnant women should be kept in jail, but the praetors vehemently objected to this idea.[152] Negotiations with the orphanage were not recorded, but later events demonstrate that its board had to yield. In 1700 a woman was released "so that some fellow prisoners may not, out of malice, take the life of her child."[153] Thereafter, children born in the house were regularly taken to the orphanage. Murders were still possible in the spinhouse, though, in the brief time they would stay with the mother. In 1707–1708 two women were told to spy on Margreth Lang, after she confided to one of them that she intended to kill her child when it was born. Margreth's daughter was taken to the orphanage soon after birth, whereupon the two spies received their freedom.[154]

In addition to the birth of illegitimate children, the prison experience included the celebration of legitimate marriage. The first took place three years after the opening of the Hamburg spinhouse, when the man with whom Maria Wageners had lived previously declared that he intended to marry her. It was decided that the two could have their wedding in the house. Maria and the child she had with her were then released, but the family had to stay away from town.[155] Several other women were married in prison by the prison preacher. Once it was recorded that the *oeconomus* and one of the *vögte* acted as witnesses.[156] In 1702 the wedding of two inmates was celebrated in the spinhouse. Johan Friedrich Holtman from Lübeck had been in prison since 1688 and had twice tried to escape without success. He was pardoned at the age of forty-four because he was willing to serve in a Danish regiment. Anna Marie Lorens, his new wife, went with him. She was thirty-three then and had been in the house since 1689. They were ordered to stay away from town, which presumably the entire Danish regiment was supposed to do. Holtman and Lorens took the oath of *uhrfeyde,* and he promised to stay with the troops, but both ran away from the lieutenant who had picked them up as soon as they had passed through the main gate.[157]

Insubordination   I am using the word insubordination to refer to disobedience, abuse, or resistance by inmates toward their superiors. This includes a broad range of behavior, from individual impertinences to large-scale revolts. Forced labor being the essence of the regime, the primary form of resistance must have been refusal to work. In our main source, the Delft logbook, this was seldom recorded, but it was mentioned several times in cases dealt with by the Amsterdam court in 1617–1618. It was also a common item in the Utrecht logbook for the 1620s, when several men were punished for it. In 1624, for example, "the cow thief" had not rasped for a week and had done too little work the week before. He claimed to have a weak arm, but after a doctor had declared him to be malingering, he was put into the cellar in chains. Women in Utrecht were also accused of having produced too little. They were usually punished with rebukes only, as in April 1625, when it is recorded that they also scolded and scratched each other.[158] The concentration of these references in the 1610s and 1620s suggests that refusal to work was regents' business, especially during the early years. It may have been that, in the course of the seventeenth century, the personnel learned to deal with unwilling inmates on their own. Alternatively, we may assume that the emphasis on productivity declined. Cheating was recorded, too, in Utrecht. Some of the raspers increased the weight of their output by wetting it, and it was reported that inmates of the Amsterdam rasphouse sometimes mixed it with sand.[159] In the latter town this was still done in the eighteenth century.[160] Since it was easily discovered, it may be taken as a sign of protest rather than as a smart way to alleviate the burden of work. It was probably not a protest when it was done with the complicity of the supervisors. A servant of the Leiden *tuchthuis* who had even assisted with carrying the sand was condemned for his offense in 1702.[161]

Other forms of insubordination were often inseparable from plans to break out of prison. Escape will be discussed below. Here we are considering cases in which escape was not the main intention, or at least this was not recorded. The evidence is too fragmentary and incidental to tell whether the character of insubordination changed during the two centuries studied. First I will consider concerted action by a larger group.

Haarlem witnessed the earliest recorded prison riot on 11 January 1613. Some inmates probably had planned it, since it broke out when its leader, Pieter Jacobs, hit the indoor father on the head with a stick. Several groups of men managed to interconnect their cages by breaking down the walls between them. Then they barricaded the main door with looms. The rebels were fully prepared to engage in a head-on confrontation, crying out that they would resist until the last man, but the riot was suppressed by force. No specific demands by the rebels were recorded.[162] The incident can be called a riot because men from more than one cage were involved. By this criterion, the sources studied disclose only a handful of riots. The relatively well-documented one which took place in the Hamburg spin-house in 1709 is discussed in the next section. Streng mentions two more riots in the spinhouse, in 1737 and 1770, and one in the *zuchthaus*, in 1774. In the last case, the repeal of certain privileges formed the immediate cause. All these revolts in Hamburg were suppressed by militia forces.[163]

It occurred more frequently that a small group of prisoners sharing a room revolted by barricading the door or by some other kind of resistance. In February 1617, for example, a few inmates of the Amsterdam rasp-house barricaded themselves in their cage after they had attacked and seriously injured the weaving master. Their leader threw soil from the latrine at anyone trying to approach them.[164] At Delft in 1739 a group of men opposed the indoor father when he came to chastize them for complaining about the food and insulting his wife recently when he had been out. This resulted in a fight in which the father himself was beaten up while two of his servants were seriously injured.[165] Another Delft case, in 1770, is memorable because of the evident clumsiness of a whole group of law enforcers, who were occupied with just two prisoners, Louis Bottenol and Hendrik van der Lubbe. Apparently, these two shared a cage by themselves then. Bottenol started the trouble by screaming loudly, and when he was told to be silent, he attacked the indoor father with a weapon made from one half of a scissors tied to a stick. The two inmates then barricaded the door of their cage. Three servants were called who found that the door could only be forced with a jack, and by 7 P.M. they had opened it far enough that a man could slip through. But each servant who approached Bottenol was hurt with the makeshift weapon. Other efforts to get at him, such as trying to hit him with a stick through a grating in the ceiling of his cage, were also unsuccessful, and it was decided to postpone the attempt to recapture the pair until the next morning. After consultation with the city's carpenters, the servants finally managed to force the door. With the help of Van der Lubbe, who had already slipped the prison offi-cials a note stating that he had tried in vain to persuade his mate to stop, they overpowered Bottenol and handcuffed him. When asked his motives, Bottenol just uttered complaints about the foot and produced a piece of mouldy bread. However, a sandwich he had kept in a box was discovered and the regents found it palatable. Apparently, there was no particular reason for the incident; events had just escalated.[166]

Bottenol's case bordered on individual resistance. When only one prisoner was involved, the resistance was recorded very infrequently. The logbook of the Hamburg *zuchthaus* has a few such cases in the 1640s. Samuel Mensendorf one day disturbed the communion, crying out that he refused to work. He cursed the founding fathers and the current house officials, calling the prison a devil's place. Another inmate also refused to work and blasphemed so seriously that, alas, his words, which were recorded, were later deleted. A third resister not only stated that he put his trust in the devil, but also cut the raspmaster on the face with a knife.[167] Apparently, the Hamburg provisors were especially offended by disobedience in the religious sphere. An inmate of the spinhouse was reported to have abused two successive ministers.[168] The Delft logbooks also refer to a few individual cases.[169]

The fact that these acts of resistance were so varied and were recorded so inconsistently precludes an elaborate analysis. One conclusion can be drawn, nevertheless. The prisoners never seem to have gained any advantage from their actions. In that sense, their behavior may be characterized as irrational and motivated by desperation or general discontent rather than by deliberate plans to force an improvement of their condition. The only deliberate objective that was constantly pursued by prisoners seems to have been to try to escape. Activities directed at breaking out, whether collective or individual, must certainly be considered rational.

Escape   The number of attempted escapes underscore the determination of many convicts, especially men, to force their way to freedom. Logbooks, such as that of the Delft regents, repeatedly refer to activities aimed at breaking out. A small minority of incarcerated managed to escape and remain free; a high percentage of successful escapes was only attained by male convicts at Delft (28%). Others were temporarily at large and then recaptured.[170] It is evident that unsuccessful attempts were much more frequent than actual escapes. It would be futile to try to quantify them. Not every such incident was reported to the board, and those that were were not recorded systematically. The perception of the superiors, who classified some activities by inmates as preparations for escape, must also have varied with time and place. Despite these reservations, it can be assumed that no day passed in early modern prisons without some inmates at least contemplating breaking out.

For the historian it is better that most attempts were unsuccessful. These incidents were documented more thoroughly, for the obvious reason that prisoners at large could not be questioned. The failure of the men and women involved to regain their freedom makes possible a qualitative analysis of this aspect of life from below. The cases reported in the sources I studied are too numerous to review them all in detail; instead I will discuss a few basic patterns, restricting myself to the most illustrative cases.

The first question is simply: how did they do it? The methods used can be grouped into three categories. The most common method then, just as today, was to try to break out without being noticed doing so. Another method, likewise practiced then and now, was to get hold of keys, by force or by some ruse, or to force the personnel into compliance. The third method, arson, is not as common today. Prisoners resorting to it hoped to create a chaos in which they could easily run away. The use of the third method is related, no doubt, to the physical circumstances of early modern prisons. They were constructed from wood to a larger extent than high-security prisons today, and much of the work equipment was also combustible.

The earliest recorded case of arson took place in Haarlem in 1615. Pieter Jacobs set fire to his cage with an unspecified "peculiar means." The fire was discovered in time, however, so that it was extinguished before there was much damage.[171] A few female prisoners in Haarlem tried this method in 1624.[172] In the same year it was tried by a group of Utrecht convicts who had obtained some coal.[173] In 1691 a woman attempted to escape from the Hamburg spinhouse by means of arson, though no details were recorded. In the same year another woman confessed that she had intended to set the house on fire, after a fellow inmate betrayed that she possessed a flint.[174] Three decades earlier, the best documented incident had occurred in the Amsterdam rasphouse. The actors were two men Lodewijk Jansen and Laurens Cornelisse, both twenty-one, who also had acquired a flint. First, they barricaded the door of their cage with a rasp saw and redwood logs. Then they set fire to their straw mattresses, with the intention of burning a hole in the ceiling. But the fire was soon discovered, and the door was forced even though the prisoners had pledged that they would suffocate or be burned rather than let anyone in. They had committed the act out of desperation, they said.[175] But in general, fires were usually discovered because of the smoke before the intended chaos could ensue, which made arson not a very effective method. It was probably obsolete already and discarded by the eighteenth century. The Delft records refer to this method just twice, but in each case it was merely tried as one of many expedients by particularly subversive inmates.[176]

Methods of breaking out, on the other hand, seem to have improved in the eighteenth century, unless this impression is just a reflection of the detail provided by the Delft sources. They show the prisoners to have been quite inventive. In 1732 two men made themselves a knife. A year later seven men were busy digging through their cage's foundation with instruments they made themselves. They used the hooks by which their hammocks were fastened to the ceiling. Understandably, almost all these activities took place at night. After the discovery of another conspiracy in January 1736 the instruments they were using were inspected and it was found that they were all made from utensils required for eating or working. A month later, three men dug a hole in the floor with unspecified instruments. They threw the mortar and sand which they dug up into the latrine, but they had to give up their project when they struck an excessively hard layer. Another group, whose cage bordered on the street, even reached the lowest depth of the house's foundation. Their instruments were made of spools and other parts of weaving looms. They intended to cover the hole they had made "very subtly," but one of the nonparticipants alarmed the indoor father. In 1751 a number of prisoners succeeded in escaping after making a hole with the spring of a pocket watch. This did not mean that inmates were allowed to keep watches; in 1738 a man received a half-year reduction for revealing that another inmate possessed such a spring. Still other versatile prisoners removed a stone from the floor with a nail recovered from the wall, broke away two irons from the latrine and removed some window clasps.[177]

Thus, prisoners in eighteenth-century Delft made escape instruments out of practically everything. Such inventiveness was seldom reported in the seventeenth century. In the Hamburg spinhouse it happened a couple of times that a few men managed to break through the walls separating their night cells. But the outer walls of these cells were apparently stronger. Three prisoners who had linked up in this way in 1682 could then only barricade themselves and try to negotiate their freedom. They were flogged instead.[178] In 1690 three men were able to break through the outer wall, too, because they had files. They reached the prison church, where they struck the grating used to separate the inmates from the audience of citizens. Two of them managed to twist through the bars, but the third, Johan Friedrich Holtman, was too fat and had to stay behind. The files had been procured—we do not learn how—by the prisoner Anna Marie Lorens, who somehow induced the porter's daughter to deliver them to the men. In the aftermath, the porter and his wife were ordered to remove their daughter from the house and to take care that she never returned. Lorens was treated to bread and water for two weeks; Holtman's punishment was not recorded. Holtman and Lorens are the couple that were married to each other and released on the promise that he would join the Danish regiment, but then they absconded.[179]

This case shows that assistance from nonprisoners, from within or without, could be a crucial factor in the success of escape attempts. This is no different from the situation today. Attempts to break out with instruments smuggled in by relatives or friends were recorded in Delft in 1726 and Amsterdam in 1746.[180] The personnel might facilitate escapes indirectly through negligence or directly by complicity, motivated by rewards of some sort. Peter Bogart, weaving master of the Utrecht *tuchthuis,* was dismissed in April 1628 because he had been away from the prison too frequently, as a result of which thirteen weavers had escaped.[181] In Hamburg Caspar Smit, Stange's precursor as master of discipline, and his wife met the same fate in 1696 for failing to notice that several prisoners' blocks had been filed off.[182] In 1703 a member of the spinhouse personnel, again, the porter's maid this time, provided escape equipment.[183] In Delft the prisoner Maria Nieuwhuis escaped in 1736 through an unspecified "secret correspondence" with a temporary servant.[184] Most criminal prisoners did not have the means to bribe a personnel member, but at least one, condemned for life at Delft, could afford it. For 100 guilders he obtained files from a servant of the house and thereupon escaped with five other men.[185]

Inmates attempted forceful escape from prison workhouses throughout their existence and the history of such incidents does not show a particular pattern over time. I will cite just two cases, from different places and periods. The first involved a group of prisoners in the Amsterdam rasphouse in April 1618. They were headed by Jan Alofs, the last person to have been blinded in Amsterdam.[186] He and three others attacked the indoor father, took his keys, and locked him up in a closet. They must have gotten the wrong keys, though, because they got no further in the escape, and at night they barricaded themselves in their cage. This incident ended when they were transferred to jail upon their own request. It was a relatively irrational demand, with a short-term advantage: no requirement to work in jail. Of course, they were questioned there. Jan Alofs was even formally threatened with torture to get him to be more detailed about his attack on the indoor father. He confessed to having hit him in the loins with the handle of a rasp saw.[187]

The second case was in Bremen. There is little information on escape attempts from that prison, but a serious and well-documented incident occurred in 1754. On the morning of 10 July, a Wednesday, when Marie Sophie Fieweks, the master of discipline's wife, was in the house church, she looked through a window and saw inmates Wilhelm Dreier and Hans Jacob Krippendorp climb a sort of rope ladder against the wall of the courtyard. But then the ladder broke and the two men were caught. Fieweks hurried to their cell, where she found her husband covered with bed clothes, his hands and feet tied, and his scarf bound tightly around his neck. His body was still warm but his eyes were blue. The cell was shared by four men and that morning at 7 a.m. the master of discipline, named Gottfried Goldstein, opened it and asked them if they wished to go to church. Two of them proceeded to go, while another inmate, Julius Tiele, quickly slipped in from his cell, whereupon the three overpowered Goldstein. Dreier and Krippendorp said they had grabbed his hands and feet, and accused Tiele of having strangled him. Tiele was lucky: he had climbed the ladder, which he had made from strings, first, and fled.[188]

Other escape attempts accompanied by violence were reported at Delft and the Amsterdam workhouse. In the latter institution in 1656 a Walloon beggar who had a knife conspired with two other men, one of whom was seventy-two years old, to escape. They did not succeed, however, and when they were interrogated, the old man said he knew his mate would rather die than serve his one-year term.[189]

Apart from the methods used, a few other aspects deserve attention. Escape attempts were mainly men's business. Women might even try to stop them. Such instances were reported in the Amsterdam workhouse in 1712 and again in 1723. In one of these, ten men beat the wife of the indoor father, who was ill, and two female prisoners said: "don't hit the mother like that."[190] At Delft in 1735 six male conspirators interrupted their breakout plan for seven weeks because they feared betrayal by the women in the room just above them, in spite of their promise to make a hole in their ceiling through which the women could join them.[191]

Occasionally, women attempted breakouts. The only large-scale collective escape from the Hamburg spinhouse during the period studied involved eight women, who ran away the night of 13 January 1671.[192] A number of female prisoners escaped from the poxhouse.[193] In 1705, Bartge Fopke almost made it from the spinhouse. She had stayed in the dining room unnoticed, so that she was locked in there at night. Then she broke her way into the courtyard, climbed a nut tree the porter had planted there, made it to the roof, and slid down along a string of ribbons she had made. She landed somewhat obtrusively, though and was noticed by a nightwatchman patrolling the area. Three years earlier another female prisoner had made a similar attempt.[194] At Delft a woman broke out in April 1756, and in August two other women escaped by way of the mad ward courtyard, but they were caught a few days later.[195]

That was about all the sources revealed. Apparently, women often felt more secure staying behind. The differences between males and females in this matter can be interpreted in terms of traditional active and passive notions about sex roles. Women did not lack the physical strength to escape, judging from the example of Bartge Fopke, but they were more inclined to accommodate to prison life. Conditions might also have been more tolerable for them. Women could use their charms with the male personnel in order to acquire favors. This must have been common, without resulting in sexual relations in most cases. Men did not usually have such possibilities of ingratiating themselves with their superiors, and therefore were more inclined to attempt radical solutions. The prevalence of breakouts among the males gave some of them an opportunity for ingratiation after all, in the form of betrayal of escape plots.

Betrayal was always a consideration because of the collective character of many escape attempts. Prisoners learned to cooperate from the beginning, but collective enterprises did not only mean cooperation. They led to conflicts as well. Informers could be motivated by the desire to avoid punishment as well as the hope of a reduction. Prisoners who betrayed a conspiracy almost always earned a recommendation for reduction from the regents. Obviously, it was in the interest of conspirators that nonparticipants would remain silent. In 1713 an Amsterdam prisoner who was the only one left when his mates had broken out was asked by the magistrates why he had failed to inform the indoor father, which would have earned him a considerable reduction. He replied that the others had threatened him and he had been afraid. A similar fear was expressed by two out of eight inmates in 1672.[196] At Delft in 1736 two men had stayed in their cage, while their five mates had successfully broken out. The two declared that when they had refused to participate, the others tied them to each other with a rope and stood them against the wall. One of the conspirators permanently watched them with a knife in his hand, and they were told that their necks would be broken upon the least suspicious movement. Meanwhile, the five men sang and danced loudly to drown out the noise of their breakout.[197] Such a serenade was apparently so common that the personnel did not bother to check on it. Of course, any statement of the two who stayed, could not be countered by the ones who had fled.

The minority who actually succeeded in escaping often stayed free for good. Courts do not seem to have been very active in tracing refugees, except in Bremen, where printed posters have been preserved with blanks for the insertion of the escapee's name.[198] In the Republic, most refugees must have disappeared into the floating population of criminals and marginals. They were only discovered when caught again for some new offense, as in the case of Little Bernard from Brussels, who had escaped from the rasphouse with four other inmates the night of 28 April 1713, and was arrested anew in January 1718. When the judges asked him if he had broken out in May 1713 together with six or seven others, he replied truthfully: "there were five of us." A few refugees stayed at large for just a brief period, though. In 1699 six Amsterdam prisoners on their way to Hoorn to be heard as witnesses overpowered their guards on the ship and fled. Five returned to the metropolis and were soon recaptured. One of Little Bernard's mates in the 1713 escape was caught again the next afternoon because he boasted to a group of people in the street that he had broken out of the rasphouse with God's help. When ten men escaped from Delft in April 1736, eight were caught the next day by the *drossaard* of the Court of Holland and provisionally confined at The Hague. They stayed there for a month until their cage at Delft was repaired.[199]

The Great Illusion   Patricia O'Brien speaks of a prison subculture in nineteenth-century France. She identifies it by some of its expressions: the use of argot in speech, making graffiti, and tattooing. Recidivists, she says, stood at the top of the hierarchy of inmates, because they were experienced in the ways of the institution. In the early modern period, in a prison such as the one at Delft, the presence of recidivists may have been less crucial to the hierarchy and their status may have been less exalted. For one thing, serious repeaters among the convict population eventually received the death penalty. Second, a number of professional criminals, even though they were serving their first term, stayed in prison for quite a substantial period. They were inside long enough to become experienced in the ways of the prison, and they were certainly viewed as leaders of a kind by their fellows. According to the records, many of them were involved in several escape attempts in a row. They must have been well aware that these undertakings were usually unsuccessful, if only because other inmates played the reductions game by betraying such plots. Maybe the frequent conspiracies should be viewed as a kind of game, too. By keeping up hopes and maintaining the myth that one day they would all be free as a result of their own efforts, these prisoners made their situation tolerable. All this meant that Coornhert's claim that rogues would rather be executed than perform forced labor was no longer valid. Several subversive inmates made exclamations to that effect in the seventeenth century. But by contrast, the cumulative experiences of generations of prisoners taught that preparations for escape kept up morale. These factors shaped the prison subculture of the early modern period.

Prison Life and
Social Tensions Outside: Hamburg 1709

Thus far the internal world of prisons has been viewed largely as a microcosm subject to its own laws. It would be wrong, however, to think that the microcosm was unaffected by what happened around it. In popular parlance today, penal institutions and asylums are often put in opposition to the rest of society as if they stood entirely apart from it. We frequently refer to psychiatric inmates being temporarily "removed from society," or to released prisoners who "return to society." This kind of terminology is very misleading. It should be avoided by historians and other scholars in all cases. In previous sections I have sometimes spoken of "society at large," to emphasize that I only meant a part of the social world: the part outside the prison. What we call society is nothing more (and nothing less) than a network of relationships between human beings, including the inmates of a prison and its personnel and people who live far away from the prison. I am referring to more than just the custom of admitting the general public as visitors, which implied contact between the world within and without. In addition to this, indoor fathers began in their job with acquired notions of labor, discipline, and morality, and convicts entered the institution with the acquired experience of a marginal existence. The microcosm continued to be affected by movements, tensions, and changing views originating outside its walls. Thus, prisons were linked socially to the rest of the world and vice versa. In the rest of this chapter, attention will be paid to a series of events in and around the Hamburg spinhouse which demonstrate in a particularly illuminating way the interdependence of internal life and great affairs of state and religion in the world at large.

The Background   The two incidents of 1709 that uprooted the prison order happened within a month of each other, in July and August. They were part of the politico-religious struggles which divided the Hamburg citizenry from the late 1670s into the 1710s. These structural conflicts have been dealt with by several of the city's historians.[200] The repercussion they had on the affairs of the spinhouse is given just a few lines in Streng's work.[201]

To try to summarize the Hamburg struggles is a hazardous enterprise, in view of a recent historian's judgment that "even many contemporaries were baffled by the bewildering variety of issues, by the shifting alliances and uneasy compromises.[202] Two major questions, however, were central: the role of religion in urban life, and the extent of the citizens' participation in the political process. In the political realm, conflicts centered around the relationship between senate and *bürgerschaft* and the accessibility of the latter's meetings to the entire citizenry. In the religious realm, the issues included the degree of tolerance extended to various religious minorities, and such classic targets of puritanically minded activists as a new opera building. In the 1680s and 1690s religious antagonisms were exacerbated by a theological division among the Hamburg parish clergy. Some of the pastors, heavily opposed by their colleagues, were known to be adherents of the movement which later came to be called Pietism. The political and religious conflicts became intertwined because the magistrates were forced to take a stand on this matter. The elites may have liked the opera, but they were also inclined to favor the cause of religious pluralism, which obliged them to defend the Pietist faction. In their turn, the Pietist pastors heavily attacked the guilds for their attitude to interlopers. Although Rückleben refuses to draw the conclusion, his study strongly suggests that the main axis of tension involved the politico-commercial elite on one side, and the lower-middle class, based in the guilds, on the other. The latter wished to assert their right as citizens to have a say in the government, and they were staunch defenders of Lutheran orthodoxy. The groups below them socially counted few citizens. The political compromise of 1699 restricted the authority of the senate vis-à-vis the *bürgerschaft*, while membership of the latter body was extended to all citizens except interlopers and servants of senators. The compromise lasted for only a decade. From 1708 to 1712 Hamburg had to allow the intervention of an Imperial Commission led by Count Schönborn. He accomplished the restoration of the senate. His presence, however, until 1716, and especially his protection of the Jesuits, increased anti-Catholic sentiments in the city. Agitation continued throughout the 1710s, culminating in the destruction of the house and chapel of the Imperial resident by a Lutheran crowd in 1719.

In this web of struggles the loyalties of the people connected with the spinhouse were not automatically given. The prisoners themselves may hardly have been interested in theological or political disputes. Most of

them were probably noncitizens, and as *unehrliche leute,* they were excluded from the world of the guilds. But according to the house ordinance, the inmates were to receive a Lutheran education during their stay.
The provisors wished to play down the guilds' notions of infamy, but they
also wanted to appease them. They were dependent on senate as well as
bürgerschaft, but they seem to have been tied in particular to the intermediate college of *oberalten.*[203] That may have influenced the position they
took. The *oberalte* first sided with the senate, but toward 1700 they began
to represent the *bürgerschaft* again, which they originally had done. Significantly, the spinhouse provisors quarrelled with a notorious anti-Pietist
minister during the 1690s, while they took a stand against religious pluralism in 1709. In the first case they were supported by the magistrates,
and in the second they found themselves opposed to the magistrates.

Magister Johann Lange was contracted to be the spinhouse's preacher in
1682.[204] At that time he was a follower of Winckler, the leader of the
Pietist faction, but he changed allegiances in 1688 after being kicked out
of the latter's house.[205] His defection may have started the conflict with
the provisors. It surfaced in March 1690, when there were disagreements
about his fee and the number of times he was to preach. Apparently a
straightforward character, Lange did not hesitate to denounce the provisors publicly from the pulpit of the spinhouse church. This matter ended
inconclusively and the next conflict came in 1693. It centered around the
prayers and hymns to be recited in the house, but there was one other
interesting issue. One of the praetors complained that Lange was interro-
gating prostitutes too conscientiously, asking them for the names of their
habitual clients. The preacher would not back down. If he could only
speak with each newly arrived prostitute in a room alone, he claimed, they
would freely confess everything, but this privilege had been denied to him
by the *jahrverwalter.* The magistrates refused to grant his request. The
praetor made it clear that asking inmates such questions constituted an
encroachment upon his judicial prerogatives, while a burgomaster cleverly
added that the minister's individual examinations were actually a Papist
procedure. Lange promised to comply with the wishes of the magistrates,
but he was suspended for unnamed reasons later that year. By 1698 he had
evidently been readmitted; his fee was even raised to four times the original amount. In spite of this, he made another public complaint about it.
His sermon of 1 September was reported to have contained the accusation
that the provisors owed him sixteen marks and that they were thieves. The
prisoners' reaction to this was left to the reader's imagination. A tumul-
tuous meeting between Lange and the magistrates followed, in which the
former denied having used the word thieves. Again, the conflict was protracted and inconclusive, only ending with Lange's death in May 1700.
This led to a final battle over his succession. Dr. Meyer, pastor of the
Jacobi parish and leader of the anti-Pietist faction, claimed the right to

designate a successor. But the provisors took a firm stand and managed to choose their own candidate.[206]

The Communion   Reimert Altwasser was taken to the spinhouse by the executioner on 25 August 1708.[207] Before his entry he had been whipped and branded for his property crimes and a term of twenty years awaited him. Born in a village near Brussels forty-four years earlier, he was one of the oldest inmates. On 2 March 1709 the prisoner's wife approached the *jahrverwalter*, Martin Goldenen, with a request that would become a heavy burden on the conscience of the provisors. She asked that a Catholic father be allowed to come to the spinhouse to present Holy Communion to Altwasser.

At other times such a request might have been considered more favorably, but with the Imperial Commission in town, it had immediate political implications. Goldenen's quick and simple reply was that to allow this would be a breach of the house's constitution. Altwasser's wife refused to accept this answer, and either she or the priest in question must have found their way to Count Schönborn. On 26 March Goldenen was called to the town hall, where he was informed of the senate's decision to comply with Schönborn's wish that the prisoner be allowed to have Communion at a neutral location. This solution might have been acceptable to the previous generation of prison administrators. In 1691 a Warsaw-born Catholic woman had been released before her term was over, because "she had not communicated for such a long time."[208] Now the senate's decree started a tug-of-war between the board of provisors and their superiors. The former tried every legal expedient to delay the matter, which caused Count Schönborn to press it with the senate once more early in July. The magistrates then decided to wait no longer and to bypass the board. The personnel of the house were ordered to hand over the prisoner on penalty of losing their jobs. On 16 July, at 4 a.m., Altwasser was picked up by a praetor's servant. Temporarily freed from his block, he went to the priest in a coach and was delivered back to the prison after two hours.[209]

Having been overruled by the senate, the provisors decided to launch a formal protest.[210] The text opens in a polemical tone, explaining that the thief Altwasser "claims to be a Roman catholic" and that he has been allowed "to perform his pretended devotion." The prisoner was "led around in a coach for his amusement, freed from his block, and taken *ad locum tertium* for the uninhibited exercise of a religion which is diametrically opposed to our fundamental urban *recesse* and constitution." The provisors speak as if they are protecting a beleaguered fortress. They have been confronted with "threatening decrees" and finally forced to allow the prisoner to be "extradited." The gist of the argument, however, is legal: the heirs of the spinhouse founder presented the institution to both the senate and the *bürgerschaft*, which means that the two bodies should decide together in matters of importance. To emphasize the exceptional character of the case, the provisors claim that Lutherans in Catholic places never enjoy similar privileges. Moreover, even their own Lutheran prisoners are not freed from their blocks during religious services. Finally, the dangers which may result from this precedent are listed: the citizens, who already have a negative view of the house, will withhold their gifts at collections still further, under the pretext that the papist religion is favored in it; similar requests for persons in jail or those publicly punished are to be expected now, which may lead to popular disturbances; the audacity of the other inmates, who are all villainous scoundrels anyway, will increase. It follows that "they are hard to restrain and [the tensions] may easily erupt into a great accident. . . . We would rather not have these evil consequences burdening our conscience."

The provisors addressed their note of protest, dated 26 July, to the college of *oberalten,* who were to induce the *bürgerschaft* to demand satisfaction from the senate. This does not mean that the parties opposing each other represented two distinct social strata. Rather, it was an internal conflict involving two groups within the urban politico-commercial elite. In 1709 the *bürgerschaft,* too, was dominated by the richer families. Five of the eight provisors who signed the note of protest could be identified. Three belonged to great merchant families and two would even become senators later.[211] One of their opponents was burgomaster Paul Paulsen, a merchant's son who had been elected into the senate as a new man without party affiliation in 1696.[212]

The Riot   The provisors' gloomy prediction came true sooner than they might have expected. We have to consider whether it might have been a self-fulfilling prophecy. The uproar, the responsibility for which the provisors had denied beforehand, broke out on Monday, 12 August. In the morning the *oeconomus* alarmed Martin Goldenen with the news that the male prisoners had entrenched themselves in their workshop and determined not to leave it. The board met immediately and Goldenen and a colleague then approached the praetors to request assistance from the militia. The militia were called and were posted in front of the workshop, but violent action was postponed. In the meantime, the female prisoners, who had been locked away in their dormitories, were contributing to the situation. A number of them yelled at the officials and warned them that the men had made weapons from nails and the rungs of spinning wheels. They also cried out that the Catholic God would soon exorcize the Lutheran devil. This caused Goldenen to note in the logbook once more that God (the Lutheran God, presumably) knew that he and his colleagues had made every conceivable effort to prevent insult to their religion and that they were not to blame for the consequences of other people's actions. At 6 P.M. four provisors went to the spinhouse to assess the situation. Finally, the militia managed to overcome the men's resistance and to drive them back to their night cells.[213]

The riot would probably not have taken place without the change of sentencing policies in the 1700s that resulted in more men staying in the spinhouse. Twelve male prisoners stayed in the house at that time and only one could convince the officials that he was not implicated in the siege. Altwasser himself was an active participant. Eleven women were reported to have yelled and encouraged the men during their siege.[214] No explicit demands were recorded other than the wish to discuss the situation in prison with the court. The men had pledged themselves not to leave the workshop unless that was accomplished. They indeed had sharp nail weapons with which they threatened the militia, and Joachim Mehtward even managed to grab the sword of one of the militiamen.[215] All male participants were provisionally punished by being deprived of their beds and obliged to stay in their cells on bread and water. On 5 September they got back their beds, and on 1 October they were readmitted to the workshop. They had been interrogated while in their cells, but it was decided that the case required a criminal investigation. As part of the criminal investigation they were interrogated anew by the praetors in November. In the meantime, the provisors also had to watch the senate endlessly delay the handling of their protest regarding Altwasser's Communion.[216]

The two rounds of interrogation preserved in the senate's archive make it possible to reconstruct the course of events which led to the uprising.[217] Discontent had been rife for some time among the male prisoners. David Steinauer was reported to have declared at the beginning of the year that the situation was unbearable and that all of them must revolt. Hans Fischer had complained to his fellows that he had been bleeding for three months due to repeated beatings by the personnel. Two others had said that they preferred to be broken on the wheel rather than to remain in prison any longer. Reimert Altwasser was sure, according to the statement of a fellow inmate, that he could never stand a term of twenty years. He hoped, therefore, to be released through the intervention of "his priest," and when this did not happen immediately, it made him rebellious. If Altwasser's Communion was only a ruse to induce the priest to help him get out of prison, the provisors were right in calling it a pretended devotion. Whatever the case with Altwasser, though, all inmates were well aware of the board's determination to maintain the Lutheran orthodoxy of prison religion. Once, it was said, when the minister had preached: "Jesus Christ will come soon," Peter Deckholt had mumbled, "the catholic God will come too and drive out the Lutheran devil." Deckholt later denied this, stating that he had only said that this God was a merciful one. But we may still conclude that the anti-Lutheran slogan was around even before the riot. Just as Altwasser reckoned on the priest's intervention, his fellow inmates hoped he could do something for them, too. Altwasser confirmed that Christian Schröder had asked him to speak to the priest on the others' behalf. He said he had told the priest that all men were ready to explode. It is not quite clear from the interrogations whether the prisoners made their weapons before or after Altwasser's Communion. Some said it was done "on the night when the work boss's child was baptized," but we do not learn when this took place. One inmate said they had their sharpened nails just to threaten that child's father, while they reckoned on the success of the priest's intervention. Indeed, the experience of unfair treatment from the work boss was mentioned as the most concrete immediate cause by two men. A few weeks before the riot, they explained, they had yelled to warn him of an intended attack (by Johann Hoyer, who became one of the participants in the siege). Instead of rewarding them, the official placed them in dark cells, where they spent eight days, for making noise. The men wanted to speak to the praetors about this injustice and Altwasser had reported it to the priest. The latter had indeed spoken with the praetors, and one of them came to the prison the morning of 12 August. When the praetor left he said he would discuss the matter with his colleague, but he did not return to the spinhouse. Thereupon, the men decided to remain in the workshop until further notice. There was no conspiracy, they said, they just wanted to complain about their situation to the authorities.

The course pursued by the male prisoners might be explained by reference to a traditional attitude and a contingent event. They manifested the naïve trust, characteristic of preindustrial subjects, in the paternalist benevolence of their rulers, who they thought would be eager to repair injustices afflicting the subjects. Altwasser's Communion provided the inmates a convenient vehicle for the transmission of their complaints. Such an explanation, however, would be insufficient. It is clear that the prisoners thought they had a particularly good chance of success. More than anything else, this proves that the social worlds within and without were interconnected. The inmates were keenly aware of the power struggles going on in the city at large. They knew that the senate, of which the praetors were members, was opposed to the faction to which the provisors belonged. This made them expect a willing ear from the magistrates. The provisors were right when they stated in their note of protest that the situation was explosive. It does not appear that they secretly encouraged the inmates to revolt in order to have their opinions confirmed. Rather, their persistent struggle to maintain orthodoxy and their eventual defeat reinforced the prisoners' conviction that they stood something to gain. That the prisoners' resistance to provisors and personnel was accompanied by a pro-Catholic attitude followed from the dynamics of the situation. The religion of the other participants in the siege was not recorded, but most of them came from Hamburg itself or Lutheran regions surrounding it. Had they been raised as catholics, they would undoubtedly have requested to see a priest, too. Their formal religion may not have meant too much to these delinquents.[218] They associated Lutheranism with the prison order that was imposed on them from above. Their terminology suggests a quasi-polytheistic perception, in which each denomination has its own deity. In this hour of need, the prisoners had more to expect from the Catholic God. Some of the women who were passive participants in the fracas shared this view.

In the end the affair just faded away. Concrete measures to ameliorate the prisoners' situation were not recorded, nor were the participants tried. The protocols containing their interrogations were handed over to the senate on 25 January 1710. The provisors admonished the inmates once more, and urged both the senate and the burgomasters to punish the guilty ones. In April the board was merely told not to impose penalties of its own authority, while a senate decree, the content of which remains unrecorded, was recited in the spinhouse.[219] Nothing further happened. The magistrates must have thought that the provisors had provoked the riot themselves, indirectly by their opposition to their superiors, or directly, in order to have their prophecy come true.

The ultimate fates of the participants had no discernible relationship to their roles in the event. The women left the house within a year or two. All but one of the men, including Altwasser, were released between 1713 and 1721, in most cases before the expiration of their terms. David Steinauer, for example, regained his freedom in 1716 because he was so attentive during the sermons and knew the right answers to all the questions from the catechism. Only Christian Schröder, who had entered the house in 1702 without a term, had to remain as late as 1736.[220] Count Schönborn became a lay cardinal in 1715. The prison records do not disclose whether he even knew what his temporary allies had been up to. Whatever the case, the magistrates may have advised him not to stir up emotions by sentencing persons to imprisonment in the city. In March 1711 the Bremen senate received a letter from their Hamburg colleagues, requesting that some *tumultuanten* might be admitted to that town's *zuchthaus* after their possible condemnation by the Imperial Commission. Bremen sent a negative reply.[221]

PART THREE:

PRISONS AND FAMILY DISCIPLINE

9

ELITES AND THE POOR
Private Confinement:
The Environment

The image of early modern prisons as pseudohouseholds was one of the dominant themes of Part Two. Vagrants, thieves, and other inmates—persons whose offense was considered connected to their lack of normal family life restraints—were punished within a paternalistic setting. This was partly a matter of symbolism. Moreover, in another, more direct way, prison life could be viewed as an alternative to an existence within the bosom of the family. Here we are referring to those persons whose own fathers, wives, or children decided they required a stay in the institution. These inmates were punished because their relatives were no longer able to discipline them, or because the relatives' reputations were suffering. Such offenders were part of the prison population from the beginning. I have identified two general changes in attitudes as background to the rise of imprisonment. The transformation of attitudes toward poverty and marginality was the most important. The other, an increase in concern over immoral behavior, was the one most directly associated with this class of potential inmates. In the course of the seventeenth and eighteenth centuries, the presence of this group affected the prison system, leading to a degree of differentiation within the system. A new type of prison regime emerged that did not include forced labor. Inmates in this group—usually consisting of members of well-to-do families only—were left to themselves, separated from the outside world as well as from the ordinary life of the prison.

We may term this type of incarceration 'private confinement' or 'imprisonment on request.' And this type of imprisonment ultimately gave rise to 'private institutions.' That is, the prisons in question were owned and managed by private proprietors and a personal contribution by the family of the inmate paid the inmate's board and other expenses. But the two uses of the term private here should not create confusion. 'Private confinement' in the sense of 'imprisonment on request' applied to the older, public institutions as well as the newer, private ones. In the case of the public institutions, imprisonment on request usually required some private contribution from the inmate's relatives, though this contribution often did not cover the inmate's complete expenses, as it did in the private institution.

There are two reasons for devoting a separate part of this book to private confinement. The first has to do with the procedure itself. Whereas in other cases the authorities had reasonably complete control over the terms of imprisonment, in this case they largely remained bystanders, merely giving their consent to a private initiative. The passive involvement of the authorities in this type of incarceration prompts an analysis of the causal mechanisms involved, including the type of behavior which was offensive to families, and considering the degree to which such behavior differed from ordinary crimes. The second reason has to do with the new regime as it differed from that of the prison workhouse. In the Dutch Republic it became linked eventually to prisons where no work was performed at all. There is no evidence to date that such institutions were established in the Empire, although future research may disclose their existence. The Hanseatic towns, in any case, continued to rely on the practice of merely having separate rooms in their *zuchthäuser* for private prisoners. In France, on the other hand, private prisons proliferated, a number of them managed by monastic orders. Thus, confinement on request made up a distinct chapter in the history of early modern imprisonment.

Documentation on this type of imprisonment mostly dates from the eighteenth century. That is understandable, since it was only then that the system had become distinct enough for the records to be inserted into separate dossiers. My archival evidence largely refers to Holland, in particular from its provincial court and the cities of Delft, Leiden, and Rotterdam. As indicated, the German towns figure in the account less prominently, but this is compensated by French data. In France a number of informative publications were devoted to the subject of private confinement at the beginning of the twentieth century, and it has been taken up anew by a few recent historians. For England, finally, there is some evidence of private madhouses, which resembled the separate institutions on the Continent.

The Rise of a System

The evolution of imprisonment on request will be discussed in two successive chapters. This one deals with the prisoners' environment. The next will treat the fate of the prisoners and explain why the system came to an end. The first section of this chapter deals with the system's structural base, beginning with its origins. The second section argues that the use of imprisonment as a tool of family discipline was associated especially with the higher—that is, wealthier—echelons of society.

Private Confinement: The Origins   In a sense, private confinement, that is, confinement on request, was the oldest form of incarceration. Justice from above developed in the later Middle Ages with the rise of the inquisitorial procedure. Before that time any type of judicial sanction, including locking someone up in jail, resulted from the initiative of a private person. Similarly, the confinement of offending monks and nuns in closed rooms was a disciplinary measure with which the secular authorities had nothing to do. It is not surprising, then, that medieval jails could also be used to detain persons who exhibited immoral or unruly behavior, though they had broken no particular criminal law. This seems to have occurred quite commonly in Italy. Pistoia's statute of 1296, for example, enabled fathers or grandfathers to incarcerate their children or grandchildren for a time if they were licentious or disobedient.[1] The 'places of chastisement' referred to in the Netherlands two centuries later (see Chapter Two) were also meant primarily for disobedient children, although troublesome spouses could also be put there. From the early sixteenth century on there are occasional references to cases of private confinement in jails. The one kept by the Officialité in Paris admitted a child in 1540 "to be corrected."[2] Eight years later, the Court of Brabant authorized Lambrecht van den Broek, a citizen of Den Bosch, to lock up his twenty-three-year-old son Melchior, whom he had sent to the Walloon regions to learn French and good manners, but who had squandered his money on gambling and prostitutes, instead. Melchior was committed to jail, escaped, and was caught again and confined in the monastery of the Celle brothers at Lier. After the death of his father in 1550 he was released. He married, and his other relatives agreed to reserve a portion of the inheritance for his children, on the condition that Melchior would leave Brabant forever.[3] This is a typical case, many more of which are documented from the late seventeenth century onward.

When prison workhouses appeared on the scene around 1600, some private prisoners were incarcerated in them. Some, like Melchior, were from families that were reasonably well-to-do. But others were children, wives, or even husbands from poorer families. There is little information on individual cases from the early period. The earliest recalcitrant inmate referred to in the Hamburg logbook was obviously a private prisoner and probably just an ordinary citizen of Hamburg. In June 1626, during the evening prayer, he suddenly exclaimed: "It is not right that women should be allowed to commit their husbands to the *zuchthaus* and such a thing is against the law. . . . When I am set free again, I will break my wife's arms."[4] We do not know whether this kind of aggressiveness had caused his imprisonment in the first place.

We have already met the richer inmates of those years, who were lodged in separate rooms and for whom board money was paid by their relatives. It has also been noted that a secret ward for prisoners from respectable families was established early on in Amsterdam. Thus, among inmates confined on request, the rich were separated from the less well-to-do from the beginning. And since hard labor was not considered a suitable career for them in the world outside, it was unnecessary to subject them to it for reformatory purposes.

The next step was the establishment of entirely separate institutions for this class of prisoners who did not work. This seems to have occurred first in the mid-seventeenth century, where the initiative was taken by enterprising private individuals. We hear of them in Delft, where an ordinance of 1662 says that ever more citizens are making a business out of lodging "the insane and other confined persons."[5] During the following decades, private institutions for the insane as well as for people who misbehaved also emerged in other places. In Amsterdam a semiprivate one was opened in 1694.[6]

Thus was the stage set toward the end of the seventeenth century. The emergence of privately managed institutions can be explained with reference to the simultaneous evolution of prison workhouses. As the latter increasingly admitted ordinary delinquents, the secret wards became tainted by association with the criminal sphere. For richer families, they were no longer honorable enough for incarceration of their black sheep. This created the need for private prisons. These institutions had the additional advantage of being tied only loosely to the place in which they were located, admitting persons from anywhere. Quite a number were established in small villages or rural areas. (Ver)beterhuis became the Dutch generic term for them, highlighting their distinctness from the prison workhouses. At the beginning of the eighteenth century this term was adopted by urban magistrates to denote the separate ward of their tuchthuis. Thus, the differentiation of private confinement led to a tripartite division between prison workhouses, urban beterhuizen, and private institutions. Poorer families continued to commit troublesome members to the first. But even then they might have to make a financial contribution, because courts and governments only supplied the deficits for their own prisoners.

Private Confinement in the Eighteenth Century: The System   A quantitative study of the dynamics of private confinement can be undertaken from the perspective of the institutions or from that of the public requiring the system. I will start with the second, because it enables us to estimate the recourse to the system within a specific population. Since every private committal in Holland needed the authorization of the magistrates, the petitions submitted to them by the inhabitants of a particular jurisdiction provide an indication of the total need for confinement. My principle data consist of series of request to the courts of Leiden and Rotterdam, from which I took samples. The data were supplemented by information from Dordrecht. These series appear more or less complete.[7] It can be calculated that the number of initial requests (i.e., excluding requests for a prolongation of confinement) by private persons in Leiden increased steadily from about two per 10,000 inhabitants per year around 1710 to about three around 1790. In Rotterdam, on the other hand, this number fluctuated without a specific pattern between one and four. However, if we add the insane committed by a separate procedure upon burgomasters' order, it would be between two and eight. In Dordrecht the number per 10,000 inhabitants could even be higher, rising to an average of thirteen per year around 1800.[8] This can partly be explained by the readiness of the Dordrecht magistrates to allow confinement at the city's expense. The only non-Dutch data available for comparison are from France. The Parisian dossiers, edited by Farge and Foucault, dating from four different years in the eighteenth century, yield a fluctuation between one-and-one-half and three initial requests by private persons per 10,000 inhabitants per year.[9] For Provence I calculated an annual average of 2.9 per 10,000.[10] These French figures are relatively close to those obtained for Leiden.

Differences between places with respect to actual committals do not necessarily imply that the number of persons causing trouble to their families also varied from place to place. We are dealing only with cases of extremely intolerable behavior. Imprisonment was, as one Rotterdam request put it, "the most bitter remedy and ultimate recourse."[11] Many more persons must have been troublesome to their families without the latter having recourse to this ultimate remedy. The prisoners were the ones whose conduct, as it may be formulated, had exceeded a threshold of unacceptability. A study of these extreme cases also sheds light on the behavior that remained below this threshold.

Next to initial imprisonment and prolongation of confinement, petitions concerned release. While one fifth of all Rotterdam requests were for release rather than imprisonment, in Leiden this category made up a mere 2 percent. This may be a reflection of a definite policy by the Leiden magistrates. Confinement was usually granted for a specific term and requests for release in both towns were almost always submitted before this term was over. These are cases in which petitioners changed their mind or experienced changed circumstances. They had to specify their motives, because the magistrates were probably reluctant to alter their original authorization. The Leiden court may have more actively discouraged such a reexamination of a prisoner's term, so that it was asked for infrequently. When the term had expired and the prisoner had been reaccepted into his former environment, it was apparently unnecessary to submit a petition.

In either case his family had to live with him again, for better or for worse. In taking back their black sheep, relatives hoped that the advantages would outweigh the disadvantages.

Although the magistrates often limited imprisonment to a term, they regularly consented to a prolongation of a stay when this was requested. Characteristically, the petitioners would claim that there was no sign of improved behavior on the part of the victim, nor much hope for the near future. If they stated their case convincingly, a prolongation was normally granted. Private confinement differed from criminal imprisonment in this regard. In the latter case, good behavior might earn an inmate a shortening of his term; in the former, an early release was uncommon and failure to repent could result into a new term. This caused rather long periods of incarceration in some cases. The average actual length of stay of those confined upon the authorization of the Court of Holland was fifteen-and-a-half years, but this group is untypical (see Chapter Ten). In Dordrecht the actual length could be ascertained in 89 percent of the cases and a third of the persons involved stayed up to one year. Seventy-nine percent stayed three years or less.[12] Because the Leiden and Rotterdam data seldom disclose when a prisoner is released, the average actual length cannot be calculated. But an informed guess is possible. In both samples initial requests decidedly outnumber prolongations, and allowing for an underregistration of the latter, we may suppose that confinements were prolonged one time on the average. Since terms, if set, usually amount to one or two years, this means that a stay normally lasted from two to four years.

Terms were not always set, though. Over the whole period the court of Rotterdam did so in 72 percent of the cases; that of Leiden in 80 percent. The petitioners themselves were less eager to have a formal limit imposed on a stay in prison. They asked for it in 49 percent and 50 percent of the cases, respectively. Especially in Leiden the petitioners tended to ask for slightly longer terms than the court eventually agreed to. These data suggest that the two parties viewed imprisonment from a different perspective. To the petitioners it was just a private matter. A family member had to be removed from sight, preferably for as long as possible. An indeterminate committal ensured the family a maximum of control. The prisoner could only be released by showing them repentance and improved behavior. The court, on the other hand, wished to keep a further measure of control beyond its initial authorization. Setting a term provided checkpoints: after one or two years, the petitioners had to plead their case anew.

The Location of Confinement   The locations of confinement referred to in the Rotterdam and Leiden samples can be grouped into three categories, along the lines of the differentiation explained above. Incarceration in the city prison workhouse was least honorable, for the victim and his family, but it was the cheapest. If petitioners could pay more, so that their relative could be admitted into the urban *beterhuis,* this was more honorable. Thus, in 1755, Abraham Hartong had been provisionally committed to the Rotterdam prison workhouse upon a complaint by his wife and a few neighbors. When three other relatives, led by Laurens Hartong, probably Abraham's brother, heard of this, they submitted a petition to have Abraham transferred to the city's *beterhuis.* The latter institution was found more suitable "to avoid shame for the family and for his improvement and correction."[13] The third possibility, a stay in a private *beterhuis,* was removed still further from infamy. It might be supposed that relatives were only prepared to commit a person to the prison workhouse if they had no other option. The Leiden and Rotterdam data confirm this. In the first town, which declined economically in the eighteenth century, the prison workhouse was increasingly used, while it happened the other way around in the second, evincing economic growth. In addition, the Leiden petitioners decreasingly opted for a private institution.[14] Thus, whereas families preferred to lock up their black sheep in the most honorable place possible, the financial difficulty of doing so acted as a counterinfluence.

The location of confinement can be considered from the supply side, too. We can examine this through a quantitative study of private confinement from the perspective of the institutions present within a particular area. Such a study is possible for Delft, which also for private confinement, became *the* prison town. It was noted that the magistrates first laid down rules in 1662 for institutions which by then were mainly admitting the insane. Toward the end of the century, persons who misbehaved were committed to these private prisons as well. The authorities increased their supervision by ruling that the names of all prisoners had to be registered at the town hall. The register was begun in 1699 and it ends with the close of the Ancien Régime in 1811.[15] It also includes private committals to the city's combined *tuchthuis* and madhouse, but that institution has been discussed already. Those committals, therefore, and the entries referring to a prolongation of confinement, were excluded from the computations below, so that our attention can be directed exclusively to the private prisons. They admitted 909 persons during the period concerned.

The residence of the court which had authorized their imprisonment was listed in 96 percent of the cases.[16] It appears that the Court of Holland and the court of The Hague together were involved in more than a third of all committals. This can be taken as an indication that the upper strata made disproportionate use of confinement in a private *beterhuis.* As a center of government, The Hague witnessed a high concentration of resident elites. The Court of Holland had jurisdiction over a part of The Hague, while it also received petitions from patrician families elsewhere in the province. The overwhelming majority of prisoners came from places relatively close to Delft: in 88 percent of the known cases the authorizing court resided in one of the present provinces of South Holland or Zeeland. Thus, despite Delft's fame as the site of a number of private institutions, it functioned as a regional center only. Apparently, the families involved wanted to hide their black sheep, but not so far away as to preclude an occasional visit.

Delft's popularity was declining in the course of the period covered by the register. Forty percent of the committals to a private prison (370) took place during the years 1699–1724. The totals were 189, 178, and 127, respectively, during the next three quarters of the century, while there were forty-two committals from 1800 to 1811 (in three cases the year of entry was missing). This decline in numbers may be related to competition which Delft faced, since 1733, from two private institutions in villages East of Leiden. The decline in the number of prisoners was parallelled by a decline in the number of institutions. Only four had a continuous existence through the eighteenth century, while all but one of the houses that did not continue were limited to the first quarter. The institution mentioned most often, De Drie Taarlingen, admitted more than a third of all prisoners. De Gekroonde Kabel, Duinkerken, Keulen were each responsible for about 15 percent of the entries, and all the others combined were responsible for about 15 percent. The latter group consisted of one named institution (Koning David, mentioned from 1721 to 1735) and thirteen that were simply listed as "the house of NN (the manager)." Only two of these admitted more than a handful of prisoners. From 1735 on there were just the four more-permanent houses, managed by successive proprietors. One of them, De Gekroonde Kabel, had always admitted men only. This was uncommon at first, because the lesser institutions and originally the other larger ones accommodated both sexes. But from the middle of the eighteenth century, there were only segregated *beterhuizen*, two for men and two for women. The last male inmates entered Keulen in 1725 and Duinkerken in 1746, while the last female inmate entered De Drie Taarlingen in 1744. Keulen and De Gekroonde Kabel admitted their last prisoners in 1798 and 1799, respectively, so from 1800 on there was only one for each sex.

A term was mentioned in the register in only 29 percent of the cases. Probably, this was not due to oversight. But it seems the courts involved had radically different policies with regard to terms. Fifty-nine Leiden prisoners out of eighty-one had a term listed, which is in line with the data from the Leiden sample. The magistrates of The Hague, on the other hand, were listed as having imposed a term upon only six of the 185 prisoners whose committals they consented to. In all cases, the terms amounted to one or two years. There is no easy explanation why one court was much stricter in this than another.

Families and Social Status

Prisoners committed to private institutions, which were expensive, belonged to relatively rich families. That is obvious. The question of the social background, therefore, is only relevant if we pose it for the entire population involved in confinement on request. Consequently, we have to return to the Rotterdam and Leiden samples. Did inmates whose relatives committed them to prison workhouses, or even urban *beterhuizen,* come from an environment similar to that of the beggars and delinquents imprisoned by the authorities? This section first inquires into the socioeconomic background of petitioners and prisoners, and analyzes family relationships between petitioners and prisoners.

Expenses   The petitions submitted in Rotterdam and Leiden seldom contain direct information on the financial circumstances of the prisoners and their families, but the costs of confinement provide a clue. Because many persons committed to a prison workhouse were unable to earn their entire living through labor, those responsible for them had to supply the deficit. In Rotterdam the amounts they paid were specified sometimes, ranging from twenty-five to sixty-five guilders a year.[17] Since a fully employed worker earned about 300 guilders a year, these sums would be high but not impossible for a lower-class family. Such a payment would be out of the question, of course, if the prospective prisoner were the household's main wage earner. Comparable specifications are lacking for the prison workhouse at Leiden, but the price of an imprisonment in the Cecilia hospital (the urban *beterhuis*) was recorded once. The son of a woman committed there agreed to contribute twelve stuivers a week, while the rest, twenty stuivers, was supplied from the Lutheran poor box.[18] This adds up to 83.20 guilders per year, which is more expensive than the highest sum mentioned for the Rotterdam prison workhouse, but not substantially more expensive. The price of a stay in the Cecilia hospital seems to have been open to negotiation with the administrators, though.[19] Higher amounts are indicated for the Rotterdam *beterhuis.* Three relatives who had committed a woman there in 1716 together were to contribute 140 guilders per year.[20] In a notarial act referring to another prisoner's stay there between 1729 and 1734, there is even talk of an accommodation fee of 100 guilders to be paid twice a year. Additional expenses amount to 659.80 guilders during that period.[21] Finally, we may deduce from the duty of seventy-five guilders imposed on imprisonment outside the city in 1771, that that amount was considered the Rotterdam *beterhuis's* missed profit or part of it.

These data can be supplemented from other sources. In Haarlem a specified sum was recorded as early as 1634. A couple was to pay twenty stuivers a week, which would be fifty-two guilders a year, when they committed their daughter to the prison workhouse for her bad behavior.[22] In the eighteenth century the accommodation-fee had risen to thirty-six *stuivers* a week.[23] Again, such amounts would be a considerable drain on the budget of a working-class family. In a number of petitions to the Utrecht court in the eighteenth century, sums varying from fifty to 120 guilders per year were mentioned, but these only concern the insane.[24] The fees required by the Dordrecht *beterhuis*, were constantly raised during the eighteenth century. In 1804 it had become 400 a year for a citizen and 425 for a noncitizen in the "first class," and 250 and 300, respectively, in the "second class." Poor relief boards from outside the town paid 175 guilders per year.[25] We may conclude that imprisonment in an urban *beterhuis* normally was beyond the means of a working-class family unless some agency provided assistance. The prices of accommodation in a private institution were seldom recorded. For a merchant's son committed to one in the 1680s, it was seventy-five guilders every three months.[26] Those responsible for Anthonia Collijns Geertsema were in arrears with their payments for her accommodation to the manager of Duinkerken. Debts increased from 700 to 2,000 guilders between June 1795 and June 1797.[27]

The Rotterdam and Leiden samples contain another indirect indication of the socioeconomic status of the prisoners and their families: literacy. Although the sources are transcripts of the original requests, it was usually recorded who signed and who made a mark. In Leiden this information is available for 800 out of a total of 880 petitioners. During the years 1680–1740, 85 percent signed and the rest made a mark. From 1745 to 1805, 86 percent signed. If we only consider the first petitioners and exclude the administrators of charitable institutions, the corresponding figures are 86 percent and 87 percent. In Rotterdam, of all petitioners, 93 percent signed in the period 1713–1756, and 90 percent in the period 1757–1801. Here the degree of literacy is slightly lower among the first petitioners, with 91 percent and 88 percent signing, respectively. We may conclude that a literacy rate of about 90 percent was common for those requesting confinement in Holland throughout the eighteenth century. This is higher than in the general adult population, but the difference becomes smaller as time progresses. So far, literacy rates before 1800 are only known for Amsterdam. The percentage of signing bridegrooms was 70 in 1680, 76 in 1730, 85 in 1780, and 88 in 1801–1806. Among brides the percentages were 42, 51, 64, and 73, respectively. Brides and bridegrooms who had been born in Leiden and Rotterdam more or less followed this general trend.[28]

In some cases there are other sources besides petitions that provide information on the financial situation of the families involved in confinement. In Leiden two tax registers were valuable, while the Rotterdam notarial archive was also useful, though less so than the tax registers. By comparing records it was possible to establish that the middle and upper classes were definitely overrepresented in the samples from the two towns.[29] In Dordrecht, on the other hand, many private prisoners seem to have come from relatively modest socioeconomic backgrounds. The occupation of 27 percent of the petitioners is known, and 77 percent of these were working people or small traders. This group is not representative of all petitioners, though. Occupations were usually revealed by those who sought to obtain a gratis confinement, claiming that their financial situation precluded a personal contribution. Petitioners whose claim was successful were concentrated in the later years of the period investigated. For some reason, committals at the expense of the town or the institution itself were granted more liberally toward the end of the eighteenth century. This also partly explains the sharp rise in the total number of committals in Dordrecht.[30] Thus, the greater involvement of workers' families in private confinement in Dordrecht at the end of the period compared to Dordrecht in an earlier period or to Leiden and Rotterdam was an exception.

This permits a conclusion with regard to the socioeconomic status of families who had recourse to private confinement in Holland. In principle, families from all social milieus did so, but most of the time the middle and upper classes used this tool of discipline to a much greater extent than the poorer classes. The cost acted as a brake, which is suggested by the data on the price to be paid. Even confinement in a prison workhouse could lead to considerable expenses. The lowest taxpayer group in Leiden in the middle of the eighteenth century accounted for 10 percent of the private petitions. This equals the percentage in Rotterdam and Leiden which made a mark under their request throughout the period investigated. It indicates a constant minority of poor and uneducated families who were on a similar socioeconomic level as prisoners committed by charitable institutions or by the authorities. In Dordrecht this group was temporarily more numerous. The fact that the percentage of those signing the request remained constant while literacy rates progressed may signify that families whose financial position was just above that of the minority hardly made use of confinement at all. They would have difficulties obtaining a gratis committal, though perhaps less so in Dordrecht, and they could not pay the cost. The group of signers, supposedly, belonged to the top half of the urban population: those who were probably literate in 1680 as well as in 1800. This group roughly comprised the lower-middle, middle, and upper classes. The analysis of the Leiden tax registers suggests that the lower-middle class made moderate use of confinement. The top quarter of the population used it twice as much.

No such detailed analysis is possible for any other country, but there is some scattered information on France. The known occupations in requests for confinement presented to the *intendant* of Provence by private persons between 1745 and 1789 yield the following figures: nobles, 14.1 percent; army and bureaucrats, 14.1 percent; merchants, 19.8 percent; bourgeois, 5.1 percent; the professions, 12.2 percent; small traders, 7.5 percent; artisans and urban workers, 17.9 percent; others, 9.3 percent.[31] This is largely in line with my Dutch data. Private prisoners in Languedoc also were reported to have been "well born" in most cases, but this conclusion is based on a sample of persons staying in several institutions in the region in 1789, rather than on a series of petitions.[32] Farge and Foucault, on the other hand, claim that in eighteenth-century Paris "these requests originated in overwhelming majority from modest milieus."[33] But they present no quantitative data to substantiate this claim, nor do they specify what "modest" means. Perhaps these findings reflect a difference between the capital and the south of France.

For the moment, I still assume that an overrepresentation of the top quarter of the population was the rule rather than the exception in Western Europe. Where this overrepresentation occurred, the annual number of initial requests seems to have fluctuated between one and four per 10,000 inhabitants, which points at a confinement rate of two to eight persons per 10,000 among the elites. If we take the median of this range, five persons per year, it amounts to 125 in a generation. Based on an average household size of five people, we can conclude that among the upper and middle classes about 6 percent of all families had one of their members or another relative confined at some point. Since imprisonment was the ultimate solution for bad behavior, lesser degrees of bad behavior must have been even more common. Among the elites, then, private confinement was always a consideration.

The Nuclear Family   Petitions for confinement yield one more type of structural information: the relationship between the prisoner and his relatives. In Holland there were often quite a number of petitioners per request: uncles, grandmothers, sons-in-law, and stepfathers signed them as well as parents or children along. In Provence, on the other hand, only one or two people, very often the parents, seem to have submitted them. At first sight this looks odd, considering established historical demographic facts. Households with one or two generations predominated in the maritime provinces of the Dutch Republic, while in the South of France in the early modern period there was a relatively large number of more complex households. However, household structure may not be that relevant.

Historians use the concept of nuclear family also with reference to power relations and emotional bonds. From the kaleidoscope of relatives who often put their signatures on Dutch petitions, we might infer that strong bonds existed between the family and a wider kinship network. A

Table 9.1

Relationship of First Petitioner to Prisoner in Private Requests

	Leiden (N = 310)			Rotterdam (N = 282)			Dordrecht (N = 314)	Provence, (N = 638)
	1680–1740	1745–1805	1680–1805	1713–1756	1757–1801	1713–1801	1734–1809	1745–1789
Wife	19%	19%	19%	18%	30%	23%	22%	2
Husband	19	11	14	22	12	18	19	9
Father	17	17	17	13	23	17	22	56
Mother	9	13	11	14	12	14	12	14
Son	3	7	5	1	2	1	4	0.3
Daughter	1	1	1	2	—	1	1	—
Brother	8	6	7	6	7	7	9	3
Sister	4	5	5	4	2	3	5	
Other	20	21	21	20	12	16	6	15.7

closer analysis, however, casts doubt on that supposition. For this analysis we have to consider the first, or principal petitioners only. Table 9.1 includes the data from my sample and comparable data from Dordrecht and Provence.[34] Holland and Provence are similar in one respect: about four fifths or more of the principal petitioners had a first-degree family relationship with the prisoner. Within this group there were marked differences. Let me first consider the Dutch towns. Dordrecht showed no significant changes over time. The most conspicuous trend in the two other towns was the decline of husbands among the petitioners. There is no easy explanation for this indication of greater tolerance of misconduct by wives in the second half of the eighteenth century. In Leiden the percentage of wives acting as first petitioner remained constant, and it increased in Rotterdam. In the latter town this resulted into a slight increase for the overall category of spouse petitioner, while spouses showed an 8 percent decline in Leiden. The overall percentage of parents increased in both towns, albeit more markedly in Rotterdam than in Leiden. In the latter town parents caught up with spouses. In cases of parents' requests, the gender of the prisoner does not determine that of the first petitioner. As a rule, mothers who were petitioners were widows, which also was true in Provence. It is remarkable that the increase in parents' requests was due to mothers in Leiden and to fathers in Rotterdam. It seems that widows who were in adverse economic circumstances were more likely to ask for confinement, but I could think of no easy explanation for this. Children and sibling petitioners were decidedly less numerous than parents or spouses, although they constituted 19 percent of the petitioners in

Dordrecht and in Leiden in the second half of the eighteenth century. In Dordrecht the percentage of the residual category—mainly consisting of unspecified and distant relatives and in-laws—was especially small in comparison with Leiden and Rotterdam; in other categories Dordrecht's percentages did not deviate markedly from those in the two other towns. The residual category consisted of distant relatives and in-laws in Provence, too.

The differences between the Dutch towns on the one hand and Provence on the other are more marked. In the French region male petitioners consistently predominated over females; there were four times as many husbands as wives, and fathers as mothers. However, male ascendancy was not the controlling principle in this disparity, but patriarchalism. More than half of the requests were made by the father, including 13 percent in which the mother was the second petitioner. Parental requests amount to 70 percent of the total. Fathers and mothers were practically never committed to prison by their children. I would like to include Paris in this comparison, but Farge and Foucault again fail to provide exact figures. They declare that committals of spouses made up a third of the family cases and that those of children accounted for more than a third.[35] This could resemble the Dutch situation, although it would indicate a greater parental initiative. Possibly the figures for Provence are not representative nationally, but reflect a more patriarchal family structure of the South of France. Patriarchy also characterized the Hanseatic towns to a certain extent. There are no quantifiable data available, but it is remarkable that married women were never called by their own name. A woman who requested to have her son committed to the Bremen prison workhouse for misconduct in 1715 signed as "the widow of Johan Lindhorn." Johan Mönnighoff, whose daughter and her husband were living with him, petitioned all by himself to have his son-in-law imprisoned. Ernst Osterman, submitting a request for the confinement of his insane mother, referred to her simply as "the widow of the citizen Noah Osterman."[36]

In the Rotterdam and Leiden samples there is one more indication of the predominance of the nuclear family. Because there were often quite a number of petitioners, a definite order of precedence can be reconstructed. It is the order adhered to in Table 9.1, whereby the first two, of course, have to be combined into 'spouse.' If someone higher up was present, he or she received precedence. Only 6 percent of the petitions submitted in Rotterdam and 15 percent of those in Leiden deviated from this 'ideal' order, and in most of these cases the first petitioner was not involved. The character of the ideal order is obvious: the controlling principle in determining the chief petitioner is the person closest to the prisoner from the perspective of the nuclear family rather than any sort of wider kinship network. The 'principle of closeness' dominated over possible patriarchal considerations. Within the nuclear family some measure of patriarchy was still visible. It is notably reflected in the percentage of female petitioners: between 36 and 45 percent.

So much for the structural aspects of family relationships as they shaped the system of private confinement. The theme of family honor occupies a prominent place in the next chapter, where the focus is on the prisoners and the behavior which prompted their relatives to commit them to prison.

10

DRUNKS, REVELLERS, AND THE INSANE
Private Confinement: The Prisoners

Who were the victims of the ultimate remedy of family discipline, and why? What was their fate once they had been securely locked away? To complete our picture of private confinement we need an answer to these questions. To a certain extent, the experience of the prisoners involved can be inferred from the discussion in Part Two. The household model, for example, and the dynamics of internal life from above and below affected private prisoners, too, when they stayed in institutions with forced labor. There is no need to repeat that story. Only the new element, the separate regime, requires attention here. The behavior which the inmates were supposed to unlearn was quite varied and complex at times. An elaborate analysis could be the starting point for a study of family life and behavioral norms, but such a study would require another book. In the present context, the crucial question is to what extent the offenses of those committed to prison by their relatives differed from the crimes for which the authorities imposed imprisonment. This question is also central to a shift in the appreciation of private confinement that manifested itself notably in France toward the end of the Ancien Régime. These considerations determine the order of the three sections of this chapter. First, I will inquire into the characteristics of the prisoners generally and their fate in private institutions. This will be followed by a discussion of behavior unacceptable to families and the way it was portrayed in different countries. The third section will discuss attempts to curb private confinement and its partial replacement by treatment for insanity.

Men, Women, and Conscience

By definition, a person's social identity is determined by his relationships to others. The prisoner's environment, therefore, and his or her position within the family also determined this identity. Two quantifiable variables, age and sex, must be considered. We have little information on the first. The petitions submitted in Leiden, Rotterdam, and Dordrecht list the prisoner's age in a few cases, and the range of recorded ages was rather broad: from sixteen to over fifty. In Provence, too, this variable is largely missing; among the known cases all ages were represented.[1] Only for Paris is the age distribution given for those committed by their parents. A mere 6.5 percent was over thirty-one, which is understandable, since parents do not live forever.[2] The prisoner's gender is known in all cases. Although there were some fluctuations in the three Dutch towns, a 1:1 ratio between male and female prisoners was the rule.[3]

The figures obtained from the Delft register, on the other hand, are quite different. Of the 909 persons committed to private institutions, only 294 were women and 608 men (with seven cases unknown). This 1:2 ratio recurred in every subpopulation; it did not vary with geographic origin or according to whether or not a term was set. Likewise, in my small sample from the Court of Holland, in which most prisoners were committed to private institutions, twenty-three out of thirty were men. Clearly, the 'prisoner elite' was overwhelmingly male. There are two possible explanations for this. It could mean that, while the threshold of unacceptibility may have been equally high with regard to the behavior of men and women, more money was spent on the first category. Consequently, they were more frequently committed to expensive institutions. Alternatively, it could mean that, among the upper social strata, the misconduct of male relatives was held to hurt the family reputation to a greater degree than female misconduct, so that the behavior of men was supervised more strictly. That would accord with the data from Provence, where many prisoners belonged to elite families and 75 percent of them were male.[4] But the basis for this alternative is uncertain.

The Separate Regime   Information on life in private prisons is derived mainly from the Court of Holland visitation reports from 1729 onward, supplemented by the case of a prisoner in the 1680s.[5] It is hard to tell what these institutions looked like in terms of outward appearance. They lacked the pompous façades which adorned prison workhouses. In Holland their names sound like those of taverns and inns, and some may have been just that. A paternalistic terminology was uncommon; it must have been associated with forced labor institutions and hence unpleasant to upper-class clients. The managers and proprietors were called landlords. These hosts made money out of imprisonment, in contrast to their colleagues who had harassed the beggar catchers a century earlier. Thus, the inmates of *beterhuizen* came from family settings, but they were not welcomed into a pseudofamily. A discussion of internal life can begin with the question to what extent the inmates' experience differed from that of prisoners who had to perform forced labor.

Since deprivation of liberty—the essence of imprisonment—characterized both regimes, it is not surprising to find that some people tried to escape from *beterhuizen,* too. The earliest recorded case was a serious one. In 1711 three inmates of the house of Abraham van Barth at Delft attempted to regain their freedom while the manager was out. They were prevented from doing so, but a servant of the house got stabbed and died. Because it was uncertain who was responsible for the killing, the Delft court condemned all three men to have the sword waved over their heads on the scaffold. Even this seemingly lenient sentence caused their relatives to submit a request for pardon. They argued that the accused had been imprisoned in the first place to prevent a public scandal. A public sentence would run counter to this purpose. The case was appealed to the Court of Holland and the High Council, and ended because the men somehow managed to escape after all from provisional detention.[6] Four years later the threat of escape haunted Abraham van Barth's house again. To the Delft court he complained that two servants of a neighbor, a man and a woman, conspired to help some of the inmates get away. The conspirators and the inmates could communicate with each other because of adjacent courtyards.[7] The fact that many inmates of private institutions were wealthy may have induced others, including personnel, to provide assistance. When three prisoners had escaped from De Drie Taarlingen in 1739, for example, the manager dismissed all his domestics.[8] Because of the wealth and social status of the prisoners in *beterhuizen,* sexual politics between personnel and inmates could be a mirror image of the situation in prison workhouses. In 1741 a man imprisoned in De Gekroonde Kabel promised a maid of the house that he would marry her and make her a respectable wife once he was free. Their contacts were discovered, however, and the maid was dismissed.[9]

Cases of violent insubordination were seldom reported in private institutions. It may have been that elite prisoners were more quiet or that the separate regime precluded collective outbreaks. In the urban *beterhuis* at Leiden, on the other hand, there was a special ward for unruly inmates, which housed not only the insane but also people who had been committed for alcoholism and the like.[10] There is little information on preventive measures and discipline in private prisons. Occasionally, a landlord was said to have "chastised" an inmate, without specifying what this amounted to.[11] Probably his upper-class clients would not have liked to see their relatives beaten. Since most of the inmates were literate, a lively correspondence was carried on between inmates and outsiders, and landlords often read and even intercepted incoming and outgoing mail.

Since no labor was performed, we might suppose that religion would be particularly emphasized as a reformatory element, but there are few references to it in the sources. Dutch private institutions being relatively small, they lacked special rooms for services. The dominant religion had no monopoly there, in contrast to the situation in prison workhouses. The Court of Holland condoned that the landlord of Nieuwenburg was a Catholic, as long as the Reformed inmates could see a preacher.[12] This also implies that visits by clergymen were considered necessary for the inmates' spiritual well-being. Similarly, when insane inmates were occasionally allowed to go in and out of the institution, this was often to visit church on Sundays. Religion may have been more central in some of the privately managed prisons in France, since quite a number of them were run by religious orders. Usually these were special convents which served as *beterhuizen* for women. In the Netherlands the town of Maastricht consented to an imprisonment in a monastery several times.[13]

In addition to the absence of a labor program, the main elements differentiating Dutch *beterhuizen* from prison workhouses were the indefiniteness of the inmate's stay and the regime of separation from the outside world in the sense that the general public was not allowed to visit the *beterhuizen* and observe the inmates. The first has been commented upon already. Although the authorizing magistrates often set a term, the prisoner's stay might always be prolonged. It seems as though especially the inmates of private institutions were the victims of repeated prolongations. That is suggested by the fates of the thirty persons making up the Court of Holland sample. They belong to three cohorts: those who were in prison in 1740, in 1770, and in 1800. Their average length of stay was eleven, twenty-two, and nineteen years, respectively.[14] Although insanity was a frequent motive for confinement, this does not account for the apparent prolongations. In the second cohort only one person was committed for this reason. His was the longest stay recorded—over forty-seven years—but, if we leave him out, the average length of stay is still nineteen years. Sometimes insanity was related to a long stay in a reverse order. A number of those committed for misconduct suffered mentally from the experience of permanent separation from the outside world. Eight of the thirty prisoners in the Court of Holland sample were reported to have become melancholic or troubled in their mind in the course of their captivity. Because the ages of four persons were mentioned, we know what years of their lives they spent in the *beterhuis*: 38–52, 45–62, 51–69, and 62–66. Only the first was released; the other three died in captivity. The mode of exit of twenty-three of the thirty prisoners is known and in thirteen cases it was death. This amounts to a considerably higher percentage than in prison workhouses for which statistical information is available.

Thus, the prospects for inmates of private institutions were not bright. The irony is that the only criminal prisoners subjected to a comparable regime of separation in the eighteenth century, the sodomites in the Amsterdam secret ward, were pitied by the administrators. These men and women from among the elites, who had been convicted of no crime at all, received less sympathy. The court did not bother with them to any great extent; the magistrates merely gave their consent to a private disciplinary measure. In institutionalizing one of their members, families seem to have been motivated primarily to conceal embarrassing conduct, rather than correct the member's behavior. As long as a public scandal was avoided, they were content.

Still, the idea of reformation played a role in the regime of separation from the outside world. This is suggested already by the very term *beter-huis*, which literally means 'house for improvement.' The managers were obliged to report on the inmates' conduct inside. Two valid reasons can be ascertained which might prompt relatives to ask for release or to refrain from seeking a prolongation and for the court to consent to this. They were repentance on the part of the prisoner and an improvement in his behavior. Since these black sheep, in captivity, were in no position to repeat the actions that had caused their misfortune, the two reasons must in practice have amounted to one and the same. Insane inmates were a special case in this respect. For the others, the experience of the separate regime was comparable to that undergone by nineteenth-century convicts subjected to solitary confinement. In this sense, the private prisons of the eighteenth century were precursors of the penitentiary—an observation also made by Farge and Foucault.[15] At least one private prisoner testified to an atmosphere of atonement. Mr. Adriaan Huisken, who had been committed to a *beterhuis* in 1758 for living an "irregular" life, drinking, and beating his wife, wrote a long letter to his former employer, the Court of Holland, in 1760, explaining that he was determined to renounce his vices: "Honorable Gentlemen. As I rather seek to find fault with myself than to excuse myself for the abuse of the talents with which Heaven has endowed me, my first intention at my sad entrance here was to inquire into the reasons for which and the ends to which I found myself imprisoned; next, to examine my conscience, subject my will, conquer my passions and to progress toward the good each time."[16] Mr. Huisken also "preached" to his fellow inmates, urging them to follow his example. He claimed they did indeed. This highlights an important difference from nineteenth-century regimes. The phrase "separation from the outside world" should be taken literally. It contrasted eighteenth-century private institutions with prison workhouses, where visitors from the general public were admitted. The separation characteristic of *beterhuizen* was not a form of solitary confinement. From the 1680s onward there are indications for the existence of a social life among inmates, mainly consisting of conversation.[17] Thus, the confrontation with one's own conscience was encouraged in a less radical manner than it would be later.

Saving the Family Honor

As the unacceptable conduct for which people were imprisoned by their families was less clearly delineated than the offenses of delinquents or beggars, it has to be briefly reviewed. The Court of Holland's dossiers may serve to introduce it. Very often, private prisoners were guilty of a combination of undesirable activities. That was certainly so in the case of Agnes van Persijn, a sixty-two-year-old lady living in the village of Valkenburg. The petition was submitted by her nephew, cornet in the army and probably her closest living relative. Agnes was an alcoholic, but she also swindled, obtaining brandy on other persons' accounts. She used to drink with ordinary people such as masons. She lodged a nightwatchman from Leiden in her house during the winter without any apparent reason. Sometimes she used indiscrete expressions. Once, when someone came and asked for her, the servants told him she was wandering about.[18] All this may lead the reader to assume that the lady was losing her faculties, but her nephew did not define her behavior in terms of insanity. He just referred to misconduct in moral terms. This also was true in the case of Jan Betua Borwater. He had previously been an embarrassment to his family while in Indonesia. He was a drunk and was considered to be licentious and dangerous. For that reason he had been imprisoned for three years in Batavia, and upon his release he was sent back to his home country. This prompted the family in Indonesia to write to his sister Cornelia, urging her to have Jan committed anew to some institution. When Jan learned this, he became furious and threatened his sister, who immediately submitted a petition for confinement.[19]

These examples illustrate the complexities involved. The prisoners were almost never guilty of just one type of offense which was clearly proscribed. Rather, each case had its own rationale and history, and we have to reconstruct the road which led the family to ask for confinement in the end. Very often the threshold of unacceptability was reached when a family felt that its reputation was on the verge of being irreparably damaged. That is why I called the concealment of a black sheep's behavior an important motive for those requesting imprisonment. This motive is plain in a number of cases in which a possible release was dependent upon measures that would continue to insure concealment. Gerard Beelaarts van Blokland, for example, only agreed to his brother's release when the latter promised to take up residence in far-away Hoorn and not to let himself called by his family name. Nicolaas van Strijen negotiated his release with his mother for five years, being unwilling to accept her condition of residence outside Holland. He was only freed after his mother died. Abraham Douglas proposed conditions for his own release. Once he suggested that he should make a journey through foreign countries to make people believe he had been abroad all the while rather than in a *beterhuis*. Johanna van der Sleiden, whose family lived in Delft and who had been committed to Duinkerken there, was in principle allowed to go out to church. But she refrained from using this privilege, because she was so well-known in town.[20]

Another motive for imprisonment is not quite the same as curbing embarrassment from a member's misdeeds, but the family reputation is involved to an equal extent. I call this motive 'anticipation of justice.' Historians of crime and punishment have shown that it was considered shameful for a respectable family and an almost unbearable embarrassment to an elite family if one of its members were to suffer a public criminal punishment. In a number of petitions for private confinement the fear is expressed that the person in question, should he continue in his harmful and semilegal activities, would fall into the hands of justice. Some of the persons in question were associating with members of the lower classes who, the petitioners thought, engaged in criminal pursuits. Others gambled away their money, which led their relatives to believe they would try to recover it by some illegal act. Imprisonment in a *beterhuis*, in a nonjudicial situation, would prevent this from happening. In most cases it is clear that the petitioners were more afraid of the prospect of punishment than the crime for which it might be imposed. The motive of anticipation of justice was an element, in a major or supplementary way, in many of the petitions submitted to the Court of Holland.

This raises the question whether the offenses private prisoners were guilty of were also crimes, and might have been punished as such. The answer must be largely negative. Alcoholism, for example, was not illegal. The supervisors of the poor in Haarlem once defined it as a *vitium*, in contrast to a *crimen;* imprisonment mainly served to ensure that the offender could no longer reach for the bottle and allow him the opportunity to improve himself.[21] Nor was madness criminal; the notion of diminished responsibility has always been associated with it. Most forms of sexual deviance, on the other hand, were liable to punishment by a court, but the sexual behavior of private prisoners was described in terms of a dubious lifestyle rather than in terms of concrete offenses. The fact that petitions for confinement were nowhere inserted in the registers of criminal trials also points to a difference of perception about the two kinds of conduct. Finally, very few private prisoners were prosecuted for a crime either before or after their confinement. Examination of all pertinent records for Leiden revealed that only two or three persons from the sample were also involved in a criminal procedure at some other time of their life.[22] In Dordrecht this was a little different. No less than eleven names from the sample were mentioned in the "book of criminal resolutions," but this was a separate register referring to minor cases only.[23]

The differentiation of noncriminal unacceptable behavior from criminality concerned all social classes, but especially the elites. Anticipation of justice as a motive for confinement was also mentioned most frequently among the elites. Indeed, it was generally accepted that the misconduct of persons from the upper and middle strata warranted preventive measures which might be denied to families of more humble status. The regents of Dordrecht's urban *beterhuis* formulated this idea explicitly. They denied a gratis confinement to a poor father whose daughter had taken some of the household's goods to a pawnshop. Since "a regular education leading to virtue is a rare phenomenon among that sort of people," they argued, if this request were granted, many other poor parents might be tempted to seek gratis confinement, to the detriment of the house.[24]

An attempt was made to quantify the types of behavior for which imprisonment was obtained. The Leiden petitioners usually made clear the main reason for the petition. The offenses in the sample from that town can be quantified as follows: alcoholism (26%), insanity (25%), licentiousness in general (14%), maltreatment (4%), sexual activities (3%), squandering money (2%), wandering about (1%), suicidal tendencies (2%), combination (7%), unclear/not mentioned (16%). Comparing these figures with requests just by spouses, there are a few differences. Notably, husbands and wives accused each other of alcoholism more often (40%) than other petitioners did. For licentiousness, referred to in the requests by terms such as "loose conduct" or "an irregular life," this is the other way around. It figures in a mere 5 percent of the requests by spouses. Children were more often accused of licentiousness by their parents. For the other offenses, there are no significant differences. Although the relationship between prisoner and first petitioner apparently influenced the frequency of requests for confinement with reference to various types of behavior, the relationship was not the major factor determining the offense mentioned. Most categories of unacceptable behavior occurred in every type of family setting. We are not dealing primarily with conflicts arising out of the situation in which people lived together but with deviant activities close relatives wanted to put a stop to.

With that established, we must downplay the importance of categorization. For one thing, the labels just given are of the historian's making. Neither the petitioners nor the court had particular recourse to labels; the former just listed what happened and the latter reacted to it. The relativity of categories becomes clearer still when the Rotterdam data are taken into consideration. In the sample from that town alcoholism figures in no less than 59 percent of petitions throughout the eighteenth century, while insanity figures in 3 to 4 percent. The latter data are biased, though, due to the use of a summary procedure for requesting imprisonment for insanity directly from burgomasters. If these requests were included in the figures, the percentage for insanity would rise to about 50 percent. But then provisional confinement in crisis situations, a phenomenon referred to in several petitions but for which there is no series of documents, would have to be included, too. In Leiden there is no evidence for the use of either of these procedures. Such considerations strongly diminish the value of a quantitative comparison of categories of unacceptable behavior.

Models for Badness   The fact remains that Rotterdam petitioners had a predilection for emphasizing alcoholism as the form of misconduct that irritated them. Moreover, for Rotterdam, the historian's labeling efforts are more problematic because the emphasis on one type of offense versus another was less marked than in Leiden. An excessive love of the bottle was mentioned as a supplementary offense in quite a number of the requests that were primarily based on some other offense. Even the mad were often reported to have fallen into their condition because of a heavy consumption of alcohol. This provides a clue. There must have been models for the description of unacceptable behavior, which varied from one town to the other. No doubt the activities listed were real and there is no reason for disbelieving the details of the stories. The prisoners had caused problems. They had made life unbearable for those around them, a phrase which literally forms the conclusion of a number of requests. If the petitioners did not actually live with the relative about whom they were petitioning, nonetheless they considered they had been hurt by the scandal owing to the relative's actions. This does not preclude, however, that the way in which the story was composed, the order in which the facts were arranged, followed a certain pattern, whether consciously or unconsciously adhered to. If the black sheep of Rotterdam families turned out to be drunks time and again, whatever else they did, too, this may have been because in that city drunkenness was considered the source par excellence of deviant behavior or because the alcoholic was the stereotyped deviant there.

Thus, in the Rotterdam model for the description of deviant behavior drunkenness had a very prominent place. This seems to have been the case in Dordrecht, too.[25] In Leiden the model apparently tended toward an emphasis on one of several types of deviance: drinking, loose living, or insanity. Towns such as Amsterdam or Utrecht may have had other models still for the description of undesirable conduct. We also do not know whether these models were cherished primarily by the magistrates. Possibly, the petitioners adhered to them to maximize their chances of success. Or it may have been the urban community's model which influenced people's perceptions of deviant behavior. International variations with respect to models must have been a function of broad cultural differences which affected rulers and ruled alike. Some international comparison is possible. We can start with a few surviving petitions to the Bremen magistrates.

These requests differ from the Dutch requests in two main ways, besides the patriarchalism already noted. First, the Bremen petitioners opened with a more elaborate introduction including copious polite formulas and phrases of modesty toward their superiors. The second difference lies in the relative prominence of religious wording. Although Dutch petitioners often referred to immorality as "godless behavior," they did so more casually than the Germans. In German petitions it was common to speak of the prospective prisoner's behavior in terms of sin and to emphasize the danger to his soul. A good example is the request submitted in 1727 by Dr. Theodorus de Hase, admittedly a minister himself, and his siblings, Cornelius and Anna Elisabeth. Their brother Paulus had been an embarrassment to his family for twelve years already, beginning with his plans to marry "a licentious female person." His guardians at the time had prevented this union and he had been sent to various schools and academies. Instead of studying, he had lived a life of drinking, dueling, and visiting prostitutes. Such accusations would be familiar to a reader of Dutch petitions. But it is also emphasized that Paul almost never went to church during those twelve years. Even worse, he had tried to infect the innocent souls of others and he had called the divine word his brother preached from the pulpit "a vicious lie." Paul, the petitioners concluded, was really a Saul. There was no other remedy but to lock him up. They had heard of the facilities at Celle, where prisoners were kept in separate rooms "without harm to the reputation of their family." There he could contemplate his sins and save himself from the abyss of eternal damnation. The Bremen magistrates gave their consent and agreed to intervene with the Hannoverian authorities.[26]

A comparable emphasis and similar phrases are found in other Bremen petitions not written by ministers. A widow who felt threatened by her son had frequently "preached" to him in an effort to change his behavior. The soul of a daughter who did nothing but drink brandy and behave violently was "running toward hell," and its course might be altered by imprisonment. Gerd Tönnies, an inhabitant of the village of Vielstedt, manifested "an unfounded hatred toward his pastor."[27] Thus, the Bremen model describing the activities of those who deserved to be confined equated unacceptable behavior and sin, and stressed the utility of imprisonment as a tool of salvation.

The Parisian petitions edited by Farge and Foucault vary in style. Their length and content seem to have depended on the status of the person addressed. Those written to the lieutenant of police were short and factual. When addressed to a count or marquis, they were somewhat more elaborate. The dossier contains just one petition written to the king. It is reverential in tone and full of circumlocutions. This is quite understandable in view of the importance of status differences under the French monarchy. Ultimately, however, every successful petition reached the royal cabinet, and that, the editors argue, was their chief common characteristic.[28] This characteristic may receive greater emphasis from them than it deserves. The editors seem to attach a quasimystical meaning to it, reminiscent of the weight attributed to the king's person by Foucault in his analysis of executions during the Ancien Régime.[29] They suggest that, because the requests ultimately went to the king, the petitioners were more readily prepared to reveal the secrets of their private lives. Telling the story to the royal father meant that it remained within the family after all. Needless to say, this argument is purely speculative. The published dossiers contain no hint that people felt this way. The Dutch and German evidence suggests a more sober conclusion. Private confinement was requested all over Western Europe. Dutch citizens petitioned just as eagerly to local or provincial courts as the French did to the royal cabinet, and the citizens of Bremen and Hamburg petitioned just as eagerly to their burgomasters and senate. There were various local and regional models for describing the offenses of black sheep, but imprisonment guaranteed the concealment of both the unacceptable behavior and the scandal it might cause.

Conclusion: Morals and Life-style   Private confinement occupied a position at the crossroads of family discipline and the authorities' desire for order. To the extent that it was used among the lower social echelons, its use may be explained by reference to the intensification of moral concern discussed in Chapter Two. The civilization offensives of the early modern period were aimed at raising the moral standards of the lower and lower-middle classes. When the administrators of charitable institutions requested imprisonment, they were exercising their disciplinary authority for the purpose of the civilization offensive. When respectable lower-class families did so, it means that they were sensitive to the offensive and wished to keep pace with it. Sometimes they were moved by more practical considerations, too, notably when the prospective prisoner's behavior endangered their financial situation. To the elites, avoidance of scandal was the most important factor. This is also made clear by anticipation of justice as a motive, which was emphasized mainly by elite petitioners. In this case, imprisonment was a preventive move rather than a remedy for misconduct. It protected a family's reputation from the stain of association with the lower classes. During the period from about 1675 to about 1800 elites submitted an especially large number of petitions. This may be explained by reference to Elias's observations on the refinement of manners among these groups in that period.[30] He shows that the French elites were constantly polishing their models of behavior and the Dutch patricians imitated them in this. The prestige of families from the upper and middle classes rested in large part on their life-style, their fancy manners, and their general ability to manage their affairs. They had to show off. When this life-style appeared to be compromised because one of their number was unable to live up to accepted standards, they were willing to consider drastic measures to hide the embarrassment. The representatives of the state, who belonged to the same social stratum, shared this outlook.

The Netherlands, France, and the End of Private Confinement

The period from the late seventeenth century to the end of the eighteenth was the heyday of confinement on request, certainly as used by elite families. Dutch evidence in the form of petitions leaves no doubt about this. In France most *affaires de famille* seem to date from that period, too. In both countries private prisons proliferated in the eighteenth century. There were eighteen houses, called by the name of their proprietor, in Paris alone.[31]

As private confinement constitutes an important part of the early modern carceral experience, primarily, its absence from histories of nineteenth-century imprisonment seems understandable. The authors of these histories could have included private confinement, since it survived to a certain extent after 1800. But it only survived in a transformed manner; the 'classical' period of confinement on request had ended by the early nineteenth century. Its demise can be explained by reference to two other phenomena: changing conceptions of political and personal liberty, and changing views of madness. I will argue that these were related and that together they reinforced the breakthrough of a medical approach to insanity.[32] Admittedly, my ideas in this section are a little speculative.

Visitations and Limitations   Concern about possible abuse of the private confinement system manifested itself from the early eighteenth century. For one thing, as a result of the spread of private institutions, which were not directly dependent on a court, quite a number of prisoners became 'invisible.' For another, there was the possibility that families could have a member locked away under false pretexts. The first problem could be solved by instituting inspections. The second was more difficult.

Reports of the visitations by commissioners from the Parlement of Paris to St. Lazare, one of the major institutions in the region keeping private prisoners, date back to 1717, and the actual visitations may have started even earlier.[33] The Court of Holland made a decision to that effect in November 1728. Henceforth, two of its members were to pay annual visits to the *beterhuizen* where prisoners were kept at its authorization, beginning during the Easter vacation of the following year.[34] The formula is significant. The court refused to assume responsibility for the fate of prisoners from other jurisdictions in these institutions. The commissioners did not automatically inspect all the province's *beterhuizen*, and where they went, they only saw the inmates whose stay had been consented to by the Court of Holland. Once, in Delft, they looked in on a private prisoner from Middelburg, but only at the explicit request of the magistrates of that town. There is no record that any particular event was the immediate cause of the decision to start visitations. Daniel Defoe's *Augusta Triumphans,* which included a passage calling for the inspection of private institutions in England, was published in 1728, too.[35] It is unlikely, however, that this writer had much influence across the North Sea. He failed even to inspire the authorities of his own country to increase their control of these institutions. The first English statue providing for the inspection of private institutions was passed in 1774.[36]

These English houses occupy a special position. In historical literature they are usually called private madhouses, but they seem to have admitted persons accused of misconduct, too. They were probably very close to Dutch private *beterhuizen.* One English husband explicitly declared that he viewed such a house as a place of correction.[37] It was with respect to these institutions that confinement under false pretexts became a standard accusation. In addition to Defoe, other eighteenth-century writers protested, too. Husbands were said to have their wives locked away in order to spend more time with mistresses, and relatives were said to have used this means to deprive a rightful heir of a family fortune. Despite the English tradition of 'the rule of law,' it must have been fairly easy to obtain the committal of a servant or a family member without intervention by a court. It remains to be investigated how frequent the abuses condemned in the contemporary literature really were.[38]

The Dutch archival evidence does not hint at such cases of blatant abuse as claimed by English writers. Occasionally, we suspect that ulterior motives beyond concealment of unacceptable behavior were involved. In 1696 a citizen of Rotterdam addressed himself to the Court of Holland to demand that his wife be formally prohibited from having him imprisoned and that he be reconfirmed in his marital power.[39] Another Rotterdam husband, who was committed to the urban *beterhuis* in October 1769 and released a year later, claimed that his wife had grossly exaggerated his misconduct.[40] In 1788 the inspector general of the fortifications at Curaçao had his wife imprisoned in a house at Delft. She in turn claimed that her husband was a drunk and lived comfortably with their son in the West.[41] Sometimes the relatives of a prisoner disagreed among themselves, which may indicate machinations by one side. In 1700 Joost van Waalwijk requested the Leiden magistrates to release his father from the Cecilia hospital, to which he had been committed by Joost's stepmother two years earlier.[42] In the same town Maria du Floo was first imprisoned by unnamed petitioners, then set free at the request of her father, and subsequently, in 1720, imprisoned anew at the request of her sister, who declared that their father had moved to an unknown location.[43] In 1770 the brother and brother-in-law of a woman were only willing to support her husband's petition for confinement on the condition that the couple's mutually owned real estate would not be mortgaged.[44] Adolf Roelofswaart was imprisoned at Delft on the Court of Holland's authorization in 1765; he was then living separately from his wife, and his father submitted the request. Three years later, when the father died, the wife petitioned for Adolf's release, complaining about the way his brothers handled the inheritance.[45] The best documented case concerns a native of Friesland, Jacobus Verfalje, who had moved to Alkmaar with his family when he was a boy. In 1736 his father obtained his imprisonment in that town's *beterhuis*, but this was contested by other relatives still living in Friesland. The contesting party accused Jacobus's father and brothers of having wanted to get control of Jacobus's property. The prisoner was set free a month later on the condition that he move to Friesland and not accuse the Alkmaar court of any irregularities.[46]

Successful machinations, of course, are unlikely to be documented. As long as the idea persisted that the preservation of a family's honor warranted the restriction of an individual's freedom, the risk of abuse of the system remained. A few cases resembling those just discussed were reported from French private prisons, too.[47] In Hamburg private confinement turned into an issue that divided the board of administrators in 1791. Provisor Sieveking made a speech in January, stating that progress obliged the administrators to renounce the traditional right of admitting prisoners at the request of their families. In the past, he claimed, many people had been arbitrarily deprived of their freedom and treated harshly. After consulting the *zuchthaus* logbooks, his colleague Brock made a speech in June, arguing that the records failed to support Sieveking's views. When Sieveking's words were published a few years later by Wagnitz, Brock felt insulted. He went through the logbooks more thoroughly, and in 1808 published his findings, thereby becoming the first historian of imprisonment in Hamburg.[48]

France was the first country where the practice of confinement on request was made subject to limitations. The system was viewed from a different perspective there, because it was associated with royal absolutism. French families could choose between two procedures when they wished to have a member imprisoned. A committal might be authorized *par ordre du roi* or *par ordre de justice*. The first procedure clearly predominated, possibly because the courts were more scrupulous than the king. At St. Lazare in 1692 the ratio of persons committed by the first method to those committed by the second was 3:2. In other known instances the percentage of judicial orders was lower still. It fluctuated between 10 percent and 25 percent in the same institution in 1733 and in the *charités* of Pontorson and Château-Thierry in the 1780s.[49] Thus, the authorization of private committals in France was largely an executive matter. As a rule, the request 'to the king' was presented to an *intendant* or other local official. In Paris most were addressed to the lieutenant of police. Every successful petition, however, passed through the office of the 'minister of the royal house.' The crucial point is that the royal order, or *lettre de cachet*, could also be used as a weapon against the king's personal opponents, from dangerous enemies of the state to small-time smugglers. The most notorious prison, of course, was the Bastille, where both Louis XIV and Louis XV kept many political opponents. It also housed a minority of prisoners committed by their families.[50] But the Bastille, which became depopulated during the second half of the eighteenth century anyway, was exceptional. Everywhere else, *prisonniers de famille* greatly outnumbered political prisoners. In Provence 81.7 percent of the *lettres de cachet* were requested by families.[51]

In spite of this figure, the association of absolutism and confinement on request made the French more sensitive to the restrictions on personal freedom associated with both. Toward the end of the Ancien Régime two ministers of the royal house attempted to impose limitations on the possibilities of obtaining *lettres de cachet*. Malesherbes, who was in office for less than a year in 1775–1776, complained that political prisoners were often victims of personal revenge by petty bureaucrats. But he defended the system in principle, blaming the philosophes for having unjustly infuriated the public. In 1784 Breteuil communicated his views to the provincial *intendants*. The mad were to be committed preferably by judicial rather than royal order. With regard to those guilty of misconduct, a clear line had to be drawn between minors and adults. The imprisonment of adults was justified only in cases of very serious damage to the honor of the family. For a spouse to be committed, both families would have to give their consent, and even if the prospective prisoner was an unmarried minor, other relatives besides the parents had to support the petition. No longer was misconduct by adults sufficient reason for their confinement.[52]

A comparison between France and the Netherlands shows unmistakably that the association of private confinement and absolutism accelerated the process by which families in France lost this disciplinary tool. There is no sign of any principled opposition to confinement on request by the Dutch around 1800. The paradox is clear: because political liberty had been accorded relatively large room in the Netherlands for two centuries, the widening of the limits of personal liberty was retarded. There were few reforms comparable to those in France. In the Netherlands on the one hand, it was unnecessary to stress the need to have numerous relatives endorse a petition, because this practice had always been fairly common. Also, the authorization of a committal had always been a judicial rather than an executive affair. On the other hand, the imprisonment of adults for misconduct remained a matter of course. Ironically, private confinement became more of an executive affair in the nineteenth century. A royal decree of 1814 reconfirmed the use of this system. Henceforth, a petition had to be submitted to the local mayor, although a court was to give final consent. In a series of requests which reached the mayor of Amsterdam between 1814 and 1820, 71 percent of the cases concerned insanity, 18 percent concerned immorality, and 11 percent concerned alcoholism. For the latter two vices, husbands, wives, and unmarried adults were still imprisoned.[53] This would have been impossible in France by then. In France, private confinement was dragged into the disrepute emanating from opposition to the *ordre du roi,* which caused the system of *lettres de cachet* to be abolished in 1790. The Civil Code of 1803, however, made it possible for fathers to have their disobedient children under twenty-one imprisoned for six months.[54] In addition to minors, there was one other category of people to whom the guarantee of personal liberty was not extended: the insane. This was the case in all countries.

Insanity and the Redefinition of Unacceptable Behavior   As noted in Chapter Two, the mad constituted the first category of deviants for whom separate institutions were established, beginning in the fifteenth century. Alternatively, they were committed to pesthouses or leprosaria, the latter usually devoid of lepers. From about 1600 the insane either were kept in separate madhouses or were locked away with other deviants again. In seventeenth-century England mad persons were sometimes committed to houses of correction.[55] They were present in French *hôpitaux généraux* and in German prison workhouses, always in separate wards, though. In the Netherlands, the Delft *tuchthuis* was combined with a madhouse. To the extent that committal for insanity in a prison workhouse was associated with the dishonorable aspect of such institutions, it is understandable that elite families were reluctant to employ them and looked for other places to house their insane. So private prisons came to admit the mad as well as other persons the elites wished to conceal, and some, in England and Delft for example, even originated as houses solely for the insane. The committal of the insane to private institutions served to save their honor and that of their families from the stains of association with marginals and criminals.

Thus, in the eighteenth century, unacceptable behavior and madness became associated. To go into the history of madness in detail would extend beyond the limits of this study. Let me just emphasize that it went through a crucial phase of secularization during the period under scrutiny and that this development stimulated the rise of a medical approach to insanity.[56] In the beginning, the cohabitation of the mad and persons guilty of misconduct retarded the evolution of the concept of mental illness. No form of treatment was administered in *beterhuizen;* just as in the case of other inmates, incarceration of the insane mainly served to conceal undesirable behavior. The houses were managed by businessmen who made a living out of guarding people. This was the case in England, too. The Court of Holland's visitation reports show that the supervision of the insane was considered primarily a judicial matter. Learning that certain persons tried to persuade Bernardus Crayevanger, an inmate of De Gekroonde Kabel, to draw up a will, in 1734 the court commissioned two of its members "to inquire into the state of his memory and sense." Without having consulted a physician, the lawyers returned from Delft reporting that Bernardus was incapable of making a testament.[57] However, attitudes were changing in this very period. From the second quarter of the eighteenth century onward, there was sometimes talk of a doctor's testimony regarding the state of mind of a prospective prisoner or an inmate whose release was being considered. Madness concealed in *beterhuizen* was gradually being drawn into the medical domain.

The evidence of numbers is even more suggestive. It was noted that the 1800 group of the Court of Holland sample was composed mostly of insane persons. A comparable development occurred in England. Around 1800 there was a decisive shift from nonmedical persons to physicians managing private institutions. At the same time the numbers of these institutions greatly expanded.[58] Thus toward the end of the eighteenth century there was a tendency to see private institutions primarily as refuges for the insane. The evidence for the Netherlands allows me to trace this development further, into the nineteenth century. Despite the persistence of the custom of confinement on request for misconduct, most *beterhuizen* were gradually transformed into houses for the mad. Presumably, this was accompanied by a gradual decline in imprisonment in these houses for misconduct; the Amsterdam percentages for the 1810s suggest that. The Dutch law of 1841 that regulated committals for insanity, introduced the term 'medical institution.' Quite a number of the houses that were allowed to bear that name were former *beterhuizen*.[59]

In this way, Dutch society caught up with countries such as France by a detour. In practice, personal liberty was now accorded an equally large domain in the Netherlands. In both countries, depriving an adult of his freedom was only considered justified in the case of someone who had broken the law or who was considered insane. But this is not the whole story. It was not simply a matter of only lawbreakers and the insane being imprisoned, and all other categories going free. To a large extent, madness was endowed with the legacy of the immorality and misconduct with which it had been associated in private institutions. It can hardly be a coincidence that the first half of the nineteenth century witnessed such an enthusiasm for 'moral treatment.'[60] Of course, this was related to an upsurge of moralism in society generally. This moralism was also manifested in the notion that delinquents should be confronted with their own conscience.

Moreover, the new view of madness was a culmination of the evolution of confinement on request. Philippe Pinel, one of the main protagonists of moral treatment, had originally developed his ideas from his experience with one of the private prisons of prerevolutionary Paris, the Maison Belhomme.[61] The career of the Marquis De Sade, who was imprisoned on moral grounds before the Revolution and later committed to the asylum of Charenton, also illustrates the connection. As the treatment of the insane after 1800 consisted of working on their conscience, many were defined as insane in the first place because their conscience was considered faulty. Masturbation and sexual promiscuity, for example, were said to lead to the loss of one's senses and bodily strength, too. Thus, the unacceptable behavior of the eighteenth century was redefined partly as mental disturbance. Considering mental derangement as a form of illness—to be treated by physicians—provided the missing link.

As late as 1886 the redefinition of unacceptable behavior was articulated in an unambiguous manner by S. A. van der Chijs. This psychiatrist wrote the history of Dordrecht's insane asylum, the former *beterhuis*, of which he had been director. Van der Chijs expressed his astonishment to discover drunks, sexual deviants, and gamblers among those committed a century earlier. He considered their presence in the institution an insult to the insane, who were guilty of no offense. Then he continued: "and yet I think that this offensiveness lies in the sound of the words rather than in the act itself. Put, in the place of 'persons of evil conduct and awfully debauched,' persons suffering from *folie morale*, dipsomaniacs, etc. Then much of what looks offensive and repelling is most certainly gone."[62]

Elite families may have been happy about the inclusion of forms of misconduct into the category of madness, and consequently their definition as illness. In this way, unacceptable behavior was not only concealed but also excused. In the eighteenth century, the public might still know about someone's stay in a private prison, which caused some minor damage to the family reputation after all. A condition which necessitated a stay in a psychiatric institution could be viewed as something which had struck the person in question without entailing any guilt.[63] So we can finally see the interconnection of the two transformations leading to the end of private confinement—changing views of personal liberty and changing conceptions of madness. The second served to neutralize opposition to the first. The possibility of defining all kinds of troublesome behavior as mental derangement made it acceptable for families to surrender the tool of imprisonment. The widening of the limits of the definition of madness was a necessary precondition for the extension of the domain of personal liberty.

PART FOUR:

THE EARLY MODERN
LEGACY

11
CROSSROADS
Bondage and the Penal System in Western Europe

Part One of this study considered the origins of the prison system from the broad perspective of Western Europe as a whole. Part Two mainly dealt with the Republic and the Empire, the core-area of the prison work-house. Part Three extended the scope of the investigation notably to France. Part Four takes up the broad perspective of the first again, in an attempt to sketch penal developments in Western Europe as a whole from the seventeenth century to the early nineteenth. The aim of this chapter is to examine the existing literature to determine whether a parallel development to that observed in the Dutch and German territories occurred elsewhere, too. To what extent was the development in other areas similar to that in the core-area and to what extent was it different? The focus will be on the evolution of imprisonment and related forms of bondage, and their role in the penal system. First, I will discuss the abortive history of transportation and galley servitude in the core-area; then, developments with respect to imprisonment and bondage generally in countries such as England and France. In the final chapter, I will present my conclusions on the evolution of the penal system in Europe.

A One-Way Course   First, we have to inquire briefly into the penal system alternatives in the core-area. Other forms of bondage than imprisonment were practiced before the first Continental prison was built. Remember that the Amsterdam judges eventually condemned their earliest candidate for incarceration to serve at the city's public works. Thus, although their institution was to become an international model, its triumph was far from assured at the outset. Little is known about public works as a form of punishment in the Netherlands. In the 1580s and 1590s a few Amsterdam convicts were forcibly employed in city extension projects.[1] Apparently, it was soon decided that it was preferable to have this job done exclusively by free workers. There are no studies referring to the application of public works penalties in other Dutch jurisdictions.

We are better informed about galley servitude by Dutch delinquents.

Already by the middle of the fifteenth century the Burgundian dukes ruling Holland and its neighboring provinces boasted a galley fleet, presumably manned by volunteers. Their Habsburg successors put convicts to this task, too, and Dutch courts might contribute to the supply of oarsmen. Thus, the college of *schepenen* at Amsterdam condemned four thieves to serve on "the king's galleys" in 1570, when the city still adhered to the Spanish side. During that decade, the other side adopted galley warfare, too, but no convicts seem to have been used as oarsmen at that time.[2] This changed in 1598, when a small galley started to patrol the great estuaries in the South of Holland. The *landdrost* of this area, who had been appointed by the Estates with special powers to arrest vagabonds and beggars, was its captain. The oarsmen were to be recruited from among "delinquents" picked up by him. He had the double task of tracing enemies of the country and rounding up vagrants, being in charge of a system which was simultaneously law enforcement and punishment. A second ship was ready in 1600, and to supply it with rowers, the Estates recommended that the courts in the province pronounce galley sentences.[3] Convicts had already been employed on the first ship. The Court of Holland and the *schepenen* of Amsterdam, Leiden, and Delft pronounced sentences to that effect. Between 1601 and 1608, the Leiden *schout* demanded a term at the galleys for forty delinquents. The court of Delft imposed this sentence forty-two times from August 1598 onward. The record of one of its convicts reveals that he was set free in May 1609 because the galleys were done away with.[4]

It is likely that the truce with the Spanish led to the abolition of the tiny galley fleet. To continue to patrol the area—while keeping an eye open for vagrants and other suspicious persons—was apparently found unnecessary. That ended the episode of galley servitude in the Republic. We do not know how many marginals rounded up by the *landdrost* or condemned delinquents actually served on the two ships, or whether the first group outnumbered the second.[5] When the galley system first went into operation, imprisonment was far from well-established in Holland; only the rasphouse was in existence and the prison at Leiden was about to be opened. During their early years, these institutions were to admit mainly marginals. The galley fleet might easily have become an alternative model for the forcible employment of marginals. When this mixture of military tasks and law enforcement did not survive into peace time, Holland went further down the road to a prison system. The prison system was well-established when hostilities with the Spanish were resumed in 1621.[6]

We may wonder whether transportation ever had a chance of becoming an alternative to imprisonment in the Netherlands. The year hostilities with Spain were resumed, the West India Company was chartered. Its counterpart in the East had been operating for two decades. In the 1620s the West India Company recruited ex-prisoners from the secret ward of the rasphouse, who served as volunteers.[7] Throughout the early modern period, signing onto a ship was to remain the most prevalent way out for those committed by their families. Shipping convicts or marginals overseas by force also occurred. I found the earliest reference to this idea in 1648. When the Estates of Holland considered plans to create new *tuchthuizen*, a few members suggested "sending a number of vagabonds and beggars to Brazil or other distant places after the example of other nations." When discussions of this possibility were resumed two months later, the majority rejected the idea. They agreed with a committee that advised that "the state in Brazil should be maintained with virtuous persons."[8] As it turned out, it was not maintained at all. Significantly, no one at the Estates meeting ever referred to Indonesia. The East India Company merely kept a network of trading posts there, and there were hardly any white settlers who could use convict labor. Manpower was needed, on the other hand, in some agrarian settlements in New Netherland. In 1652 about twenty-five boys and girls who were over fourteen and not learning a trade were sent there by the supervisors of the poor at Amsterdam.[9] There is no evidence, however, that convicts were ever transported to New Netherland.

The only experiment with transportation to a colony as a form of punishment took place toward the end of the seventeenth century. In 1684 the governor of Surinam approached the Amsterdam magistrates with the suggestion that an occasional delinquent whom they intended to condemn to a *tuchthuis* might be handed over to him instead. The matter was raised at the meeting of the Estates, which authorized Amsterdam as well as other towns to adopt this form of punishment. Those subjected to it were "to labor at the discretion of the lord governor and the council" at the colony's public works. Shipping costs had to be paid by the court that pronounced the sentence.[10] This may have discouraged the other towns, which are not known to have sent persons to Surinam. Possibly, Amsterdam had a contract with the governor. But its court only pronounced about fifty transportation sentences. Twelve delinquents who had been punished on the scaffold were sent to Surinam, six of whom had to serve a term in the rasphouse first.[11] Besides convicts, the colony received a few dozen poor boys and girls during this period.[12] At the beginning of the 1690s, however, the Amsterdam court stopped imposing transportation penalties.[13] No records survive which might disclose the reason or reasons why.

This abortive project ended the history of transportation in the Netherlands. Its failure may have been due partly to an insufficient demand for it. Convicts were employed only at the colony's public works; they were not sold to private settlers, as English convicts would be in America. On the other hand, the failure of transportation was also due to the idea that there was just no room for it alongside the 'traditional' penalty of imprisonment. Transportation was seen as an alternative to imprisonment from the beginning. Both the governor of Surinam and the Estates of Holland explicitly referred to persons who would normally receive a prison sentence. The clerks of the Amsterdam court had no word for the transportation penalty and called it "confinement," considering the whole country of Surinam as a place of detention. Commelin in 1693 inserted a reference to the colony into the margin of his description of the rasphouse. The fact that six delinquents sentenced to be transported overseas were first committed to this institution is especially illuminating. Whether the Amsterdam magistrates feared depopulation of the rasphouse or considered rasping a more appropriate punishment, the end result was the same. With regard to penal bondage, the Dutch steered a one-way course.

To a large extent, the same can be said for the Empire. The German states did not found overseas colonies, nor did they keep a galley fleet. Still, the possibility existed of subjecting convicts to bondage under foreign supervision. Until the middle of the eighteenth century, the authorities in Franken had contracts with Venice and Genoa to send oarsmen to those cities.[14] At that time Hamburg tried the expedient of transportation. In 1752 the senate allowed an agent named Decke to take four men and five boys who had been transferred from the *zuchthaus* to the spinhouse because of sodomy to Rotterdam and from there to Nova Scotia, together with a few women who would also be willing to go. It was soon found that almost all inmates of the spinhouse were desirous of leaving for America. The *speisemeisterin* protested that four young women who wished to be put on the list were absolutely needed in the house's kitchen. Eventually, fifty-four prisoners, male and female, left on two successive shipments, the second bound for South Carolina. To its dismay, the senate soon learned that they had all escaped upon their arrival in Holland. This caused the magistrates to decline a request from a captain in 1753, although another one received six women and two children. Another request in 1773 was declined with unambiguous arguments. It was stated, among other things, that transported prisoners effected an undue evasion of their deserved punishment and that this would lower the fear of justice.[15]

Clearly, the Hamburg magistrates saw transportation as a form of pardon, not from the death penalty but from imprisonment. The prisoners themselves considered it a special favor, judged from their eagerness to obtain it. This is in accord with the incidental character of transportation. As in the Dutch Republic, imprisonment was so well integrated into the penal system that there was no room for the colonial solution. There is no information on whether other German states sent offenders overseas during the early modern period. In the first half of the nineteenth century, however, several states, including Hamburg, briefly experimented with transportation.[16]

One other form of bondage, public works, enjoyed a moderate vogue in the Empire well into the eighteenth century. It was practiced by several states alongside and sometimes intertwined with imprisonment. Hamburg had known the *karrenstrafe* between 1609 and 1630. Chained to a cart, convicts had to clean the streets and collect the contents of citizens' latrines. Upon the abolition of this punishment, the *bürgerschaft* recommended putting delinquents to forced labor at the ramparts instead, but it is not known whether the senate followed this advice.[17] In Bremen, on the other hand, public works remained in use into the eighteenth century. The documents referring to it are a little ambiguous, though. In 1717 there was talk of delinquents going around with a cart. In 1724, three women requesting the release of their husbands stated that the men had been condemned "*ad operas publicas* in the *zuchthaus*" and were actually working at the ramparts. They were probably soldiers. A document dated 1732 speaks of "slaves" who were cleaning bridges and helping at the fortifications. They were either thieves or pardoned deserters.[18] Possibly, public works was mainly used as a military punishment in Bremen.

Scattered references in the literature suggest that delinquents were employed at public works elsewhere in Germany, too. In seventeenth-century Nürnberg they were cleaning the streets in a chain gang, but this penalty does not seem to have survived the establishment of a prison workhouse there.[19] In Prussia at the beginning of the eighteenth century, the employment of convicts at fortifications was very common. The creation of more prisons was seen as supplementary to public works, and imprisonment was considered a special form of *opus publicum*.[20] In the first half of that century, chained convicts worked at several fortresses in Schleswig-Holstein, even though there were also *zuchthäuser* in the territory.[21] The intertwining of imprisonment and public works at a few other places in Germany in the second half of the eighteenth century has been noted already. Sometimes only women were actually incarcerated, while the men condemned to imprisonment were employed outside. In the Hannoverian territories imprisonment evolved out of the *karrenstrafe,* which had been practiced there from the seventeenth century.[22] In Harburg, a town close to Hamburg, public works was still very much in use as late as 1791. This can be inferred from a report presented to its neighbor city. Those subjected to the penalty had to do all kinds of work at the ramparts or clean the streets and bridges of the fortress.[23] Thus, the course taken by the German territories was a little more variegated than that pursued in the Netherlands.

Penal Bondage in England   Developments in the two most populous countries of Western Europe, England and France, were more complex than in the Dutch and German territories. Although England pioneered imprisonment, it was slow to grant this form of penal bondage a monopoly. The role of the bridewells during the first 150 years of their existence should not be underestimated, though. Traditionally, it has been argued that the original enthusiasm for them faded away by the early seventeenth century. Recent research is proving this view to have been mistaken. New bridewells, or houses of correction as they came to be called, were founded throughout the seventeenth century and at the beginning of the eighteenth. The nature and intensity of confinement in these institutions were not substantially altered during that period.[24] Schematically, we may distinguish three phases in the evolution of bondage in England in the early modern period. During the first phase, houses of correction dominated but as a rule they never admitted serious offenders. During the second phase, starting around 1720, the impact of houses of correction declined, while transportation of felons considerably increased in importance. In the third phase, during the last quarter of the eighteenth century, imprisonment, this time also for felons, was increasingly used as a penal sanction. Offenders were subjected to it in houses of correction as well as in some of the old jails, and a few new prisons were built, too.

The first phase, the longest, is the one we know least about. There is almost no quantitative information from archival research on the specific categories of offenders committed to houses of correction. Many were vagrants, as they were on the Continent in the early days. A considerable portion of prisoners, on the other hand, was from the settled population: wage servants committed upon a complaint by their masters. These offenders were punished for disobedience, breach of contract, or the embezzlement of goods or materials belonging to their employers. Other transgressions of the law for which a stay in a house of correction was commonly used were petty theft, prostitution, and a host of other morals offenses and misdemeanors such as unlicensed selling of beer. Presently, no more than this rough indication of types of offenses can be given.[25]

Just as on the Continent, the English institutions had close connections with the poor relief system. They were also reported to have had a paternalistic character, although they merely had masters instead of fathers and mothers. A phenomenon peculiar to English law was the sharp distinction between formal criminal procedures at the assizes or quarter sessions on the one hand, and those in church courts and a number of summary jurisdictions, on the other. Until well into the eighteenth century, the confinement of offenders in houses of correction largely belonged to the latter sphere. Although a minority of delinquents guilty of less serious felonies were condemned to imprisonment, most inmates of houses of correction were petty offenders who had been tried summarily.[26] This type of legal procedure, without a formal trial or a jury, was a task for the justices of the peace. They routinely sent 'disorderly' persons to houses of correction, as the Essex J. P. William Holcroft did.[27] This practice can be compared with that in the Empire in the seventeenth century, when a committal to prison was usually considered a police measure belonging to the executive sphere. Despite the association of English prisons with summary procedures, the penal character of the these institutions was evident. From about 1600, separate workhouses for the nonoffending poor were created, as they were in many Dutch and German towns in a later period.

Three major differences between the English prison system and that on the Continent can be identified. First, a considerably larger number of houses of correction were opened in England than *tuchthuizen* in the Netherlands or *zuchthäuser* in the Empire. The number of county bridewells alone was estimated at about seventy by 1630, while a century and a half later the national total was about 170.[28] This would suggest a more prominent role for the bridewells than for their Continental counterparts, but the two other differences lessen the plausibility of such a view. The second difference concerns length of stay, which was always particularly short in England. In the seventeenth century, a stay of over a month was considered exceptionally long and was accorded to just a tiny minority of prisoners. Most English inmates spent only a few weeks in the house and a large number merely some days. Later, when the imposition of terms became common, these were still a matter only of weeks or months.[29] The shortness of terms is related, no doubt, to the predominance of summary convictions.

The third English peculiarity concerned the activities of inmates. Absence of a prison regime of forced labor, was not uncommon. On the Continent forced labor was seen as the essence of the prison regime, and normally it was imposed on prisoners, though there were exceptions to this rule. This was less true in England. Evidently, contemporaries knew about this difference between the two systems, Englishmen advocating that their countrymen take the Amsterdam rasphouse for an example.[30] Sometimes, English J. P.s considered it to be at their discretion whether offenders should work or not. William Holcroft sentenced some thieves to the Barking house of correction with hard labor and others without labor.[31] The situation also differed from one institution to the other. The London Bridewell certainly had a labor program, and so had the larger institutions outside the metropolis. The master of the Preston house of correction was dismissed in 1703 for—among other charges—failing to put the inmates to work.[32] This case shows that, even when the authorities wanted a labor regime, it was not always provided. Elsewhere there were facilities for work but no real prison regime, and inmates were simply told to do some job if they wished to get food at all. In other houses the facilities were completely absent. Quite a number of county bridewells were actually no more than shacks where an occasional offender was locked up from time to time. Thus, upon a closer inspection, the astonishingly intensive spread of houses of correction over England is a mirage. Despite this, Innes stresses the symbolic value of the numerous nominal prisons. According to her, they testified to a widespread local belief in the system, which she thinks surpassed that on the Continent. Even if many of these institutions only had an occasional prisoner, law enforcement agents wished to have the possibility of imprisonment always at hand.[33] However, that argument fails to take the Dutch and German supralocal network into account. Small towns and outlying rural jurisdictions regularly sent offenders to far-away prisons. In England, despite the central government's injunctions, the system remained substantially more local than in the Dutch and German territories. A result of the network was that Continental offenders from insignificant places were subjected to a prison regime.

The second phase in the evolution of penal bondage in England was introduced by the Transportation Act of 1718. Instead of adapting the bridewell system to make room for an influx of felons, British authorities favored the colonial solution. Transportation had already been practiced for a century when the act was passed. It was made possible by James I's decree in 1615. Pointing to "the severity of our laws," the king expressed the wish that "justice be tempered with mercie." Notorious malefactors could not benefit from his wish, but lesser offenders were allowed to live, be "corrected," and perform a "profitable service to the Commonwealth."[34] Thus, transportation began as an unofficial legal sanction: as the condition for a royal pardon or a new form of commutation of the death penalty. At first, it had only limited application. In the second half of the seventeenth century there were attempts to make more use of it, but they did not succeed, partly because of resistance from the colonists.[35] The act of 1718, authorizing courts to sentence certain offenders to a stay in the West for seven or fourteen years, made transportation a penalty in its own right for the first time. Pardoned capital convicts continued to be sent to the colonies, too. More important for the success of transportation was that the government consented to pay for the shipment of the transportees now.[36] From then on, the use of the penalty increased. Almost half of the women and three fifths of the men condemned to a noncapital punishment for a property offense in Surrey between 1722 and 1749 were transported.[37]

Thus, during most of the eighteenth century, Britain steered a course away from imprisonment. From about 1720 onward, houses of correction, although still used, lost their distinctness to a certain extent. Bridewells and jails tended to converge; notably, the former increasingly admitted persons awaiting trial.[38] Condemned offenders who were not punished primarily by physical means were removed to the colonies now. Transportation was not only practiced by English courts but by Irish courts, and to a lesser extent Scottish courts as well. In all, some 50,000 British convicts were shipped to the West between 1718 and 1775. While a fair share of the Irish were vagrants, most of the others were thieves who had been charged with grand larceny; 20 percent of these were women. Felons transported to America were sold by contractors to work with private employers. Most were bought by operators of medium-sized plantations, who also owned a small number of black slaves. The price of a convict averaged about a third that of an African. The larger slaveholders, who had no use for convict labor, protested against the system and suggested, though in vain, that English courts adopt galley servitude or public works as punishments.[39]

Although the third phase of penal bondage in England might seem to begin with the American Revolution, this is not quite so, for two reasons. First, transportation did not completely disappear at that time; it was discontinued during the Revolutionary War period, but was revived at the end of the 1780s. The fact that in the interim potential transportees were kept in hulks on the Thames to work on its shores shows that they continued to be considered a category apart. Second, imprisonment was already on the increase from the 1750s. It was imposed on almost 10 percent of the noncapitally punished property offenders in Surrey during the third quarter of the eighteenth century.[40] Of course this is still a modest percentage compared to the number imprisoned in Amsterdam. Transportation rose to unprecedented heights in the same period, partly because of an increasing reluctance on the part of the courts to routinely apply the death penalty. The crucial year was 1772. In their reply to a request from a Berlin judge by the name of Schmidt, the London magistrates explained that prisons had been neglected because transportation had demanded all their energies.[41] However, the penal policies were changing at that very time: in Surrey the figures for transportation dropped considerably during the four years preceding the Revolution.[42] It is clear that, even without the Revolutionary War, imprisonment would have risen in importance compared to transportation. Beattie convincingly argues that John Howard and his fellow reformer Jonas Hanway merely provided a justification for a movement which was already in progress.[43]

It is unnecessary to deal at length with the third phase of the evolution of penal bondage in England, because this phase which continued after 1800 is relatively well-understood. In spite of Botany Bay, transportation gave way to imprisonment as the major form of bondage. Average terms of incarceration became longer. The word "penitentiary" was invented, and the first experiments with solitary confinement were tried, but before 1800 only a few new penal establishments were built.[44] Houses of correction, which remained legally distinct institutions well into the nineteenth century, partly absorbed the increasing numbers of criminal prisoners. The relative weight of imprisonment among all punishments again can be illustrated with the Surrey figures. By 1800 it accounted for over 60 percent of noncapital sentences for property offenses among men, and close to 80 percent among women.[45]

Penal Bondage in France   Whereas the English evolution can best be understood as constituting three sequential phases, the history of bondage in early modern France may be dealt with synchronically, because it was associated with three different institutions: the *hôpitaux généraux*, the *dépôts de mendicité*, and the galleys. Transportation was adopted only after 1800, except for a few shipments, mainly of women discharged from hospitals, in the 1660s, the 1680s, and 1719–1720.[46] In historical literature there is no indication of the use of public works as a penalty to any significant extent. The closed wards of the *hôpitaux généraux* were the first prisons, as I define them, in France. Apart from the experiments discussed in Chapter Two, French imprisonment started around 1650; almost a hundred years later than in England. The earliest galley sentences, on the other hand, date back to the fifteenth century. With regard to penal bondage overall, then, the French were first. The three institutions will be reviewed successively.

Royal edicts of 1656, organizing the *hôpitaux généraux* system in Paris, and 1662, ordering the establishment of them in all major towns of the kingdom, accelerated the process of institution building.[47] Vincent de Paul and his followers had in mind asylums of a sort for pooling charitable resources, although they also cherished the distinction between the deserving and the undeserving poor. The French government was primarily keen on keeping beggars from the streets, but it was only in 1724 that the administration was prepared to bear the cost for this.[48] The *hôpitaux généraux* became hybrid institutions: places of confinement for some, hospitals in the modern sense for the sick, asylums for the insane and infirm, and shelters for people who entered them for a comfortable old age. Thus, they were multipurpose institutions to a much greater extent than the Dutch and German institutions that combined a prison with a voluntary workhouse. There is little information on the percentage of inmates of these French hospitals who were actually incarcerated. From 1724 to 1733, at Caen 23 percent entered after an arrest, and at Bayeux 58 percent did so. About a quarter these figures are children under ten, though. Moreover, these years represent a brief episode of more active policing and increased use of confinement following another royal edict.[49] A 1777 listing of the population of the *hôpital général* at Rouen, one of the largest, conveys a different impression. It categorized the 2,005 inmates according to their physical condition or their tasks within the building, rather than according to the agency through which they had been committed. Just fifty-two *"filles de police"* are recognizable as prisoners.[50] As a rule, only the *hôpitaux* in the larger towns had the facilities for housing large numbers of prisoners. The others lacked the personnel to guard them and often there were no separate, closed wards, either.[51] In the smaller *hôpitaux* probably no more than a handful of people were incarcerated. When the *prévôtal* court of Auvergne sentenced a few female thieves to be confined in an *hôpital général* in the region, the administrators protested, arguing that they were unable to prevent escapes.[52] We have to conclude that these French institutions were decidedly less penal in character than prisons in the Netherlands, Germany, or England were.

Paris, to be sure, was the major exception. For one thing, the city did not boast an actual general hospital. There were several physically distinct institutions, which were only joined administratively. Two had a relatively strict regime: the *Salpêtrière* for women, and *Bicêtre,* originally for only men, but since the early eighteenth century also including syphilitic women. Even these two were no mere places of detention. Each had a separate ward, *la force,* which was in fact a prison within the institution. Inmates confined to *la force* seem to have been called *"les correctionnaires,"* although it is not clear from the available data whether the two categories were one and the same. In 1661 *Bicêtre* had 116 *correctionnaires* of a population of 1,400; in 1789 this had become 665 out of 4,196. In addition, several hundreds of those listed as venereal patients, both male and female, were also prisoners. The *Salpêtrière* housed between 6,500 and 8,000 women during the second half of the eighteenth century, some 800 to 1,200 being confined to *la force.* The *Salpêtrière* prison was subdivided into four sections, which were only imperfectly separate, though.[53] Clearly, even though a minority of the inmates of both institutions were incarcerated, the prisons within them were among the largest in Europe at the time. Riots in the *Salpêtrière* prison were reported in 1737, when 160 inmates escaped, 1739, 1750, and 1758. The women rebelling in 1750 cried out that they would rather be hanged or shot than be imprisoned any longer. However, it seems that not all of these women performed forced labor, since raw wool was provided to just some of them. There is little information on a labor program at *Bicêtre,* but at any rate it is unlikely that the syphilitics were put to work.[54]

It should be noted that a fair number of prisoners were committed at the request of their families. The two *forces,* therefore, were not just criminal prisons, but were penal institutions to a significant extent. A large share of their inmates, male and female, were admitted on a police order. The Parisian police who patrolled the streets at night routinely picked up suspect persons and charged them with vagabondage or petty theft. The lieutenant had the authority to pass judgment on the persons arrested by his men, which he did in monthly sessions. In May 1759, for example, lieutenant Bertin judged forty-five women and sixteen men. Thirty-three of the women and fifteen of the men he sentenced to confinement. In the closing years of the Ancien Régime a new prison was created to keep first offenders sentenced by this summary court.[55] Prostitutes constituted another distinct category of inmates; they were committed to the *Salpêtrière,* a number of them also on a police order. Women condemned for prostitution stayed in prison between three and ten months; an early release was possible on the basis of good behavior. This resembled Dutch reduction practices. It is not surprising that Benabou takes issue with historians who situate the rise of imprisonment in the nineteenth century. For women, she concludes, it definitely started in the eighteenth.[56] The regular criminal courts, on the other hand, pronounced few prison sentences, although the frequency rose from the middle of the century on. Almost 5 percent of food thieves judged on appeal by the Parlement of Paris between 1750 and 1790 were condemned to an *hôpital*.[57]

In addition to Paris, the towns of Alsace-Lorraine may have taken a divergent road in the second half of the eighteenth century, possibly influenced by their German neighbors. French historians of crime and repression have not yet extended their research to this region. It was noted in Chapter Seven that the Metz magistrates requested information from Hamburg because they intended to found a prison. A new *zuchthaus*, which could accommodate a hundred prisoners, was reported to have been erected at Strasbourg in the 1760s. There were three workrooms, which were arranged in such a way that one man could oversee them all to check on whether the inmates were busy.[58]

The *dépôts de mendicité* were inaugurated in the 1760s as a substitute for the *hôpitaux généraux*, especially in the provinces. Henceforth, arrested beggars and vagrants were to be committed to these institutions. Unlike the *hôpitaux*, they had no ties with charity or poor relief, as their name clearly testified. Still, they resembled the provincial *hôpitaux* to the extent that they did not constitute a smooth-running, efficient prison system. *Dépôts de mendicité* were routinely established in long-deserted castles or other decrepit buildings from which it was often easy to escape. Epidemics occurred frequently, while in some *dépôts* the inmates were actually starved to death. Nevertheless, it was thought that people would want to enter voluntarily; at least, the government warned against this. Although the *dépôts* had been set up only for the confinement of marginals, insane persons and syphilitics were soon housed there, too. The numbers of inmates varied between 100 and 200. Vagrants usually served a term of three to six months; a minority of recidivists received galley sentences. The authorities contracted with private companies to provide the inmates with work, but sometimes there were no work facilities. The *dépôts* met with opposition from various sides, and during Turgot's ministry they were temporarily closed.[59] The *dépôts de mendicité* simply appeared on the scene too late to play any significant role in the development of imprisonment.

Although Benabou restricted her argument about imprisonment in eighteenth-century France to women, men were subjected to it, too. The country even had three criminal prisons, at Toulon, Brest, and Rochefort, from the 1750s. Following the Amsterdam rasphouse and the Hamburg spinhouse, they were the next European places of detention exclusively reserved for criminals. The courts masked this form of incarceration behind a galley sentence. That is, the courts continued to impose galley sentences but these translated into prison sentences. It is to the galleys, then, that we must turn to see the overall evolution, not only of penal bondage generally but also of imprisonment.

By the middle of the sixteenth century galley servitude became a regular penal sanction in France, supported by the weight of legal tradition. Originally, legislators primarily had vagabonds in mind for this punishment, and royal edicts threatening them with it were repeatedly proclaimed until 1764.[60] In the seventeenth and eighteenth centuries, however, vagrants made up only a small minority of convict oarsmen. Galley sentences were pronounced more frequently from the 1660s when Colbert embarked upon an ambitious scheme of expanding the Mediterranean fleet. The wars óf Louis XIV ushered in the heyday of convict rowing. We are amply informed about the use of the system from 1680 until the abolition of the galleys in 1748 through Zysberg's recent study. He divides this whole era into two periods which contrasted markedly. After the War of the Spanish Succession galleys became progressively less useful, which gradually caused the government to become indifferent to the sentencing policies of the country's courts. In the second period, as a result, penal considerations prevailed over political ones in the exercise of justice. This was paralleled by a change in the composition of the galley population. Between 1680 and 1715 nearly 45 percent of convicts were condemned by a court-martial, in almost all cases for desertion. During the years 1716–1748 the share of military offenses dropped to below 5 percent, while common law crimes (45%) and smuggling (44%) made up nearly all the rest. In general, a wide array of higher and lower courts were always involved. The annual average number of entries into the register was 1,057 in the first period and 678 in the second. The figures for nonmilitary offenders, however, were 582 and 646, respectively.[61] Thus, there was a dual evolution of galley servitude from a military to a penal institution: with regard to the system's purposes and with regard to the crimes of the men condemned to serve. After 1715 the courts routinely continued to sentence offenders to galley servitude, but fewer people were needed aboard ships. As a result, oarsmen became workers. During the winter season the convicts had always stayed in Marseille harbor, where many of them labored in the arsenals. In addition, some were hired out to serve private merchants on their ships, and a few were hired out to citizens ashore. Such practices became more common in the second period. During the years 1720–1740, some 15 percent of the convicts worked for one textile company alone. Others spent their days in the arsenal's hospital: when judges put penal considerations before military ones it meant that they no longer cared when the condemned were too weak to serve as oarsmen or workers.[62]

The entry books of the administrators at Marseille do not reveal the relative importance of galley servitude among the judgments of individual courts. Few data are available for the years in question. In two rural regions East of Bordeaux during the period 1696–1789, 21.2 percent of the sentences included a term at the galleys and another 12.4 percent were to the galleys for life.[63] Of the food thieves judged by the Parlement of

Paris, during the years 1700–1724, 13.7 percent received a galley sentence, and during the years 1725–1749, 17.2 percent received a galley sentence. There were few serious delinquents among this group, and only three were condemned for life.[64] The percentage given a life term was considerably greater among all convicts sent to Marseille. In this respect, French judges were harsher than their colleagues in Holland and Hamburg whose prison sentences are known. This harshness declined in Zysberg's second period. From 1680–1715, 64.7 percent of the convicts whose term is known were condemned for life. From 1716–1748 this figure was 25 percent. A mere 0.3 percent and 0.2 percent in the respective periods received a term under three years. No wonder, then, that more than half of those arriving at Marseille never returned. In the two periods, 51.7 percent and 53.2 percent died during their servitude. For the rest, the actual length of stay may be compared with the original term. From 1680–1715 about three quarters of them left before their term was over, and only about one in seven stayed longer than their term. Most of the convicts who left before their terms were over, however, were serving life sentences. If we leave these out, at least 38 percent stayed for less than their original term and at least 36 percent stayed longer. From 1716–1748 this had become at least 56 percent staying less and 2.9 percent staying longer among all convicts who lived to be released, and 50 percent staying less and 3.3% longer among those not sentenced for life. We are not informed whether good behavior during servitude played any role in obtaining an early release. On the contrary, many oarsmen seem to have been obliged to buy their freedom or offer a replacement. Pardons were often granted on the condition of service in the army, especially during the War of the Spanish Succession. However, since buying one's freedom was mainly characteristic of the first period, and in the second there were few wars, we may still conclude that somewhat of a system of routine reduction, comparable to that instituted in Holland, developed after 1715.[65]

It is a pity that comparable information is not available for the second half of the eighteenth century, because that is the crucial period from the point of view of this book. In 1748 the galleys were abolished and the complex at Marseille dismantled. That completed the evolution from a military to a penal institution that had begun in 1715. The law did not change and courts continued to pronounce galley sentences. Beginning in the 1750s, those convicts were put to work in the naval arsenals (*bagnes*) at Toulon, Brest, and Rochefort. They carried heavy loads, turned wheels, drove pumps, or pulled cables. They were also employed in joinery, drilling, or caulking. A few assisted in building ships. At night they slept in barracks, where they were chained to their beds. This punishment survived the Revolution and continued to be used until 1854.[66] A few figures are available for the second half of the eighteenth century. In a sample of offenders judged by the *prévôtal* courts and condemned in the majority of cases for second degree theft, 57 percent were committed to the *bagnes* or a *maison de force* in 1758; 52 percent in 1773; 60 percent in 1783; and 47 percent in 1789.[67] The Parisian Parlement imposed a 'galley' sentence on 24.7 percent of the food thieves in the years 1750–1774, and 35 percent in 1775–1790.[68] Among all judgments by the Parlement of Paris, 37.1 percent were 'galley' sentences in the 1770s, and 50.4 percent in the 1780s. The corresponding figures for the parlements of Toulouse and Nîmes in about the same period were 53.1 percent and 41.1 percent, respectively.[69] Although the *bagnes* were labor camps rather than buildings, they are quite comparable to Dutch and German prison workhouses. By a detour, penal imprisonment had reached France, too. Considering the evolution of the galleys and the emergence of the *bagnes,* even for his own country, Foucault is decidedly wrong in situating the birth of the prison system in the nineteenth century.

Other Countries   For the rest of Europe our information is less detailed. Developments in Spain resembled those in France as far as galley servitude is concerned. From the sixteenth century on, Spanish courts routinely condemned delinquents to serve as oarsmen, and the Inquisition supplied some rowers, too. It seems that the majority were kept beyond their term, but no exact figures are available. From the early eighteenth century onward, an increasing number of convicts as well as slaves worked in naval arsenals, as the galley fleet campaigned less frequently. The Bourbon government abolished the galley fleet in the same year as its Northern neighbor. From then on, the number and variety of public works facilities expanded. Convicts had already been employed in the mercury mines at Almadén and in military garrisons and forts in North Africa from the sixteenth century. After 1748 they worked at naval arsenals, on the construction of roads and canals, or in the Caribbean on public works or in the service of private individuals.[70] While the Spanish monarchy was among the first in Europe to introduce forced labor for serious delinquents, the country was relatively late to embark upon a repressive policy toward groups that were traditionally associated with the rise of prison workhouses. Although critical views of the poor were expressed in the sixteenth and seventeenth centuries, and a women's prison was established at Madrid, no further institutional arrangements were made. Troublesome vagrants and gypsies were whipped and banished or sent to the galleys. The older notions of charity remained stronger here than elsewhere, partly because they were adhered to by many of the elites. It was only in the second half of the eighteenth century that church leaders as well as laymen favored a more repressive approach toward what they too called the undeserving poor, and initiated a secularization of relief. The prison workhouse of San Fernando just outside Madrid was opened in 1766; it admitted vagrants, beggars, and prostitutes. A decade later a number of towns established so-called *hospicios*. During the 1780s, when the San Fernando institution began to admit property offenders and other serious delinquents, the confinement of marginals shifted entirely to the *hospicios*. In many respects, these institutions repeated the experience of Spain's northern neighbors a century and a half earlier.[71]

Italian states continued to rely on galley servitude as the preferred form of bondage throughout the early modern period. A few prison-like institutions were established, though. From 1703 Rome boasted one. It was set up in a ward of St. Michael's hospital, and admitted male juvenile delinquents up to eighteen years of age, convicted of theft or comparable crimes. Offenders above that age were to be sent to the galleys. This prison's regime included forced labor and a welcome upon entry. In 1735 a ward for women was added. A comparable type of prison workhouse seems to have been opened in Milan in 1766.[72] Figures for committals to these institutions are not available. Elsewhere in Italy, jails continued to be used for penal purposes sometimes. Between 1585 and 1672 the court of Padova sentenced a number of offenders—the number fluctuated between 2 percent and 8 percent of the court's convictions—to a stay in the *carcere*. In Padova and Brescia the overwhelming majority of sentences in the seventeenth century included a term on the galleys.[73] A Venetian law of 1669 made it possible for convicts unable to serve as oarsmen to be enlisted in the army instead. Imprisonment was another possibility. Just as France and Spain, eighteenth-century Italy witnessed the decline of galley warfare, but there was no clear-cut connection with penal reform. It seems that an increasing number of convicts were detained ashore, as ever fewer of them were needed aboard ships. In the end, the words *galera* and *prigione* became almost synonymous. Imprisonment gained ascendancy out of necessity, but the prisons had no work program. Venetian plans around 1790 aimed at the introduction of forced labor outdoors as an alternative to imprisonment. Facilities for public works were established in the Republic's overseas territories.[74]

In still other countries imprisonment developed gradually during the early modern period. The major Swiss towns, for example, had a prison workhouse in the eighteenth century. Bern also boasted a separate house for serious delinquents.[75] Elsewhere in Switzerland carceral institutions were usually combined with orphanages or almshouses. Such was the case in St. Gallen, where seventy-two out of 371 inmates of the closed ward during the period 1750–1798 were property offenders.[76] Scandinavia was generally slow about instituting imprisonment, despite the early foundations at Copenhagen and Stockholm. The second prison workhouse of the Danish-Norwegian kingdom, for women only, was opened at Trondheim in 1647.[77] Although various *tuchthuser* were established in Sweden, outside the capital they functioned merely as asylums for wandering orphans and other poor children.[78] In the second half of the seventeenth century the Swedes tried other expedients, too. Delinquents performed public works in silver and copper mines, at fortifications, and in the Stockholm harbor; some were transported to the Baltic dominions or even to New Sweden. In 1698 it was decided to establish a separate rasphouse and spinhouse in the capital for convicts of both sexes, but this project was only realized in 1724.[79]

Developments in the provinces of the Southern Netherlands, some of which were briefly noted in earlier chapters, implied a mixture of the experiences of their Dutch and French neighbors. A *tuchthuis* was opened in a few Flemish cities in the first half of the seventeenth century. The Bishopric of Liège, on the other hand, followed the French model. From the late 1680s on, several prison like institutions were established as 'houses of force' within the framework of an *hôpital général* system. The prisoners were mostly marginals and juvenile offenders.[80] Galley servitude was used in the Southern Netherlands at least until the beginning of the eighteenth century. The Austrian government did not keep a fleet in these parts, but, when robber bands were rounded up in the Aalst region during the 1740s, those arrested were, among other punishments, sent to the galleys.[81] Imprisonment increased in importance during the eighteenth century. From about 1720 on, the Brussels *tuchthuis* increasingly kept thieves and other delinquents sentenced by the court.[82] Some cities must also have consented to the admission of foreign offenders, because the court of Mechelen sentenced a few persons to be committed to a *tuchthuis*, an institution which that town lacked.[83] The new provincial prison of Flanders at Ghent, which became a model in its turn, and that of Brabant at Vilvoorde were opened in 1776 and 1779, respectively.[84] Thereafter, the court of Antwerp sentenced beggars to one or two weeks in its own workhouse, while delinquents were sent to Vilvoorde for a year or more. Theresia Verschueren, a recidivist who had already been whipped and banished from town, was condemned to no less than twenty years in September 1779.[85] Thus, long-term imprisonment had become a feature of the Southern Netherlands, too.

Long-Term Changes in the Penal System   The complex history of penal bondage in its various forms stretches over more than four centuries. This history was far from being a unilinear development, and the ultimate triumph of imprisonment was by no means prefigured from the start. Galley servitude and public works preceded it on the European scene and transportation came into play in several instances. The experiences of the countries discussed differed from each other. Overviewing them, we can conclude that imprisonment faced an almost permanent competition, varying in intensity with time and place, from other forms of bondage. Originally, the galleys were its foremost competitors. That it was Northern Europe that introduced forced labor in closed buildings was partly due to the fact that the naval solution was a well-established tradition in the South. In the end, however, that tradition could not sustain itself. Besides the fact that they were becoming obsolete, the galleys had another major disadvantage as a penal option. Rowing on these ships was considered unsuitable for women. No doubt, this consideration contributed to the eventual replacement of galley punishment with imprisonment. Transportation was the only other form of bondage applicable to both sexes.

It is not surprising, therefore, that after 1800 the competition mainly came from that direction. Transportation survived the first experiments with penitentiaries and solitary confinement. The number of British and Irish offenders sent to Australia between 1787 and 1868 was three times as high as the number transported to America in the period 1718–1775. These were men and women convicted for property offenses ranging from picking pockets to highway robbery. Some four thousand were condemned for political crimes.[86] France, which hardly had used transportation previously, introduced it in the 1850s as a substitute for the *bagnes*. From then until 1938 some 52,000 convicts were shipped to Guyana and another 20,000 to New Caledonia. They performed forced labor in several large settlements in these colonies. Three quarters had been condemned for property offenses and all but about a thousand were men. It is only with the advantage of hindsight that we can call this an 'old-fashioned' type of punishment. French advocates of transportation in the Third Republic predicted a glorious future for it, claiming that the days of the prison would soon be over.[87] In the southern United States, convict chain gangs worked at road construction well into the twentieth century.[88] It is possible that new forms of bondage as alternatives to imprisonment will be introduced in the future.

12

CONCLUSION

Imprisonment, Mentalities, and Social Change

The final chapter returns to the framework outlined in the first: a process-oriented approach to the history of imprisonment and repression generally. We have gone from the theoretical to the empirical, and now come back to theory again. Chapter Two discussed the emergence in the late sixteenth century of imprisonment and other spatial solutions to problems of marginality, deviance, and crime, and explained this development with reference to pacification and state formation processes. The empirical data in parts Two and Three corroborated this thesis, but they also raised new problems. Other factors besides state formation have to be taken into consideration to discover the social context of the evolution of systems of discipline and punishment.

One problem—the question of whether the exploitation of the labor force in the service of capitalist production was the main impetus behind the emergence and spread of imprisonment—can now be reviewed in the light of the evidence on the economics of imprisonment and the relationship of imprisonment to the other forms of bondage. Early modern prison workhouses were pseudohouseholds rather than capitalist manufactories, and penal considerations prevailed over economic ones, the prison administrators accepting a modest loss. By contrast, economic motives seem to have played a role in the introduction of other penalties. Transportation also cost the English government money, but it was cheaper than building new prisons, and in America convicts earned profits for private employers. Ekirch argues that the British preferred transportation to the Continental example of putting delinquents to forced labor in prison workhouses because they associated the latter practice with state tyranny. But he admits that constitutional liberties were only paid lip service, since they were so easily sacrificed abroad.[1] We must conclude that the crucial difference between transportation and imprisonment lay in the commercial priorities guiding the first and the importance of the household model for the second. A comparable argument can be made with regard to galley servitude. In Spain and in France until 1715 the need for able-bodied oarsmen determined the fate of convicts. Strong men were kept longer than their term: precisely the practice which Rusche wrongly associates with prison workhouses. To be sure, the problem of manning a war fleet is not just an economic one and it can hardly be said that the specialized training inculcated into oarsmen contributed to the discipline of the labor force in the interest of capitalist production. Generally, however, it seems that rulers who desired financially expedient solutions above all, favored forms of bondage other than imprisonment. This is even more understandable when we consider that these forms were penal sanctions from the outset, while prison workhouses were originally meant as solutions to problems of marginality and immorality rather than crime. For such institutions the household model seemed most appropriate.

Imprisonment certainly became a criminal punishment, though, and as such, its evolution should be viewed as part of the evolution of bondage generally. A major trend in the history of penal systems in Europe was the shift from public spectacles to privately inflicted punishment, which began in the seventeenth century and gained momentum in the period 1770–1870. The proliferation of prison workhouses represented a crucial phase in that shift. The very existence of carceral institutions meant that attention was deflected from the scaffold to some extent, but the new penalty still had a considerably public character. The same can be said for other forms of bondage. The French public could not see the oarsmen when they were at sea, but in the port of Marseille they freely interacted with this group. The galley convicts were also displayed publicly in other areas of France, primarily through the use of 'the chain' as they journeyed toward Marseille. Processions of between 200 and 400 convicts tied together by the neck in pairs departed twice a year from three different starting points. The Paris chain took about a month to reach Marseille, during which the convicts marched about 500 kilometers and completed their journey by boat. At every stop along the way the procession was shown in the marketplace. Although local inhabitants often kept a low profile, fearing that their carts would be confiscated, the chain was an effective teaching device. The custom was practiced by all Mediterranean states keeping galleys. In France it was abolished with the fleet, but Spanish convicts continued to be led to the arsenals in this way after 1748.[2]

To a lesser extent, this type of ritual also characterized transportation in Britain. London convicts went in procession from Newgate to Blackfriars, where they embarked. Convicts from Southwark joined them a little further down the Thames. From Bristol jail, criminals sentenced to transportation rode on horseback to Bideford, chained two by two. Crowds were reported to watch the spectacle. A few rich convicts escaped the infamy of such rituals by paying for the privilege of traveling in a coach.[3] Apart from this theatrical accompaniment to transportation, English houses of correction were just as open to visitors as Continental prison workhouses. That is attested, among others, by Ned Ward's account of a visit to the London Bridewell.[4] The processions of criminals condemned to transportation are documented for the eighteenth century only, which probably means they were discontinued in the nineteenth. Galley chains usually disappeared with the punishment of which they were part; in the Spanish case, presumably, they did not survive the abolition of forced labor on the arsenals in 1818. Prisons featured the most conspicuous shift with respect to publicity. Everywhere they were closed to the curious public around 1800; henceforth, only selected persons with a professional interest were admitted. This was a major step in the privatization of punishment.

. Another question, which is difficult to answer from the available evidence, refers to the interrelationship of the evolution of imprisonment, alternative forms of bondage, and the penal system generally to changing sensibilities vis-à-vis the physical treatment of offenders. Did the judges, the executive authorities, or the general public of the early modern period reflect on the suffering inherent in various types of punishment? Few voices articulating feelings on this point have come down to us from the days when prison workhouses were first established. Casual hints about imprisonment being an alternative to the scaffold have been noted in Amsterdam and Hamburg around 1600. It is understandable that few such arguments were recorded at the time, since imprisonment was not really considered a penal sanction. Its subsequent evolution in that direction, although complicated by problems such as that of infamy, does not seem to have generated major debates on the physical treatment of offenders. Most people found disciplinary beatings a normal and acceptable procedure, and the pumping myth was widely believed. Neither does the literature on alternative forms of bondage, such as galley servitude, reveal anything like a lively discussion of this subject. We have to wait until the end of the eighteenth century to find expressions of moral concern about certain forms of forced labor. The deadly work of glass-polishing in the Nürnberg prison, for example, met with criticism from opposition groups in the late 1790s.[5] This was a special case. There is no record of a principled opposition to forced labor as such—on the Continent at least— during the early modern period. Certainly, imprisonment was never seen as a threat to the bodily integrity of delinquents. Reformers around 1800 were concerned with matters such as fresh air, diet, and the separation of the sexes, rather than the physical treatment of the inmates.

The link between the rise of imprisonment and changing sensibilities with regard to physical treatment of convicts is largely implicit. In the end, the existence of prison workhouses and their use for penal purposes paved the way for the decline of more direct forms of physical punishment. Before that happened, however, the scaffold and confinement coexisted for over two hundred years. At first, each was imposed on different categories of offenders, but from the middle of the eighteenth century, the two largely served as alternatives. For England, Beattie explains the increasing frequency of imprisonment partly with reference to a declining confidence in physical punishment.[6] By the early nineteenth century, British reformers simply considered the prison as synonymous with an absence of the infliction of pain—though perhaps without regard for what happened inside the institutions.[7] The fact that prison life was largely hidden from public view helped to sustain such notions. In other countries the situation was comparable. The triumph of imprisonment after 1800, the building of penitentiaries, the experiments with solitary confinement, the panoptic principle: these phenomena are very well-known and they are not my subject. They formed part of the transformation of repression generally between 1770 and 1870, which was related in turn to a new phase in state formation processes.[8]

Paradoxes   The developments dealt with here, to emphasize it once more, were not unilinear. The history of forms of punishment other than the scaffold was one of recurrent experiments, retreats, and new beginnings. In the European core-area, two paradoxes were inherent in the evolution of imprisonment. First, although the existence of prison workhouses contributed to an eventual diminishment of emphasis on the physical element in the penal system, at the beginning these institutions represented an intensification of repression. The intensity of repression increased, not in the sense that every offender received harsher treatment, but rather that new groups of people became its target. They were marginals, the attitudes toward whom had changed for the negative, and undisciplined persons whom their families shunned. Policies attuned to the change of mentalities concerning marginals confirm the growth of a stronger justice from above, and consequently bolster state authority. The paradox can be explained: it was the subsequent evolution of prison workhouses, rather than their first appearance on the scene, which was related to changes in the penal system. We have to wait until the later seventeenth century, and in most regions until the eighteenth century, to find authorities confidently relying on less severe forms of repression for the more traditional offenders. As this confidence spread, the imprisonment penalty was extended to thieves and comparable delinquents.

The second paradox is implied by the combination of old and new models. Although, originally, committal to a prison workhouse was not an official criminal sanction, a stay there was certainly punitive. Securing the punitive character of these institutions received priority over exploitation of their economic potential. For the authorities and the administrators, penal considerations prevailed over economic ones. Thus, from the start, imprisonment contributed to the renewal of modes of repression, and in that sense the system might be termed innovatory. However, the application of this new form of punishment took place in a rather traditional context. Its model was the household rather than the manufactory. This paradox can be explained if we realize that the family became more important as a model within society generally in the course of the early modern period. The closely knit but hierarchically structured unit of father, mother, children, and servants was viewed by governments as a microcosm reflecting their own ideal relationship with their subjects. Criminals and marginals—the latter increasingly considered as delinquents, too—were seen as obstructing this paternalistic order. They were not perceived so much in economic terms, as a reservoir of potential manpower, as in moral terms, as persons who had broken away from the disciplining bonds of the family. For these outsiders forced labor was seen as an exercise in discipline, rather than an opportunity to become accustomed to an industrial routine.

This view also makes it understandable why the authorities were prepared to offer the opportunity of imprisonment as a tool to families who had problems with troublesome members, including the insane. These individuals had broken away from traditional bonds, too. The evidence on private confinement shows that the connections between the one type of deviance and the other were hazy and ill-defined in the early modern period. Even the borderlines between insanity and immorality were not always clearly defined—the same people were alternately denoted in terms of the one or the other. The rise of a medical approach to madness served to differentiate it from unacceptable behavior generally, and in the nineteenth century insane asylums became distinct institutions. Some of the traditional forms of immorality, however, had been drawn into the medical domain during this process. Redefined as illnesses, they were less harmful to the reputation of those exhibiting them, and more important, of their families. Early modern private confinement prefigured this development.

A final observation is on the ironies of history. One period's ideals were the anxieties of another. Nineteenth-century advocates of imprisonment in lonely cells were queasy about physical suffering and wished punishment to be directed at the mind of an offender. Early modern judges had fewer scruples about meting out physical punishments, but they found solitary confinement an unbearable torment. For private prisoners, on the other hand, to be alone and think about one's sins was thought to be a suitable pastime. Nowadays, both corporal punishment and solitary confinement, or 'sensory deprivation,' are widely considered forms of torture and unacceptable. Even routine imprisonment has come under attack. Experiments are being undertaken in several countries at present to 'divert' the treatment of offenders from the penal system to an external agency. Alternatively, offenders who are still tried by a court are sentenced to work for nonprofit organizations. To a certain extent, these practices repeat the experience of four centuries ago. Had the concept been current, contemporaries might well have viewed the committal to a prison work-house as a form of 'diversion.' In the beginning, the courts largely considered these institutions as external agencies. Rather than belonging to the sphere of justice, the houses were associated with charity and served the general public good. Their purpose was to divert juvenile and other non-serious offenders away from the penal system. Inmates were to do useful work and be spared the taint of infamy. The purposes of imprisonment four hundred years ago parallel modern arguments in favor of diversion. That prison workhouses eventually became firmly associated with the penal system may serve as a warning.

NOTES

There are two bibliographies: of printed sources (A) and of secondary literature (B). In the notes, (A) or (B) preceding an author's name indicate in which bibliography to look for the work.

Chapter One. Introduction

1. See, for example, (B) Ignatieff 1983: 183.
2. In the Netherlands the works of Hallema constitute the main example. See also (B) Eggink 1958.
3. See (B) Spierenburg 1984a: 183–185; 1987: 439.
4. (B) Perrot 1975: 81; Perrot (ed.) 1980.
5. (B) Ignatieff 1978. It should be stressed that he modified his views in later publications. Ignatieff 1983 is an excellent review article in which he is critical of the revisionist approach, including his own, but adheres to the nineteenth-century perspective. In his contribution to Petit 1984 he is much more aware of the longer-term process involved.
6. Other recent studies on imprisonment and prisons in the nineteenth century that should be mentioned include (B) Petersen (1978), Ruller (1981), and the contributions by Franke, Faber, Diederiks, and Leonards to Faber et al. (1989) for the Netherlands; the articles by Digneffe and Dupont-Bouchat (1982) for Belgium; O'Brien (1982) for France; Mecklenburg (1983) for Germany; Henriques (1972) and the contributions by Tomlinson and DeLacy to Bailey (1981) for England; Kaczynska (1988) for Poland; and Rothman's follow-up study (1980) for America.
7. See (B) Spierenburg 1987.
8. (B) Rusche 1933 is an outline of this theory. He then expanded it into a more elaborate work, which was edited by Kirchheimer and first published in an English translation (Rusche and Kirchheimer 1939). Because Rusche was the actual author, whenever I refer to it in the text, I will use only his name.
9. (B) Lis and Soly 1979: 116–129; 1984: 166–185.
10. (B) Treiber and Steinert (1980: 83) note the inconsistency, too. The problem may be partly solved if we assume that Foucault thought that the *hôpitaux généraux* and workhouses he dealt with in *Histoire de la Folie* did not serve penal purposes at all, so that he could neglect them in *Surveiller et Punir*.
11. See also (B) Weiss 1987, a review article whose author shows an awareness of the longer-term process.
12. (B) Spierenburg 1984a.
13. See especially (B) Innes 1987 and Beier 1985: 164–169. Both historians are still engaged in research on the subject.
14. See (B) Faber 1983; Spierenburg 1984a; Pol 1987; and a forthcoming books by Jüngen and Boomgaard.
15. I have concentrated less on Lübeck than I had originally intended, because most of its archival records have been kept in the DDR and became available only as I was completing my manuscript. All but a few documents referring to the Danzig prison were destroyed during World War II.
16. They all may have done so, but the records are no longer extant in many cases.
17. I did consult an early Utrecht logbook. On Groningen, (B) Kampman (1984 and 1986) provides additional data. Ample information on the early history of Copenhagen's prison is given in Olsen 1978.
18. During my research I found that Hallema is frequently wrong on points of detail. Investigators can use his work to direct them to specific records, although he often fails to

specify his sources. In all cases where Hallema and I studied the same events, I have based my study on the original records. In a few cases I refer to documents published by Hallema when I could determine their authenticity.

19. See, among others, (B) Innes 1987: 42; Rosenfeld 1906: 3.

20. Compare (B) Spierenburg 1987: 440–441. The famous etchings of *carceri d'invenzione* by Piranesi of course represented jails rather than prisons. See Piranesi 1967. The part devoted to the early modern period in Harding et al. 1985 also largely deals with jails.

21. On the *maisons de correction* in 19th-century France see (B) Gaillac 1971.

22. On the *Roggenkiste* see SAH, Senatsakten: Cl. VII, Lit. Mb, nr. 2, vol. 2. In the 17th century, convicts performing public works stayed there, too.

23. (B) Sheehan 1977: 234; Innes 1980; DeLacy 1986: 31–32. On the altogether different conditions in the jail of early modern Seville, see Perry 1980: 75–94.

24. GAH, Burg. Resol.: 20 March 1734 (fo. 35) and 23 November 1754 (fo. 92 vs).

25. GAA, 5059: nr. 32, pp. 226, 329; index also refers to p. 459, which is missing.

26. The word 'voluntary' is used in a practical, formal sense. A prison is an institution with an involuntary membership because its inmates are physically prevented from getting out. In a more general sense all members of society are restrained by forces around them. A poor man may have no other choice but to enter a workhouse. Even a king, as Norbert Elias brilliantly demonstrates, can be 'imprisoned' in his own court.

27. (B) Pike (1983) uses the concept of penal servitude for approximately the same group of penalties. This term, however, refers primarily to forced labor other than to restrictions on a person's freedom.

28. See, among others, (B) Foucault 1960; Lis and Soly 1979; Geremek 1987. Schwartz 1988 uses the concept in a slightly different sense, specifically referring to a wave of arrests of beggars in France in 1724–1733.

Chapter Two. Idleness and Labor

1. (B) Treiber and Steinert 1980.

2. (B) Jong 1986: 95.

3. Quoted in (B) Künzel 1986: 41.

4. (B) Hoyt 1966: 125, 371.

5. (B) Jong 1986: 104.

6. (B) Dolsperg 1928: 17–23; Nève and Coppens 1987.

7. (A) Mabillon 1987. Compare (B) Sellin 1926, and Mendez and Pavarini 1987. Ariès (1981: 66) mentions a form of confinement that, because of its religious context, can be considered related. Certain offenders were locked up in rooms in the churchyard, sometimes in close proximity to immured female hermits.

8. (B) Jetter 1966: 8, 39.

9. (B) Gutton 1970: 223–224.

10. A prohibition on leaving is more germane, in speaking of imprisonment, than an obligation to enter. In his discussion of Italian hospitals in the 15th and early 16th centuries, Geremek only refers to the second. The word *renfermement*, therefore, would seem too strong. He makes it clear that only the sick and invalid were admitted to hospitals, while the poor whom magistrates wanted to punish were sent to the galleys. Cf. (B) Geremek 1973: 209–211.

11. GAA, 5020: nr. A, fos. 113v and 128.

12. (A) Wagenaar VIII: 203.

13. On the problem of the origins of madhouses see (B) Spierenburg 1988a: 212–213.

14. (B) Garnsey 1970: 148–150.

15. Compare (B) Streng 1890: 14.

16. (B) Pugh 1970; Bellamy 1973: 162–176.

17. (B) Franzoi 1975; Scarabello 1979: 9–10.

18. (B) Seggelke 1928: 40–153.

19. Information from Jan Boomgaard, from his forthcoming book.

20. (A) Wagenaar 1760–1768, VIII:271.

21. GAR, Stadsarchief I: nr. 1214.

22. See Hallema's introduction to (A) Hout 1927: 72.

23. Compare (B) Schilling 1987.
24. (B) Elias 1969, 1: 89–109.
25. (B) Burke 1978: 207–243.
26. (B) Flandrin 1979: 174–242.
27. (B) Muchembled 1988: 154–174.
28. For a summary, see (B) Spierenburg 1988a: 300–301, 311–314.
29. (B) Beattie 1986: 495–496; Innes 1987: 84.
30. See among others (B) Scherpner 1962; Gutton 1974; Mollat 1978; Lis and Soly 1979; Geremek 1987.
31. (B) Ricci 1983: 167–168.
32. (B) Ricci 1983: 158; Pullan 1971: 373; Engrand 1984: 515.
33. (B) Gutton 1970: 125–218.
34. (B) Biraben 1974: 511.
35. (B) Mollat 1978: 256–302. See also Geremek 1976: 189–237. For the Netherlands, see Blockmans and Prevenier 1977: 55–56.
36. (B) Scherpner 1962: 54–63; Sachsse and Tennstedt 1980: 49–50, 56–58.
37. (A) Liber 1862; (B) Scherpner 1962: 49–50; Sachsse and Tennstedt 1980: 51–56; Chrisman 1988. A recent study devoted entirely to the book is Jütte 1988. He presents data from German archives showing that several of the tricks mentioned in it were actually practiced by beggars (70–105).
38. Translated from the Dutch edition originally published in Antwerp in 1563. See (A) Fielen 1914: 20, 21, 41.
39. (B) Hartung 1986: 94; Jütte 1988: 59–60.
40. (B) Beier 1985: 4–8, 114.
41. (B) Manen 1913: 8–11.
42. (B) Fischer 1979: 155–160, 181–182, 225.
43. (B) Lis and Soly 1979: 87; Geremek 1987: 159–230.
44. (A) Erasmus 1965: 254.
45. (B) Gutton 1970: 266–286; Davis 1975: 56.
46. (B) Gutton 1970: 296.
47. (A) Mémoires 1837: 247–256, 273–284.
48. (B) Gutton 1970: 295–302.
49. (B) Delumeau 1957: 403–416. Geremek (1987: 271) seems to consider this an episode of asylum rather than imprisonment (see, however, p. 273, and Geremek 1973: 212–213). On Italian hospitals generally, see Pullan 1971: 362–371. See also Ferrante 1983.
50. (B) Callahan 1971: 4.
51. (B) Pike 1983: 5. Pike says it was opened in 1622, although its founder, Madre Magdalena de San Jeronimo, had laid out the program in 1608 (see Manuel Serrano Y Sanz, *Apuntes para una biblioteca de escritoras Espanoles,* 1401–1833, vol. 270 of *Biblioteca de autores Espanoles,* Madrid 1903: 304–306). At the instigation of Madre Magdalena, several houses for converted prostitutes were established in Spain from the late 16th century onward. These institutions were also prison-like. I owe this information to Mary Elizabeth Perry, whose article on this subject is due to appear in *Women and Criminal Justice,* 2, 1 (Fall 1990).
52. (B) Olsen 1978: 23–24.
53. (B) Hippel 1898: 431–432; Sothmann 1970: 23–24, 66–67, 119.
54. (B) Beier 1985: 149–150.
55. (B) Beier 1985: 164–166; Innes 1987: 52–61; Leonard 1965: 30–40, 98–101; Slice 1936: 50–51; Dolsperg 1928: 97.
56. (B) Slice 1936: 61; Sellin 1944: 21.
57. (B) Beier 1985: 165–166.
58. (B) Leonard 1965: 112–115; Slice 1936: 52–53; Innes 1987: 62–77.
59. (B) Zysberg 1984: 81–83, and 1987: 63–64; Pike 1983: 4, and 1976: 701; Cozzi 1980: 379–381.
60. (B) Cozzi 1980: 382, 395; Scarabello 1979: 48–50.
61. (B) Pullan 1971: 298–306.
62. (B) Garnsey 1970: 104–134.
63. (B) Pike 1983: 27–45. The mines at Almadén were not quite public; they belonged to the house of Fugger.
64. All dates are based on archival sources I consulted or on local studies close to the

sources. See the notes in this chapter and the next. For Brussels: (B) Bruneel 1966a: 40–52 and Stroobant 1900: 253. The latter author gives a chronological overview of foundations of European prisons, but he is not always correct. In secondary publications various dates are often mentioned for the same institution, partly because it is sometimes unclear which was the opening year; administrators could be appointed before a prison was opened or an ordinance promulgated when it was already in operation. The Swiss *schellenwerke* of the early 17th century were no prisons but places of detention for offenders performing public works. Some of them later evolved into prison workhouses, which is the reason why (A) Wagnitz (2: 277–286) thought that Bern had a *zuchthaus* since 1615. The first Swiss *zuchthaus*, combined with an orphanage, was opened at Zürich in 1637: (B) Mayer 1987: 64–65.

65. (B) Hippel 1898. Hippel 1932 is a reprint of this article; Hippel 1897–1898 is a separate publication of the part about Lübeck. See also Seggelke 1928; Dolsperg 1928; Schmidt 1947.

66. (B) Traphagen 1935: 112–113.

67. (B) Weber 1941 and 1961: 45–46.

68. (B) Radbruch 1950: 116–129.

69. Especially see (B) Leonard 1965: 30–40.

70. (B) Slack (1988: 120–121) confirms that Catholic leaders supported the project in principle, although he feels they were suspicious of some of the details.

71. (B) Scherpner (1962: 216) is the only non-Dutch author who acknowledges this.

72. GA Antwerpen, Vierschaar: nr. 1823 (22 June 1609).

73. GA Antwerpen, Vierschaar: nrs. 1645 and 1822 (first dossier). In the first half of the 17th century, the Antwerp prison was alternately referred to as *dwinghuis* or *tuchthuis*, or even through a contamination, *duchthuis*. The records do not disclose the date of its opening, but the ordinance and the contract with the first *huismeester*, Jacob Jansen Boy, are dated 9 February 1613. Since Boy is shown to have been functioning until 1619, I assume he kept prisoners from the first year of his contract. (B) Hallema 1931 is based on a few documents from Vierschaar 1645, and as always, he has errors of detail.

74. Compare the case of Geneva, where the *hôpital général* was a voluntary institution in the sixteenth century, but later became prison-like. See (B) Lescaze 1985.

75. (B) Chill 1962: 405–412; Hufton 1974: 139–143.

76. (B) Olsen 1978: 12.

77. (B) Dahlberg 1898: 36–53; Wieselgren 1895: 22–41. The exact date of opening of the prison workhouse at Stockholm is not mentioned by these authors. Its ordinance dates from 1622, the contract with the first master of discipline was dated 24 April 1624, and the first recorded committals took place in 1625–1626.

78. (B) Sellin (1944: 18–22) did not find it and neither did I in my sources or more recent literature.

79. A standard Dutch/ Low German language, understood from Bruges to Novgorod, had been developed in the later Middle Ages as a result of commercial and administrative contacts within the Hanse-network. See (B) Schildhauer 1984: 217–219.

80. "*. . . dat wij tho erholding guder Policeij undt afstellung des muthwilligen gesindes nah dem Exempel der Erbarn von Amstellredam ein tuchthuss anthorichten gemeinet*": SAB, 2-D. 18. d, dossier 1a.

81. (B) Jetter 1966: 21–38; Davis 1975: 37; Mollat 1978: 328.

82. (B) Loose 1982: 197–200; Whaley 1985: 14.

83. (B) Schwarzwälder 1975: 209.

84. (B) Lescaze 1985: 49–52.

85. (B) Davis 1975: 61–62. See also Davis 1981.

86. There is disagreement on his exact role. (B) Ehrle (1881: 27–34) demonstrates that Vives influenced the reform at Bruges. This author merely assumes that he discussed his ideas with the Ypres magistrates, too. The reform at Ypres took place in 1525 and *De subventione pauperum* was published in 1526. Thus, Rusche and Kirchheimer (1939: 39), attributing the Ypres reform to Vives, state something which is unproven. Gutton (1974: 103–104), on the other hand, goes too far when he denies Vives's influence on any of the Flemish cities.

87. (B) Manen 1913: 24–26. Amsterdam, though, did not follow the example of centralization of poor relief at that time.

88. (B) Jetter 1966: 117–119.

89. (A) Mémoires 1837: 245.

90. (B) Thomas 1964: 59.
91. Compare (B) Raeff 1983: 91.
92. See (B) Herwaarden 1978: 27; Fischer 1979: 162–163, and the literature referred to by these authors.
93. (B) Fischer 1979: 163–165. Beier (1985: 14–15) relates "fear about vagrancy" in England to a growth in the number of vagrants between 1560 and 1640. But that growth, too, came after the change of mentalities.
94. "Means of orientation" is understood here in the sense used by Norbert Elias in his discussion of sources of power. See (B) Elias 1971.
95. (B) Spierenburg 1984a: 1–12.
96. For a more elaborate discussion of this argument, see (B) Spierenburg 1983.
97. See (B) Loose 1982 and Schwarzwälder 1975. In 1761 English troops entered Bremen, which resulted in a temporary closure of the *zuchthaus,* because they used it as a hospital for wounded soldiers: SAB, 2-D. 18. d, dossiers 10 and 12 (1761–1762); also see (B) Heineken 1983: 94–98.
98. (B) Geremek 1974: 350.
99. I found the earliest use of the word confinement in a resolution by the Amsterdam council in 1600: GAA, 5025: nr. 8, p. 643. An Amsterdam sentence of 1657 still used the word banishment; after that time, the term was no longer used in Amsterdam. Rural courts continued to use the term a little longer, but by the 18th century it had become obsolete. The Delft magistrates, writing to Zierikzee in 1736, spoke of "men and women confined (or banished) into the *tuchthuis,*" using both terms just to be sure (GAD, St. Joris: nr. 69). The antiquarian (A) Le Long (1732: 770) was clearly old-fashioned (and no lawyer) when he referred to persons banished into the rasphouse.
100. (A) Hout 1927: 85. My emphasis.
101. (B) Dekker 1988: 6–7.
102. (B) Kent 1986: 200–205.

Chapter Three.   The Period of Experimentation

1. GAA, 5061: nr. 276, fos. 125–v and 129.
2. GAA, 5061: nr. 276, fo. 140v.
3. GAA, 5025: nr. 6, p. 226.
4. See (B) Roodenburg (1987: 83) for the case of the sick child. So far, no record has been found of complaints to the magistrates.
5. GAA, 5025: nr. 6, pp. 270–1: resolution of 12 Nov. (A) Wagenaar (8: 234) mentions the resolution, too, but mistakenly dates it 26 Oct.
6. GAA, 5061: nr. 569, fo. 78.
7. (A) Coornhert 1630 (original edition 1587). For a more elaborate analysis of Coornhert's work, see my contribution to (B) Fijnaut and Spierenburg 1990.
8. The college numbered nine *schepenen.* The names of those in office in 1589 are given by (A) Wagenaar (12: 245); information on them is provided by (B) Elias, Johan 1963. Five *schepenen* clearly belonged to the faction which came into power in 1578; one of them, Pieter Willemsz Vriend, became a rasphouse regent in 1601. Two of them frequently held a burgomastership during the 1610s, when a Calvinist faction was in power.
9. (A) Hooft 1925: 81–82.
10. GAL, Stad: nr. 6522.
11. (B) Elias, Johan, 1963, vol. 1: nr. 31. On Jan Spiegel's authorship, see my contribution to Fijnaut and Spierenburg 1990.
12. (B) Elias, Johan, 1963 vol. 1, nr. 78. For the sake of uniformity, I will call him Egberts, although this is not a surname but a patronym.
13. Compare (B) Elias (Norbert) 1971: 79–113.
14. The *vroedschapsresoluties* between Nov. 1595 and Feb. 1596 contain no items connected with the *tuchthuis.* Burgomasters' resolutions for that period are not extant. In 1597 Jan van Hout was told that the magistrates had been unable to agree on the matter. See (A) Hout 1927: 78. In March 1598 burgomasters authorized the regents to draw up an ordinance for the house and to determine the penalties for infractions. See Handvesten 1748, 1: 293–294. There are no records to tell whether they did so immediately. A text discovered in

the Danzig archive and published by Von Hippel has been incorrectly held to be the oldest set of rules. See (B) Hippel 1932: 39–47. In fact, it must be dated after 1607 and possibly after 1656. Von Hippel dated it *before* 1656 because he thought that the house's rasping mill mentioned in the text was dismantled in that year. However, it was *erected* in 1656. There might have been a small, hand-operated mill inside the house, to which a court record of 1617 seems to refer (GAA, 5061: nr. 571, fo. 138). In any case, the text dates from after 1607 because it refers to female regents, who were first appointed in that year. See (A) Wagenaar, 8: 248. The original is no longer extant in the Danzig archive. We only have Von Hippel's High German translation. He informs us that it was added to the Danzig prison ordinance of 1639. See (B) Hippel 1898: 644. It is not quite clear whether Von Hippel translated the text himself or whether this had been done in 17th-century Danzig. Upon my inquiries of professors Reinhard and Wolfgang von Hippel and the University Library at Göttingen, I was informed that Robert von Hippel's papers do not contain research notes.

15. (A) Wagenaar 1760–1768, 8: 234.
16. See his contribution to (B) Fijnaut and Spierenburg 1990.
17. (A) Handvesten 1748, 1: 293.
18. (A) Hout 1927: 79–81.
19. GAA, 5025: nr. 8, p. 313.
20. (A) Wagenaar 1760–1768, 8: 256.
21. GAA, 5023: nr. 2, fo. 189–vs.
22. (A) Pontanus 1614: 137. Pontanus received this information from the regents, who explained that the citizens in question wished to remain anonymous.
23. (A) Wagenaar 1760–1768, 8: 257.
24. (A) Pontanus 1614: 137. The original Latin edition was published in 1611.
25. GAA, 5025: nr. 8, p. 643; (A) Bontemantel 1897, 1: 281; ms. by Schaap in GAA, 5059: nr. 41 (1595 and 1603). The idea may have come from Jan van Hout, who had drawn a "secret corridor" in his plan for the Leiden prison: (A) Hout 1927: 96.
26. (A) Brandt 1704: 245.
27. GAA, 345: nr. 3 (dossier with various papers). That it was a standard protocol follows from the fact that the word 'mother' has been filled out with a different hand, while room for the insertion of the prisoner's name and that of other relatives has been left open. Room was also left open for the specific year of release.
28. (A) Ordnung 1598.
29. (A) Pontanus 1614: 132.
30. (A) Baudartius 1624: vol. I, book 5: p. 40.
31. See (B) Spierenburg 1984a: 189.
32. (A) Brandt 1704: 237–243.
33. (A) Brandt 1704: 585; (B) Allard 1899: 104–105.
34. (A) Brandt 1704: 579–581; (B) Allard 1899: 112–114.
35. (A) Brandt 1704: 584–585; (B) Allard 1899: 130–131. Vezekius also escaped from the Haarlem prison. When he was recaptured in 1623, he declared that this had been possible because he had found "an old key of the indoor father." See his own account in: GA Nijmegen, Familie-archief Biesman: nr. 16. I owe this reference to Rudolf Dekker; see also his contribution to Fijnaut and Spierenburg 1990, showing that a few other remonstrant ministers were arrested during the 1620s and imprisoned in the fort of Loevestein.
36. (A) Grevius 1624.
37. GAL, Stad: nr. 6522 includes a dossier with documents relating to the planning and building of the *tuchthuis*. The exact date of its opening is not mentioned, but the last note on its construction is dated 20 January 1600. The documents edited by Hallema (A: Hout 1927) also form part of this dossier.
38. Leeuwarden: (B) Eekhoff 1846: 22–27; Groningen: Kampman 1986: 20–21; Middelburg: Teijlingen 1883: 96. The date of the opening of the Utrecht *tuchthuis* is unclear. According to GAU, Resolutiën Vroedschap, the decision to erect it was made 3 Nov. 1614. According to Van Buchell (Stad: nr. 1043, fo. 1) the first stone was laid in 1616.
39. (Copies in) GAL, Stad: nr. 6524.
40. GAH, Vroeds. resol.: 25 April 1609 (fo. 301–v) and Kast 7-2-3-2.
41. GAD, Stad: nr. 872. The sources do not reveal when exactly the spinhouse was opened. A register listing its finances (GAD, Stad: nr. 475) begins in 1622. The earliest criminal sentence that included imprisonment dates from 1624.
42. ARA, HvH: nr. 59, fo. 205v–209; GAD, Stad: nr. 1217.

43. GAD, Card system of criminal sentences.

44. See (A) Ordnung 1598. The German legal author Jakob Bornitz, writing in 1602, spoke of the "carcer, vulgo *Zuchthaus*" that existed "apud Belgos" (quoted in (B) Hippel 1898: 441–442).

45. The first *vorsteher* were appointed on 16 February 1608, when it was noted that the *zuchthaus* had not been built yet (SAB, 2-D. 18. d: copies in dossiers 1a, 2 and 7). It must have been opened before 26 October 1608, because in a letter dated 26 Oct. 1611, an inmate says that he is now in his fourth year of imprisonment (ibid.: dossier 6b1). Thus, the prison was already opened when the ordinance of 1609 was promulgated. The ordinance has traditionally, but incorrectly, as it turns out, been considered the starting point of the prison.

46. (B) Ebeling 1935: 17–38, 72–77; Streng 1890: 15–19. These authors are in disagreement on the exact date of opening. However, an archival document (SAH, 242-1-I: nr. A25) clearly states that the building was completed in 1618.

47. (B) Bruns 1915: 188–204.

48. AHL, Bürgerschaft: nr. 120-1, p. 125 and Senate: nr. 1, dossier 1.

49. AHL, Bürgerschaft: nr. 120-1, p. 130. This ms. mentions the word *zuchthaus* for the first time in 1631, when the provisors refused admittance to a woman who had been in jail. Thus, (B) Brehmer (1883: 22) is incorrect in considering 1632 as its date of opening. It is also clear that there was only an almshouse and no *zuchthaus* in 1601. Assuming that Wetken's house was used as a prison ward immediately after its confiscation, I take 1613, also mentioned by Hippel (1898: 623), as the year of opening of the Lübeck *zuchthaus*.

50. (A) Hainhofer 1834: 11.

51. (B) Irsigler and Lasotta 1984: 30; Reekers 1981: 35 (note 7).

52. SAB, 2-D. 18. d: dossier 1a (21 April 1621).

53. GAD, Stad: nr. 15-1, fo. 352v and nr. 1219.

54. (B) Innes 1987: 56.

55. GA Antwerpen, Vierschaar: nrs. 1645 and 1822. On 29 March 1624, Ambrosius Pots was contracted as the new work boss.

56. (B) Schilling and Diederiks 1985: 47.

57. I consulted four editions of Reinking(k)'s work (see Bibliography A). The passage on prison workhouses was only revised slightly in the 1632 edition. The passages are identical in the editions of 1632 and 1659. Therefore, the passage should also be the same in the 1651 edition, which I was unable to locate. In 1659 the foreword is that of the 1651 edition. On Hippolythus à Lapide, see (B) Walker (Mack) 1971: 17.

58. GAH, Oud-Rechterlijk Archief: nr. 66-2. The last sentence in the register is dated 26 November 1615.

59. Ibid.: fos. 175v, 183, 190, 193v, 225v.

60. SAB, 2-D. 18. d: dossier 1a.

61. (B) Grambow (1910: 27) expresses the same opinion.

62. On matters of jurisdiction in early Bremen, see (B) Hiemsch 1964: 11–51. The *obergericht*, which exercised high jurisdiction, actually consisted of a committee from the senate, but the prison ordinance only mentioned "the council."

63. SAB, 2-D. 18. d: dossier 6c (1610, 1612, 1615, 1617, 1619).

64. We can only guess whether the bishop drew on any existing tradition. (A) Dellaporta 1593 has no criminal faces among his c. 40 descriptions of facial types. Most of them are pairs of opposite character traits. The sections *de iracundi, mendacis, malevoli verifigura* come closest (pp. 489–492, 512–513, 516–517).

65. A very preliminary study is (B) Kottmann 1986. He considered the years 1607 and 1781 and concluded that almost all cases concerned conflicts between citizens.

66. SAB, 2-D. 18. d: dossier 6b1 (26 Oct. 1611).

67. SAB, 2-d. 18. d: dossier 6b1 (3 May 1616).

68. GAA, 5061: nr. 291, fo. 19–v and nr. 571, fo. 14–v. The Bremen letter speaks of Herman, the son of Jürgen Hilcken of Hildesheim. The Amsterdam records speak of Harmen Hilcken from Hillims or Hillesom near Bremen. No doubt, the same person is meant.

69. GAA, 5061: nr. 571, fo. 14–v, 100–v, 108.

70. GAA, 5061: nr. 291, fo. 171.

71. GAA, 5061: nr. 571, fo. 150v.

72. For a comparable case, see GAH, Oud-Rechterlijk Archief: nr. 66-2, fos. 201v and 218v; GAA, 5061: nr. 533, fo. 1. Another is in GAH, ibid.: fo. 199–vs.

73. The prison archive (SAH, 242-1-I) contains two copies: nrs. A12 and A13. The text

published in (B) Streng (1890: 173–193) has a few minor variations and was presumably taken from another archival source. A consequential variation, however, is that Streng leaves out the second "I am" in the translation of the Latin motto. This has caused later historians to assume that the motto's two parts refer to one and the same group.

74. SAH, 242-1-I: nrs. A12 and A13 *("der andere Theil")*.
75. SAH, 242-1-I: nr. A14-1, fo. 55.
76. Ibid.: fos. 5v and 25.
77. Ibid.: fo. 67.
78. Ibid.: fos. 13 and 17–v.
79. See, for example, Marten Kollat (ibid., fos. 14–v and 19v) and Hennig Thomsen (ibid., fos. 64v–66v, 76–77v, 81).
80. To be sure, the ordinance stipulated that the porter should only allow them to leave the house if they had a token from the *oeconomus* or the schoolmaster.
81. SAH, 242-1-I: nr. A14-1, fo. 115–v.
82. (B) Beier 1985: 141.
83. SAH, 242-1-I: nr. A14-1, fo. 43v. See also fo. 64.
84. Ibid.: fo. 43v. See also fo. 29.
85. Ibid.: before fo. 1.
86. Ibid.: fo. 67v. For other gifts by ordinary citizens, see fos. 1v, 41, 58v, 117, 121v–123v, 139v.
87. Ibid.: fo. 143.
88. SAB, 2-D. 18. d: dossier 1a.
89. SAB, P. 1 s. 22. c. 1. c: p. 82.
90. They are: Peter Koster (SAB, P. 1. s. 22. c. 1. c); an anonymous author of the *"Stadt-bremische Geschichte"* (excerpts in SAB, 2-D. 18. d: dossier 7); Johann Renner's successor (SAB, DDR: 2308/ 6926). Renner died in 1583 (see (B) Schwarzwälder 1975: 266); subsequent events were added to his chronicle in another hand. The provisors of the Hamburg *zuchthaus* inserted remarks about heavy thunderstorms without damage to the house into their log-book three times in the period studied (SAH, 242-1-I: nr. A14-1).
91. SAB, 2-D. 18. d: dossier 7.
92. *"wegen der Einwohner unbändigen Uppigkeiten und Sünden"*: SAB, DDR: nr. 2308/ 6926.
93. *"durch Gottes unerforschliche Verhängnus"*: SAB, 2-D. 18. d: dossier 7.
94. A third conclusion, that God had aimed his rage more specifically at the institution's wicked inmates (which would mean that he preferred them to be capitally punished instead of imprisoned and hence would also imply a criticism of imprisonment), was unlikely, since the master of discipline and his wife perished, too.
95. Koster mentions Reinking as having written about he Bremen *zuchthaus* generally. He mentions one other author who did so, too: Maximilian Faust in his *Consilia pro Aerario*. I was unable to find a copy of this book, but based on my bibliographical research, it had only one edition, published in Frankfurt in 1641. (A) Wagnitz (2: 58) mentions the lightning strike of 5 August 1647 without further comment.

Chapter Four.   In the Margins of Settled Life

1. See, especially, (B) Hufton 1974; Küther 1983; Schubert 1983; Beier 1985.
2. GAH, Vroeds. Resol.: 13 July 1590 (fo. 77), 17 Nov. 1597 (fo. 72), 11 April 1598 (fo. 90v); Burg. Resol.: 4 Dec. 1598 (fo. 193v), 24 April 1604 (fo. 9).
3. For Haarlem: GAH, Vroeds. Resol.: 5 Sept. 1609 (fo. 4v) and Burg. Resol.: 18 Sept. 1609 (fo. 139).
4. See, for example, (B) Reekers 1981: 38–40.
5. GAA, 5020: nr. H, fo. 61v; (A) Placaetboek 1658, 1: 481–486.
6. (A) Handvesten 1748: 461–462.
7. GAA, 5020: nr. H, fo. 116–120v.
8. (A) Handvesten 1748: 460–461.
9. GAA, 5020: nr. I, fo. 22–27.
10. (A) Handvesten 1748: 457.
11. GA Antwerpen, Vierschaar: nr. 1645 (contract, 9 Feb. 1613).

12. GAD, Stad: nr. 2001-II, fos. 43v (1692), 55v (1694) (renewed on 3 June 1715: fo. 141v); nr. 2027 (undated ordinance).

13. SAB, DDR: nr. 1203/ 3490, dossier 12. An archivist later fixed the date at 1598, which is impossible because Bremen had no prison then.

14. SAB, DDR: nr. 1203/ 3490, dossier 8.

15. SAB, DDR: nr. 1203/ 3490, dossier 10.

16. AHL, Bürgerschaft: nr. 120–1, pp. 115, 124, 140–141.

17. SAH, 242-1-I: nr. A14-1, fo. 2–v. Alternatively, a *vogt* was denoted as *(pragger) faget*.

18. SAH, 242-1-I: nr. A14-1, fo. 7v.

19. (B) Ebeling 1935: 49.

20. GAH, Kast 7-2-3-28; see also Burg. Resol.: 13 Feb. 1695 (fo. 66v).

21. GAH, Burg. Resol.: 29 Sept. 1615 (fo. 45v).

22. SAH, 242-1-I: nr. A14-1, fo. 1.

23. (A) Mémoires 1837: 251.

24. SAH, 242-1-I: nr. A14-1, fos. 33v–35 and 87v–88. Knopf's name is alternatively spelled Knoop or Knop.

25. Ibid.: fo. 32–33.

26. Ibid.: fo. 84v.

27. Ibid.: fo. 83–84. Presumably, Knopf had coins worth 16 Reichsthaler with him upon his arrest.

28. Ibid.: fo. 86–89.

29. Ibid.: fo. 91–92. The case of Claus Knopf also demonstrates that nonresident beggars were in fact imprisoned in the *zuchthaus*. The decrees of 1699 and 1712 restricting admission to resident beggars (see (B) Streng 1890: 31–32) may have been temporary measures. Ebeling (1935: 47–48) refers to the imprisonment of nonresident beggars around the same time.

30. On beggars' companies and the problem of their reality, see (B) Hufton 1974; Burke 1987: 63–75; Jütte 1988: 62. On the literature of rogues, see Kraemer 1944. Dutch painters always portrayed beggars in stereotypical scenes of merriment, never in a situation of repression. See Reinold 1981: 33, 129–172.

31. (B) Voss 1958: 5. The head-provost was also denoted as "a special kind of *schout*": (A) Dapper 1663: 420; Gebouwen 1736: 350.

32. (A) Handvesten 1748: 457.

33. (A) Handvesten 1748: 460–461.

34. SAH, 242-1-I: nr. A14-1, fo. 106.

35. (B) Voss 1958: 6, 12.

36. GAA, 5020: nr. I, fo. 45–46v.

37. GAA, 5020, nr. K, p. 111. The reward was 100 Flemish pounds.

38. GAA, 5020: nrs. M, fos. 199 and 228v; O, fo. 231; P, fo. 257; S, fo. 55; T, fo. 7. I did not study Amsterdam urban legislation after 1750.

39. (B) Spierenburg 1984a: 129.

40. GAA, 5061: nr. 366, fo. 32.

41. (A) Mémoires 1837: 249.

42. Compare (A) Montchrétien (1889: 349), who wrote about the same time that the true poor are the members of Christ and to give to them is to give to Him and is not a waste.

43. (B) Gutton 1970: 356–361, 442–449.

44. (B) Hufton 1974: 220–221; Farge and Zysberg 1979: 997.

45. (B) Beier 1985: 139.

46. (B) Ebeling 1935: 50.

47. (B) Streng 1890: 34.

48. (B) Wolf 1963: 11–12.

49. *"geringer oder vornehmerer Pöbel"*: (B) Sothmann 1970: 116–118.

50. (B) Haesenne-Peremans 983: 25–26.

51. (B) Gutton 1970: 359–360.

52. GAA, 347: nr. 562. There are no indications as to whether the listing includes all beggars supervised in the city or only those who appeared before one of the two commissioners.

53. The sources are a little confusing sometimes in their terminology. The institution opened in 1654 was called the *nieuwe werkhuis* at first, but, predictably, the word *nieuw* was soon dropped. In 1782, when the old workhouse and the spinhouse were combined in a

new building, this was called the *nieuwe werkhuis*. The term *willige rasphuis*, which Bonteman-tel (c. 1660) clearly used to refer to the secret ward of the rasphouse, was considered synon-ymous with the workhouse in (A) Gebouwen 1736.

54. (B) Oldewelt 1942: 31–33. The counts performed under Oldewelt's supervision are not always accurate (see Spierenburg 1984a: 209), but in this case the margin of error must have been small.

55. For years of dearth, see (B) Faber (J. A.) 1976.

56. (A) Handvesten 1748: 456.

57. On the punishment of beggars and gypsies in Amsterdam, see (B) Faber 1983: 74–77; Spierenburg 1978: 90, 214 and 1984a: 129–130, 174. On the repression of gypsies and other vagrants in Brabant, see Eerenbeemt 970 and 1968: 119–148. For France, see Asséo 1974: 63. In Lyon, however, gypsies were condemned to the galleys or to banishment, see Gutton 1970: 180–183. On the criminalization of gypsies generally, see Florike Egmond, paper prepared for the Third IAHCCJ-Conference, Paris, Oct. 1988.

58. The Delft entry books are analyzed in chapter 7. Delfland had a *landdrost* with eight men to chase after marginals since the late seventeenth century: (copy in) GAH, Kast 7-2-3-23: dossier Delft.

59. SAB, 2-D. 18. d: dossier 6a. The series was apparently bound in the 19th century, when it was entitled *"Bürgschaften für entlassene Prüflinge."*

60. SAB, 2-D. 18. d: dossier 10 (1 May 1743).

61. Compare (B) Sharpe 1984: 118.

62. (A) Koning 1616 (unpaginated). See also (B) Zalm 1979: 102–113. This author deals with two other lottery-plays: Samuel Coster's *Spel van de Rijke Man* also adheres to the distinction between the deserving and undeserving poor. Jan van Hout's *Loterij-spel* presents only the first group.

63. GAH, werkhuis: nr. 12. For a comparable instruction to the Amsterdam *buurtmees-ters:* (A) Handvesten 1748: 462–463.

64. GAH, Kast 7-2-3-2 (ordinance of 1612.) The only other reference to such a custom was found in Leiden in 1662: GAL, nr. 6526.

65. GAH, Burg. Resol.: 18 January 1634 (fo. 153v).

66. Ibid.: resolutions of 6 March 1640, 16 Nov. 1649, 13 Dec. 1679, and 26 April 1684. The supervisors' right of imprisonment was also mentioned by Langendijk in the middle of the 18th century: Handschriften: nr. 153, dossier R: fo. 26.

67. GAH, Handschriften: nr. 153, dossier R: ms. Langendijk, fo. 18–24. The gate and the statue are now in the Frans Hals Museum at Haarlem. I relied both on Langendijk's description and my own observation.

Chapter Five.   Prisons and the Imagination

1. (A) Baudartius (1624, vol, I, book 5, p. 40) is the only one to provide the sculpture's symbolic meaning, which appears to have become forgotten. Wagenaar (8: 239) was not even sure of the identity of the animals; he speaks of "lions, tigers and other wild animals." Both authors translate the motto; for other translations: Hooft, (PC), 1976: nr. 362 (p. 810); Gebouwen 1736: 342. On the motto's history, see (B) Boas 1917. The gate and the inscription were first mentioned by (A) Pontanus (1614: 139).

2. On the back side of a contract by which the regents bought an adjacent house was written: "the gate will be set there" (GAA, 345: nr. 3, 25 April 1634). This may have referred to a relocation of the original gate to a more convenient spot or to the construction of the second gate. In any case, the latter was first mentioned by (A) Dapper (1663: 425). It still was in place in Wagenaar's (8: 239) time. But today only the first gate survives intact. The second gate lions, but not the raspers, are preserved in the dépôt of the Amsterdam Historical Museum.

3. *"Schrik niet; ik wreek geen quaat, maar dwing tot goet; straf is myn hant, maar lieflyk myn gemoet"*: (A) Hooft, (PC.), 1976: nr. 7 (p. 89). The spelling here is that of the actual inscrip-tion. In 1782 it was transferred to the new combined spinhouse and workhouse (Howard 1789: 73), but today gate and inscription are back at the original spot.

4. (A) Dapper 1663: 418.

5. (A) Zesen 1664: 433.
6. (A) Commelin 1693: 515.
7. (A) Guide 1701: 88; Guide 1753: 212.
8. (A) Howard 1792: 52.
9. "*Kan man doch Löwen und Bären zähmen: Sollte man dann die muthwilligen Buben auch nicht zwingen*": (A) Reinkingk 1659: 842.
10. (A) Wagenaar, 8: 240, 260, 264. De Lairesse's painting is now in the Amsterdam Historical Museum.
11. (A) Gool 1750, 2: 303.
12. (B) Muller 1985: 34.
13. I am indebted to Paul Schulten for this interpretation.
14. (B) Spierenburg 1987: 443.
15. (A) Brown 1682: 18.
16. (copy in) GAL, Stad: nr. 6525. (A) Bowrey (1927: 38–39) says that he had to pay two stuivers to get into the Amsterdam spinhouse in 1698.
17. GAL, Stad: nrs. 6527 and 6528. An additional difference between the two towns was that Leiden accorded a part of the income from the boxes to the *schout* and his deputies and the prison's indoor father, while no one received a share in Amsterdam. This may have caused Leiden officials to encourage visitation.
18. GAA, 5059: nr. 34, p. 367.
19. (B) Elias, Johan, 1963: nr. 171. Bontemantel had married in 1646, which suggests that the other children may have been older. He was not a *schepen* in 1663.
20. SAH, 242-1-I: nr. A29–1, p. 88.
21. For special interest in notorious female delinquents, see GAH, Kast 7-2-2-6 and 7-2-2-8; GAD, Stad: nr. 2001-II, fo. 140-v (8 April 1715).
22. The Haarlem rules in: GAH, Werkhuis: nr.12, instruction for the *cipier* (undated, probably late 17th century). See also Burg. Resol.: 26 November 1615 (fo.50). For Bremen: SAB, 2-D.18.d: dossier nr.4 (17 May 1695). For Leiden: GAL, Stad: nr.6528.
23. GAD, St. Joris: nr. 59–1, fo. 62.
24. See, for example, an incident in 1801: GAD, St. Joris: nr. 59-2, fo. 208-v.
25. GAU, Stad: nr. 1043, fo. 13 v-14.
26. GAD, St. Joris: nr. 59–1, fo. 132v-133.
27. (B) Streng 1890: 89–90.
28. (B) Ebeling 1935: 58, 114–116.
29. (B) Spierenburg 1988a: 214–215.
30. (A) Mumen 1616. The Hamburg *zuchthaus* was praised in a brief rhymed description: see (B) Ebeling 1935: 40–42.
31. For the full titles of its various editions, see Bibliography A. Note that the word *wonderlijk*, translated here as "amazing," also means "miraculous."
32. The preface actually says "Raspus," which may be a misprint; further on he is consistently called Raspinus.
33. GAA, 5061: nr. 282, fo. 284-v. Nr. 283 should list his punishment (a whipping on the scaffold, according to the *Historie*), but the index is lacking a Frans.
34. GAA, 5061: nr. 285, fo. 77–78v.
35. (A) Pontanus 1614: 134–136.
36. See (B) Walker, Daniel, 1977.
37. (A) Lipsius 1605.
38. See the original Latin edition (Johannes Isacius Pontanus, *Rerum et Urbis Amstelodamensium Historia*, Amsterdam 1611): 99–100. Three observers in the 1660s still referred to the exhibition of false crutches in the rasphouse: (A) Fokkens (1662: 279–280); Dapper (1663: 428); and the Hamburg traveler Christian Knorr von Rosenroth (quoted in (B) Ebeling 1935: 110). By that time, arrested beggars were imprisoned in the workhouse.
39. They are the editions kept in the library of the GAA and at Marburg. The latter forms part of a convolute; it is undated, but its spelling and the length of pages prove that it is a different edition.
40. Edition kept at Strasbourg. The Ghent copy may be the same edition, but it lacks the epilogue and an explanation of a plate.
41. (A) Koning 1616 (unpaginated).

42. (A) Baudartius, 1624: vol. I, book 5, pp. 40–42.

43. (A) Fokkens 1662: 279–280. The crutches were also referred to by Bowrey (1927: 42), who visited the rasphouse as late as 1698.

44. (A) Vondel (ed. van Lennep and Unger): 351–353 (verse for regent Jacob Hinlopen Vermaas), and 1982: 123 (verses 747–751).

45. (A) Montchrétien 1889: 107 (original ed.: Rouen 1615).

46. (A) Mémoires 1837: 250–251. According to (B) Chill (1962: 417), the "Cour des Miracles" became a kind of fortress, which was demolished in 1667.

47. (B) Kraemer 1944: 261 et seq. See also Dupille 1971. She uses "Cour des Miracles" as a generic term for a retreat of beggars and rogues. However, it is clear from her account that only the one referred to here was actually called by that name. Her earliest reference to the term "Cour des Miracles" dates from 1603 (31–41).

48. (A) Hainhofer 1834: 11.

49. Reproduced in (B) Hirth 1897: nr. 1636. In Amstelodamum Maandblad (1939: 182) A.W. refers to two versions of this sheet with slightly different wordings of the text. He ascribes the plate to Simon Frisius. See also F. Muller, Beredeneerde Beschrijving van Nederlandsche Historieplaten. Vol. 4. Amsterdam 1882: nrs. 1417 C and D.

50. Reproduced in (A) Scheible 1850: nr. 51.

51. Reproduced in (A) Scheible 1850: nr. 88. Augsburg was biconfessional then, but in 1629–31 the emperor was able to favor the Catholics: (B) Warmbrunn 1983: 162–164.

52. (A) Krausoldus 1698.

53. GAA, 5059: nr. 41 (city chronicle, middle of 17th century).

54. (B) Pol 1988: 122–123, 128; GAH, Kast 2-24-7 (I am indebted for the archival reference to Rudolf Dekker).

55. (A) Fokkens 1662: 283–285.

56. Notably, he refers to the Dutch edition of the *History of amazing miracles*, which, in fact, does not include the pumping story. See (B) Schama 1988: 35. On imprisonment generally there are more errors.

57. (A) Brown 1682: 18. The dates in the text refer to the years when the authors visited Amsterdam or claimed they did.

58. (A) Misson 1691, 1: 21.

59. (A) Mountague 1696: 174; Bowrey 1927: 42; Zetzner 1913: 17.

60. (A) Blainville 1743, 1: 36.

61. The entire passage devoted to the rasphouse is quoted from a manuscript in (B) Ebeling 1935: 117–118.

62. (A) Wagenaar 1760–1768: 8: 243.

63. (A) Howard 1792: 58.

64. (B) Hippel 1898: 492.

65. (B) Hallema 1936: 33–38. Hallema also suggests that the free-thinker Adriaan Koerbagh died in the water cellar. This is probably based on a misreading of Meinsma 1896: 316–324. Koerbagh's interrogations and sentence are in GAA, 5061: nrs. 318 (fos. 115v and 118v) and 586 (fo. 91, which has a blank where the judgment ought to be inserted).

66. (B) Sellin 1944: 72.

67. (A) Dapper 1663: 426.

68. (A) Wagenaar 1760–1768: 8: 242. Some people must have called it a "water-cellar" though, since this name appears in (B) Nieuwenhuijs (1820: 303). Nieuwenhuijs does not refer to the pumping myth and explains that a layer of cement protects this cellar from becoming moist. The workhouse also had a dark pit; in 1612 its regents determined that the beggar Hendrik Aarse had to sit there each Saturday: GAA, 5061: nr. 366, fo. 30.

69. (A) Gebouwen 1736: 345–346.

70. "On a aboli l'usage depuis quelques années": (A) Misson 1698, 1: 30.

71. See the works cited above and (B) Sellin 1944: 70–71. Schama (1988: 34) also refers to a manuscript account kept at the Bodleian Library, Oxford, by Robert Bargrave, dated 1634, but in his notes the date has been changed into 1652–1653.

72. See (B) Moes 1891: 102. Moes quotes the entire passage devoted to the rasphouse. Neither did (A) Evelyn (1983: 21), who saw the rasphouse in August 1641, refer to the myth.

73. See (B) Vámbéry 1915. Vámbéry gives a German translation of the entire passage concerning the rasphouse.

74. This story, about a Strasbourg beggar who preferred the fruits of begging to an inheritance, does not appear in the two versions of the *Liber Vagatorum* (A: Liber 1862; Fielen 1914) that I consulted.

75. (A) [Historie-] Miracula 1617: 24–29.

76. The ordinance is published in (B) Pietsch 1931: 77. Von Hippel (1898: 644) explains that the Danzig archive contained a manuscript combining its prison ordinance, a description of the Amsterdam rasphouse (the one discussed in chapter three, which did not refer to the water punishment), and passages from Pontanus and from the (German) Miracula San Raspini. The records consulted by Von Hippel and Pietsch are no longer extant.

Chapter Six.   The Prison as a Household

1. The difference in meaning between 'household,' used in the chapter title, and 'family,' appearing in the first section subtitle, should be noted. While the idealized prison community was viewed as a kind of (morally regenerating) family, the institutions were run more or less as complex households.

2. In 20th-century Dutch historiography it has become customary to denote the ruling patricians as *regenten*. In the time of the Republic this was never done, and a burgomaster or council member would certainly have felt offended by it. It would be better if historians quit this anachronistic usage.

3. There was also a board of *alten* in Hamburg. In 1698 it was said that its members (referring to the spinhouse) had always belonged to the town's *oberalten* (SAH, 242-1-I: nr. A29-1, p. 168). The division of tasks between *alten* and *provisoren* remains unclear, but only the latter, led by the *jahrverwalter*, actually managed the institution's affairs.

4. In Amsterdam in 1659 one of the regents had to visit the rasphouse every day to judge cases. The Leiden magistrates found that twice a week was enough: GAL, Stad: nr. 6525.

5. GAH, werkhuis: nr. 12, second document.

6. (A) Hout 1927: 77 (date corrected from the original document in GAL, Stad: nr. 6522).

7. GAH, werkhuis: nr. 12, first document.

8. GAD, St. Joris: nr. 59-2, fo. 79.

9. GAH, Handschriften: nr. 153, dossier R; werkhuis: nr. 2.

10. GAL, Stad: nr. 6525: (A) Wagenaar, 8: 248–249, 266–267.

11. "in den standt der Oberkeit": SAH, 242-1-I: nr. A14-1, front page, and fo. 110 v. in addition to the provisors, the *alten* were bound by the agreement.

12. SAH, 242-1-I: nr. A14-1, fo. 133v.

13. GAL, Stad: nr. 6525.

14. GAH, Werkhuis: nr. 12; see also Kast 7-2-2-7, containing a dossier which confirms that most instructions in 1686 have been approved.

15. *Tuchtmeester*, also called *gardiaan:* (A) Wagenaar, 8: 250.

16. See, among others, GAD, St. Joris: nr. 59-1, fos. 57 and 58v–59; GAD, Stad: nr. 1242; (B) Bouricius 1927: 27–35 and 151–154.

17. In Hamburg these functions regularly appear in the records of the *zuchthaus* as well as the *spinnhaus*. It seems though, that the words *werkmeister* and *zuchtmeister* were sometimes used interchangeably. The term *fabriqueur* is used in Bremen in 1749: SAB, 2-D. 18. d: dossier 10. The other functions are mentioned at an earlier date: Ibid.: dossiers 4 and 5. I will refer to the *zuchtmeister/zuchtvogt* as 'master of discipline.'

18. SAH, Senatsacten: Cl. VII, Lit. Mb, nr. 2, vol. 3g. The two personnel members were interrogated after a prison riot.

19. SAB, 2-D. 18. d: dossiers 6b1 (30 Sept. 1726) and 5 (1754–1757).

20. GAA, 345: nr. 3 (undated document in 18th-century handwriting).

21. GAA, 5061: nr. 354, fo. 35.

22. SAB, 2-D. 18. d: dossier 4 (1748: art. 18).

23. (A) Wagenaar (8: 266) still used this term. See also GAL, Stad: nr. 6525 (1659).

24. From now on, therefore, I will refer to him as the "indoor father."

25. SAH, 242-1-I, nr. A28 (art. 3 of the *oeconomus*'s instructions); SAB, 2-D 18. d: dossier 4 (1748).

26. (B) Pietsch 1931: 44–45; Hippel 1898: 645–646.

27. (B) Doering 1926: 39; (A) Wagnitz, 1: 238 and 3: 32; (B) Schmidt 1915: 41/275, 81/315; Eichler 1970: 143–144; Stekl 1978: 152–153. Wolf (1963: 12) mentions no paternalistic titles for Potsdam.

28. (B) Hufton 1974: 148–149.

29. (B) Spierenburg 1988a: 38–49 (on households) and 302–304 (on brothels).

30. (B) Otis 1985: 83.

31. GAA, 5023: nr. 2, fo. 182–183v. The word journeymen (*"gesellen"*) is also used by S. Egberts and in (A) Ordnung 1598.

32. (B) Macdonald 1981: 85–88.

33. SAH, 242-1-I: nr. A14-1, fos. 3 and 4v.

34. SAH, 242-1-I: nr. A14-1, fos. 128 v–132, 134, 136, 137v–139. Compare 18th-century Bedford, where the jailkeeper was usually assisted by his wife: (B) Stockdale 1977: passim.

35. GAD, St. Joris: nr. 59-1, fo. 72v–73 (1736). For other advertisements, see fo. 101–107v and nr. 59-2, fo. 152–153v.

36. (B) Goffman 1961: 7.

37. GAA, 345: nr. 3 (undated dossier). See also (A) Gebouwen 1736: 344.

38. (Copy in) GAL, Stad: nr. 6525.

39. GAA, 5061: nr. 354, fos. 31v–39v and 75.

40. SAB, 2-D. 18. d: dossier 6a.

41. GAD, St. Joris: nr. 59–1, fo. 76–77. This situation was institutionalized in 1743: GAD, Stad: nr. 1242 (fourth contract, art. 11). The regents of the Amsterdam resphouse had a private servant, too: (A) Wagenaar, 8:249.

42. GAD, St. Joris: nr. 59-1: fo. 101–107v.

43. GAD, Stad: nr. 1242.

44. GAD, Stad: nrs. 2002–24, (1757), 21–2, 14-3, 21-3, 4-4 and fo. 99v–101; St. Joris: nr. 69, 14-3-1757 and nr. 59-1, fo. 91-2.

45. GAD, St. Joris: nr. 59-1, fo. 117–119.

46. GAD, St. Joris: nr. 59-2, fo. 152.

47. See (B) Adler 1924: 60–61.

48. (B) Rusche and Kirchheimer 1939: 24–33.

49. The Dutch Republic, pioneering in imprisonment, has traditionally been considered not to have been a champion of mercantilism. Rusche anticipates this objection with the argument that the high wages in Holland ensured that every effort was made to draw upon the available labor reserves: (B) Rusche and Kirchheimer 1939: 42. In a recent article, however, Klein (1989) defends the thesis that Dutch authorities adopted mercantilist policies.

50. (B) Rusche and Kirchheimer 1939: 46–52.

51. GAH, Kast 7-2-3-1.

52. GAH, Grote Lade 5-2-4.

53. GAH, Kast 7-2-3-16 (lesser values omitted).

54. GAH, Werkhuis: nr. 3 (last document, 7 Oct. 1664).

55. GAH, Kast 7-2-3-21.

56. GAH, Kast 7-2-2-5.

57. GAH, Werkhuis: nr. 13 (10 December 1710).

58. GAH, Grote Lade 7-8-9-b.

59. GAH, Grote Lade 7-8-9-1. See also the monthly accounts over approximately the same period: GAH, Werkhuis: nr. 18.

60. GAH, Grote Lade 7: Bundel 10, Letter a (lesser values omitted).

61. GAH, Vroeds. Resol.: 22 Sept. 1784 (fo. 65–66).

62. GAH, Burg. Resol.: 24 March 1786 (fo. 27 v–31v, art. 18 and 22).

63. All documents in SAB, 2-D. 18. d: dossier 1a.

64. (B) Kampman 1984: 67–68.

65. GAL, Stad: nr. 6527.

66. GAD, Stad: nr. 2010 (dossier 17).

67. GAA, 5059: nr. 24, p. 308 and nr. 27, pp. 136 and 206; (A) Wagenaar, 8: 265.

68. GAD, Stad: nr. 2001-II, fo. 112v–113. For further financial details about the Delft

prison, see St. Joris: nrs. 125 et seq., 144, 180, 340, 347–55. In 1758 the institution was said to own a capital of over 16,000: St. Joris: nr. 59-1, fo. 97. Basing himself on a few misinterpreted data, (B) Bouricius (1927: 30) thought that the *tuchthuis*'s textile business was thriving in the 18th century; his opinion is reproduced in Wijsenbeek-Olthuis 1987: 74–75.

69. Regents' complaint in: GAA, 5059: nr. 72; specification of the subsidies in: ARA, 3.20.52: nr. 465.

70. SAB, 2-D. 18. d: dossier 6a.

71. (B) Grambow 1910: 41–46.

72. SAB, 2-d. 18. d: dossier 1a (1799).

73. (B) Pietsch 1931: 41–43, 59–65; Verhoeven 1978: 49; Schmidt 1915: 87–88, 321–322; Stier 1988: 171–176; Reekers 1981: 36–37, 43: Wolf 1963: 13; Schubert 1983: 295–296, 299–301.

74. GAD, St. Joris: nr. 69 (11 Sept. 1713 and 14 Dec. 1761); Stad: nr. 2001-II, fos. 47v–54, 129, 142v.

75. GAH, Werkhuis: nr. 13 (3 June 1760).

76. (A) Dapper 1663: 419–420. In St. Gallen sales were reported to have been problematic too: (B) Mayer 1987: 199.

77. (B) Fokker 1862: 65–99.

78. GAA, 5024: 1612–47 (1 Sept. 1612). Published text, with a few minor errors, in (B) Ebeling 1935: 25–26.

79. GAD, Stad: nr. 872.

80. (Copy in) GAL, Stad: nr. 6524.

81. (B) Ebeling 1935: 23–30.

82. Many were held in 1661–3: SAB, 2-N. 3. a.

83. SAB, 2-D. 18. d: dossier 1a (5 June 1618; 16/6 Oct. 1645) and dossier 7 (1647, 1650).

84. (B) Streng 1890: 66.

85. (B) Schmidt 1915: 34–38; Doering 1926: 27.

86. GAA, 5020: nr. H, fo. 99v–100v.

87. GAA, 5020: nr. K, fo. 123v–124v.

88. GAA, 5020: nrs. *m.*, fo. 227 (1655) and P, fo. 121 (1675). Brandy had already been mentioned in 1626: marginal remark in nr. H, fo. 99v.

89. GAA, 347: nrs. 42 et seq. contain the permits for the years 1742–1771. See also (A) Wagenaar 1760–1768, 8: 257–257, 261–262.

90. GAD, Stad: nr. 1224.

91. GAL, Stad: nr. 8979. The entire series, covering the years 1703–1810, ends with nr. 8991.

92. (B) Pietsch 1931: 30; Ebeling 1935: 57.

93. See, for example, Amstelodamum Maandblad (1938): 63; SAB, 2-D. 18. d: dossier 1a (25 Nov. 1716).

94. With some variations, these arguments are put forward by (B) Eichler 1970: 144–145; Sachsse and Tennstedt 1980: 122; Reekers 1981: 63–64. See also Lis and Soly 1979: 117 (who argue in a similar vein but admit that the economic benefit was rather a question of expectations than of practical success).

95. SAH, 242-1-I: nr. A14-1, fos. 55, 61, 93.

96. See the contract with Johan Schnakenborg in Bremen, 30 Oct. 1646: SAB, 2-D. 18. d: dossier 1a.

97. GAD, Stad: nr. 1242 and 2010–1013; St. Joris: nr. 59-1, fos. 1–7, 8–12, 17, 20, 34–36, 57–59, 94–98. At the end of the 18th century, the indoor father may have had a private business as well. In 1788 Willem Maas obtained permission to start a worsted manufactory of his own in prison and it was said that his brother had done the same previously: St. Joris: nr. 59-2, fo. 98 v.

98. GAD, Stad, nr. 1242.

99. GAA, 5059: nr. 72; ARA, 3.20.52: nr. 465.

100. (B) Sothmann 1970: 72–79.

101. (B) Reekers 1981: 49–50.

102. (B) Wolf 1963: 27–32. See also Eichler 1970: 138.

103. Quoted in (B) Reekers 1981: 41.

104. See Conley 1981, and the contributions by Petchesky and Shelden to Greenberg 1981.
105. (A) Dapper 1663: 428; Wagenaar 1760–1768, 8: 236.
106. GAH, Werkhuis: nrs. 13 (3 June 1760) and 18; Grote Lade 7-8-9-1.
107. (A) Wagenaar 1760–1768, 8: 260–261.
108. (A) Dapper 1663: 419–420; Bontemantel 1897, 1: 281.
109. GAL, Stad: nr. 6529.
110. An inventory of 1712–1713 lists two *raspbanken* and one *rasp,* "which are no good": GAD, St. Joris: nr. 59-1, fo. 57v (see also fo. 60, where the *raspbank* is used for a barricade). Also in 1713 an inmate hit another on the head with a redwood log (GAD, Stad: nr. 2120a, fo. 15).
111. SAB, 2-D. 18. d: dossiers 1a and 10 (30 Oct. 1646) and dossier 1a (23 Jan. 1669).
112. SAB, 2-D. 18. d: dossiers 4 (1724 and 1748), 6c (23 Febr. 1702), 6b1 (August 1782).
113. SAH, 242-1-I: nrs. A25, A12, and A13; see also A14-1, fos. 74v, 110, 136v.
114. (B) Streng 1890: 58–64, 91.
115. Data from a preliminary investigation in Dutch archives; for Arnhem, see (B) Verhoeven 1978: 41.
116. (B) Hippel 1898: 646; Pietsch 1931: 38; Doering 1926: 24; Sothmann 1970: 66–84; Eichler 1970: 146.
117. (B) Reekers 1981: 40–42; (A) Wagnitz 1791–1794: 3: 10.
118. (B) Lieberknecht 1921: 34–35, 105–108; Eichler 1970: 146–147.
119. (B) Sothmann 1970: 106–108, 126, 159–164. The author does not inform us when exactly glass polishing was introduced and presents her data in a slightly chaotic fashion.
120. Additionally, (A) Wagnitz (1791–1794: 2: 7) refers to "milling cotton" in the Augsburg prison in the 1790s.
121. (B) Vries 1976: 98–110; Lis and Soly 1979: 104–108, 144–159.
122. (B) Baxandall 1986: 12–26.
123. (A) Battus 1650: 286–290. The book went through numerous editions; I consulted the oldest possessed by the Amsterdam university library.
124. (B) Schaefer 1937: 341–352.
125. (B) Nie 1937: 37.
126. (B) Schaefer 1937: 326, 331, 337.
127. GAA, 347: nr. 562 (nr. 2757 of the book).
128. For a serious case, see GAL, Oud, Rechterlijk Archief: nr. 4, Correctieboek N, fos. 100–102. See also (A) Posthumus 1914, 4: nr. 274 and (B) Nie 1937: 126, 274.
129. (B) Nie 1937: 21–22.
130. GAH, werkhuis: nr. 3.
131. (B) Doorman 1940: 82.
132. Ibid.: 106, 110.
133. GAA, 5020: nr. H, fo. 146.
134. Document nr. 2 in (B) Hallema 1935: 142–143.
135. (A) Handvesten 1748: 294–295. Copies in GAH, Kast 7-2-3-23 and GAL, Stad: nr. 6526. The date was 11 May 1602.
136. The only exception in the 1602 privilege by the Estates of Holland was the provision that any other town in Holland wishing to erect a *tuchthuis* was allowed to let its prisoners rasp as much wood as was needed within that town. The Estates of Friesland and Groningen granted similar monopolies to their provincial *tuchthuizen* in 1663 and 1669, respectively. (B) Hallema 1935: documents 7 and 8; Kampman 1986: 24–25.
137. *Keuren* of 23 Aug. 1646; 12 Dec. 1657; 2 Jan. 1660. The first (and a marginal remark on the second) in GAA, 5020: nr. L, fo. 272. Copies of all three in GAH, Kast 7-2-3-23 (with references to the Amsterdam *keurboeken;* for the second and third: N, fos. 50 and 123; (book N is missing in the Amsterdam archive). The third has been published in (A) Handvesten 1748: 295 (also in (B) Hallema 1935: nr. 4).
138. GAA, 5025: nr. 21, fo. 161v; GAA, 5059: nr. 27, p. 311; (B) Vis 1943: 16–18, 24–27; (A) Wagenaar 1760–1768, 8: 237.
139. (B) Hallema (1935: 137–139) even speaks of a lawsuit between the parties in the 1670s, but he fails to specify his sources. Such a lawsuit is unlikely; I did not find any reference in the archives of the Court of Holland, the High Council, or the committee of

justice of the Estates of Holland. The text of Hallema's article is completely useless. It even conflicts with the documents which he publishes at the end, giving only vague and unspecified references. I was able to trace some of these documents in the Amsterdam archive and they turned out to have been published with only a few spelling errors. Therefore, I take the others, which could not be traced, to be authentic as well.

140. GAA, 5059: nr. 25, pp. 459–60 and nr. 27, p. 311.
141. GAA, 5024: Gemene Missiven, nr. 7: fo. 8v; GAL, Stad: nr. 6526.
142. See the documents, nrs. 6 and 9–18 in (B) Hallema 1935.
143. (A) Posthumus 1918, 5: nr. 576.
144. (B) Lootsma 1950: 184–187.
145. (B) Vis 1943: 89–90.
146. (B) Woude 1972, 1: 320–322.
147. (B) Vis 1943: 31–36.
148. (B) Hallema 1935: nrs. 27–30. Another document (undated, 18th century: GAR, Oud Stadsarchief: nr. 2149) reveals that Rotterdam dye traders were obliged to accept rasped and chopped wood from prison according to a fixed ratio. Strangely, it concerned a trader whose colleagues accused him of exceeding his ratio of rasped wood.
149. GAH, Werkhuis: nr. 15. See also Kast 7-2-3-26 (1760s).
150. (A) Handvesten 1748: 295–297; also in (B) Hallema 1935: nr. 19. (A) Wagenaar (1760–1768, 8: 237–239) mentions a comparable agreement for 1763.
151. (B) Nie 1937: 41.
152. (B) Hallema 1935: nr. 20.
153. (B) Hallema 1935: nrs. 20–26.
154. (B) Hippel 1932: 42 (art. 22); (A) Dapper 1663: 426.
155. (A) Wagenaar 1760–1768, 8: 243–244. Jews were not eligible for these jobs.
156. (A) Howard 1792: 57–58. For the Republic, he confirms that rasping is "in many places performed at the mills, much cheaper" (45).
157. In 1798 rasping was still listed as one of its activities, but "weaker inmates" worked for the city's stocking factory. See the document published in (B) Hallema 1929: 198–206.
158. (B) Vis 1943: 36.
159. SAB, 2-D. 18. d: dossier 11.
160. (A) Wagnitz 1791–1794, 2: 47–48, 201. "Between 0 and 16 prisoners" rasped at Magdeburg (2: 204–205).
161. (A) Wagnitz 1791–1794 (1: 262, 269–273; 2: 47–48, 87, 96, 144–148) lists Zwickau, Leipzig, Bremen, Erfurt, Gotha, and Hamburg. In the latter town deer horn was also rasped. For Copenhagen, see SAB, 2-D. 18. d: dossier 1a (nr. 31, 1799). The Bremen records, and in some cases Wagnitz himself, confirm that just a few inmates were actually involved in rasping. In the prison workhouse at Brussels rasping was discontinued in 1739: (B) Bruneel 1966b: 223–224.
162. (B) Vries 1976: 252.
163. (B) Woude 1972, 2: 315–318. "Industrial windmills" do not include those used for milling grain, which were much older.
164. (B) O'Brien (1982: 183–184) reaches a similar conclusion for 19th-century French prisons.
165. (B) Houlbrooke 1984: 153–155.

Chapter Seven. Thieves, Prostitutes, and Aggressors

1. (A) Wagnitz 1791–1794, 2: 229; (B) Saam 1936: 80; Eichler 1970: 146; Lieberknecht 1921: 105–108; Stekl 1978: 62; Doering 1926: 12–13.
2. Documents published by Hallema in Jaarboek Oranjeboom (1957): 179–185. See also (B) Eerenbeemt 1968: 105–106.
3. Rijksarchief in Gelderland, Hof van Gelre: nr. 4842.
4. Rijksarchief Overijssel, Resoluties Ridderschap en Steden: nr. 199.
5. (B) Emmermann 1921: 1–12.
6. (A) Wagnitz (3 vols, 1791–1794) lists 44 *zuchthäuser*, and a few more, not mentioned by him, appear in historical literature. Recently, (B) Stier (1988: 218–221) counted 77, but some of these may not have been real prisons.

7. There were three prisons in Amsterdam and one each in sixteen other towns. The latter include Dordrecht and Schiedam, whose houses do not seem to have functioned as *tuchthuizen* in the eighteenth century. Between 1740 and the end of the Ancien Régime, one more *tuchthuis* was established, at Den Bosch in 1808. See (B) Eerenbeemt 1968: 106–111; Jacobs 1988: 28.

8. GAD, St. Joris: nr. 59-1, p. 12. Their report was not recorded.

9. (B) Stroobant 1900: 198.

10. (A) Blok 1909: 121–122, 170–171.

11. SAB, 2-D. 18. d: dossier la (contains all documents referred to).

12. (B) Streng 1890: 59.

13. (B) Emmermann 1921: 8.

14. (B) Hippel 1898: 648.

15. SAH, Senatsakten, Cl. VII, lit. Mb, nr. 2, vol 3a.

16. (B) Schmidt 1915: 65/ 299.

17. GAA, 5061: nr. 571, fo. 69.

18. GAA, 5061: nr. 268.

19. GAA, 345: nrs. 1 (passim) and 3 (dossiers 1797–1811 and 1806). See also (B) Faber 1983: 196 (referring to GAA, 345: nr. 2).

20. GAU, Stad: nr. 1043, fos. 11 and 16v.

21. GAH, Burg, Resol.: 20 June 1651 (fo. 162v), 12 Aug. 1660 (fo. 176v), 15 May 1766 (fo. 49v) and Vroeds. Resol: 4 April 1795 (fo. 44v).

22. ARA, Gedeputeerden Haarlem: nr. 843.

23. Zierikzee/ 1715: GAD, St. Joris: nr. 69 (referred to in dossier 1736); new general contract with Zierikzee (1736): GAD, Stad: nr. 1237; Court-martial and Generality Lands: GAD, St. Joris: nr. 69 (13 Nov. 1750); Tholen: GA Tholen, V: nr. 592. In the second half of the 18th century Tholen also confined a few offenders at Middelburg.

24. GAD, St. Joris: nr. 69 (14 Dec. 1725).

25. GAD, St. Joris: nr. 119 and Stad, nr. 1237.

26. Court of Holland: GAD, St. Joris: nr. 69 (5 Nov. 1751 and 9 Dec. 1760); The Hague: Ibid.: 16 Jan. 1777.

27. ARA, HvH: nr. 4686. It is impossible to count the total number of prisoners, since most courts stating they had them gave specifications on a separate list. These lists have not been preserved.

28. SAH, 242-1-I: nr. Cl-2, pp. 153–155, 185.

29. (B) Reekers 1981: 67. (A) Wagnitz (1791–1794 3, 22–24) explicitly mentions that foreign delinquents were admitted into the *zuchthäuser* at Halle and Frankfurt/ Oder. This was probably a policy in other places, too.

30. SAB, 2-d. 18. d: dossier 6c.

31. (A) Spaan 1698: 398–405.

32. (A) Mieris 1770: 381.

33. (A) Riemer 1730: 646. On a list of inmates of The Hague's *tuchthuis* in 1752 ten were committed on request and twelve were condemned offenders (GA's Gravenhage, Oud Archief: nr. 5919). In later decades, the institution's capacity may have become insufficient.

34. On these plans: (A) Resolutien Holland 1647 (19 Dec.), 1648 (18 March, 27–28 Nov., 10–11 Dec.), 1649 (12 March, 17–18 March, 6 May, 12 May), 1709 (16 April, 16–17 May, 15 June, 29 Aug., 30 Aug., 23 Oct., 20 Dec.), 1716 (23 June, 25 July, 29 Aug.), 1722 (12 June); ARA, Gedeputeerden Haarlem: nr. 843; GAH, Vroeds. Resol.: 30 Nov. 1648 (fo. 74v) and 17 April 1649 (fo 93v-94).

35. (B) Kampman 1986: 35, 102.

36. (A) Commelin 1693: 507.

37. (B) Bruinvis 1908: 2–7.

38. GAH, Handschriften: nr. 153, dossier R: fo. 6–7; Ned. Herv. Diaconie: nrs. 23 and 24; Burg. Resol.: 24 March 1786 (fo. 27v-31v); Vroeds. Resol.: 27 Febr. 1786 (fo. 12 et seq.).

39. GAD, St. Joris: nr. 69 (4 Oct. 1797). See also nr. 59–2, fo. 160v.

40. (A) Wagenaar 1760–1768, 8: 472–477.

41. SAB, 2-D. 18. d: dossier la; (B) Heineken 1983: 95.

42. (B) Streng 1890: 64, 195–196.

43. (B) Eerenbeemt 1977: 38.

44. (B) Lis 1976; Stroobant 1900: 221–239.
45. (B) Stekl 1978: 82–87.
46. (A) Wagnitz 1791–1794, 2: 71–74, 95, 185, and passim. For Spandau: report in AHL, Senate: nr. 1, dossier 5.
47. (B) Streng 1890: 171; SAB, 2-D. 18. d: dossier 1a (record nr. 31, dated 1799, report IV on Hamburg). See also the report on the Hamburg *zuchthaus* from the 1770s in AHL (Senate: nr. 1, dossier 5), stating that there were about 500 inmates but with a rapid turnover: c. 1,500 per year.
48. Compare the discussion (B) Marzahn 1984: 28–29. The high numbers he gives for Norwich and Liverpool also refer to voluntary workhouses. That is likewise the case with his figures (between 0.5% and 2%) on the ratio of inmates to the general population. If would be futile to calculate a ratio of prisoners for an individual town, since inmates were often recruited from wandering groups.
49. (B) Beier 1985: 166.
50. GAU, Stad: nr. 1043, fo. 33v-37v.
51. (B) Moes 1899: 4; (A) Fokkens 1662: 284; Bowrey 1927: 38–39; Wagenaar 1760–1768, 8: 258, 261, 265; Howard 1789: 73 and 1792: 60–61.
52. (B) Stier 1988: 65.
53. SAB, 2-D. 18. d: dossiers 6a (calculations by Schönhülde, 1764) and 6b1 (1782); (A) Howard 1792: 68; Wagnitz 1791–1794, 2: 45.
54. SAB, 2-D. 18. d: dossier 1a, record nr. 31.
55. In a verse ascribed to a prisoner, the rasphouse was also seen as an alternative to the scaffold. See (A) Opschriften 1682: 19.
56. (A) Dapper 1663: 426.
57. (A) Bontemantel 1897, 1: 278–279.
58. (A) Wagenaar 1760–1768, 8: 248.
59. GAA, 5061: nr. 354, fo. 31v-39v.
60. The first in 1740: GAA, Bibliotheek: nr. B54, 15 Oct. 1740.
61. (A) Wagenaar 1760–1768, 8: 248; GAA, 345: nr. 3, dossier 1777.
62. (A) Bowrey 1927: 42; ARA, 3.20.52: nr. 465 (dossier 1743–1752); (A) Wagenaar 1760–1768, 8: 248; GAA, 345: nr. 3 (dossier 1777); (A) Howard 1789: 73 (1785 and 1787); Howard 1792: 57–58 (1776, 1781, 1783); (B) Faber 1983: 194. Faber's supposition that the number never rose much over 50 during the period 1733–1790 is not confirmed.
63. Compare (B) Spierenburg 1984a: 82.
64. (B) Rusche and Kirchheimer 1939: 65.
65. (B) Sellin 1944: 73; Hallema 1958: 190–191. Even the term *"opslag"* (extension) was hardly used at all. Among contemporaries, (A) Dapper (1663: 427) and Wagenaar (1760–1768, 8: 251; but another term is used on p. 243) used it once, but judicial records seldom did so.
66. (A) Bontemantel (1897, 1: 281) confirms that a possible lengthening of a prisoner's term normally followed upon a demand by the *schout*.
67. (A) Hout 1927: 80; GAA, 5061: nrs. 570, fo. 4v and 571, fo. 69. In Utrecht in 1624 an inmate serving a term of 6 years was told that if he behaved well he might be released after 3 years: GAU, Stad: nr. 1043, fo. 8v.
68. GAA, 5061: nr. 268.
69. (A) Bontemantel 1897, 1: 280–284. He also mentioned a few prisoners who were pardoned by burgomasters at the request of persons of high status, but these were exceptional cases and *schepenen* usually protested.
70. (B) Faber 1983: 194.
71. GAA, 345: nr. 3 (1777).
72. Data collected by Jan Verwoerd and Alex de Boer, under Faber's supervision, from GAA, 345: nr. 1. See also (B) Faber 1983: 191–193.
73. Quoted in (B) Ebeling 1935: 29.
74. (B) Streng 1890: 68–69; Ebeling 1935: 42–43.
75. SAH, 242-1-I: nr. A28 and Senatsakten, C1. VII, Lit. Mb, nr. 2, vol 3a.
76. The mixed cases: SAH, 242-1-I: nr. C1-2, pp. 160 and 192. On burgomaster's order: two cases in 1671–1673 and three in 1693–1694. In addition, the logbook (A29-1, p. 128) mentions the college's consent to a committal in 1693 of a woman at the request of her

father, who was living in Copenhagen. Since she does not turn up in the entry book, she may not have been admitted after all.

77. Sources: SAH, 242-1-I: nr. C1, vol. 1 et seq.
78. (B) Streng 1890: 97; Ebeling 1935: 63.
79. Counts are missing for 1672, 1759, and 1771–1773.
80. SAH, 242-1-I: nr. C1-1 (case nr. 41).
81. SAH, 242-1-I: nr. C1-1 (case nr. 63).
82. SAH, 242-1-I: nr. C1-1 (case nr. 52).
83. SAH, 242-1-I: nr. C1-1 (case nr. 13) and A29-1, p. 36. She must have been pregnant for about a week when she was flogged.
84. The three longest: SAH, 242-1-I: nrs. C1-1, pp. 105, 160, and C1-2, p. 29.
85. SAH, 242-1-I: nr. C1-2, p. 134 and A29-1, pp. 156–158.
86. SAH, 242-1-I: nrs. A29, p. 199 and A34 (listing the gifts); (B) Streng 1890: 94–96, 203, 207.
87. Quoted in (B) Ebeling 1935: 53.
88. (B) Streng 1890: 48. On pp. 38–52 he discusses selected cases of imprisonment in the *zuchthaus* since 1650. Entry books of the *zuchthaus* before 1790 are no longer extant.
89. (B) Streng (1890: 77–78) presents a series of figures.
90. SAH, Senatsacten, Classis VII, Lit. Mb, vol. 31.
91. (A) Wagnitz 1791–1794, 2: 144.
92. Only the minimum necessary for the substantiation of my thesis is presented here. A more complete series of figures and an explanation of how they were derived are given in my paper presented at the World Historical Congress in Madrid, August 1990.
93. GAA, 347: nr. 39.
94. Two volumes: GAD, Stad: nr. 2120a. (A) Howard (1792: 52) counted 90 inmates at Delft in the 1770s and 47 men and 36 women in 1781. He did not specify whether they were *tuchtelingen* or *bestedelingen*.
95. (A) Fokkens (1662: 281–285) and Dapper (1663: 418) mentioned women committed at the request of relatives as a minority category in the spinhouse's public part. In the confession books, 1651–1683, they made up a mere 1%: (B) Spierenburg 1978: 177.
96. SAH, 242-1-I: nr. C1-2, pp. 207–210.
97. (B) Spierenburg 1984a: 19.
98. That was recorded in Friesland: (B) Huussen 1985: 137.
99. GAD, Stad: nr. 2001-II (2 April 1696).
100. SAH, 242-1-I: nr. C1-2, p. 1.
101. SAH, 242-1-I: nr. C1-2, p. 211.
102. (B) Grambow 1910: 44–45.
103. (B) Stier 1988: 130–132.
104. SAH, 242-1-I: nr. A29-1, fo. 30–37.
105. SAH, 242-1-I: nr. C1-1, p. 63.
106. SAH, 242-1-I: nr. C1-1, p. 205, and C1-2, pp. 55, 105, 122.
107. SAH, 242-1-I: nr. C1-1, pp. 121, 144, 147, and C1-2, p. 68 and A29-1, p. 44.
108. SAH, 242-1-I: nr. C1-2, p. 300.
109. SAH, 242-1-I: nr. C1-2, p. 131. She stayed for more than three years after the expiration of her term. If we exclude this exceptional case, there are 15 women from the "after expiration" group who stayed in the poxhouse. Subtracting the number of days their cure lasted from the numbers of days served beyond imposed term, the average remainder is 133 days.
110. SAH, 242-1-I: nr. C1-2, p. 212.
111. That was also recorded in Celle a couple of times: (B) Emmermann 1921: 41. For pardons: pp. 28–29.
112. See (B) Spierenburg 1987: 445–446 (from Jüngen 1979).
113. See (B) Faber 1983; Spierenburg 1978 and 1984a. I am grateful to Sjoerd Faber for sharing figures with me that were not included in his book.
114. For a specification, see (B) Spierenburg 1987: 446–447.
115. That life sentences were exceptional is illustrated by the case of a woman in the 1650s. She received one only because her lifelong banishment was commuted to imprisonment: GAA, 5061: nrs. 309, fo. 250 and 581, fo. 234v.
116. GAD, card inventory with excerpts of the sentence books.

117. (B) Hoeven 1982: 21–24 and 35.
118. (B) Valkering 1984: 105.
119. (B) Kalshoven 1988: 68–69.
120. (B) Verhoeven 1978: 56–57.
121. (B) Graaff 1954: 222–223 and information from Ton van Weel.
122. From a project of the section of social history of the Leiden history department (figures kindly provided by Heiko Tjalsma) and from (B) Kampman 1986: 53–56.
123. (B) Spierenburg 1984a: 13–42 and the literature referred to there. Among the publications which appeared after I completed the manuscript, Blok 1981 should be mentioned.
124. (B) Wissell 1971: 185, 225–231.
125. (B) Wissell 1971: 262–269.
126. (B) Wissell 1971: 269–271.
127. (B) Bade 1982: 15.
128. See also (B) Raeff 1983: 105 et seq. Toward the end of the 18th century this tension became more complex, as indicated by the fact that journeymen often went on strike against their masters because of questions of honor. In those cases, the patriciates of Imperial cities tended to defend the journeymen against the masters, who dominated the guilds: Griessinger 1983: 162–165, 173. See also Griessinger 1981.
129. (B) Walker, Mack, 1971: 105.
130. Compare (B) Bade 1982: 1–3.
131. There are 8 overlaps when we compare the 40 towns on Walker's map (p. 23) with the 44 German places Wagnitz lists as having a *zuchthaus*. However, Walker's map shows "towns mentioned in the text," among which are a few non-home towns, such as Bremen.
132. SAB, 2-D. 18. d: dossiers 1a and 10 (each contains an identical copy of the agreement, 80 Oct. 1646).
133. SAB, 2-D. 18. d: dossier 1a (series later numbered 15: 1–17) The series contains remarks by an investigator in 1875 and one of the pieces he refers to is no longer there. Also, some of the dates have apparently been added later (one of which is incorrect).
134. SAB, 2-D. 18. d: dossier 10 (4 Oct. 1651).
135. SAB, 6, 1-B. 42.
136. SAB, 2-D. 18. d: dossier 10 (25 Aug. 1671).
137. SAB, 2-D. 18. d: dossier 5 (on the problems with the guilds) and dossier 1a (4 Febr. 1735; on a plan to raise the *zuchtvogt*'s status). It should be noted that the *ehrlichkeit* of personnel supervising prisoners and other offenders at forced labor had been proclaimed in the Imperial Trades Edict of 1731 (clause 4). See the text of the edict in (B) Walker, Mack, 1971: 440.
138. (A) Wagnitz (1791–1794 2: 56–57) says that, while the Bremen *speisevater* was a respected citizen, the master of discipline usually came from outside Bremen, because natives were reluctant to perform the task. The present incumbent is a former prison servant from Celle.
139. SAB, 2-D. 18. d: dossier 1a (21 April 1621; 11 Jan., 21 March, 12 Aug. 1622).
140. SAB, 2-D. 18. d: dossier 1a (6 Oct. 1648) and DDR: nr. 1212/ 3501. The phrase about the absence of a workhouse cannot have meant that the construction of the third *zuchthaus* was not yet completed. In the first of Koster's cases (see note 143) the offender in question stayed in the newly built *zuchthaus* until 1652.
141. SAB, 2-D. 18. d: dossiers 1a (8 May 1715) and 7 (17 July 1715); also in the *Wittheitsprotocollen* of 1715 (SAB, 2-P. 6. a. 9. c. 3. b. 26: pp. 142 and 251). They yield no more information than this.
142. SAB, 2-D. 18. d: dossiers 6a (14 Aug. 1726) and 4 (31 Oct. 1727). Vol. 30 of the *Wittheitsprotocollen* (1724–1748) is missing.
143. SAB, P. 1. S. 22. c. 1. c. The cases mentioned: pp. 82–83, 364; other cases: 418, 445–446.
144. SAB, 2-D. 18. d: dossiers 6c (11/ 16 June 1694 and Dec. 1742/ Feb. 1743) and 6b1 (28 July 1727).
145. SAB, 2-D. 18. d: dossier 6b1 (1647–1648 and 25 Nov. 1754).
146. SAB, 2-D. 18. d: dossier 6a (31 Jan. 1766).
147. (A) Wagnitz 1791–1794, 2: 46. On punishment and criminal justice in Bremen in the first half of the 19th century, see (B) Freest/ Marzahn 1988.
148. SAB, 2-D. 18. d: dossier 6b1 (2 Feb. 1774).

149. SAH, 242-1-I: nr. A14-1, fos. 6v, 13v, 78v.
150. SAH, 242-1-I: nr. A14-1, fo. 154.
151. SAH, 242-1-I: nr. C1-1, p. 23.
152. SAH, 242-1-I: nr. C1-1, p. 203 and C1-2, pp. 197, 205.
153. On persons not admitted to the *zuchthaus,* see SAH, 242-1-I: nr. C1-1, p. 76 and C1-2, pp. 134 and 28 July 1697. For an example of a stay in the *zuchthaus* and one in the spinhouse afterwards, see C1-2, p. 157.
154. SAH, 242-1-I: nr. C1-2, p. 209.
155. (B) Hippel 1898: 644–648: Pietsch 1931: 37–40. Meye (1935: 49) calls it a separate house, with reference to a city description of 1809.
156. (A) Wagnitz, 1791–1794, 3: 41.
157. AHL, Bürgerschaft: nr. 120-1, p. 130; (B) Brehmer 1883: 22; Hippel 1898: 628. What I am calling jail was the *fronereij,* a term also used in Hamburg. It means a jail which is frequented by the executioner or even where he lives.
158. (B) Hippel 1898: 628–630.
159. AHL, Senate: nr. 1, dossiers 1 (1686), 2 (1724–1725), 3 (committee and designs, 1759–1774), 4 (committee and appointment of the new prison's first provisors, 4 April 1778) and Bürgerschaft, nr. 120-7 (reorganization, 1777–1778). From 1778 there was the *zucht-* und *spinnhaus* on the one hand, and the *St. Annen armen- und werckhaus* on the other. (A) Wagnitz (1791–1794 3: 47–48), who lists only one prison for Lübeck, must have referred to the former. The latter institution remained in existence well into the 19th century: (B) Pelc 1986: 147–150. In 1785 there were plans to erect still another prison, either for drunks or for beggars: AHL, Bürgerschaft: nr. 120-9 (16 Sept. and Oct. 1785).
160. (B) Schmidt 1915: 48/ 282; Doering 1926: 27; Stekl 1978: 285.
161. (B) Hippel 1898: 656–657.
162. (B) Emmermann 1921: 9.
163. See, among others, (B) Reekers 1981: 44; Wilbertz 1979: 92; Sothmann 1970: 126, *Anhang;* Lieberknecht 1921: 105–108; Wolf 1963: 22; Stekl 1978: 67; Stier 1988: 78–86; Schlue 1957: 17–18.
164. (A) Wächter 1786: 199. The Bonn prison was actually split into a *zuchthaus* and a *polizei-arbeitshaus* in the 1790s: (B) Schlue 1957: 60–66.
165. (A) Wagnitz 1791–1794, 2: 149 and 1: 341.
166. SAB, 2-D. 18. d: dossier 1a.

Chapter Eight. The Prison Experience

1. (B) O'Brien 1982: 9. Priestley 1985 is valuable, too, in this respect, but the ego-documents he draws on were almost all written by atypical, middle-class prisoners.
2. On the other hand, these sources are not so detailed that they allow us to follow individual prisoners minutely from the moment of entry. There is no point, therefore, in comparing my data with Goffman's observations on the "moral career" of inmates of total institutions. Compare (B) Stekl (1978: 203), who claims that the mechanisms observed by Goffman characterized Austrian *zuchthäuser* from the 18th century. Stekl's huge chapter on institutional life, however, is somewhat disappointing. It is based almost entirely on ordinances and prescriptions. For details on the real life of galley convicts around 1700, see Zysberg 1987: chapter 5.
3. Exact measures were taken in the rasphouse by J. A. Kool in 1844, shortly before a reconstruction project destroyed the inside architecture of the 17th and 18th centuries. See (B) Kool 1865: 197–207.
4. GAA, 5061: nr. 354, fo. 35–38.
5. Compare Corbin in (B) Petit 1984: 151–156.
6. (A) Wagenaar, 8: 259.
7. In Hamburg the night rooms were called *"koyen."* In Bremen they were indeed called cells: SAB, 2-D. 18. d: dossiers 1a (15 Jan. 1788) and 5 (interrogations on the murder of Goldstein, 1754–1757). Although I found no references to men sharing beds in the Dutch Republic, this practice may not have been entirely unknown, since it was recorded in Alkmaar in 1807 (information from Herman Franke).

8. (A) Hout 1927: 81, 97; (B) Hippel 1932: 39–42 (arts 5 and 21); Hallema 1953b: 187; compare Hallema 1935: 178 (document nr. 22).

9. The fixed amount of rasped wood for strong men was said to be 45 pounds per man per day in 1680 and 150 pounds per man per week in 1788: SAB, 2-D. 18. d: dossier 1a (nrs. 9 and 27). Presumably, in the first case per pair was actually meant.

10. One has been preserved in the Amsterdam Historical Museum.

11. GAH, Grote Lade 5-2-4.

12. Delft: GAD, Stad: nr. 2120a, pp. 2, 13, 24, 150, and St. Joris: nr. 59-1, fos. 119v and 128. Bremen: SAB, 2-D. 18. d: dossiers 1a (ordinance, art. 5) and 6b1 (30 Sept. 1726). Danzig: (B) Pietsch 1931: 53–54. Spandau: Schmidt 1915: 46/ 280. See also O'Brien 1982: 165–168 for 19th-century France.

13. GAD, Stad: nr. 2120a, pp. 26 and 40; GAD, Oud-Rechterlijk Archief: nr. 50, fo. 230v.; (B) Faber 1983: 194–195.

14. SAB, 2-D. 18. d: dossier 4 (1748, art. 19).

15. SAH, 242-1-I: nrs. C1-2, p. 102 and A29-1, pp. 142, 144–148, 153–154.

16. At Delft, Jan Hoogeveen, convicted for sodomy in 1730, was lodged in a separate room. He was given the choice to work or to pay for his stay out of his own pocket. He died in 1738: GAD, Stad: nr. 2120a, p. 6.

17. GAA, 5059: nr. 72. Presumably "too many prisoners" referred to the 7 or 8 staying there toward the end of the century, as compared to the 2 or 3 at the beginning. It is no coincidence that the regents spoke of a period of 20 years, since sodomy trials were conducted in Amsterdam from 1730 onward.

18. GAD, St. Joris: nr. 59-1, fo. 130v and 59-2, fo. 8v.

19. GAD, St. Joris: nr. 59-2, fo. 23–25v.

20. (A) Handt-boecxken 1635. This copy is a convolute in which the earlier compilation is bound together with a selection from the letters of the apostles. The title pages of both editions include the phrase quoted. For the rest, there are no references to any specific tie with the rasphouse. The 1599 edition is mentioned, with the complete title, in Long 1732: 770–771. The same texts were mentioned as reading material in the Stockholm prison in 1624: (B) Wieselgren 1895: 35.

21. "Int jaer 1651 den 27 junius ben ick hier gecomen / A la Rochelle."

22. Amsterdam: (A) Dapper 1663: 428. Haarlem: GAH, Kast 7-2-2-6 and 7-2-2-8; Werkhuis: nr. 12; Handschriften: nr. 153 (dossier R, fo. 25); see also Burg. Resol.: 16 March 1623. On restrictions during services at Delft: GAD, St. Joris: nr. 59-1, fo. 124.

23. Also in Amsterdam and Delft: (A) Wagenaar, 8: 245; GAD, St. Joris: nr. 59-1, p. 22 and fo. 99.

24. SAH, 242-1-I: nr. A14-1, fos. 27-v and 55v.

25. SAB, 2-D. 18. d: dossier 1a (1646 and 1680); SAH, 242-1-I: nr. A29-1, pp. 38 and 95–97.

26. SAH, 242-1-I: nr. A36-1.

27. SAH, 242-1-I: nr. A29-1, p. 98.

28. SAH, Senatsacten, C1. VII, Lit. Mb, nr. 2, vol. 3d.

29. (B) Emmermann 1921: 14.

30. GAH, Burg. Resol.: 22 Feb. 1614 (fo. 6vs).

31. GAD, St. Joris: nr. 59-1, p. 45.

32. (A) Howard 1792: 49–50.

33. (B) Streng 1890: 85.

34. (A) Wagnitz 1791–1794, 2: 53.

35. (A) Wagnitz 1791–1794, 2: 4–5, 13, 211–212 and 3: 63; (B) Stier 1988: 105–106.

36. At the level of the administrators, at least, the Reformed had no monopoly in Haarlem. It was determined in 1682 that the board should consist of four Reformed and three Mennonite regents: GAH, Handschriften: nr. 153 (dossier R, fo. 15–16).

37. SAH, 242-1-I: nr. C1-2 (29 Sept. 1713); (B) Streng 1890: 91, 96–97.

38. (B) Lieberknecht 1921: 45.

39. (A) Wagenaar 1760–1768, 8: 266.

40. (A) Howard 1792: 47.

41. (copy in) GAL, Stad: nr. 6525.

42. ARA, 3.20.52: nr. 465.

43. (A) Wagenaar 1760–1768, 8: 244.

44. GAD, St. Joris: nr. 59-1, fo. 58 and Stad: nr. 1242.
45. GAD, St. Joris: nr. 59-2, fo. 12 and nr. 69: 27 May 1775.
46. SAB, 2-D. 18. d: dossiers 1a (nr. 27: 1788), 4 and 10 (1749, art. 8); (B) Grambow 1910: 39–40. See also Stekl (1978: 265–269) for the diets of Austrian prisoners in the second half of the 18th century.
47. (B) Streng 1890: 91, 215–219.
48. GAD, St. Joris: nr. 59-1, fo. 109-v.
49. GAD, St. Joris: nr. 59-1, fos. 130v, 131, and 134v.
50. GAD, St. Joris: nr. 59-2, fo. 13.
51. SAB, 2-D. 18. d: dossier 4 (1695, art. 2; 1748, art. 8 and 10).
52. GAA, 5059: nr. 72. An inmate in 1723 was drunk when he was taken from the rasphouse (GAA, 5061: nr. 381, fo. 54v).
53. (A) Wagenaar 1760–1768, 8: 243.
54. GAD, St. Joris: nr. 59-2, fos. 63, 82v, 93v–94v.
55. GAH, Burg. Resol.: 10 Jan. 1708 (fo. 10); GAD, St. Joris: nr. 59-1, fo. 125.
56. GAL, Stad: nr. 6528; SAB, 2-D. 18. d: dossier 4 (1748: 145. 6).
57. GAH, werkhuis: nr. 12.
58. (B) Stier 1988: 130.
59. (A) Hout 1927: 82–83; Dapper 1663: 426.
60. GAA, 5061: nr. 335, fo. 14v–16v. Other cases: nrs. 320, fo. 135v and 571, fo. 47v.
61. GAD, St. Joris: nr. 59-1, fo. 86v and 59-2, fo. 76.
62. GAH, Burg. Resol.: 10 April 1688 (fo. 45v).
63. SAH, 242-1-I: nrs. A12/ A13 (*Raspelmeister,* art. 1) and A28 (*Zuchtmeister,* art. 1).
64. SAH, 242-1-I: nr. C1-2, p. 1.
65. SAH, 242-1-I: nr. C1-2, pp. 184–185.
66. SAB, 2-D. 18. d: dossier 1a (see also: 4 Feb. 1735).
67. Ibid.: ordinance of 1680, art. 10.
68. GAD, St. Joris: nr: 59-1, fos. 81 and 85.
69. SAH, 242-1-I: nr. C1-2, p. 168; (B) Streng 1890: 54–55.
70. GAD, St. Joris: nr. 59-1, fos. 137 and 139v–140v; GAH, Burg. Resol.: 14 March 1661 (fo. 52).
71. SAH, 242-1-I: A29-1; C1-1; C1-2 (passim). (B) Streng (1890: 56) mentions a case in the *zuchthaus* in 1743 where a prisoner was flogged by an unmasked fellow inmate.
72. For England: (B) Slice 1936: 64; Stockdale 1977: 43–44.
73. SAB, 2-D. 18. d: dossier 6b1 (1747–1748).
74. (B) Stekl 1978: 204.
75. (A) Wagnitz, 2: 53–54 and 3: 60–61; (B) Streng 1890: 55; Schmidt 1915: 54–55/ 288–289; Lieberknecht 1921: 38–39, Emmermann 1921: 45; Jetter 1971: 102; Schubert 1983: 303; Stier 1988: 81, 99–101.
76. GAD, St. Joris: nrs. 59-1, fos. 60v, 82, 140, 112–114, and 59-2, fo. 169–v; SAH, 242-1-I: nrs. C1-1, p. 109 and C1-2, p. 184.
77. GAD, St. Joris: nr. 59-2, fo. 202v–204v. The name of the court was "committee of justice" then, but the regents used the word *schepenen.*
78. Officially, this seems to have been the case in England, too, but a tip for the keeper usually gained people admittance: (B) Beier 1985: 168.
79. GAD, St. Joris: nr. 59-2, fos. 30–37, 41–42, 53.
80. GAD, St. Joris: nr. 59-2, fo. 23–25v. She did not reappear in the logbook. The court records (Oud-Rechterlijk Archief: nr. 51, fo. 169v, where she is called Anna Maria Wijnmaalen) confirm that in 1772 she had been condemned to imprisonment and banishment, each for 8 years, for prostitution. She was then 20 years old and living with her mother and sister. A marginal remark referred just to her pardon on the centennial day, but St. Joris: nr. 118 reveals that she was released on 4 April 1778. The 1765 ceremony: St. Joris: nr. 59-1, fo. 129v–130v. In 1767 the Court of Holland allowed a Haarlem prisoner to stay in the *tuchthuis* as a servant, his banishment being commuted to a confinement: GAH, Werkhuis: nr. 14.
81. GAD, St. Joris: nr. 69 (dossier 1736). See also dossier 1757 (16 Dec.) and Stad, nr. 2120a, p. 183 for recommendations for reduction to other courts by the regents.
82. By the court of The Hague: GAD, St. Joris: nr. 69 (16 January 1777).
83. GAD, St. Joris: nrs. 59-2, fo. 56 and 69 (dossier 1782).

84. (B) Spierenburg 1978: 183.
85. Compare GAA, 345: nrs. 1, pp. 1–6 and 3 (dossier 1777).
86. If the parallellism would be pursued, we would have to liken hell to capital punishment. However, one Polish 15th-century author compared a stay in hell to one *in carcere perpetuo:* (B) Bylina 1987: 1237.
87. GAH, Burg. Resol.: 4 March 1648 (fo. 60v).
88. GAA, 5059: nr. 34, p. 367.
89. SAH, 242-1-I: nr. C1-1, nrs. 27, 30, 43. The earliest references to medical attention for prisoners are in the records of the Hamburg *zuchthaus:* nr. A14-1, fos. 16vs, 55, 121.
90. The 1602 plague epidemic in Amsterdam did not strike the rasphouse: (A) Pontanus 1614: 136–137; Historie 1612. No prison epidemics are mentioned in the sources or the literature I studied, except in the case of the prison at Waldheim, which was ravaged by four severe epidemics between 1719 and 1755: (B) Jetter 1971: 96. Plague epidemics also struck the institution at Copenhagen in its early years, but most victims were children from the asylum associated with the prison: Olsen 1978: 104–107.
91. SAH, 242-1-I: nr. C1-1, p. 88.
92. SAH, 242-1-I: nr. A29-1, p. 100.
93. SAH, 242-1-I: nr. C1-2, pp. 8, 110, 133, 230.
94. SAH, 242-1-I: nr. A29-1, pp. 139–140 and C1-2, p. 121.
95. SAH, 242-1-I: nr. A29-1, p. 149 and C1-2, p. 130.
96. GAH, Burg. Resol.: 3 Dec. 1706; 10 Jan. 1708; 18 March 1751 (fos. 158v, 10, 27v).
97. Document published in (B) Hallema 1953b: 188.
98. (B) Streng 1890: 29; Lieburg 1982.
99. GAD, St. Joris: nr. 59-1, fo. 133.
100. GAD, St. Joris: nr. 118. The register actually ends in 1804, but its bad state prohibited quantification for the period after 1791.
101. (B) Faber 1983: 199.
102. (B) Diederiks 1982: 51–52.
103. SAH, 242-1-I: nrs. C1-1, p. 56 and C1-2, p. 120.
104. SAH, 242-1-I: nrs. C1-1 and C1-2. A deceased inmate in Bremen was buried at the cemetery of the Stephen's church, close to the prison: SAB, 2-D. 18. d: dossier 6d (2 Jan. 1690).
105. GAD, St. Joris:: nr. 59-2, fo. 49v.
106. GAD, St. Joris:: nr. 59-1, fo. 128v.
107. AHL, Bürgerschaft: nr. 120-9 (1701).
108. SAH, 242-1-I: nr. C1-1, p. 159.
109. SAH, 242-1-I: nr. C1-1, p. 44.
110. SAH, 242-1-I: nr. C1-1, p. 106.
111. (B) Mayer 1987: 214.
112. GAD, St. Joris: nr. 69, dossier 1800 (report of 31 Oct.).
113. SAH, 242-1-I: nr. A29-1, pp. 198–200.
114. For a few exceptions, see: GAD, St. Joris: nr. 59-2, fo. 49; GAA, 5061: nrs. 328, fo. 162v–163v and 593, fo. 108v.
115. GAD, St. Joris: nr. 69 (dossier 1799).
116. SAH, 242-1-I: nr. A14-1, fo. 93v–94.
117. SAH, 242-1-I: nrs. A29-1, p. 201 and C1-2, pp. 168 and 200.
118. GAD, Stad: nr. 2120a, fos. 15 and 17.
119. GAA, 5061: nrs. 316, fos. 63 and 70, and 585, fo. 20.
120. GAU, Stad: nr. 1043, fo. 77v.
121. GAA, 5061: nrs. 398, fo. 182–186v, and 399, fo.4.
122. GAD, St. Joris: nr. 59-1, fo. 70–1.
123. GAD, Stad: nr. 2120a (pp. 31 and 106) and Oud-Rechterlijk Archief: nr. 51, fos. 63, 82v.
124. (B) Ebeling 1935: 55.
125. It was only between 1643 and 1645, when the spinhouse was being rebuilt after a fire, that men and women stayed together in the rasphouse: (A) Wagenaar 1760–1768, 8: 246.
126. (B) Kappen 1987: 329.

127. (B) Zysberg 1987: 161–162.
128. GAD, St. Joris: nr. 59-2, fo. 42v–43. The only other reference to sodomy in early modern prisons is in (B) Streng 1890: 55. According to him, nine inmates of the *zuchthaus* were transferred to the spinhouse because of this offense in 1744.
129. *"met andere vrouwluyden in een hok geseten hebbende, veele vuyle gyligheeden van tijt tot tijt pleegden"*: ARA, HvH: nr. 300 (24 November 1746). Unfortunately, this was in a period when almost nothing was recorded in the logbook of the Delft regents.
130. (B) O'Brien 1982: 62–63, 90–108, 208–209.
131. (B) Mayer, 1987: 185–189.
132. (B) Stier 1988: 111, 153.
133. Other cases reported in the literature involved a governor of the London Bridewell who was accused of being the father of an inmate's child in 1630, and a male inmate and a female inmate of the Groningen prison in 1669: (B) Beier 1985: 168; Kampman 1986: 99. French galley convicts in the first half of the eighteenth century were reported to have been surrounded by prostitutes when they stayed in the harbor: Zysberg 1987: 156–160.
134. SAH, 242-1-I: nr. A14-1, fo. 137.
135. SAH, 242-1-I: nr. C1-2, p. 117; (B) Streng 1890: 55–57.
136. GAD, St. Joris: nr. 59-1, fo. 116–v.
137. GAD, St. Joris: nr. 59-1, fos. 102–v and 108.
138. GAD, St. Joris: nr. 59-2, fo. 22v.
139. The case is referred to in the logbook (GAD, St. Joris: nr. 59-2, fos. 194v and 205) and in the *fiscaalboek* of the Delfland court (ARA, 3.03.08: Oud-Rechterlijk Archief Delfland, nr. 4: 19 March and 2 April 1801; copy in GAD, St. Joris: nr. 69, 19 March 1801). The Delfland court merely notified the Delft regents by letter. They recorded the reception of the letter in question without further comment. The two remaining cases of confirmed personnel-inmate sex are found in GAD, St. Joris: nrs. 59-1, fo. 137v; 59-2, fo. 123; 69 (13 Dec. 1790).
140. GAD, Oud-Rechterlijk Archief: nr. 51, fo. 150–154 and St. Joris: nr. 59-1, fo. 141–142.
141. SAH, 242-1-I; nr. A29-1, p. 139.
142. Ibid.: pp. 172–183, 195–197, 201, and nr. C1-2, pp. 128, 142, 150. (B) Streng (1890: 89) devotes just a few lines to the case.
143. The logbook (A29-1, p. 182) says that the child was found; the entry book (C1-2, p. 142) says that Anna Glotz voluntarily showed it to the provisors. Possibly, both events took place, one shortly after the other.
144. GAD, Stad: nr. 2002–19 (24 Nov. 1738, 23 Feb. and 15 April 1739) and St. Joris: nr. 59-2, fo. 144–v.
145. GAD, St. Joris: nr. 59-2, fo. 308.
146. In 1791 it was stated that released women often failed to pick up their children: GAD, St. Joris: nr. 69 (dossier 1791).
147. SAH, 242-1-I: nrs. C1-1, p. 55[1] and C1-2, pp. 41 and 143.
148. SAH, 242-1-I: nr. C1-2, pp. 183–184.
149. SAH, 242-1-I: nrs. A29-1, p. 131 and C1-2, p. 16. A29-1 fixes the execution at 27 August; C1-2 at 3 September.
150. SAH, 242-1-I: nr. C1-2, p. 110.
151. SAH, 242-1-I: nrs. A29-1, pp. 155–159 and C1-2, pp. 134, 138, 289.
152. SAH, 242-1-I: nr. A29-1, pp. 156–158.
153. SAH, 242-1-I: nr. C1-2, p. 161.
154. SAH, 242-1-I: nr. C1-2, pp. 214, 218, 234. Also p. 234 (and (B) Streng 1890: 28–29) for comparable problems in the *zuchthaus*.
155. SAH, 242-1-I: nr. C1-1, p. 23.
156. SAH, 242-1-I: nrs. C1-1, pp. 40, 96, 125 and A29-1, p. 155. See also (B) Streng 1890: 75–76.
157. SAH, 242-1-I: nrs C1-1, p. 204; C1-2, p. 1; A29-1, p. 202. A comparable case took place in the Utrecht *tuchthuis* in 1624: GAU, Stad: nr. 1043, fo. 5.
158. GAU, Stad: nr. 1043, fos. 23v–24 and 59v.
159. GAU, Stad: nr. 1043, fos. 9 and 40v.
160. (A) Wagenaar 1760–1768, VIII: 242.
161. GAL, Oud-Rechterlijk Archief: nr. 28, fo. 93v.

162. GAH, Oud-Rechterlijk Archief: nr. 66-2, fo. 224.

16f. (B) Streng 1890: 58, 88–89.

164. GAA, 5061: nr. 571, fo. 138.

165. GAD, St. Joris: nr. 59-1, fo. 80-v.

166. GAD, St. Joris: nr. 59-1, fo. 137v–140. Further trouble with Bottenol (then called Bodinot) is recorded in 59-2, fo. 16.

167. SAH, 242-1-I: nr. A14-1, fos. 127v, 140, 146v–147.

168. Reviewed in (B) Spierenburg 1988b: 284.

170. Apart from entry books, quantitative evidence is available for Brussels. In 20 years in the 18th century for which there were records, 81 persons, including 6 women, escaped: (B) Bruneel 1966b: 249.

171. GAH, Oud-Rechterlijk Archief: nr. 66-2, fo. 267v.

172. GAH, Burg. Resol.: 6 March 1624.

173. GAU, Stad: nr. 1043, fo. 4v.

174. SAH, 242-1-I: nr. Cl-2, pp. 1 and 34–35. No connection between the two cases was recorded.

175. GAA, 5061: nrs. 314, fos. 166, 182; 584, fo. 100v–102v; 585, fo. 114v.

176. GAD, St. Joris: nr. 59-2, pp. 16 and 202v.

177. GAD, St. Joris: nr. 59-2, fos 65v, 67–68, 70–72, 81–v, 83, 84–v, 112–114, 125v–127v and Stad: nr. 2120a, p. 184. The 1733 case is the only reference to prisoners sleeping in hammocks, which may have been used in periods of overcrowding when there was too little room in a cage for a mattress for each inmate.

178. SAH, 242-1-I: nr. A29-1, pp. 83–86.

179. SAH, 242-1-I: nrs. Cl-1, pp. 202 and 204; Cl-2, pp. 1 and 14; A29-1, pp. 96 and 98.

180. GAD, St. Joris: nr. 59-1, fo. 63–64; GAA, 5061: nr. 407. fo. 14(2) and 14(3). The 1726 case is expounded more elaborately in (B) Spierenburg 1988b: 281–282.

181. GAU, Stad: nr. 1043, fo. 87v–88.

182. SAH, 242-1-I; nr. A29-1, pp. 137–138.

183. SAH, 242-1-I: nr. Cl-2, pp. 166, 184, 188.

184. GAD, Stad: nr. 2120a, p. 177.

185. GAD, Oud-Rechterl. Archief: nr. 51, fo. 92 and Stad: nr. 2120a, p. 56.

186. On Jan Alofs: (B) Spierenburg 1984a: 75.

187. GAA, 5061: nrs. 291, fo. 172–174 and 533, fo. 2v–3. Other cases in the rasphouse: GAA, 5061: nrs. 291, fo. 170v–171v and 571, fo. 136–139. In the second case the prisoners also obtained a temporary transfer to jail.

188. SAB, 2-D. 18. d: dossier nr. 5 (1754–1757).

189. GAA, 5061: nr. 311, fo. 191–193. Delft case in (B) Spierenburg 1988b: 281.

190. GAA, 5061: nrs. 366, fo. 29v-32v and 381, fos. 60 and 67v.

191. GAD, St. Joris: nr. 59-1, fo. 68v–69v.

192. SAH, 242-1-I: nrs. A29-1, pp. 16–17 and Cl-1, pp. 2 et seq. Also in (B) Streng 1890: 74. The women first had enjoyed themselves in the spinhouse, so their determination was apparently not that great.

193. SAH, 242-1-I: nr. Cl-1, p. 68.

194. SAH, 242-1-I: nr. Cl-2, pp. 198 and 202.

195. GAD, St. Joris: nr. 59-1, fo. 88–89v.

196. GAA, 5061: nrs. 367, fo. 105v and 320, fo. 72.

197. GAD, St. Joris: nr. 59-1, fo. 75–v.

198. SAB, 2-D. 18. d: dossier 6b1 (17 August 1746).

199. GAA, 5061: nrs. 348, fos. 73v–85, 159v–162, 182, 184v, 214v, 216; 367, fos. 98v, 104v–105. 116v–117; 375, fo. 232–233; GAD, St. Joris: nr. 59-1, fo. 74–75v.

200. (B) Rückleben 1970; Loose 1982: 277–286; Whaley 1985: 56–63 and passim. The following paragraph is based on these works.

201. (B) Streng 1890: 84–85, 88. He has a few errors of detail.

202. (B) Whaley 1985: 13.

203. See Chapter 6, note 3.

204. SAH, 242-1-I: nr. A29-1, p. 80.

205. (B) Rückleben 1970: 83–93, 98–99.

206. SAH, 242-1-I: nr. A29-1, pp. 95–99, 116–119, 154, 160–167, 175, 184–192.

207. SAH, 242-1-I: nr. C1-2, p. 245. In the entry book his name is spelled Altwähser; in the other sources it is Altwasser. Sometimes his first name is Germanized into Reinhold.

208. SAH, 242-1-I: nr. C1-1, p. 203.

209. SAH, 242-1-I: nrs. A29-1, pp. 216–220 and C1-2, p. 245.

210. The text is referred to in the logbook but not inserted there. It survives in SAH, Senatsacten: C1. VII, Lit. Mb, nr. 2, vol. 3d. Seven appendices (A-G) are referred to, both there and in the logbook, but I was unable to trace them.

211. They are: Frans von Som (a); Jürgen Westphalen (b); Vincent Moller (c); Jacob Volckmann (d); Johan Adrian Boon (e). I looked for the names in the index of (B) Reissmann 1975 with the following results: The families of (a) and (b) had become great merchants in the course of the 17th century (p. 272); (c) was a merchant trading with Flanders in 1715 (p. 163); someone with the same name as (d) is listed, without a date, as a senator (p. 225); (e) was the son of a senator in 1682 and was later elected into the senate himself (p. 157).

212. (B) Rückleben 1970: 299.

213. SAH, 242-1-I: nr. A29-1, pp. 220–222a.

214. They are listed in the entry book: SAH, 242-1-I: nr. C1-2 (the nonparticipant on p. 202).

215. SAH, 242-1-I: nr. C1-2, p. 210.

216. SAH, 242-1-I: nr. A29-1, pp. 222b–223.

217. SAH, Senatsacten: C1. VII, Lit. Mb, nr. 2, vol. 3g.

218. They shared such an attitude with a number of Dutch robbers. See (B) Egmond 1986: 75–76.

219. SAH, 242-1-I: nr. A29-1, pp. 225–226, 233.

220. SAH, 242-1-I: nr. C1-2, pp. 211, 253.

221. SAB, 2-D. 18. d: dossier 6a (11 March 1711).

Chapter Nine.   Elites and the Poor

1. Seggelke 1928: 49.

2. Fosseyeux 1929: 39.

3. Document published in Ysselt 1920.

4. SAH, 242-1-I: nr. A14-1, fo. 3v.

5. GAD, Stad: nr. 2010-3 (excerpt from *keurboek* nr. 8, 18 Dec. 1662). That not just the insane were committed is confirmed by the imprisonment of Willem Bolnes, Vermeer's brother-in-law, in the house of Taarling for misconduct in the 1660s: (B) Montias 1989: 154–170.

6. GAA, 5020: nr. R, fo. 40v–41: "kwaadaardige en hardnekkige personen."

7. For an earlier analysis of the Leiden data, see my contribution to (B) Diederiks et al. 1985; for the Leiden and Rotterdam data: Spierenburg 1986. The Dordrecht series was analyzed, under my supervision, by Jannemieke Geessink; see Geessink 1987 and 1989. See these articles generally for problems of sources and method.

8. (B) Geessink 1987: 54.

9. See (B) Farge and Foucault 1982. In their introduction they state that they suspect the archives in question to be incomplete, but this is probably compensated for by the fact that the dossiers also include cases where a committal was refused or not put into effect. With few exceptions, the Dutch dossiers refer only to actual cases of imprisonment, as far as initial requests are concerned.

10. See (B) Emmanuelli 1974. His series, assuming it is complete, counted 1,052 initial requests by families during 1745–1789. In 1778–1787 the population of Provence was about 676,000 (see *Histoire de la population française,* ed. by Jacques Dûpaquier, Paris 1988, 2: 76). I could not calculate the figure for Normandy from Quétel 1978, because on page 131 this author says he has 1,723 cases, while on page 140, where he divides them into men and women, the total adds up to 1,273.

11. GAR, Schepenen: nr. 283, fo. 320.

12. (B) Geessink 1987: 40.

13. GAR, Schepenen: nr. 283, fo. 162.

14. (B) Spierenburg 1986: 122–123.

15. Two volumes: GAD, Stad: nrs. 2031 and 2031a.
16. See the table in (B) Spierenburg 1984b: 48.
17. Amounts referred to subsequently in the text are in guilders, unless otherwise mentioned.
18. GAL, Secretarie: nr. 9328, fo. 236–237.
19. Compare GAL, Secretarie: nr. 9303, fo. 138.
20. GAR, Schepenen: nr. 280, fo. 198–199.
21. GAR, Notarieel: nr. 2129, fo. 1045.
22. GAH, Burg. Resol.: 1634 (fo. 188v).
23. GAH, Werkhuis: nr. 14 (undated document, after 1747).
24. GA Utrecht, Bewaarde Archieven II: nr. 2635.
25. (B) Geessink 1987: 33–34.
26. (B) Garrer 1929: 30–31.
27. ARA, HvH: nr. 4930, dossiers 1795 and 1797.
28. (B) Woude 1980: 261–262; Diederiks 1982: 356.
29. In detail in (B) Spierenburg 1986: 127–130.
30. (B) Geessink 1987: 86–87, 131–136.
31. (B) Emmanuelli 1974: 376.
32. (B) Castan 1980: 269.
33. (B) Farge and Foucault 1982: 9. In note 2 (p. 364) they explain, again without specification, that "a socio-professional analysis" of their sources shows that from half to two thirds of the petitioners were *"gens de petite condition."* They opposed their findings to Emmanuelli's, referring to a nonexistent page of his article, though.
34. Figures for Dordrecht and Provence from (B) Geessink 1987: 78 and Emmanuelli 1974: 373. Emmanuelli seems to have computed one category of relatives per request. Most frequently, this was one person and sometimes a group, usually consisting of two persons, such as the parents-in-law. Therefore, I combined the categories "parents" and "father." I also had to calculate the percentages anew: in the text, Emmanuelli says that the total was 642, but his numbers add up to 638.
35. (B) Farge and Foucault 1982: 23.
36. SAB, 2-D. 18. d: dossier 6b1 (27 Feb. 1715; 7 Sept. 1730; 11 April 1178). In Hamburg, too, unlike in Holland, married women, were always called by their husband's surname.

Chapter Ten.   Drunks, Revellers, and the Insane

1. (B) Emmanuelli 1974: 376.
2. (B) Farge and Foucault 1982: 157 (table) and 165.
3. For more-detailed data, see (B) Spierenburg 1986: 136-6 and Geessink 1987.
4. (B) Emmanuelli 1974: 375. The same percentage is reported for Normandy, where, there is no information on social status, however: Quétel 1978: 140, 147. On the other hand, among the prisoners committed to a private institution in the Leiden sample, only 56% were male; in the Rotterdam sample this group numbered just a few cases.
5. ARA, HvH: nrs. 4929, 4930, 6086, 6087; (B) Garrer 1929.
6. GAD, Oud-Rechterlijk: nrs. 50, fo. 155v–147 and 123; ARA, HvH: nr. 5659, fo. 90 and Hoge Raad: nr. 806, fo. 75–79v.
7. GAD, Stad: nr. 2002–13, fo. 42v.
8. ARA, HvH: nr. 6087, dossier 1739.
9. ARA, HvH: nr. 6087, dossier 1743 (referring to 1741). A similar case in the prison at St. Gallen in 1766 involved the master of discipline's daughter and a man from Zürich who had been committed by his family. The woman got pregnant. See (B) Mayer 1987: 187–188.
10. GAL, Secretarie: nrs. 9328, fos. 265–266 and 9337, fos. 122–123.
11. ARA, HvH: nr. 4930, dossier 1790; (B) Garrer 1929: 23–24.
12. ARA, HvH: nr. 6087, dossier 1743.
13. (B) Jansen 1978: 86. This author is unclear about the character of his sources and gives few exact figures. Therefore, the Maastricht data could not be considered for my quantitative analysis.

14. The average for the 1800 group is biased because I fixed the year of exit for three prisoners at 1811. These three were still in the *beterhuis* at the last visitation in 1810. In 1811 the Court of Holland was abolished and its private prisoners could not be traced in other archives.

15. (B) Farge and Foucault 1982: 355.

16. ARA, HvH: nr. 6086, dossier 1760.

17. In various dossiers of the Court of Holland sample. For the 1680s: (B) Garrer 1929.

18. ARA, HvH: nr. 6087, dossier 1740.

19. ARA, HvH: nr. 6086, dossier 1762.

20. ARA, HvH: nrs 4929 (dossier 1753), 6087 (dossiers 1735–40 and 1732), 6086 (dossier 1763).

21. GAH, Werkhuis: nr. 14 (undated document, after 1747).

22. See my more elaborate analysis of the Leiden sample in (B) Diederiks et al. 1985: 131–132.

23. (B) Geessink 1987: 116.

24. Quoted in (B) Geessink 1987: 64.

25. (B) Geessink 1987: 103–107.

26. SAB, 2-D. 18. d: dossier 6b1 (30 Sept. 1727). It is unclear where exactly the petitioners wished to confine their brother. They speak of a *"zucht-oder verbesserungshaus."* The latter word is the exact equivalent of the Dutch *beterhuis*, but I cannot tell whether it refers to a separate ward of the prison workhouse at Celle or to a separate institution there. If it was the latter, we would have evidence for the existence of at least one private prison in the Empire.

27. SAB, 2-D. 18. d: dossier 6b1 (27 Feb. 1715; 30 April 1731; 20 March 1767).

28. (B) Farge and Foucault 1982: 353–355.

29. Compare (B) Foucault 1975 and my criticism of this position in Spierenburg 1984a: 203.

30. (B) Elias 1969, vol. 1.

31. (B) Funck-Brentano 1903: xxxvii–xxxviii.

32. I agree with (B) Szasz (1961) that "mental illness" does not really exist. Consequently, the medical view of insanity has to be explained historically.

33. (B) Vié 1930: 138–142.

34. ARA, HvH: nr. 291 (11 Nov. 1728).

35. See (B) Hunter and Macalpine 1963: 265–267. Strangely, this work is not discussed in Bender 1987, despite ample attention paid to Defoe.

36. (B) Parry-Jones 1972: 9.

37. (B) Byrd 1974: 44.

38. On the accusation of abuse: (B) Parry-Jones 1972; Byrd 1974: 40–44; on similar criticism in the 17th century: Beier 1985: 169. See also Christianson 1985 on the crown's prerogative, contested in the Stuart period, of jailing persons who refused to pay taxes.

39. GAD, Stad: nr. 2022, first page.

40. GAR, Schepenen: nr. 283, fo. 322–323.

41. ARA, HvH: nr. 4930, dossier 1790.

42. GAL, Secretarie: nr. 9297, fo. 64.

43. GAL, Secretarie: nr. 9309, fo. 238v.

44. GAL, Secretarie: nr. 9334, fo. 230.

45. ARA, HvH: nr. 6086 (dossiers 1770 and 1768).

46. GA Alkmaar, Oud-Rechterlijk Archief: nr. 10, fo. 97–101v and Notarieel Archief: nr. 525, fos. 99 et seq. and 103A et seq. See also (B) Loo 1984: 100–105. I am indebted to Mr. Van Loo for providing me with these references.

47. (B) Quétel 1981b.: 76–79.

48. (A) Wagnitz 1791–1794, 2: 165–174; Brock 1808.

49. (B) Sérieux and Trénel 1931: 454–456.

50. (B) Petitfils 1975: 54; Quétel 1981a: 29–39.

51. (B) Emmanuelli 1974: 357–358.

52. (B) Funck-Brentano 1903: xlii–xlv; Sérieux 1932: 453–462; Farge and Foucault 1982: 357–363.

53. See Diederiks and Spierenburg in (B) Petit 1984: 43–44, 50.

54. (B) Sérieux 1932; 462; Schnapper 1980. This method was used by fathers until 1914; it was formally abolished in 1935.

55. (B) Fessler 1956.
56. For an overview of the history of madness in preindustrial Europe, see (B) Spierenburg 1988a: Chapter 6.
57. ARA, HvH: nr. 6087, dossier 1734.
58. (B) Parry-Jones 1972: 6–28, 282–284.
59. (B) Binneveld and van Lieburg 1979.
60. On moral treatment, see (B) Binneveld 1985: 16–22.
61. (B) Jetter 1971: 11–27.
62. (B) Chijs 1886: 25.
63. Of course, this changed again with the further breakthrough of a medical approach to insanity, in the form of a biologically oriented psychiatry, in the second half of the nineteenth century. By then, being called insane was no longer acceptable to a family, because the defect was hereditary. The age of moral treatment was a transitional era, in which moral and medical terms were fused and physicians acquired control over the mad.

Chapter Eleven.   Crossroads

1. See Chapter 3.
2. Figures for Amsterdam in (B) Jüngen 1979: 60–61. On galley warfare in the Netherlands, see Lehmann 1984. Lehmann's study is purely technical and he does not say who manned the Dutch galleys.
3. (B) Hallema 1953a: 69–83.
4. GAD, Oud-Rechterlijk Archief: nr. 53. The total number of sentences was counted from a card system that included abstracts from the criminal records.
5. (B) Hallema (1953a: 81–2) supposes that the majority of oarsmen were vagrants arrested by the *landdrost,* but he fails to document this.
6. King Louis Napoleon suggested including galley servitude for burglary in the penal code of 1809. This idea was vehemently opposed because the penalty was considered contrary to Dutch national character. The opponents even thought it had never been practiced in the Netherlands. See (B) Binsbergen 1949: 25.
7. See Chapter 3.
8. (A) Resolutien Holland: 10 Jan. 1648 (p. 364) and 18 March 1648 (pp. 470–472).
9. (B) Voss 1958: 15.
10. (A) Handvesten 1748: 578–579. Quoted formula in: GAA, 5061: nr. 595, fo. 44v.
11. The 12 delinquents who were punished on the scaffold form an absolute number. In addition, about forty delinquents who had not been punished on the scaffold must have been sent to Surinam, since two cases entered my sample of nonpublic punishments.
12. (B) Voss 1958: 28–30.
13. To be concluded from my sample of nonpublic punishments. In 1694, beggars were still threatened with transportation to Surinam upon their second arrest; when the ordinance in question was reissued in 1697, the reference to transportation was dropped: GAA, 5020: nr. R, fos. 37v and 94.
14. (B) Schubert 1983: 292–293.
15. (B) Streng 1890: 79–82. See also SAH, 242-1-I: nr. A41, where the first document (1751) is on the recruitment of settlers to Nova Scotia. But it does not speak of convicts.
16. SAH, 242-1-I: nr. A41; (B) Hippel (Reinhard) 1986: 441.
17. (B) Ebeling 1935: 3–17.
18. SAB, 2-D. 18. d: dossiers 1a (1 Sept. 1717); 6b1 (7 Oct. 1724); 6a (1732).
19. (B) Sothmann 1970: 66–67.
20. (B) Schmidt 1915: 12–13/ 246–247, 60/ 294; Reekers 1981: 52.
21. (B) Falck 1838: 773–774.
22. (B) Wilbertz 1979: 93. At Wesel forced labor at the ramparts was discontinued when the town founded a *zuchthaus* in 1776: Reekers 1981: 35.
23. (B) Ebeling 1935: 67–72.
24. See, especially, (B) Innes 1987 and Beattie 1986: 492–493. The phases I distinguish are based on a combination of the chronologies by these authors. Innes's article is the main reference for the evolution of houses of correction; Beattie (Chapters 9 and 10) gives a detailed account of the history of punishment in England, 1660–1800.
25. (B) Innes 1987: 45, 47–58, 68; Sharpe 1984: 180; Beattie 1986: 492–500. The

tentativeness of these conclusions is illustrated by Innes's formulation: "imprisonment in bridewell *must* have been one of the penal sanctions most commonly deployed to punish offences of this kind" (45; my emphasis).

26. From 1706 to about 1718, though, a first wave of felons was sentenced to houses of correction is relatively large numbers: (B) Beattie 1986: 492–494; Innes 1987: 88–89.

27. James Sharpe, The judicial world in its local context: the evidence of English Justices' notebooks, a paper presented at the 16th IAHCCJ-colloquium, Paris, 18–19 December 1987, with reference to his publication of Holcroft's notebook.

28. (B) Innes 1987: 62.

29. (B) Innes 1987: 85, 88.

30. (B) Beattie 1986: 550.

31. Paper by Sharpe (see note 27).

32. (B) DeLacy 1986: 36.

33. (B) Innes 1987: 76, 91–92.

34. Quoted in (B) Smith 1947: 92–93.

35. (B) Beattie 1986: 473–483.

36. (B) Ekirch 1987: 17; Beattie 1986: 504.

37. (B) Beattie 1986: 507.

38. (B) Innes 1987: 95–96.

39. (B) Ekirch 1987: 26–27, 43, 48–51, 112–114, 124, 138. This author provides an excellent analysis of the entire system.

40. (B) Beattie 1986: 520–539.

41. (B) Schmidt 1915: 65/ 299.

42. (B) Beattie 1986: 546.

43. (B) Beattie 1986: 568. On Howard, see Morgan 1977.

44. (B) Beattie 1986: 573–618; Ignatieff 1978: 28–132; Innes 1987: 98–111; DeLacy 1986: 79–94; Whiting 1979: 24–30.

45. (B) Beattie 1986: 612.

46. (B) Benabou 1987: 85–89; Schwartz 1988: 28–34. In 1719–1720 a number of smugglers and marginals were transported, too.

47. (B) Deyon 1975: 41.

48. (B) Hufton 1974: 139; Schwartz 1988: 13.

49. (B) Schwartz 1988: 95–96.

50. (B) Hufton 1974: 150.

51. (B) Hufton 1974: 155–157; Fairchilds 1976: 29–37; Jones 1982: 61; Schwartz 1988: 41–44.

52. (B) Cameron 1981: 158.

53. Quétel 1981a: 181–185; Benabou 1987: 79–80, 407–414.

54. (B) Williams 1979: 233–234; Benabou 1987: 82–83.

55. (B) Williams 1979: 232, 235.

56. (B) Benabou 1987: 84–85. See also pp. 89–95 on a few smaller prisons where prostitutes were confined.

57. (B) Farge 1974: 84.

58. Report to Lübeck: AHL, Senate; nr. 1, dossier 5.

59. (B) Schwartz 1988: 154–242; Hufton 1974: 230–244; Jones 1982: 140–155; Gutton 1970: 452–457. In some cases, such as at Dijon, plans to establish a *dépôt* did not materialize and beggars continued to be committed to the *hôpital:* Bigorre 1967: 42–44.

60. (B) Deyon 1975: 42.

61. (B) Zysberg 1987: 64–116.

62. (B) Zysberg 1987: 117–148.

63. (B) Ruff 1984: 59.

64. (B) Farge 1974: 84.

65. (B) Zysberg 1987: 364–371. Percentages of terms were calculated from table 14 (p. 373; see also p. 65 for information leading to the inference that in the first period 13.8% of the terms are missing). For mortality figures, see table 11 (p. 349). Reductions and longer stays are calculated from tables 13 and 15 (pp. 369, 374). These calculations cannot be precise because Zysberg groups the terms into crude categories, sometimes comprising more than one year.

66. André Zysberg in (B) Spierenburg 1984b: 111–120.

67. (B) Castan 1976: 347–352.
68. (B) Farge 1974: 84.
69. Calculated from the tables in (B) Castan 1980: 279, 281. See p. 273 of Castan's study for a specification of the table sources.
70. (B) Pike 1983.
71. (B) Callahan 1971; Pike 1983: 54–57.
72. (B) Sellin 1929; Scarabello 1979: 189.
73. (B) Cozzi 1980: 217–218.
74. (B) Scarabello 1979: 184; Cozzi 1980: 322–323, 427.
75. (A) Wagnitz 1791–1794, 2: 237–283.
76. (B) Mayer 1987: 99–100.
77. (B) Olsen 1978: 39.
78. Information kindly provided by Bengt Ankarloo from his research notes.
79. (B) Wieselgren 1895: 142–162.
80. (B) Haesenne-Peremans 1983: 17–45.
81. (B) Maes 1947: 450–451; Vanhemelryck 1981: 216.
82. (B) Bruneel 1967: 42, 56.
83. (B) Maes 1947: 36–37, 459.
84. (B) Stroobant 1900: 221–239; Lis 1976: 155; GA Antwerpen, Vierschaar: nr. 1645 (dossiers 1770s).
85. GA Antwerpen, Vierschaar: nrs. 282, 283, 1822 (dossiers on individual committals, 1779–1793; the cited case is in nr. 282, 25 September 1779).
86. (B) Shaw 1966; Rudé 1978.
87. (B) Pierre 1982; Wright 1983: 129–152.
88. (B) Sellin 1976: 163–176.

Chapter Twelve.   Conclusion

1. (B) Ekirch 1987: 3, 20, 118. Beattie (1986: 502), on the other hand, argues that Englishmen in 1718 found imprisonment not severe enough compared to transportation.
2. (B) Zysberg 1987: 19–39; Pike 1983: 18, 77.
3. (B) Smith 1947: 124; Ekirch 1987: 92–93.
4. (A) Ward 1955: 105–111.
5. (B) Sothmann 1970: 150–151, 159–164, 223. See also appendix 1 with Paul Wolfgang Merkel's criticism in 1798. To be sure, Merkel only opposes the subjection of prostitutes and marginals to this form of labor and to imprisonment in the *zuchthaus* generally.
6. (B) Beattie 1986: 450–637.
7. (B) McGowen 1984.
8. For a discussion of that transformation and its relationship with state formation, see (B) Spierenburg 1984a: 183–207.

LIST OF ARCHIVAL SOURCES

Only the main series and documents used are listed here. They appear in the following order: country, record office, archive (sometimes the archive has its own number), inventory number. All abbreviations used in the notes are explained. Records consulted and not listed here have been given a complete reference in the notes.

Netherlands

Algemeen Rijks-Archief, **The Hague (ARA)**

3.03.01: *Hof van Holland* (HvH)

Nrs. 4929–4930, 6086–6087: Reports on the visitations to private prisoners committed at the authorization of the Court of Holland, 1729–1810.

3.20.52: *Familie-Archief Slingelandt/ De Vrij Temminck*

Nr. 465: Documents concerning the Amsterdam rasphouse, mid-18th century.

Gemeente-Archief Amsterdam **(GAA)**

345: Archive of the rasphouse (3 nrs.).

347: Archive of the spinhouse and the workhouse.

Nr. 39: Entry book of the spinhouse, 1678–1725.
Nrs. 116–125: Entry books of the workhouse, 1654–1754.
Nr. 562: Supervision of beggars, 1597–1598

5020: *Keurboeken* (A–T), 15th century to 1750

5059: *Handschriften*

Nrs. 24–40: Manuscripts by Hans Bontemantel, c. 1650 to c. 1672.
Nr. 72: *Memorie van de Regenten van het mannen Tuchthuijs,* c. 1750.

5061: *Oud-Rechterlijk Archief*

Nr. 268: *Examinatie Boeck,* 1658.
Nrs. 276–533: *Confessieboeken,* 1588–1811.

Gemeente-Archief Delft **(GAD)**

Stadsarchief I (Stad)

Nr. 2120a: *Register van Tuchtelingen,* Vol. 1: 1675–1733; Vol. 2: 1733–1752.
Nrs. 2031–2031a: Registers of private prisoners, 1699–1811.

Archief van het St. Jorisgasthuis (St. Joris)

Nr. 59 (3 vols.): Logbooks of the regents, 1677–1812.
Nr. 69: Various dossiers, 1664–1804.
Nr. 118: *Rekeningenboek der gevangenen,* 1759–1796.

Gemeente-Archief Haarlem **(GAH)**

Aalmoezeniers-Armen en Werkhuis (Werkhuis)

Nrs. 1–18: Archive of the prison workhouse.

Kasten en Laden: provisional inventory of various dossiers.

Burgemeestersresoluties (Burg. Resol.), 1598–1786
Vroedschapsresoluties (Vroeds. Resol.), 1590–1796
Handschriften
Nr. 153: Manuscripts by Pieter Langendijk, mid-18th century.
Oud-Rechterlijk Archief
Nr. 66-2: *Derde Register van den criminele sententiën,* 1602–1615.

Gemeente-Archief Leiden (GAL)

Stadsarchief, 1574–1816 (Stad)
Nr. 6522: Various dossiers on the Amsterdam rasphouse and the Leiden *tuchthuis,* c. 1590 to c. 1600.
Nrs. 6524–6529: Archive of the Leiden *tuchthuis.*
Secretarie-Archief
Nrs. 9290–9348 and 1021–1026: *Gerechtsdagboeken,* 1680–1805.

Gemeente-Archief Rotterdam (GAR)

Schepenen-archief (Schepenen)
Nrs. 280–285: Requests for confinement, 1712–1801.

Gemeente-Archief Utrecht (GAU)

Stadsarchief II (Stad)
Nr. 1043 *Notulen van regenten van het tuchthuis,* 1616–1633 (private logbook by Arend van Buchell).

German (Federal Republic)

Staatsarchiv Bremen (SAB)

2-D.18.d: *Zuchthaus*
(dossiers with documents which can be identified only by their date)
Nr. 1a: *Einrichtung und Ordnung,* 1604–1801.
Nr. 4: *Speisevater oder Oekonom,* 1695–1867.
Nr. 5: *Zuchtvogt oder Zuchtmeister,* 1711–1862.
Nr. 6: *Züchtlinge* (subdivided a–d).
Nr. 7: *Bau und Besserung,* 1608–1869.
Nr. 10: *Arbeit,* 1646–1769.
Nr. 11: *Raspmühle,* 1750.
Nr. 12: *Englische Besatzung,* 1761.
Revidiertes Verzeichnis des am 26.3.1987 aus der Deutschen Demokratischen Republic zurückgekehrten Schriftgutes (DDR)
Nr. 1203/ 3490: *Armenpflege und Armenwesen.*
Nr. 2308/ 6926: *Renner's Chronik.*

Staatsarchiv Hamburg (SAH)

111-1: *Senatsacten*
Classis VII, Lit. Mb, nr. 2 (*Gefängnisse*):
Vol. 2: *Roggenkiste*
Vol. 3: *Spinnhaus* (subdivided a–u)
242-1-I: *Gefängnisverwaltung*
Nr. A12: *Ordnung des Zuchthauses,* 1622 (also in A13).
Nr. A14-1: *Zuchthaus, Verwaltungsprotokollen, Band I,* 1625–1680.

Nr. A28: *Ordnung des Spinnhauses,* 1669.
Nr. A29-1: *Spinnhaus, Verwaltungsprotokollen, Band I,* 1670–1751.
Nr. A36-1: *Stellenbuch der Kirchen im Spinnhause,* 1682.
Nr. A41: Dossiers on transportation.
Nr. C1: *Spinnhaus, Aufnahmebücher:*
    Vol. 1: 1669–1688.
    Vol. 2: 1689–1715.

Archiv der Hansestadt Lübeck (**AHL**)

  Bürgerschaft II (Bürgerschaft)

Nr. 120: *St. Annen Armen- und Werckhaus* (subdivided 1–12).

  Senatsarchiv-Interna: Zucht- und Spinnhaus (Senate)

Nr. 1: *ältere Einrichtungen, neue Planung* (5 dossiers, numbered 1–5).

Belgium

Gemeente-Archief Antwerpen (**GA Antwerpen**)

  Archief van de Vierschaar (Vierschaar)

Nr. 1645: Documents relating to the *dwinghuis,* 1612–1779.
Nr. 1822: Documents relating to imprisonment, 1624–1793.

BIBLIOGRAPHY

A differentiation has been made between printed sources (A) and secondary literature (B). Part A includes works published before 1800 as well as contemporary manuscripts edited and published after that date. Because of the rarity of a number of these publications, the library where I consulted them has been listed in all cases (UB = University Library of Amsterdam).

A. Printed Sources

Battus, Carolus. 1650. *Secreet-boeck van vele diversche en heerlicke consten in veelderleye materien.* . . . Amsterdam (UB).

Baudartius, Gulielmus. 1624. *Memoryen ofte Cort Verhael der Gedenck-weerdichste so kercklicke als werltlicke gheschiedenissen.* . . . *Tweede editie, grootelicx vermeerdert.* 2 vols. Arnhem (Historical Institute, Amsterdam).

Blainville, J. de. 1743–1745. *Travels through Holland, Germany, Switzerland and other parts of Europe.* 3 vols. London (Koninklijke Bibliotheek, The Hague).

Blok, P. J., ed. 1909 *Relazioni Veneziane: Venetiaansche berichten over de Vereenigde Nederlanden van 1600–1795.* Den Haag (Historical Institute, Amsterdam).

Bontemantel, Hans. 1897 *De regeeringe van Amsterdam, soo in't civiel als crimineel en militaire, 1653–1672.* Ed. G. W. Kernkamp. 2 vols. Den Haag (Historical Institute, Amsterdam).

Bowrey, Thomas. 1927. *The papers of Thomas Bowrey, 1669–1713.* Ed. Richard Carnac Temple. London (UB).

Brandt, G[eeraert]. 1704. *Historie der Reformatie en andere kerkelyke geschiedenissen in en ontrent de Nederlanden.* Vol. 4. Rotterdam (UB).

Brock, Johann Franz. 1808. *Hamburgische Werk- und Zuchthaus-Sachen.* Hamburg (Staatsarchiv, Hamburg).

Brown, Edward. 1682. *Naukeurige en Gedenkwaardige Reysen van Edward Brown, M. Dr. afgesonden van 't Collegie tot Londen . . . door Nederland. . . . Uit het Engels vertaald door den Heer Jacob Leeuw.* Amsterdam (UB).

Commelin, Casparus. 1693. *Beschrijvinge van Amsterdam.* 2 vols. Amsterdam (UB).

Coornhert, Dirck Volkertszoon. 1630. "Boeventucht." *Idem, Wercken.* Vol. III. Amsterdam: 384–388 (UB).

D[apper], O[lfert]. 1663. *Historische Beschryving der Stadt Amsterdam.* Amsterdam (UB).

Dellaporta, Giambattista. 1593. *De humana physiognomonia.* Hanoviae (UB).

Erasmus, Desiderius. 1965. *The Colloquies of Erasmus.* Translated by Craig R. Thompson. Chicago: University of Chicago Press.

Evelyn, John. 1983. *Diary.* Selected and edited by John Bowle. Oxford, New York (UB).

Fielen. 1914. "Der Rabauwen oft der Schalcken Vocabulaer, ooc de beueysde manieren der bedeleeren oft bedelerssen. . . ." Victor de Meyere and Lode Baekelmans, eds., *Het boek der rabauwen en naaktridders. Bijdrage tot de studie van het volksleven der 16e en 17e eeuwen.* Antwerpen (Dutch Institute, Amsterdam).

Fokkens, M[elchior]. 1662. *Beschrijvinge der wijdt-vermaarde Koop-stadt Amstelredam.* Amsterdam (UB).

Gebouwen. 1736. *Gebouwen, gezichten en oudheden der stad Amsterdam.* Met figuuren. Haarlem (UB).

Gool, Johan van. 1750–1751. *De nieuwe schouburg der Nederlantsche kunstschilders en schilderessen.* 2 vols. Den Haag (UB).

Grevius, Johannes. 1624. *Tribunal reformatum, in quo . . . rejecta et fugata tortura. . . . Quam captivus scripsit in Ergastulo Amsterodamensi.* Hamburgi (UB).

Groot-Placcaatboek en Charterboek van Vriesland. 1768–1793. 5 vols. Leeuwarden (UB).

Guide d'Amsterdam, Le. 1701. Amsterdam (UB).

Guide, Le, ou nouvelle description d'Amsterdam. 1753. Amsterdam (UB).

Hainhofer, Philipp. 1834. *Reise-Tagebuch enthaltend Schilderungen aus Franken, Sachsen, der Mark Brandenburg und Pommern im Jahr 1617.* [Beiheft zu] Baltische Studien, Zweiter Jahrgang. Stettin (UB).

Handt-Boecxken, Een cleyn, waer in begrepen zijn vier stucken: het eerste is ghenaemt Proverbia/ de spreuken Salomonis. 'T tweede Ecclesiastes/ de Prediker. Het Derde Sapientia, 't Boeck der Wijsheyt. 't Vierde Ecclesiasticus/ ofte Jesus Syrach. De welcke gedruckt zijn ten nutte ende profijte van den Tuchthuyse binnen der Stede van Amstelredam opgherecht. 1635. Amsterdam (UB).

Handvesten ofte privilegien ende octroyen mitsgaders willekeuren, costumen, ordonnantien en handelingen der stad Amstelredam. 1748. 3 vols. Amsterdam (Gemeentearchief, Amsterdam).

Historie Van de wonderlijcke Mirakelen/ die in menichte ghebeurt zijn/ ende noch dagelijcx ghebeuren/ binnen de vermaerde Coop-stadt Aemstelredam: In een plaets ghenaempt het Tucht-huys, gheleghen op de Heylighe-wegh. Hier achter is noch by ghevoeght een wonderlijck Mirakel van S. Justitia. 1612. t' Amstelredam, By Marten Gerbrantsz. (Gemeente-archief, Amsterdam and Koninklijke Bibliotheek, The Hague: Knuttel, nr. 2032).

Histoires admirables des miracles estranges, qui sont advenus en grand nombre, & adviennent encores journellement en la marchande & fameuse ville d'Amsterdam, en un lieu appelé Tuchthuys, situé sur la saincte voye. Auquels, est adjousté sur la fin encore un miracle tres admirable de S. Iustitia. 1612. À Leyden, par Theodore Iohannes. (Koninklijke Bibliotheek, The Hague: Knuttel, nr. 2033).

Miracula San-Raspini, Das ist: [Ku]*rtze und Historische Beschreibung der Wunderlichen Mirackel oder Wunderwerck/ so in der weitberhümbten Kauff- und HandelStatt Amsterdam/ an einem Orth auff dem heiligen Weg gelegen/ so gemeiniglich das Zuchthauss genannt wirdt/ an vielen fürgangen/ und noch täglich fürgehen. Mit zugefügter Beschreibung eines wunderbaren Mirackels/ so von der heiligen Iustitia geschehen. Alles auss Niderländischer Verzeichnuss in hochteutscher Spraach beschrieben. Getruckt im Jahr nach Christi Geburt M.DC. XIII.* 1613(Gemeente-archief, Amsterdam).

Miracula San-Raspini, Das ist: Kurtze und Historische Beschreibung der Wunderbarlichen Mirackel unnd Wunderwerck/ so in der weitberümbten Kauffund HandelStatt Amsterdam/ an einem Ohrt auff dem heiligen Weg gelegen/ so gemeiniglich das Zuchthauss genannt wirdt/ an vielen fürgangen/ und noch täglich fürgehen. Mit zugefügter Beschreibung eines wunderbaren Mirackels/ so von der heiligen Iustitia geschehen. Alles auss Niderländischer Verzeichnuss in hochteutscher Sprach beschrieben. Getruckt im Jahr [missing]. No date. (University Library, Marburg).

Miracula San Raspini Redivivi, Das ist: Historische Beschreibung der Wunderlichen Mirackel oder Wunderwerck/ so in der weitberhümbten Kauff- und HandelStatt Amsterdam/ an einem Orth auff dem heiligen Weg gelegen/ so gemeinglich das Zuchthauss genannt wirdt/ an vielen fürgangen/ und noch täglich fürgehen. Mit zugefügter Beschreibung eines wunderbaren Mirackels/ so von der heiligen Iustitia geschehen. Ietzo auffs neu in Truck verfertigt/ und mit der Statt Bremen Zuchthauss vermehret. Getruckt im Jahr nach Christi Geburt/ M.DC.XVII. 1617. (Bibliothèque Nationale et Universitaire de Strasbourg, Section Droit and University Library, Ghent).

Hooft, Cornelis Pietersz. 1925. *Memoriën en adviezen.* Vol. II. Ed. H. A. E. van Gelder. Utrecht.

Hooft, Pieter Corneliszoon. 1976. *Briefwisseling.* Ed. H. W. van Tricht. Vol. I, 1599–1630. Culemborg (Historical Institute, Amsterdam).

Hout, Jan van. 1927. "Rapporten en adviezen betreffende het Amsterdamsche tuchthuis uit de jaren 1597 en '98." Ed. A. Hallema in *Bijdragen en Mededelingen van het Historisch Genootschap* 48: 69–98 (Historical Institute, Amsterdam).

Howard, John. 1789. *An account of the principal lazarettos in Europe, with various papers relative to the plague: together with further observations on some foreign prisons and hospitals and additional remarks on the present state of those in Great Britain and Ireland.* First ed. Warrington (UB).

Howard, John. 1792. *The state of the prisons in England and Wales . . . and an account of some foreign prisons and hospitals.* Fourth ed. London (UB).

Koning, Abraham de. *'t Spel van Sinne. Vertoont op de Tweede Lotery van d'Arme Oude Mannen ende Vrouwen Gast-Huys. Tot Lof, Eere en Leere der Wijt-Beroemder Coopstadt Amstelredam.* 1616. Amsterdam (UB).

Krausoldus, Fridericus. 1698. *Discursus juridico-politicus ex principiis juris divini, naturalis, gentium & civilis depromptus de Miraculis, et egregiis usibus S. Raspini. Von denen Wunderwercken und vortreflichen Nutzbarkeiten des Rasps- oder Zucht-Hauses.* Martisburgi (Koninklijke Bibliotheek, The Hague).

Liber Vagatorum. Le livre des gueux. 1862. Ed. P. Ristelhuber. Strasbourg (University Library, Strasbourg).

Lipsius, I. 1605. *Lipsii Heylige Maghet van Halle. Hare weldaden ende Miraculen ghetrouwelick ende ordentlick uutgheschreven. Uut de Latijnsche in onse Nederlantsche tale overgheset deur eenen Lief-hebber der eere sijns Salichmakers; tot bespottinghe der Pauselicke Roomsche Afgoderije.* . . . Delft (Koninklijke Bibliotheek, The Hague).

Long, Isaac le. 1732. *Boek-zaal der Nederduytsche Bybels.* Amsterdam (Instituut voor Neolatijn, Amsterdam).

Mabillon, Jean. 1987. "überlegungen zu den Gefängnissen der religiösen Orden," (translated from the French by Peter Wettman) in *Kriminologisches Journal*, 2 (Beiheft): 79–87 (personal copy).

"Mémoires concernans les pauvres que l'on appelle enfermez." 1837. *Archives curieuses de l'histoire de France depuis Louis XI jusqu'à Louis XVIII.* Eds. M. L. Cimber and F. Danjou Ière. Série, Tome 15: 243–284 (University Library, Leiden).

Mieris, Frans van. 1770. *Beschryving der stad Leyden.* Vol. II. Leiden (UB).

Misson, Maximilien. 1691, 1698. *Nouveau voyage d'Italie fait en l'année 1688.* 2 vols. First ed. Den Haag 1691 (Koninklijke Bibliotheek, The Hague). Second ed. Den Haag 1698 (ibidem).

Montchrétien, Antoyne de. 1889. *Traicté de l'oeconomie politique. Avec introduction et notes par Th. Funck-Brentano.* Paris (UB).

Mountague, William. 1696. *The delights of Holland, or a three months travel about that and the other provinces.* London (UB).

Mumen, Sebastian. [1616]. *Bremer Zuchthauss/ Ein kurz und warhaftig Gespräch zweyer Personen/ darinn eigentlich angezeiget wird/ was ordnung und gute disciplin im Zuchthause zu Bremen gehalten worden. . . . Gestellet durch* Sebastian Mumen Vördensem. . . . Bremen (University Library, Bremen).

Opschriften, Koddige en ernstige opschriften op luyffens, wagens, glazen, uythangborden, en andere taferelen. 1682. Amsterdam (UB).

Ordnung der fürtrefflichen hoch und weiterümbten Kauffstadt Amsterdam in Hollandt/ mittelst welcher doselbsten die Bettler gentzlich abgeschaffet/ und die armen unterhalten werden. 1598. Hamburg (Gemeente-archief, Amsterdam).

Placaetboek, Groot, vervattende de Placaten . . . van de . . . Staten Generaal . . . ende . . . Staten van Hollandt . . . mitsgaders . . . Staten van Zeelandt. 1658–1797. 10 vols. Den Haag, Amsterdam (Gemeente-archief, Amsterdam).

Pontanus, Johannes Isacius. 1614. *Historische beschrijvinghe der seer wijt beroemde coop-stadt Amsterdam.* Amsterdam (UB).

Posthumus, N. W. ed. 1914 and 1918. *Bronnen tot de geschiedenis van de Leidsche textielnijverheid.* Vol. 4: Den Haag (1914) and Vol. 5: Den Haag (1918) (Library of Erasmus University, Rotterdam).

Reinkingk, Theodorus. 1619, 1622, 1632, 1659. *Tractatus de regimine seculari et ecclesiastico.* . . . Giessen (1619); Basel (1622; editio altera); Marburg (1632; editio secunda); Francofurti ad Moenum (Johannes Martinus Porssius) (1659); (all editions: University Library, Tübingen)

Resolutien van de Heeren Staaten van Holland en Westvrieslandt, genoomen in haar Edele Groot Mog. Vergaderinge. 1647–1649, 1709, 1716, 1722 (UB).

Riemer, Jacob de. 1730. *Beschrijving van's Graven-Hage.* Vol. 1. Delft (UB).

Scheible, J. 1850. *Die fliegenden Blätter des XVI. und XVII. Jahrhunderts in sogenannten Einblatt-Drucken. . . . Aus den Schätzen der Ulmer Stadtbibliothek wort- und bildetreu herausgegeben.* Stuttgart (UB).

Spaan, Gerard van. 1698. *Beschrijvinge der stad Rotterdam en eenige omleggende dorpen.* Rotterdam (UB).

Vondel, Joost van den. 1657–1660. *De werken van Joost van der Vondel. Uitgegeven door J. van Lennep, herzien en bijgewerkt door J. H. W. Unger.* Leiden s.a. (Dutch Institute, Amsterdam).

Vondel, Joost van den. 1982. *Inwydinge van 't stadhuis t'Amsterdam.* Ed. Saskia Albrecht, et al. Muiderberg (UB).

Wächter, Carl Eberhard. 1786. *Ueber Zuchthäuser und Zuchthausstrafen.* Stuttgart (UB).

Wagenaar, Jan. 1760–1768. *Amsterdam in zyne opkomst, aanwas, geschiedenissen, voorregten, koophandel, gebouwen, kerkenstaat, schoolen, schutterye, gilden en regeeringe* (quarto edition). 13 vols. Amsterdam (Historical Institute, Amsterdam).

Wagnitz, H[einrich] B[althasar]. 1791–1794. *Historische Nachrichten und Bemerkungen über die merkwürdigsten Zuchthäuser in Deutschland. Nebst einem Anhange über die zweckmässigste Einrichtung der Gefängnisse und Irrenanstalten.* 2 Bände, 3 vols. Halle (UB).

Ward, Ned. 1955. *The London spy.* Ed. with notes and introduction by Kenneth Fenwick. London (British Library).

Zesen, Filip von. 1664. *Beschreibung der Stadt Amsterdam.* Amsterdam (UB).

Zetzner, Johann Eberhard. 1913. *Aus dem Leben eines strassburger Kaufmanns des XVII. und XVIII. Jahrhunderts. 'Reiss-Journal und Glücks- und Unglücksfälle' von Johann Eberhard Zetzner, 1677–1735.* Ed. Rudolf Reuss. Strassburg (Koninklijke Bibliotheek, The Hague).

B. Secondary Literature

Adler, Max. [1924]. *Fabrik und Zuchthaus. Eine sozialhistorische Untersuchung* (Kulter- und Zeitfragen, Heft 10). Leipzig.

Allard H. J. 1899. *"Hoe een Jezuïet en twee predikanten uit het Amsterdamsche tuchthuis ontsnapten." Jaarboekje van Alberdingk Thijm:* 86–131.

Ariès, Philippe. 1981. *The hour of our death.* New York.

Asséo, Henriette. 1974. "Marginalité et exclusion. Le traitement administratif des Bohémiens dans la société Française du 17e siècle." In *Problèmes socio-culturels en France au 17e siècle.* Présenté par Robert Mandrou. Paris: 11–87.

Bade, Klaus J. 1982. "Altes Handwerk, Wanderzwang und Gute Policey. Gesellenwanderung zwischen Zunftökonomie und Gewerbereform." *Vierteljahrschrift für Sozial- und Wirtschaftsgeschichte* 69: 1–37.

Bailey, Victor, ed. [1981]. *Policing and Punishment in 19th-century Britain.* London.

Baxandall, Michael. [1986]. *Schilderkunst en leefwereld in het quattrocento. Een inleiding in de sociale geschiedenis van de picturale stijl.* [Nijmegen].

Beattie, J[ohn] M. 1986. *Crime and the Courts in England, 1660–1800.* Oxford.

Beier, A[ugustus] L. 1985. *Masterless Men. The Vagrancy Problem in England, 1560–1640.* London, New York.

Bellamy, John. 1973. *Crime and Public Order in England in the Later Middle Ages.* London, Toronto.

Bender, John. [1987]. *Imagining the Penitentiary. Fiction and the Architecture of Mind in 18th-century England.* Chicago, London.

Bigorre, Alain. 1967. *L'admission du malade mental dans les éstablissements de soins de 1789 à 1838.* (Medical thesis, Dijon).

Binneveld, Hans. [1985]. *Filantropie, repressie en medische zorg. Geschiedenis van de inrichting-spsychiatrie.* Deventer.

Binneveld, J. M. W. and M. J. van Lieburg. 1979. *Psychiatric Reform in the Netherlands in the 19th century.* Rotterdam (Centrum voor Maatschappijgeschiedenis 7).

Binsbergen, Willem Cornelis van. 1949. *Algemeen karakter van het Crimineel Wetboek voor het Koningrijk Holland.* Utrecht.

Biraben J.-N. 1974. "Les pauvres et la peste." In Michel Mollat (ed.), *Etudes sur l'histoire de la pauvreté.* Tome II. Paris: 505–518.

Blockmans, W[im] P., and W. Prevenier. 1977. "Poverty in Flanders and Brabant from the 14th to the mid-16th Century." *Acta Historia Neerlandicae* 10: 20–57.

Blok, Anton. 1981. "Infame beroepen." *Symposion* 3: 104–128.

Boas, M. 1917. "De spreuk van de rasphuispoort." *Jaarboek Amstelodamum* 15: 121–9.

Bouricius, L. G. N. 1927. *Geschiedenis van het geneeskundig gesticht voor krankzinnigen het St. Jorisgasthuis en het daarmede verbonden geweest zijnde tuchthuis binnen Delft.* Delft.

Brehmer, W[ilhelm]. 1883–1884. "Correktionshaft." *Mittheilungen des Vereins für Lübeckische Geschichte und Alterthumskunde* 1: 22–23 and 60–62.

Bruinvis, C. W. 1908. *De gevangenissen en inzonderheid het tuchthuis te Alkmaar.*

Bruneel, C. 1966a. "Un épisode de la lutte contre la mendicité & le vagabondage. La maison de correction (tuchthuys) de Bruxelles." *Cahiers Bruxellois* 11: 29–72.

Bruneel, C. 1966b. "A rude école. Le régime pénitentiaire de la maison de correction de Bruxelles." *Cahiers Bruxellois* 11: 213–249.

Bruneel, C. 1967. "Les prisonniers de la maison de correction de Bruxelles. Etude statistique." *Cahiers Bruxellois* 12: 40–68.

Bruns, Friedrich. 1915. "Zur Geschichte des St. Annenklosters." *Zeitschrift des Vereins für Lübeckische Geschichte und Alterumskunde* 17: 173–204.

Burke, Peter. 1978. *Popular culture in early modern Europe.* New York.

Burke, Peter. 1987. *The historical anthropology of early modern Italy. Essays on perception and communication.* Cambridge.

Bylina, Stanislaw. 1987. "L'enfer en Pologne médiévale, 14e-15e siècle." *Annales ESC* 42: 1231–1244.

Byrd, Max. 1974. *Visits to Bedlam. Madness and Literature in the 18th Century.* Columbia, S.C.

Callahan, William J. 1971. "The problem of confinement: An aspect of poor relief in 18th-century Spain." *Hispanic American Historical Review* 51: 1–24.

Cameron, Iain A. [1981]. *Crime and repression in the Auvergne and the Guyenne, 1720–1790.* Cambridge.

Castan, Nicole. 1976 "La justice expéditive." *Annales ESC* 31: 331–361.

Castan, Nicole. 1980. *Justice et répression en Languedoc à l'époque des Lumières.* Paris.

Chill, Emanuel. 1962. "Religion and mendicity in 17th-century France." *International Review of Social History* 7: 400–425.

Chrisman, Miriam U. 1988. "Printing and the evolution of lay culture in Strasbourg, 1480–1599." R. Po-chia Hsia, ed., *The German People and the Reformation.* Ithaca, London: 74–100.

Christianson, Paul. 1985. "John Selden, the Five Knights' case and discretionary imprisonment in early Stuart England." *Criminal Justice History* 6: 65–87.

Chijs, S. A. van der. 1886. *Geschiedenis van Dordrecht's krankzinnigenhuis.* Dordrecht.

Conley, John. 1981. "Revising conceptions about the origin of prisons: the importance of economic considerations." *Social Science Quarterly* 62, 2: 247–258.

Cozzi, Gaetano, ed. [1980]. *Stato, societa e giustizia nella Repubblica Veneta, sec. 15–18.* Roma [1980].

Daalen, A. P. A. van, and E. C. de Vroedt. 1980. *Politie en justitie in Delft. Van schout tot commissaris, van rakker tot agent* (Archive of Delft).

Dahlberg, Bror Hermann. 1898. *Bidrag till Svenska fattiglagstiftningens historia.* Upsala.

Davis, Natalie Zemon. 1975. "Poor relief, humanism and heresy." *Idem, Society and culture in early modern France.* Stanford: 17–64.

Davis, Natalie Zemon. 1981. "The sacred and the body social in 16th-century Lyon." *Past and Present* 90: 40–70.

Dekker, R[udolf] M. 1988. "Getrouwe broederschap. Organisatie en acties van artbeiders in preïndustrieel Holland." *Bijdragen en Mededelingen betreffende de Geschiedenis der Nederlanden* 103: 1–19.

Delacy, Margaret. 1986. *Prison Reform in Lancashire, 1700–1850. A Study in Local Administration.* Stanford.

Delumeau, Jean. 1957. *Vie économique et sociale de Rome dans la seconde moitié du 16e siècle.* Tome I. Paris.

Deyon, Pierre. [1975]. *Le temps des prisons. Essai sur l'histoire de la délinquance et les origines du système pénitentiaire.* Lille, Paris.

Diederiks, Herman. 1980. "Patterns of Criminality and Law Enforcement during the Ancien Régime: The Dutch Case." *Criminal Justice History* 1: 157–174.

Diederiks, Herman. 1981. "Punishment during the Ancien Régime. The case of the 18th-century Dutch Republic." In Louis A. Knafla, ed., *Crime and Criminal Justice in Europe and Canada.* Waterloo, Ont.: 273–296.

Diederiks, Herman. 1982. *Een stad in verval. Amsterdam omstreeks 1800, demografisch, economisch, ruimtelijk.* Amsterdam.

Diederiks, Herman, et al., eds. 1985. *Armoede en sociale spanning. Sociaal-historische studies over Leiden in de 18e eeuw.* Hilversum.

Digneffe, Françoise, and Marie-Sylvie Dupont-Bouchat. 1982. "A propos de l'origine et des transformations des maisons pour jeunes délinquants en Belgique au 19e siècle." *Déviance et Société* 6: 131–165.

Doering, Heinz W. L. 1926. "Das alte Münchener Zuchthaus. Ein Studie zur Entwicklung des Gefängniswesens in Bayern von der Carolina bis Feuerbach." Diss., University of Erlangen.

Dörner, Klaus. 1969. *Bürger und Irre. Zur Sozialgeschichte und Wissenschaftssoziologie der Psychiatrie.* s.l.

Dolsperg, Franz Doleisch von. 1928. *Die Entstehung der Freiheitsstrafe, unter besonderer Berücksichtigung des Auftretens moderner Freiheitsstrafe in England.* Breslau.

Doorman, G. 1940. *Octrooien voor uitvindingen in de Nederlanden uit de 16e–18e eeuw.* Den Haag.

Dupille, Chantal. [1971]. *Historie de la Court de Miracles.* [Paris].

Dupont-Bouchat, Marie-Sylvie. 1981, 1982, 1984. "Le pénitencier de St. Hubert (3 vols; vol. 2 with Françoise Digneffe). *Saint-Hubert d'Ardenne-Cahiers d'Histoire* 5 (1981): 161–182; 6 (1982): 139–186; 7 (1984): 165–196.

Ebeling, Albert. 1935. *Beiträge zur Geschichte der Freiheitsstrafe.* Breslau-Neukirch.

Eekhoff, W. 1846. *Beschrijving van Leeuwarden.* Vol. II.

Eerenbeemt, H. F. J. M. van den. 1968. *In het spanningsveld der armoede. Agressief pauperisme en reactie in Staats-Brabant.* Tilburg.

Eerenbeemt, H. F. J. M. van den. 1970. *Van mensenjacht en overheidsmacht. Criminogene groepsvorming en afweer in de Meierij van 's Hertogenbosch, 1795–1810.* Tilburg.

Eerenbeemt, H. F. J. M. van den. 1977. *Armoede en arbeidsdwang. Werkinrichtingen voor "onnutte" Nederlanders in de Republiek, 1760–1795. Een mentaliteitsgeschiedenis.* Den Haag.

Eggink, Jan Willem. 1958. *De geschiedenis van het Nederlandse gevangeniswezen.* Assen.

Egmond, Florike. [1986]. *Banditisme in de Franse tijd. Profiel van de Grote Nederlandse Bende, 1790–1799.* s.l.

Ehrle, Franz. 1881. *Beiträge zur Geschichte und Reform der Armenpflege* (Ergänzungshefte zu den "Stimmen aus Maria-Laach" 17). Freiburg i.B.

Eichler, Helga. 1970–1971. "Zucht- und Arbeitshäuser in den mittleren und östlichen Provinzen Brandenburg-Preussens." *Jahrbuch für Wirtschaftsgeschichte* 127–147.

Ekirch, A. Roger. 1987. *Bound for America. The transportation of British convicts to the colonies, 1718–1775.* Oxford.

Elias, Johan E. 1963. *De vroedschap van Amsterdam, 1578–1795.* 2 vols. 2d ed. Amsterdam.

Elias, Norbert. 1969. *über den Prozess der Zivilisation. Soziogenetische und psychogenetische Untersuchungen.* 2 vols. 2d ed. Bern, München.

Elias, Norbert. [1971]. *Wat is sociologie.* Utrecht, Antwerpen.

Emmanuelli, François-Xavier. 1974. "Ordres du roi et lettres de cachet en Provence à la fin de l'Ancien Régime." *Revue Historique:* 357–92.

Emmermann, Carl. 1921. *Das Zuchthaus zu Celle.* (Diss. Jur., University of Göttingen.

Engrand, Charles. 1984. "Mendier sa vie au 18e siècle: de la résignation à la révolte. Amiens, 1764–1789." *Revue de Nord* 66: 515–529.

Fairchilds, Cissie C. 1976. *Poverty and Charity in Aix-en-Provence, 1640–1789.* Baltimore, London.

Faber, J. A. 1976. *Dure tijden en hongersnoden in preïndustrieel Nederland.* (Inaugural lecture, Amsterdam.)

Faber, Sjoerd. 1983. *Strafrechtspleging en criminaliteit te Amsterdam, 1680–1811. De nieuwe menslievendheid.* Arnhem.

Faber, S[joerd], et al. 1989. *Criminaliteit in de negentiende eeuw.* Hilversum.

Falck, R. 1838. *Handbuch des Schleswig-holsteinischen Privatrechts. Des dritten Bandes zweite Abteilung.* Altona.

Farge, Arlette. 1974. *Délinquance et criminalité. Le vol d'aliments à Paris au 18e siècle.* [Paris].

Farge, Arlette, and Michel Foucault. [1982]. *Le désordre des familles. Lettres de cachet des archives de la Bastille.* [Paris].

Feest, Johannes, and Christian Marzahn, eds. 1988. *Criminalia. Bremer Strafjustiz, 1810–1850* (Beiträge zur Sozialgeschichte Bremens 11, University of Bremen).

Ferrante, Lucia. 1983. "L'onore ritrovato. Donne nella casa del soccorso di S. Paolo a Bologna, sec. 16-17." *Quaderni Storici* 53: 499–527.

Fessler, A. 1956. "The management of lunancy in 17th-century England. An investigation of quarter-sessions records. *Proceedings of the Royal Society of Medicine* 49: 901–907.

Fischer, Thomas. 1979. *Städtische Armut und Armenfürsorge im 15. und 16. Jahrhundert. Sozialgeschichtliche Untersuchungen am Beispiel der Städte Basel, Freiburg i. Br. und Strassburg.* Göttingen.

Flandrin, Jean-Louis. 1979. *Families in Former Times. Kinship, Household and Sexuality.* Cambridge.

Fokker, G. A. 1862. *Geschiedenis der loterijen in de Nederlanden.* Amsterdam.

Fosseyeux, Marcel. 1929. *"Les maisons de correction à Paris sous l'Ancien Régime." Bulletin de la Société de l'Histoire de Paris et de l'Ile-de-France* 56: 36–47.

Foucault, Michel. *Folie et déraison. Histoire de la folie à l'age classique.* Paris.

Foucault, Michel. 1975. Surveiller et punir. Naissance de la prison. [Paris].

Frank, Michael. date? *Kriminalität, Strafrechtspflege und sozialer Wandel. Das Zuchthaus Detmold, 1752–1801.* (forthcoming).

Franzoi, Umberto. 1975. *Les prisons de la République de Venise.* Venezia.

Funck-Brentano, Frantz. 1903. *Les lettres de cachet à Paris. Etude suivie d'une liste des prisonniers de la Bastille, 1659–1789.* Paris.

Fijnaut, Cyrille and Pieter Spierenburg, eds. 1990. *Scherp toezicht. Van 'Boeventucht' tot 'Samenleving en Criminaliteit.'* Arnhem.

Gaillac, Henri. 1971. *Les maisons de correction, 1830–1945.* s.l.

Garnsey, Peter. 1970. *Social Status and Legal Privilege in the Roman Empire.* Oxford.

Garrer, A. H. 1929. *In een beterhuis van 1682 tot 1692.* Haarlem.

Geessink, Jannemieke. 1987. "Confinement op verzoek in Dordrecht, 1734-1809." Thesis, Erasmus University Rotterdam, History.)

Geessink, J[annemieke]. 1989. "Opsluiting op verzoek in Dordrecht." *Kwartaal & Teken* (Gemeentearchief Dordrecht) 15: 3–7.

Geremek, Bronislaw. 1973. "Renfermement des pauvres en Italie, 14e–17e siècle. Remarques préliminaires." *Histoire économique du monde Mèditerranéen, 1450–1640. Mélange en l'honneur de Fernand Braudel.* Vol. I. Toulouse 1973: 205–217.

Geremek, Bronislaw. 1974. "Criminalité, vagabondage, paupérisme: la marginalité à l'aube des temps modernes." *Revue d'Histoire Moderne et Contemporaine* 21: 337–375.

Geremek, Bronislaw. [1976]. *Les marginaux Parisiens aux 14e et 15e siècles.* [Paris].

Geremek, Bronislaw. [1987]. *La potence ou la pitié. L'Europe et les pauvres du moyen âge à nos jours.* [Paris].

Goffman, Erving. 1961. *Asylums. Essays on the social situation of mental patients and other inmates.* Garden City, N.Y.

Graaff, H. H. A. de. 1954. "Enige opmerkingen over de invloed van het oud-vaderlandse en het Franse recht op de vrijheidsstraffen voor militairen." *Tijdschrift voor Strafrecht* 63: 221–235.

Grambow, Otto. 1910. "Das Gefängniswesen Bremens." Diss. Göttingen. Borna, Leipzig.

Greenberg, David, ed. 1981. *Crime and Capitalism. Readings in Marxist Criminology.* Palo Alto.

Griessinger, Andreas. *Das symbolische Kapital der Ehre. Streikbewegungen und kollektives Bewusstsein deutscher Handwerksgesellen im 18. Jahrhundert.* Frankfurt a. M.

Griessinger, Andreas, and Reinhold Reith. 1983. "Obrigkeitliche Ordnungskonzeptionen und handwerkliches Konfliktverhalten im 18. Jahrhundert. Nürnberg und Würzburg in Vergleich. In Rainer S. Elkar, ed., *Deutsches Handwerk im Spätmittelalter und früher Neuzeit.* Göttingen: 117–180.

Gutton, Jean-Pierre. 1970. *La société et les pauvres. L'exemple de la Généralité de Lyon, 1534–1789.* Paris.

Gutton, Jean-Pierre. 1974. *La société et les pauvres en Europe, 16e–18e siécles.* Paris.

Haesenne-Peremans, Nicole. 1983. *Les pauvres et le pouvoir. Assistance et répression au Pays de Liège.* Kortrijk-Heule

Hallema, A. 1929. "Eenige officieele bescheiden over den staat der stedelijke gevangenissen van Amsterdam in het jaar 1798." *Jaarboek Amstelodamum* 26: 187–206.

Hallema, A. 1931. "Het Antwerpsche tuchthuis. Een Hollandsche navolging." Antwerpsch Archievenblad: 3–26.

Hallema, A. 1935. "De gevangenisarbeid in concurrentie met het particuliere bedrijfsleven en de strijd om het Amsterdamsche tuchthuismonopolie ten tijde der Republiek." *Economisch-Historisch Jaarboek* 19: 114–201.

Hallema, A. 1936. *In en om de gevangenis.* Den Haag.

Hallema, A. (1953a). "Vlaardingen en Dordrecht als oudste Nederlandse galeiendepots." *Tijdschrift voor Geschiedenis* 66: 69–94.

Hallema, A. (1953b). "Het Amsterdamse tuchthuis in 1710." *Jaarboek Amstelodamum* 45 (1953): 183–192.

Hallema, A. 1958. *Geschiedenis van het gevangeniswezen. Hoofdzakelijk in Nederland*. Den Haag.

Harding, Christopher, et al. [1985]. *Imprisonment in England and Wales. A Concise History*. London.

Hartung, Wolfgang. 1986. "Gesellschaftliche Randgruppen im Spätmittelal-ter. Phänomen und Begriff." In: Bernhard Kirchgässner and Fritz Reuter, eds., *Städtische Randgruppen und Minderheiten*. Sigmaringen: 49–114.

Heineken, Christian Abraham. 1983. *Geschichte der freien Hansestadt Bremen von der Mitte des 18. Jahrhunderts bis zur Franzosenzeit*. Bearbeitet von Wilhelm Lührs. Bremen.

Henriques, U[rsula] R. Q. 1972. "The rise and decline of the separate system of prison discipline." *Past and Present* 54: 61–93.

Herwaarden, Jan van. 1978. *Opgelegde bedevaarten. Een studie over de praktijk van het opleggen van bedevaarten, met name in de stedelijke rechtspraak, in de Nederlanden gedurende de late middeleeuwen*. Assen, Amsterdam.

Hiemsch, Jan. 1964. *Die bremische Gerichtsverfassung von der ersten Gerichtsordnung bis zur Reichsjustizgesetzgebung, 1751–1879*. Bremen.

Hippel, Reinhard von. 1986. "Zur Verortung der Spezialprävention/ Sozialtherapie: Mass-regel oder Strafvollzug?" In Hans Joachim Hirsch, et al., eds., *Gedächtnisschrift für Hilde Kaufmann*. Berlin, New York: 433–449.

Hippel, R[obert] von. 1897–1898. "Zur Geschichte des Werk- und Zuchthauses zu St. An-nen." *Mittheilungen des Vereins für Lübeckische Geschichte und Alterthumskunde* 8: 146–158.

Hippel, R[obert] von. 1898. "Beiträge zur Geschichte der Freihesitsstrafe. *Zeitschrift für die gesamte Strafrechtswissenchaft* 18: 419–494 and 608–666.

Hippel, R[obert] von. 1932. *Die Entstehung der modernen Freiheitsstrafe und des Erziehungs-Strafvollzugs* (Schriften der Thüringischen Gefängnisgesellschaft, Heft 2). Jena 1932 (sticker over: Eisenach 1931).

Hirth, Georg. [1897]. *Kulturgeschichtliches Bilderbuch aus drei Jahrhunderten*. Band III. Leipzig, München.

Hoeven, Anton van den. 1982. "Ten exempel en afschrik. Strafrechtspleging en criminaliteit in Haarlem, 1740–1795." Thesis, University of Utrecht, History.

Houlbrooke, Ralph A. 1984. *The English family, 1450–1700*. London, New York.

Hoyt, Robert S. [1966]. *Europe in the Middle Ages*. 2d ed. New York.

Hufton, Olwen H. 1974. *The poor of 18th-Century France, 1750–1789*. Oxford.

Hunter, Richard and Ida Macalpine, eds., 1963. *Three Hundred Years of Psychiatry, 1535–1860. A History Presented in Selected English Texts*. London.

Huussen, A[rend] H. 1985. "Politie in Friesland gedurende de 18e en in het begin van de 19e eeuw: van gewestelijke naar nationale status." *Redenen van wetenschap. Optellen over de politie 40 jaar na het Politiebesluit 1945*. Arnhem: 127–143.

Ignatieff, Michael. 1978. *A Just Measure of Pain. The Penitentiary in the Industrial Revolution, 1750–1850*. New York.

Ignatieff, Michael. 1983. "State, civil society and total institution: A critique of recent social histories of punishment. In: David Sugarman, ed., *Legality, Ideology and the State*. London: 183–211.

Innes, Joanna. [1980]. "The King's Bench prison in the later 18th century: law, authority and order in a London debtor's prison." In John Brewer and John Styles, eds., *An Ungovernable People. The English and their Law in the 17th and 18th Centuries*. London. 250–298.

Innes, Joanna. "Prisons for the poor. English bridewells, 1555–1800." In Francis Snyder and Douglas Hay, eds., *Labour, Law and Crime. An historical Perspective*. London, New York: 42–122.

Irsigler, Franz, and Arnold Lasotta. 1984. *Bettler und Gaukler, Dirnen und Henker. Randgruppen und Aussenseiter in Köln, 1300–1600*. Köln.

Jacobs, Beatrix C. M. 1988. "Arme vrouwen in een gevangenpoort." *Over het onderbelichte. De vrouw in studie en beroep, vroeger en nu* (University of Tilburg): 28–37.

Jansen, J. C. G. M. 1978. "Waanzin en repressie. De zinnelozen en hun behandeling in Maastricht in de 18e eeuw." *Studies over de Sociaal-Economische Geschiedenis van Limburg* 23: 63–97.

Jetter, Dieter. 1966. *Geschichte des Hospitals. Band I: Westdeutschland von den Anfängen bis 1850*. Wiesbaden.

Jetter, Dieter. 1971. *Zur Typologie des Irrenhauses in Frankreich und Deutschland, 1780–1840*. Wiesbaden.

Jones, Colin. 1982. *Charity and Bienfaisance. The Treatment of the Poor in the Montpellier Region, 1740-1815*. Cambridge.

Jong, Mayke de. [1986]. *Kind en klooster in de vroege middeleeuwen. Aspecten van de schenking van kinderen aan kloosters in het Frankische Rijk, 500-900*. Amsterdam.

Jüngen, Jean. 1979. "Een stad van justitie. Een verkenning van misdaad en maatschappij in Amsterdam in de tweede helft van de 16e eeuw." Thesis, Free University Amsterdam, Law.

Jütte, Robert. 1988. *Abbild und soziale Wirklichkeit des Bettler- und Gaunertums zu Beginn der Neuzeit. Sozial-, mentalitäts- und sprachgeschichtliche Studien zum Liber Vagatorum (1510)*. Köln, Wien.

Kaczynska, Elzbieta. 1988. "Punished people. Prisons and the penal system in the kingdom of Poland in the years 1815-1914." *IAHCCJ-Newletter* 12 (December): 49-59.

Kalshoven, Hans. 1988. "Criminaliteit en strafrechtspleging in Enkhuizen, 1654-1810." Thesis, University of Amsterdam, History.

Kampman, Jacqueline. 1984. "Het tuchthuis in Groningen, 1601-1811." *Gronignse Volksalmanak* (1984): 64-81.

Kampman, Jacqueline. 1986. "De tuchthuisstraf te Groningen. Een onderzoek naar het gebruik van de tuchthuisstraf binnen de strafrechtspraak." Thesis, University of Groningen, History.

Kappen, O. Moorman van. 1987. "Willem van der Pauw's 'De disciplina ergastulorum' (1773)." *Straffen in Gerechtigheid. Opstellen over sancties en executie, uitgegeven ter nagedachtenis aan prof. mr. W. H. A. Jonkers*. Arnhem: 321-331.

Kent, Joan R. 1986. *The English Village Constable, 1580-1642. A Social and Administrative Study*. Oxford.

Klein, P[eter] W. 1989. "De Nederlandse handelspolitiek in de tijd van het mercantilisme. Een nieuwe kijk op een oude kwestie?" *Tijdschrift voor Geschiedenis* 102: 189-212.

Kock, P. M. J. 1903. "Het 's Gravenhaagse tuchthuis." *Die Haghe*: 195 et seq.

Kool, J. A. 1865. "Bijdrage tot de geschiedenis van het vroegere gevangeniswezen." *Schat der Gezondheid* 8: 161-184 and 193-208.

Kottmann, Peter. 1986. "Die Protokolle des bremer Kämmereigerichts von 1600 bis 1800." *Historical Social Research/ Historische Sozialforschung* (Quantum Information) 40 (October): 72-83.

Kraemer, Erik von. 1944. *Le type du faux mendiant dans les littératures romanes depuis le moyen âge jusqu'au 18e siècle* (Societas Scientiarum Fennica, nr. XIII. 6). Helsinki.

Künzel, Rudi. [1986]. "Bloed, vuur en draken. Enkele geloofsvoorstellingen en elementen van een agrarisch gekleurd wereldbeeld bij geestelijken in de 13 e en 14 e eeuw." In Gerard Rooijakkers and Theo van der Zee, eds., *Religieuze volkscultuur. De spanning tussen de voorgeschreven orde en de geleefde praktijk*. Nijmegen: 36-53.

Küther, Carsten. 1983. *Menschen auf der Strasse. Vagierende Unterschichten in Bayern, Franken und Schwaben in der zweiten Hälfte des 18. Jahrhunderts*. Göttingen.

Langbein, John H. 1977. *Torture and the Law of Proof. Europe and England in the Ancien Régime*. Chicago, London.

Lehmann, L. Th. [1984]. *Galleys in the Netherlands*. Amsterdam.

Leonard, E. M. 1965. *The Early History of English Poor-Relief*. London.

Lescaze, Bernard. [1985?] "Pouvoirs publics, charités privées. L'hôpital dans la cité au 16e siècle." In *Sauver l'âme, nourrir le corps. De l'hôpital général à l'hospice général de Genève, 1535-1985*: 49-76.

Lieberknecht, Herbert. 1921. *Das altpreussische Zuchthauswesen bis zum Ausgang des 18. Jahrhunderts*. Charlottenburg.

Lieburg, M[art] J. Van. 1982. "De syfilitische patient in de geschiedenis van het Nederlandse ziekenhuiswezen voor 1900." *Tijdschrift voor Sociale Geschiedenis* 26: 156-79.

Lis, Catharina. 1976. "Sociale politiek in Antwerpen, 1779." *Tijdschrift voor Sociale Geschiedenis* 5: 146-166.

Lis, Catharina, and Hugo Soly. 1979. *Poverty and Capitalism in Preindustrial Europe*. Hassocks.

Lis, Catharina, and Hugo Soly. 1984. "Policing the early modern proletariat, 1450-1850." In David Levine, ed., *Proletarianization and Family History*. Orlando: 163-228.

Loo, H. van. 1984. *De geschiedenis van het geslacht Verfaille in Nederland*. Bergen.

Loose, Hans-Dieter, ed. 1982. *Hamburg. Geschichte der Stadt und ihrer Bewohner. Band I: Von den Anfängen bis zur Reichsgründung*. Hamburg.

Lootsma, S. 1950. *Historische studiën over de Zaanstreek. Tweede bundel*. Koog a.d. Zaan.

Macondald, Michael. *Mystical Bedlam. Madness, Anxiety and Healing in 17th-Century England*. Cambridge.

Maes, Louis Th. 1947. *Vijf eeuwen stedelijk strafrecht. Bijdrage tot de rechts- en cultuurgeschiedenis der Nederlanden*. Antwerpen.

Manen, Charlotte Aleida van. 1913. *Armenpflege in Amsterdam in ihrer historischen Entwicklung*. Leiden.

Marzahn, Christian. 1984. "Das Zucht- und Arbeitshaus. Die Kerninstitution frühbürgerlicher Sozialpolitik." In Christian Marzahm and Hans-Günther Ritz, eds., *Zähmen und Bewahren. Die Anfänge bürgerlicher Sozialpolitik*. Bielefeld: 1–68.

Mayer, Marcel. 1987. *Hilfsbedürftige und Delinquenten. Die Anstaltsinsassen der Stadt St. Gallen, 1750-1798*. St. Gallen.

Mecklenburg, Frank. 1983. *Die Ordnung der Gefängnisse. Grundlinien der Gefängnisreform und Gefängniswissenschaft in der ersten Hälfte des 19. Jahrhunderts in Deutschland*. Berlin.

Meinsma, K. O. 1896. *Spinoza en zijn kring. Historisch-kritische studiën over Hollandsche vrijgeesten*. Den Haag.

Melossi, Dario, and Massimo Pavarini. 1981. *The Prison and the Factory. Origins of the Penitentiary System*. London.

Mendez, Emilio Garcia, and Massimo Pavarini. 1987. "Einleitung zum Text von Jean Mabillon." *Kriminologisches Journal* 2 (Beihelft): 73–78.

Meye, Albrecht. 1935. *Das Strafrecht der Stadt Danzig von der Carolina bis zur Vereinigung Danzigs mit der preussischen Monarchie, 1532-1793*. Danzig.

Moes, E. W. 1891. "Amsterdamsche vondelingen." *Amsterdamsch Jaarboekje*: 96–103.

Moes, E. W. 1899. "Vorstelijke bezoeken te Amsterdam." *Amsterdamsch Jaarboekje*: 1–8.

Mollat, Michel. 1978. *Les pauvres au moyen âge. Etude sociale*. [Paris].

Montias, John Michael. [1989]. *Vermeer and his milieu. A web of social history*. Princeton, N.J.

Morgan, Rod. 1977. "Divine philanthrophy. John Howard reconsidered." *History* 62: 388–410.

Muchembled, Robert. 1988. *L'invention de l'homme moderne. Sensibilités, moeurs et comportements collectifs sous l'Ancien Régime*. [Paris].

Muller, Sheila D. 1985. *Chariy in the Dutch Republic. Pictures of Rich and Poor for Charitable Institutions*. Ann Arbor.

Nève, P. L. and Coppens, E. C. 1987. "Ut commissa defleat. De vrijheidsberoving in het canonieke recht tot 1300." In: *Straffen in gerechtigheid. Opstellen over sancties en executie, uitgegeven ter nagedachtenis aan prof. mr. W. H. A. Jonkers*. Arnhem: 333–347.

Nie, Willem Leendert Johannes de. 1937. *De ontwikkeling der Noord-Nederlandsche textielververij van de 14e tot de 18e eeuw*. Leiden.

Nieuwenhuijs, C[hristianus] J[ohannes]. 1820. *Proeve eener geneeskundige plaatsbeschrijving (topographie) der stad Amsterdam*. Vol. 4. Amsterdam.

Noordam, D[irk] J[aap]. 1985. "Criminaliteit van vrouwen in Leiden in de 17e en 18e eeuw." *Leids Jaarboekje*: 36–46.

O'Brien, Patricia. [1982]. *The Promise of Punishment. Prisons in 19th-Century France*. Princeton. N.J.

Oldewelt, W. F. H. 1942. "Het aantal bedelaars, vondelingen en gevangenen te Amsterdam in tijden van welvaart en crisis." *Jaarboek Amstelodemum* 39: 21–34.

Olsen, Olaf. 1978. *Christian IVs tugt- og børnehus. Anden forögede udgave. s.l.*

Otis, Leah Lydia. 1985. *Prostitution in Medieval Society. The History of an Urban Institution in Languedoc*. Chicago, London.

Parry-Jones, William Ll. 1972. *The trade in Lunacy. A Study of Private Madhouses in England in the 18th and 19th Centuries*. London, Toronto.

Pelc, Ortwin. 1986. "Die Armenversorgung in Lübeck in der ersten Hälfte des 19. Jahrhunderts." In *Zeitschrift des Vereins für Lübeckische Geschichte und Altertumskunde* 66: 143–88.

Perrot, Michelle. 1975. "Délinquence et système pénitentiarie en France au 19e siècle." *Annales ESC* 30, 1: 67–91.

Perrot, Michelle, ed. 1980. *L'impossible prison. Recherches sur le système pénitentiare au 19e siècle. Débat avec Michel Foucault*. Paris.

Perry, Mary Elizabeth. [1980]. *Crime and society in early modern Seville*. Hanover, N.H., London.

Petersen, M. A. 1978. *Gedetineerden onder dak. Geschiedenis van het gevangeniswezen in Nederland van 1795 af, bezien van zijn behuizing*. Leiden.

Petit, Jacques G., ed. 1984. *La Prison, le Bagne et l'Histoire*. Genève.

Petitfils, Jean-Christian. 1975. *La vie quotidienne à la Bastille du moyen âge à la Révolution*. s.l.

Pierre, Michel. [1982]. *La terre de la grande punition. Histoire des bagnes de Guyane*. Paris.

Pietsch, Günter. 1931. "Das Zuchthauswesen Alt-Danzigs." Diss. Jur., Göttingen. Danzig.

Pike, Ruth. 1976., "Crime and punishment in 16th-century Spain." *Journal of European Economic History* 5, 3: 689–704.

Pike, Ruth. 1983. *Penal servitude in early modern Spain*. Madison, London.

Piranesi, Giovanni Battista. [1976]. *A critical study. With a list of his published works and detailed catalogues of the Prisons and the Views of Rome*. By Arthur M. Hind. 2d ed. [London].

Pol, Lotte C. van de. "Vrouwencriminaliteit in Amsterdam in de 2e helft van de 17e eeuw." *Tijdschrift voor Criminologie* 29: 148–155.

Pol, Lotte C. van de. [1988]. "Beeld en werkelijkheid van de prostitutie in de 17e eeuw." In Gert Hekma and Herman Roodenburg, eds., *Soete minne en helsche boosheit. Seksuele voorstellingen in Nederland, 1300–1850*. Nijmegen: 109–44.

Priestley, Philip. 1985. *Victorian Prison Lives. English Prison Biography, 1830–1914*. London, New York.

Pugh, Ralph B. 1970. *Imprisonment in medieval England*. Cambridge.

Pullan, Brian. 1971. *Rich and Poor in Renaissance Venice. The Social Institutions of a Catholic State, to 1620*. Oxford.

Quétel, Claude. 1978. "Lettres de cachet et correctionnaires dans la Généralité de Caen au 18e siècle." *Annales de Normandie:* 127–159.

Quétel, Claude. [1981a]. *De par le roy. Essai sur les lettres de cachet*. Toulouse.

Quétel, Claude. [1981b]. "En maison de force au siècle des Lumières." In *Marginalité, déviance, pauvreté en France, 14e–19e siècles (Cahier des Annales de Normandie 13)*. Caen: 43–79.

Radbruch, Gustav. 1950. *Elegantiae juris criminalis. Vierzehn Studien zur Geschichte des Strafrechts*. Basel.

Raeff, Marc. [1983]. *The Well-Ordered Police State. Social and Institutional Change through Law in the Germanies and Russia, 1600–1800*. London.

Reekers, Stephanie. 1981. "Die Manufakturen in den Zucht- und Fabrikhäusern Westfalens im 18. Jahrhundert." *Westfälische Forschungen* 31: 34–72.

Reinold, Lucinda Kate. 1981. "The representation of the beggar as rogue in Dutch 17th-century art." Thesis, UC Berkeley, available from University Microfilms.

Reissmann, Martin. 1975. *Die hamburgische Kaufmannschaft des 17. Jahrhunderts in sozialgeschichtlicher Sicht*. Hamburg.

Ricci, Giovanni. 1983. "Naissance du pauvre honteux: entre l'histoire des idées et l'histoire sociale." *Annales ESC* 38, 1: 158–77.

Roodenburg, Herman. [1987]. "Een soorte van duivelsche afgoderije. De bestrijding van toverij door de gereformeerde kerkeraad te Amsterdam. 1580–1700." In Marijke Gijswijt-Hofstra and Willem Frijhoff, eds. *Nederland betoverd. Toverij en hekserij van de 14e tot de 20e eeuw*. Amsterdam: 80–93.

Rosenfield, Ernst. 1906. "Zur Geschichte der ältesten Zuchthäuser." *Zeitschrift für die Gesamte Strafrechtswissenschaft* 26: 1–18.

Roth, Robert. 1981. *Pratiques pénitentiaries et théories sociale. L'exemple de la Prison de Genève, 1825–1862*. Genève.

Rothman, David J. 1971. *The Discovery of the Asylum. Social Order and Disorder in the New Republic*. Boston, Toronto.

Rothman, David J. 1980. *Conscience and convenience. The Asylum and its Alternatives in Progressive America*. Boston.

Rudé, George. 1978. *Protest and Punishment. The Story of the Social and Political Protesters Transported to Australia, 1788–1868*. Oxford.

Rückleben, Hermann. 1970. *Die Niederwerfung der hamburgischen Ratsgewalt. Kirchliche Bewegungen und bürgerliche Unruhen im ausgehenden 17. Jahrhundert*. Hamburg.

Ruff, Julius R. [1984]. *Crime, Justice and Public Order in Old Regime France. The Sénéchaussées of Libourne and Bazas, 1696–1789*. London.

Ruller, Sibo van. 1981. "Het aantal gevangenen in Nederland sinds 1837. Een analyse van 140 jaar gevangenisstatisieken." *Tijdschrift voor Criminologie* 23: 209–223.

Rusche, Georg. 1933. "Arbeismarkt und Strafvollzug. Gedanken zur Soziologie der Strafjustiz." *Zeitschrift für Sozialforschung* 2: 63–78.

Rusche, Georg, and Otto Kirchheimer. 1939. *Punishment and Social Structure.* New York.
Saam, Günther. 1936. *Quellenstudien zur Geschichte des deutschen Zuchthauswesens bis zur Mitte des 19. Jahrhunderts.* Berlin, Leipzig.
Sachsse, Cristoph, and Florian Tennstedt. 1980. *Geschichte der Armenfürsorge in Deutschland vom Spätmittelalter bis zum Ersten Weltkrieg.* Stuttgart.
Scarabello, Giovanni. 1979. *Carcerati e carceri a Venezia nell' età moderna.* Roma.
Schaefer, Gustav. 1937. "Die Farbhölzer." *Ciba-Rundschau* 10, Basel, (February): 326–352.
Schama, Simon. 1988. *Overvloed en onbehagen. De Nederlandse cultuur in de gouden eeuw* [original title: *The Embarrassment of Riches*]. Amsterdam.
Scherpner, Hans. [1962]. *Theorie der Fürsorge. Herausgegeben von Hanna Scherpner.* Göttingen.
Schildhauer, Johannes. 1984. *Die Hanse, Geschichte und Kultur.* Stuttgart.
Schilling, Heinz, and Herman Diederiks, eds. 1985 *Bürgerliche Eliten in den Niederlanden und in Nordwestdeutschland. Studien zur Sozialgeschichte des europäischen Bürgertums im Mittelalter und in der Neuzeit.* Köln, Wien.
Schilling, Heinz. 1989. "History of crime or history of sin. Some reflections on the social history of early modern church discipline." In E. I. Kouri and Tom Scott, eds., *Politics and Society in Reformation Europe. Essays for Sir Geoffrey Elton on his 65th birthday.* London: 289–310.
Schlue, Helmuth. 1957. *Die Geschichte des bonner Zuchthauses und des bonner Arbeitshauses.* Bonn.
Schmidt, Eberhard. 1915. *Entwicklung und Vollzug der Freiheitsstrafe in Brandenburg-Preussen bis zum Ausgang des 18. Jahrhunderts Ein Beitrag zur Geschichte der Freiheitsstrafe (Abhandlungen des kriminalistischen Instituts an der Universität Berlin.* Dritte Folge, zweiter Band, Heft 2). Berlin.
Schmidt, Eberhard. 1947. "Neue Forschungen über den Ursprung der moderen Freiheitsstrafe." *Schweizerische Zeitschrift für Strafrecht* 62: 171–193.
Schnapper, Bernard. 1980. "La correction paternelle et le mouvement des idées au 19e siècle, 1789–1935." *Revue Historique:* 319–349.
Schubert, Ernst. 1983. *Arme Leute. Bettler und Gauner im Franken des 18. Jahrhunderts.* Neustadt a.d. Aisch.
Schwartz, Robert M. [1988]. *Policing the Poor in Eighteenth-Century France.* Chapel Hill, London.
Schwarzwälder, Herbert. [1975]. *Geschichte der freien Hansestadt Bremen. Band 1:Von den Anfängen bis zur Franzosenzeit, 1810.* Bremen.
Scull, Andrew T. 1979. *Museums of Madness. The Social Organization of Insanity in 19th-Century England.* London.
Seggelke, Günther. 1928. *Die Entstehung der Freiheitsstrafe.* Breslau.
Sellin, J. Thorsten. 1926–1927. "Dom Jean Mabillon. A prison reformer of the 17th century." *Journal of the American Institute of Criminal Law and Criminology* 17: 581–602.
Selling, J. Thorsten. 1929–1930. "The house of correction for boys in the hospice of Saint Michael in Rome." *Journal of the American Institute of Criminal Law and Criminology* 20: 533–553.
Selling, J. Thorsten. 1944. *Pioneering in Penology. The Amsterdam Houses of Correction in the 16th and 17th Centuries.* Philadelphia.
Selling, J. Thorsten. *Slavery and the Penal System.* New York.
Sérieux, Paul, and Lucien Libert. 1914–1915, 1916. "Le régime des aliénés en France au 18e siècle d'après des documents inédits": *Annales Medico-Psychologiques* (1914–1915): 43–76, 196–219, 311–323, 470–497, 598–627; (1916): 74–98.
Sérieux, Paul and M. Trénel. 1931. "L'internement des aliénés par voie judiciaire (sentence d'interdiction) sous l'Ancien Régime." *Revue Historique de Droit Français et Etranger:* 450–86.
Sérieux, Paul. 1932. "L'internement par ordre de justice des aliénés et des correctionnaires sous l'Ancien Régime d'après des documents inédits." *Revue Historique de Droit Français et Étranger:* 413–462.
Sharpe, J[ames] A. 1984. *Crime in Early Modern England, 1550-1750.* London, New York.
Shaw, A[lan] G[eorge] L[ewers]. 1977. *Convicts and the Colonies. A Study of Penal Transportation from Great Britain and Ireland to Australia and Other Parts of the British Empire.* Melbourne.

Sheehan, W. J. [1977]. "Finding solace in 18th-century Newgate." In J. S. Cockburn, ed., *Crime in England, 1550–1800.* Princeton: 229–245.

Slack, Paul. 1988. *Poverty and Policy in Tudor and Stuart England.* London, New York.

Slice, Austin van der. 1936–1937. "Elizabethan houses of correction." *Journal of the American Institute of Criminal Law and Criminology* 27: 45–67.

Smith, Abbot Emerson. 1947 *Colonists in Bondage. White Servitude and Convict Labor in America, 1607–1776.* Chapel Hill.

Sothmann, Marlene. 1970. *Das Armen-, Arbeits-, Zucht- und Werkhaus in Nürnberg bis 1806.* Nürnberg.

Spierenburg, Pieter. 1978. "Judicial violence in the Dutch Republic. Corporal punishment, executions and torture in Amsterdam, 1650–1750. Thesis, University of Amsterdam.

Spierenburg, Pieter. 1983. "Model prisons, domesticated elites and the state: the Dutch Republic and Europe." In Göran Rystad, ed., *Europe and Scandinavia. Aspects of the Process of Integration in the 17th Century.* Lund: 219–235.

Spierenburg, Pieter. 1984a. *The Spectacle of Suffering. Executions and the Evolution of Repression: From a Preindustrial Metropolis to the European Experience.* Cambridge.

Spierenburg, Pieter, ed. 1984b. *The Emergence of Carceral Institutions. Prisons, Galleys and Lunatic Asylums, 1550–1900.* Rotterdam (Centrum voor Maatschappijgeschiedenis 12).

Spierenburg, Pieter. 1986. "Imprisonment and the family. An analysis of petitions for confinement in Holland, 1680–1805." *Social Science History* 10, 2: 115–146.

Spierenburg, Pieter. 1987. "From Amsterdam to Auburn. An explanation for the rise of the prison in 17th-century Holland and 19th-century America." *Journal of Social History* (Spring): 439–461.

Spierenburg, Pieter. 1988a. *De verbroken betovering. Mentaliteitgeschiedenis van preïndustrieel Europa.* Hilversum.

Spierenburg, Pieter. 1988b. "Gevangenis en verzet. Op zoek naar onvrede met tuchthuizen in de 17e en 18e eeuw." In René van Swaaningen, et al, eds., *A tort et à travers. Liber amicorum Herman Bianchi.* Amsterdam: 273–285.

Stekl, Hannes. 1978. *Österreichs Zucht- und Arbeitshäuser, 1671–1920. Institutionen zwischen Fürsorge und Strafvollzug.* Wien.

Stier, Bernhard. 1988. *Fürsorge und Disziplinierung im Zeitalter des Absolutismus. Das Pforzheimer Zucht- und Waisenhaus und die badische Sozialpolitik im 18. Jahrhundert.* Sigmaringen.

Stockdale, Eric. 1977. *A study of Bedford prison, 1660–1877.* London, Chichester.

Streng, Adolf. 1890. *Geschichte der Gefängnisverwaltung in Hamburg von 1622–1872.* Hamburg.

Stroobant, Louis. 1900. "Le rasphuys de Gand. Recherches sur la répression du vagabondage et sur le système pénitentiaire établi en Flandre au 17e et 18e siècle." *Handelingen der Maatschappij van Geschied- en Oudheidkunde te Gent* III, 2: 191–307.

Szasz, Thomas S. 1961. *The Myth of Mental Illness. Foundations of a Theory of Personal Conduct.* s.l.

Tanghe, Fernand. [1986]. *Sociale grondrechten tussen armoede en mensenrechten. Van de middeleeuwen tot de Franse revolutie.* Antwerpen.

Teijlingen, D. G. van. 1883. "Enige bladen uit de geschiedenis van het oude tuchthuis te Middleburg." *Archief Zeeuws Genootschap* 5: 89–124.

Thomas, Keith. 1964. "Work and leisure in preindustrial society." *Past and Present* 29: 50–66.

Traphagen, Wilhelm. 1935. *Die erstein Arbeitshäuser und ihre pädagogische Funktion.* Berlin.

Treiber, Hubert, and Heinz Steinert. 1980. *Die Fabrikation des zuverlässigen Menschen. über die 'Wahlverwandtschaft' von Kloster- und Fabrikdisziplin.* München.

Valkering, Ton. 1984. "De criminele vonnissen in Alkmaar, 1680–1795." Thesis, University of Amsterdam, History.

Vámbéry, Rustem. 1915–1916. "Das Amsterdamer Tuchthuis in ungarischer Beleuchtung." *Zeitschrift für die Gesamte Strafrechtswissenschaft* 37: 106–109.

Vanhemelryck, Fernand. 1981. *De criminaliteit in de Ammanie van Brussel van de late middeleeuwen tot het einde van het Ancien Régime, 1404–1789.* Brussel.

Verhoeven, Karel. 1978. "Het provinciaal tuchthuis te Arnhem vanaf de oprichting in 1710 tot de Bataafse omwenteling in 1795." Thesis, University of Nijmegen, Law.

Vié, Jacques. 1930. *Les aliénés et les correctionnaires à Saint-Lazare au 17e et au 18e siècles.* Paris.

Vis, D. s.a. *Drie eeuwen verf. Een en ander uit de geschiedenis van de Zaanse verfindustrie, 1643–1943*. Wormerveer.

Voss, H. O. Heerma van. 1958. "De armenzorg te Amsterdam in de 17e eeuw." Thesis, University of Amsterdam, History; copy at Gemeente-archief.

Vries, Jan de. 1976. *The economy of Europe in an age of crisis, 1600–1750*. Cambridge.

Walker, D[aniel] P. [1981]. *Unclean Spirits. Possession and Exorcism in France and England in the Late 16th and Early 17th Centuries*. London.

Walker, Mack. 1971. *German Home Towns. Community, State and General Estate, 1648–1871*. Ithaca, London.

Warmbrunn, Paul. 1983. *Zwei Konfessionen in einer Stadt. Das Zusammenleben von Katholiken und Protestanten in den paritätischen Reichsstädten Augsburg, Biberach, Ravensburg und Dinkelsbühl von 1548 bis 1648*. Wiesbaden.

Weber, Hellmuth von. 1941. "Die Entstehung des Zuchthauswesens in Deustchland im 17. und 18. Jahrhundert." In *Abhandlungen zur Rechts- und Wirtschaftsgeschichte. Festschrift Adolf Zycha*. Weimar: 427–468.

Weber, Hellmuth von. 1961. "Calvinismus und Strafrecht." In Paul Bockelmann and Wilhelm Gallas, eds. *Festschrift für Eberhard Schmidt zum 70. Geburtstag*. Göttingen: 39–53.

Weiss, Robert P. 1987. "Humanism, labour exploitation or social control? A critical survey of theory and research on the origin and development of prisons." *Social History* 12, 3: 331–350.

Whaley, Joachim. *Religious Toleration and Social Change in Hamburg, 1529–1819*. Cambridge.

Whiting, J. R. S. 1979. *A house of correction*. Gloucester.

Wieselgren, Sigfrid. 1895. *Sveriges fängelser och fångvård. Från äldre tider till våra dagar. Ett bidrag till Svensk kulturhistoria*. Stockholm.

Williams, Alan. [1979]. *The police of Paris, 1718–1789*. Baton Rouge, London.

Wilbertz, Gisela. 1797. *Scharfrichter und Abdecker im Hochstift Osnabrück. Untersuchungen zur Sozialgeschichte zweier 'unehrlicher' Berufe im nordwestdeutschen Raum vom 16. bis zum 19. Jahrhundert*. Osnabrück.

Wissell, Rudolf. 1971. *Des alten Handwerks Recht und Gewohnheit. Zweite, erweiterte und bearbeitete Ausgabe, herausgegeben von Ernst Schraepler. Band I*. Berlin.

Wolf, Werner. 1963. *Zur Geschichte des Armen- und Arbeitshauses in Potsdam*. Potsdam.

Woude, Adrianus Maria van der. *Het Noorderkwartier. Een regionaal-historish onderzoek in de demografische en economische geschiedenis van Westelijk Nederland van de late middeleeuwen tot het begin van de 19e eeuw*. 3 vols. Wageningen.

Woude, A[drianus] M[aria] van der. 1980. "De alfabetisering." In *Algemene Geschiedenis der Nederlanden*, Vol. VII. Haarlem: 256–264.

Wright, Gordon. 1983. *Between the Guillotine and Liberty. Two centuries of the Crime Problem in France*. New York, Oxford.

Wijsenbeek-Olthuis. Thera. 1987. *Achter de gevels van Delft. Bezit en bestaan van rijk en arm in een periode van achteruitgang, 1700–1800*. Hilversum.

Ysselt, A. Sasse van. 1920. "Maatregelen die een vader oudtijds kon nemen tegen zijn verkwistende zoon." *Taxandria* 27: 84–91.

Zalm, Leo van der. 1979. "Ondertekend-Brederood. Een onderzoek naar het beeld van de arme en de bedelaar in de literatuur van de 16e en vroeg-17e eeuw, in samenhang met ontwikkelingen in de armenzorg." Thesis, University of Amsterdam, Dutch.

Zysberg, André. [1987]. *Les galériens. Vies et destins de 60,000 forçats sur les galères de France, 1680–1748*. Paris.

INDEX